Dominican Republic and Haiti
country studies

Federal Research Division
Library of Congress
Edited by
Richard A. Haggerty
Research Completed
December 1989

On the cover: View of mountains, Hispaniola

Second Edition, First Printing, 1991.

Library of Congress Cataloging-in-Publication Data

Dominican Republic and Haiti : country studies / Federal Research
Division, Library of Congress ; edited by Richard A. Haggerty. —
2d ed.
    p. cm. — (Area handbook series, ISSN 1057-5294)
(DA Pam ; 550-36)
    "Research completed December 1989."
    Rev. ed. of : Area handbook for Dominican Republic and Area
handbook for Haiti / coauthors, Thomas E. Well . . . [et al.].
1976.
    Includes bibliographical references (pp. 401–431) and index.
    ISBN 0-8444-0728-3
    1. Dominican Republic. 2. Haiti. I. Haggerty, Richard A.,
1954-   . II. Library of Congress. Federal Research Division.
III. Area handbook for Dominican Republic. IV. Area handbook
for Haiti. V. Series. VI. Series : DA Pam ; 550-36.
F1934.D64   1991   91-9495
972.93—dc20   CIP

Headquarters, Department of the Army
DA Pam 550-36

For sale by the Superintendent of Documents, U.S. Government Printing Office
Washington, D.C. 20402

Foreword

This volume is one in a continuing series of books prepared by the Federal Research Division of the Library of Congress under the Country Studies—Area Handbook Program sponsored by the Department of the Army. The last page of this book lists the other published studies.

Most books in the series deal with a particular foreign country, describing and analyzing its political, economic, social, and national security systems and institutions, and examining the interrelationships of those systems and the ways they are shaped by cultural factors. Each study is written by a multidisciplinary team of social scientists. The authors seek to provide a basic understanding of the observed society, striving for a dynamic rather than a static portrayal. Particular attention is devoted to the people who make up the society, their origins, dominant beliefs and values, their common interests and the issues on which they are divided, the nature and extent of their involvement with national institutions, and their attitudes toward each other and toward their social system and political order.

The books represent the analysis of the authors and should not be construed as an expression of an official United States government position, policy, or decision. The authors have sought to adhere to accepted standards of scholarly objectivity. Corrections, additions, and suggestions for changes from readers will be welcomed for use in future editions.

Louis R. Mortimer
Chief
Federal Research Division
Library of Congress
Washington, D.C. 20540

Acknowledgments

The authors wish to acknowledge the contributions of Jan Knippers Black, Howard I. Blutstein, Kathryn T. Johnston, David S. McMorris, Frederick P. Munson, and Thomas E. Weil, who wrote the 1973 editions of *Dominican Republic: A Country Study* and *Haiti: A Country Study*. Their work lent perspective to several chapters of the present volume. The authors also are grateful to individuals in various agencies of the United States government and international and private institutions who gave their time, research materials, and special knowledge to provide information and perspective. These individuals include Ralph K. Benesch, who oversees the Country Studies-Area Handbook Program for the Department of the Army.

The authors also wish to thank those who contributed directly to the preparation of the manuscript. These include Richard F. Nyrop, who reviewed all drafts and served as liaison with the sponsoring agency; Sandra W. Meditz, who reviewed drafts and provided valuable advice at all stages of production; Dennis M. Hanratty, who contributed useful and substantive comments on several chapter drafts; Vincent Ercolano, who edited the Dominican Republic chapters; Richard Kollodge, who edited the Haiti chapters; Martha E. Hopkins, who edited portions of the manuscript and managed editing; Marilyn Majeska, who also edited portions of the manuscript and managed production; Barbara Edgerton, Janie L. Gilchrist, and Izella Watson, who did the word processing; Alice Craig Harvey, who compiled the index; and Diann J. Johnson and Linda Peterson, of the Printing and Processing Section, Library of Congress, who prepared the camera-ready copy under the supervision of Peggy Pixley.

David P. Cabitto, Sandra K. Ferrell, and Kimberly A. Lord provided invaluable graphics support. David P. Cabitto designed the cover illustration, and Kimberly A. Lord prepared the illustrations for the title page of the chapters on Haiti. Map drafts were prepared by Harriett R. Blood, David P. Cabitto, and Kimberly A. Lord. Various individuals, libraries, and public agencies provided photographs.

Finally, the authors would like to thank several individuals who provided research support. Arvies J. Staton supplied information on ranks and insignia, and Karen Sturges-Vera wrote the geography sections in chapters 2 and 7.

Contents

Page

Foreword iii

Acknowledgments v

Preface xv

Introduction xvii

Dominican Republic: Country Profile xxvii

Chapter 1. Dominican Republic: Historical
    Setting 1
        Richard A. Haggerty

THE FIRST COLONY 3
HAITI AND SANTO DOMINGO 8
SANTANA AND BÁEZ: THE CAUDILLOS TAKE
   CHARGE 12
    The Infant Republic 12
    Annexation by Spain, 1861–65 16
    The Contest for Power, 1865–82 18
ULISES HEUREAUX, 1882–99 18
RENEWED CONFLICT, 1899–1916 21
OCCUPATION BY THE UNITED STATES, 1916–24 24
THE ERA OF TRUJILLO 27
THE POST-TRUJILLO ERA 31
    Transition to Elected Government 31
    Civil War and United States Intervention, 1965 32
    Joaquín Balaguer, 1966–78 33
    Antonio Guzmán, 1978–82 34

Chapter 2. Dominican Republic: The Society and
    Its Environment 37
        Patricia Kluck

GEOGRAPHY 40
    Natural Regions 40
    Drainage 41
    Climate 43
POPULATION 44
    Size and Growth 44

Migration 45
Urbanization 47
RACIAL AND ETHNIC GROUPS 49
Ethnic Heritage 49
Modern Immigration 50
Haitians 52
URBAN SOCIETY 52
The Elite 52
The Middle Sector 55
The Urban Poor 56
RURAL SOCIETY 58
Sugar Plantations 60
Mixed Farming 62
FAMILY AND KIN 64
RELIGION 67
SOCIAL WELFARE 68
Education 68
Health and Social Security 70

Chapter 3. Dominican Republic: The Economy .. 75
Daniel J. Seyler

GROWTH AND STRUCTURE OF THE ECONOMY 77
ECONOMIC POLICY 82
Fiscal Policy 82
Monetary and Exchange-Rate Policies 85
LABOR 87
Formal Sector 87
Informal Sector 89
AGRICULTURE 89
Land Tenure and Land Policy 90
Land Use 92
Farming Technology 92
Crops 94
Livestock 100
Forestry and Fishing 101
INDUSTRY 101
Manufacturing 101
Mining 106
Construction 108
Energy 109
SERVICES 111
Tourism 111
Banking and Financial Services 113
Transportation 115
Communications 118

FOREIGN ECONOMIC RELATIONS 119
   Foreign Trade 119
   Balance of Payments 122
   Foreign Debt 122
   Foreign Assistance 124

Chapter 4. Dominican Republic: Government and Politics 127
Howard J. Wiarda

THE SYSTEM OF GOVERNMENT 130
   Constitutional Development 130
   The Executive 132
   The Legislature 133
   The Judiciary 136
   Public Administration 137
   Local Government 139
   The Electoral System 139
POLITICAL DYNAMICS 141
   The System of Dominican Politics 141
   Political Developments since 1978 142
   Interest Groups 144
   Political Parties 151
   The Mass Media 154
FOREIGN RELATIONS 156

Chapter 5. Dominican Republic: National Security 161
Melinda Wheeler Cooke

HISTORY AND DEVELOPMENT OF THE ARMED
   FORCES 164
THE ROLE OF THE MILITARY IN PUBLIC LIFE 169
   Missions 170
   Manpower 172
   Defense Spending 172
ARMED FORCES ORGANIZATION, TRAINING, AND
   EQUIPMENT 174
   The Army 175
   The Navy 179
   The Air Force 180
   Ranks, Uniforms, and Insignia 181
INTERNAL SECURITY AND PUBLIC ORDER 181
   Crime 186
   The National Police 187
   The Criminal Justice System 189

Haiti: Country Profile 195

Chapter 6. Haiti: Historical Setting 201
Richard A. Haggerty

SPANISH DISCOVERY AND COLONIZATION 203
FRENCH COLONIALISM 205
French Settlement and Sovereignty 205
Colonial Society: The Conflicts of Color and Class ... 206
THE HAITIAN REVOLUTION 207
The Slave Rebellion of 1791 207
Toussaint Louverture 209
INDEPENDENT HAITI 213
Christophe's Kingdom and Pétion's Republic 215
Boyer: Expansion and Decline 218
DECADES OF INSTABILITY, 1843-1915 219
THE UNITED STATES OCCUPATION, 1915-34 224
POLITICS AND THE MILITARY, 1934-57 227
FRANÇOIS DUVALIER, 1957-71 232
JEAN-CLAUDE DUVALIER, 1971-86 235

Chapter 7. Haiti: The Society and Its
Environment 239
Frederick J. Conway

GEOGRAPHY 243
POPULATION 245
Demographic Profile 245
Migration 246
Fertility and Family Planning 248
SOCIAL STRUCTURE 248
The Upper Class 250
The Middle Class 251
Peasants 252
Urban Lower Class 254
GENDER ROLES AND FAMILY LIFE 254
THE LANGUAGE QUESTION 257
French and Creole 257
Changes in Language Use 260
Creole, Literacy, and Education 261
RELIGIOUS LIFE 265
Voodoo 265
Roman Catholicism 267
Protestantism 268
EDUCATION 269
Primary Schools 270

Secondary Education 273
Higher Education 273
HEALTH 274
Nutrition and Disease 274
Acquired Immune Deficiency Syndrome 274
Health Services 275
Welfare 276

Chapter 8. Haiti: The Economy 279
Daniel J. Seyler

GROWTH AND STRUCTURE OF THE ECONOMY 282
ECONOMIC POLICY 286
Fiscal Policy 286
Monetary and Exchange-Rate Policies 287
LABOR 288
AGRICULTURE 290
Land Tenure and Land Policy 291
Land Use and Farming Technology 293
Crops 295
Forestry 300
Livestock and Fishing 301
INDUSTRY 302
Manufacturing 302
Construction 307
Mining 307
Energy 308
SERVICES 309
Banking and Financial Services 309
Transportation and Communications 311
Tourism 314
FOREIGN ECONOMIC RELATIONS 314
Foreign Trade 314
Balance of Payments 317
Foreign Debt 318
Foreign Assistance 318

Chapter 9. Haiti: Government and Politics 323
Glenn R. Smucker

BACKGROUND: FROM DUVALIER TO AVRIL,
1957–89 326
THE CONSTITUTIONAL FRAMEWORK 330
THE GOVERNMENTAL SYSTEM 332
Governmental Institutions 333

The Functions of the State 334
Urban Dominance, Rural Stagnation 335
POLITICAL DYNAMICS 337
Power Maintenance 337
Army Politics: Force and Counterforce 337
The President as Strongman 339
Perceptions of Democracy 340
The Mass Media 341
INTEREST GROUPS 342
The *Tonton Makout* Network 342
Political Parties 342
The Upper and the Middle Classes 344
Other Groups 345
FOREIGN RELATIONS 346

Chapter 10. Haiti: National Security 351
Georges A. Fauriol

THE MILITARY IN HAITIAN HISTORY 354
ARMY POLITICS IN THE TWENTIETH CENTURY 355
François Duvalier, 1957–71 356
Jean-Claude Duvalier, 1971–86 357
The Post-Duvalier Period 359
THE ROLE OF THE ARMED FORCES 361
MILITARY SPENDING AND FOREIGN ASSISTANCE ... 364
ARMED FORCES ORGANIZATION AND
STRUCTURE 365
THE JUDICIAL SYSTEM AND PUBLIC ORDER 372
The Legal Framework 372
Public Order 374

Appendix A. Tables 379

Appendix B. Caribbean Basin Initiative 393

Bibliography 401

Glossary 433

Index 437

List of Figures
1 Dominican Republic: Administrative Divisions, 1989 xxvi
2 Dominican Republic: Topography and Drainage 42
3 Dominican Republic: Estimated Population Distribution
by Age and Sex, 1990 44
4 Dominican Republic: Transportation System, 1989 116
5 Dominican Republic: Structure of the Government, 1989 ... 134

6 Dominican Republic: Organization of the Armed Forces,
  1989 177
7 Dominican Republic: Officer Ranks and Insignia, 1989 ... 182
8 Dominican Republic: Enlisted Ranks and Insignia, 1989 .. 183
9 Dominican Republic: Organization of the National Police,
  1989 188
10 Haiti: Administrative Divisions, 1989 194
11 Haiti: Topography and Drainage 242
12 Haiti: Population Distribution by Age and Sex, 1982 246
13 Haiti: Employment by Sector, 1983 290
14 Haiti: Estimated Gross Domestic Product (GDP) by Sector,
   Fiscal Year (FY) 1987 292
15 Haiti: Transportation System, 1989 312
16 Haiti: Civil Jurisdictions and Governmental Institutions,
   1989 332
17 Haiti: Organization of the Armed Forces, 1989 368
18 Haiti: Officer Ranks and Insignia, 1989 370
19 Haiti: Enlisted Ranks and Insignia, 1989 371

Preface

Like their predecessors, these studies represent an attempt to treat in a compact and objective manner the dominant contemporary social, political, economic, and military aspects of the Dominican Republic and Haiti. Sources of information included scholarly books, journals, monographs; official reports of governments and international organizations; numerous periodicals; the authors' previous research and observations; and interviews with individuals who have special competence in Dominican, Haitian, and Latin American affairs. Chapter bibliographies appear at the end of the book; brief comments on sources recommended for further reading appear at the end of each chapter. To the extent possible, place-names conform with the system used by the United States Board on Geographic Names (BGN). Measurements are given in the metric system; a conversion table is provided to assist readers unfamiliar with metric measurements (see table 1, Appendix A). A glossary is also included.

Although there are numerous variations, Spanish surnames generally consist of two parts: the patrilineal name followed by the matrilineal one. In the instance of Joaquín Balaguer Ricardo, for example, Balaguer is his father's surname and Ricardo, his mother's maiden name. In nonformal use, the matrilineal name is often dropped. Thus, after the first mention, just Balaguer is used. A minority of individuals use only the patrilineal name.

Creole words used in the text may be presented in forms that are unfamiliar to readers who have done previous research on Haiti. The Creole orthography employed in this volume is that developed by the National Pedagogic Institute (Institut Pédagogique National—IPN), which has been the standard in Haiti since 1978.

Introduction

SINCE THE SIGNING of the Treaty of Ryswick between the kingdoms of Spain and France in 1697, the island of Hispaniola (La
Isla Española) has played host to two separate and distinct societies that we now know as the nations of Haiti and the Dominican
Republic. At first encounter, and without the benefit of historical
background and context, most students or observers find it incon-
gruous that two such disparate nations—one speaking French and
Creole, the other Spanish—should coexist within such limited confines. When viewed in light of the bitter struggle among European
colonial powers for wealth and influence both on the continent and
in the New World, however, the phenomenon becomes less puz-
zling. By the late seventeenth century, Spain was a declining power.
Although that country would maintain its vast holdings in mainland North America and South America, Spain found itself hard
pressed by British, Dutch, and French forces in the Caribbean.
The Treaty of Ryswick was but one result of this competition, as
the British eventually took Jamaica and established a foothold in
Central America. The French eventually proved the value of Caribbean colonization, in an economic as well as a maritime and strategic sense, by developing modern-day Haiti, then known as
Saint-Domingue, into the most productive colony in the Western
Hemisphere, if not the world.

Although the other European powers envied the French their
island jewel, Saint-Domingue eventually was lost not to a colonial
rival, but to an idea. That idea, inspired by the American Revolution and the French Revolution, was freedom; its power was such
as to convince a bitterly oppressed population of African slaves that
anything—reprisal, repression, even death—was preferable to its
denial. This positive impulse, liberally leavened with hatred for
the white men who had seized them, shipped them like cargo across
the ocean, tortured and abused them, and forced women into concubinage and men into arduous labor, impelled the black population of Saint-Domingue to an achievement still unmatched in
history: the overthrow of a slaveholding colonial power and the
establishment of a revolutionary black republic.

The saga of the Haitian Revolution is so dramatic that it is surprising that it has never served as the scenario for a Hollywood
production. Its images are varied and intense: the voodoo ceremony
and pact sealed in the Bois Cayman (Alligator Woods) in anticipation of the slave revolt of 1791; the blazing, bloody revolt itself;

foreign intervention by British and Spanish forces; the charismatic figure of François-Dominique Toussaint Louverture, his rise and fateful decision to switch his allegiance from Spain to France, his surprisingly effective command of troops in the field, the relative restraint with which he treated white survivors and prisoners, the competence of his brief stint as ruler; the French expedition of 1802, of which Toussaint exclaimed, "All France has come to invade us"; Toussaint's betrayal and seizure by the French; and the ensuing revolution led by Jean-Jacque Dessalines, Henri (Henry) Christophe, and Alexandre Pétion.

Given the distinctive and auspicious origins of the Haitian republic, there is some irony in that the Dominicans commemorate as their independence day the date of their overthrow of Haitian rule. The Dominican revolt, however, came as a response to annexation by a Haitian state that had passed from the promise of orderly administration under Toussaint to the hard-handed despotism of Dessalines and had then experienced division, both racial and political, between the forces of Christophe and Pétion. By the time of its conquest of Santo Domingo (later to become the Dominican Republic), Haiti had come under the comparatively stable, but uninspired, stewardship of Jean-Pierre Boyer. Although viewed, both at the time and today, by most Dominicans as a crude and oppressive state dominated by the military, the Haiti that occupied both eastern and western Hispaniola from 1822 to 1844 can itself be seen as a victim of international political and economic isolation. Because they either resented the existence of a black republic or feared a similar uprising in their own slave-owning regions, the European colonial powers and the United States shunned relations with Haiti; in the process, they contributed to the establishment of an impoverished society, ruled by the military, guided by the gun rather than the ballot, and controlled by a small, mostly mulatto, ruling group that lived well, while their countrymen either struggled to eke out a subsistence-level existence on small plots of land or flocked to the banners of regional strongmen in the seemingly never-ending contest for power. To be sure, the French colonial experience had left the Haitians completely unprepared for orderly democratic self-government, but the isolation of the post-independence period assured the exclusion of liberalizing influences that might have guided Haiti along a somewhat different path of political and economic development. By the same token, however, it may be that Western governments of the time, and even those of the early twentieth century, were incapable of dealing with a black republic on an equal basis. The United States occupation of Haiti (1915–34) certainly brought little of lasting value to the country's political culture or institutions, in part because the Americans saw the Haitians as uncivilized lackeys and treated them as such.

Both nations of Hispaniola share—along with much of the developing world—the strong tendency toward political organization built upon the personalistic followings of strongmen, or caudillos, rather than on more legalistic bases, such as constitutionalism. This similarity in political culture helps to explain the chronologicallystaggered parallels between the brutal regimes of Rafael Leónidas Trujillo Molina (1930–61) in the Dominican Republic and that of the Duvaliers—François Duvalier (1957–71) and his son, Jean-Claude Duvalier (1971–86)—in Haiti. Both regimes lasted for approximately thirty years; both were headed by nonideological despots; both regimes sustained themselves in power by employing terror and ruthlessly suppressing dissent; both drew the ire of an international community that ultimately proved incapable of directly forcing them from power; and both left their countries mired in political chaos and internal conflict upon their demise. One may only hope that the unstable situation in Haiti after the fall of the Duvalier regime will resolve itself without further analogy to Dominican history—that is, without a civil war. As of late 1990, however, the outcome of the situation remained extremely unpredictable.

Lieutenant General Prosper Avril took power in Haiti in September 1988, ousting the highly unpopular military regime led by Lieutenant General Henri Namphy. Avril, a product of the Haitian military tradition and the Duvalierist system, initially gave assurances that he would serve only as a transitional figure on the road to representative democracy. Whatever his personal feelings or motivations, however, Avril by his actions proved himself to be simply another corrupt Haitian military strongman. Having scheduled elections for 1990, he arrested and expelled leading political figures and declared a state of siege in January of that year. These actions triggered demonstrations, protests, and rioting among a population weary of exploitation and insincere promises of reform. Despite his public rhetoric, Avril presided over a military institution that perpetuated the Duvalierist traditions of extortion, graft, and price-gouging through state-owned enterprises. At the same time, the military made no substantive effort to address the problem of political violence. By early 1990, Haitians had had enough of promises; many decided to take action on their own, much as they had during the uprising of 1985 that swept Jean-Claude Duvalier from power.

Violent demonstrations began in earnest in early March 1990, ostensibly in response to the army's fatal shooting of an eleven-year-old girl in Petit Goâve. Streets blazed across Haiti as demonstrators ignited tires and automobiles, chanted anti-Avril slogans, and fought with army troops. Avril soon recognized the untenable nature of his position; the United States ambassador reportedly influenced the general's decision to step down in a private meeting held on March 12. Avril's flight from Haiti on a United States Air Force transport added his name to a long list of failed Haitian strongmen, and it left the country under the guidance of yet another military officer, Major General (subsequently promoted to Lieutenant General) Hérard Abraham.

Consultations among civilian political figures produced a provisional government headed by a judge of the Court of Cassation (supreme court), Ertha Pascal-Trouillot, a woman little-known outside legal circles. Judge Pascal-Trouillot reportedly accepted the post of provisional president after three other supreme court judges declined; she was sworn in on March 13. Appointed along with her was a nineteen-member Council of State, made up of prominent civic and political leaders. Although the new government announced no clear definitions of the powers of the council vis-à-vis the provisional president, some reports indicated that the president could exercise independent authority in some areas. The most compelling reality, however, was that all powers of the provisional government had been granted by the Haitian Armed Forces (Forces Armées d'Haïti—FAd'H), which would provide the government's only mandate—and perhaps its major political constituency—until valid popular elections could be held.

The Permanent Electoral Council (Conseil Electoral Permanent—CEP) scheduled local, legislative, and presidential elections for sometime between November 4 and November 29, 1990. The prospects for their successful implementation, however, appeared highly problematical at best. Seemingly unchecked political violence, which conjured up for many the horrible images of the bloody election day of November 1987, presented the major obstacle to free and fair balloting. Negotiations between the FAd'H and the CEP sought to establish security mechanisms that would prevent a recurrence of the 1987 tragedy. Popular confidence in these efforts, however, did not appear to be very great.

In a larger sense, the utter absence of any democratic tradition, or framework, in Haiti stacked the odds heavily against a smooth governmental transition. Economist Mats Lundahl has referred to Haiti as a hysteretic state, "not simply one where the past has shaped the present, but also one where history constitutes one of the strongest obstacles to change." Several conditions prevailing in Haiti gave substance to this definition. Among the wide array of personalistic political parties, only three—Marc Bazin's Movement for the Installation of Democracy in Haiti (Mouvement pour l'Instauration de la Démocratie en Haïti—MIDH), Serge Gilles's National Progressive Revolutionary Haitian Party (Parti National-al Progressiste Révolutionnaire Haïtien—Panpra), and Sylvio C. Claude's Christian Democrat Party of Haiti (Parti Démocrate Chré-tien d'Haïti—PDCH)—displayed any semblance of coherent programs or disciplined party apparatus. The odyssey of the Haitian military, from dominant power before the Duvaliers to subordinate status under the dynastic dictatorship, left uncertain the intentions of the FAd'H under Abraham's leadership. The return of such infamous Duvalierist cronies as former interior minister Roger LaFontant and persistent rumors that Jean-Claude himself was contemplating a return to the nation he had bled dry for fifteen years provoked outrage among a population that wanted nothing so much as to rid itself of the remaining vestiges of that predatory regime. According to some observers, internal conditions had approached, by the late summer of 1990, a sort of critical mass, which, if not defused by way of fair and free elections, could explode into generalized and ultimately futile violence.

In July one of the more responsible political leaders, Sylvio Claude, exhorted Haitians to block the return of undesirables by seizing the international airport outside Port-au-Prince. In a speech on Radio Nationale, he declared, "Instead of letting [the army] go kill you later, make them kill you now." Among the figures targeted by Claude for such action was former president Leslie F. Manigat, not previously considered a controversial figure by most observers. Perhaps in response to such rabble-rousing, the provisional government announced on August 1 that Manigat would be barred from returning to his native Haiti.

In late July, the Council of State issued a communiqué, laying down four conditions that it deemed necessary for holding successful elections. First, effective legal action had to be initiated against those who had participated in the November 1987 attacks and other political murders; second, a general climate of public security needed to be established in order to encourage voters to go to the polls; third, the public administration should be purged of entrenched, corrupt bureaucrats; and fourth, some checks had to be established over the powers of the rural section chiefs (*chefs de section*), so that the rural population could vote in an atmosphere free of coercion and intimidation. It was not clear what action the Council would take if these conditions had not been met by November.

In the Dominican Republic, events unfolded along a much more predictable path. Although Dominican politics were boisterous, and physical clashes—occasionally punctuated by gunfire—between the members of contending political parties were not unusual, the democratic system established after the 1965 civil war and the United States intervention continued to function with comparative efficiency (especially when compared with that of Haiti). The elections of May 16, 1990, however, demonstrated the manifold weaknesses of this system. The most glaring example of the lack of institutionalization in Dominican politics was that the major contenders for the presidency were the same two men who had opposed each other in the elections of 1966, namely, Juan Bosch Gaviño and incumbent Joaquín Balaguer Ricardo. Despite almost a quarter of a century of relatively free political organization and competition, the two modern-day caudillos, both octogenarians, still sallied into the arena flying their own personalistic banners rather than those of truly established parties. The one party that had displayed some level of institutionalization, the Dominican Revolutionary Party (Partido Revolucionario Dominicano—PRD), had split into antagonistic factions—each with its own caudillo—and never presented a serious challenge to the two elder statesmen.

The elections themselves, like most during the post-civil war era, were lively, controversial, and bitterly contested. Despite debilitating national problems, such as a chronic shortage of electricity, rising inflation, and persistent poverty, President Balaguer retained enough support in a presidential race contested by sixteen political parties (some running in coalition) to eke out a narrow victory over Bosch. The final tally showed Balaguer with 678,268 votes against Bosch's 653,423. Like most Dominican politicians before him, Bosch did not accept defeat with magnanimity; he lashed out at Balaguer and the Central Electoral Board, accusing both of fraud during balloting that impartial observers had judged to be fair and orderly. Bosch's early public statements exhorted his followers to stage public protests against the alleged electoral fraud. Early fears of widespread street violence initiated by disgruntled Bosch supporters proved unfounded, however, and Balaguer's reelection was confirmed by the Board on June 12, 1990.

Although it traditionally bends a little around election time, the Dominican democratic system showed few signs of breaking completely. Economic developments, however, will exercise a decisive impact on the nation's future stability. In that regard, Balaguer's reelection could prove to be a storm warning for the republic. At eighty-one years of age, Balaguer reportedly retained his enthusiasm for hands-on administration of government policy. The major economic aspects of that policy, however, did not promise a significant degree of improvement in the short term. Balaguer, since his days as a protégé of Trujillo, has believed in the liberal application of funds to public works projects—the construction of schools, housing, public buildings—in order to boost employment and purchase political support. Such gratuitous expenditures, however, largely served to exacerbate the government's fiscal problems, while masking to only a limited degree the consistently high levels of unemployment prevailing in the republic. Another tenet of Balaguer's economic creed was a refusal to submit to an economic adjustment program dictated by the International Monetary Fund (IMF—see Glossary). By ruling out an IMF-mandated program, Balaguer avoided further short-term austerity measures, such as devaluation and price increases on subsidized items; this enabled him to stand on a platform of economic nationalism and to proclaim his opposition to economic hardship imposed from abroad (that is, from the United States, which is strongly identified with the IMF throughout Latin America). In the long run, however, his obstinacy diminished Dominican standing with foreign creditors, and it limited any new infusions of capital needed to sustain the impressive growth of nontraditional exports achieved during the latter 1980s. This, in turn, would hinder the accumulation of foreign exchange needed to finance the imports required to sustain industrial development. Moreover, although an austerity program undoubtedly would pinch still further an already hard-pressed population, it might also help to balance the budget, to stabilize domestic prices, and to boost exports, all highly desirable potential results.

If the Dominican situation demonstrated anything to Haitians, it was that democracy is not a panacea for domestic turmoil. As Winston Churchill observed, it is the worst political system "except for all the others." Since Trujillo's death, Dominicans have struggled to adjust to an imperfect system, under less than ideal conditions; the final outcome of this process is still in doubt. For Haitians, the small step represented by valid elections could be their first lurch along a much longer road to peace and stability.

August 21, 1990

* * *

In the months following completion of research and writing of this book, significant political developments occurred in Haiti. On December 16, 1990, over 60 percent of registered voters turned out to elect political neophyte Jean-Bertrand Aristide president of Haiti. Aristide, a Roman Catholic priest and an advocate of liberation theology (see Glossary), registered an overwhelming first-round victory against a number of opponents. His popular identification as an outspoken opponent of the regime of Jean-Claude Duvalier apparently moved some 67 percent of voters to select Aristide as their leader. More traditional politicians such as Marc Bazin, Louis Dejoie, and Sylvio Claude trailed badly, reflecting their lack of appeal beyond the upper and middle classes. Aristide's victory came as a result of what was arguably the first free and fair election in Haitian history.

Right-wing backlash against the election of the radical leftist Aristide expressed itself in a coup attempt led by Duvalierist Roger Lafontant on January 6, 1991. Assisted by a small contingent of army personnel, Lafontant seized the National Palace, took prisoner Provisional President Pascal-Trouillot, and announced over the state-run television station his control of the government. Lafontant's pronouncement turned out to be decidedly premature, however, as loyalist army forces stormed the palace twelve hours later on the orders of FAd'H commander Abraham. Lafontant and those of his fellow conspirators who survived the fighting were captured and incarcerated. The coup also ignited violent street demonstrations in which mobs lynched at least seven people they accused of Duvalierist ties or sympathies. Violence continued in the interim between the elections and the presidential inauguration on February 7, 1991. Particularly intense anti-Duvalierist demonstrations took place on the night of January 26, leaving more than a dozen dead. On the night of February 1, 1991, suspected Duvalierists set fire to an orphanage in Port-au-Prince administered by Aristide.

Aristide's inauguration on February 7, 1991, was a gala event, befitting its historic nature. As expected, the new president delivered a spellbinding inaugural address. In it, he renounced his US$10,000 a month salary as a "scandal in a country where people cannot eat." Although the address was short on specifics of policy, its tone was one of gratitude and support for the poverty-afflicted constituency that had provided such a striking electoral mandate. The address was also conciliatory with regard to the military. Aristide described a "wedding between the army and the people," and hinted that the army would henceforth function as a public security force in order to lessen the threat emanating from right-wing forces such as those directed by Lafontant.

Beyond his rhetorical outreach to the rank and file, Aristide moved quickly to shore up his rule in the face of possible opposition from within the officer corps of the FAd'H. In his inaugural address, he called on General Abraham to retire six of the eight highest-ranking generals as well as the colonel who commanded the Presidential Guard. The appeal reflected Aristide's surprisingly powerful position, based on his overwhelming electoral victory and his demonstrated popular support, which extended even to the ranks of the military. The fact that Abraham complied with the request confirmed the already rather obvious disarray of the FAd'H and the general unwillingness of the institution to reassume political power in Haiti.

On February 9, Aristide proposed René Préval as Haiti's prime minister. Préval, a Belgian-trained agronomist and close associate of the president, was subsequently approved by the National Assembly. Although Aristide won a smashing personal victory in his presidential race, no one party or movement achieved a majority in the assembly. This fact promised a certain degree of stalemate and inertia in the legislative process under the Aristide administration. Such a situation did not seem conducive to the development of programs to deal effectively with the country's many severe problems. At the same time, however, an assembly based on coalition and compromise should serve to check any temptation by the new government toward heavy-handed or even authoritarian rule. In any case, the assembly was a new institution in a new government in what many hoped would be a new and democratic Haiti.

March 14, 1991   Richard A. Haggerty

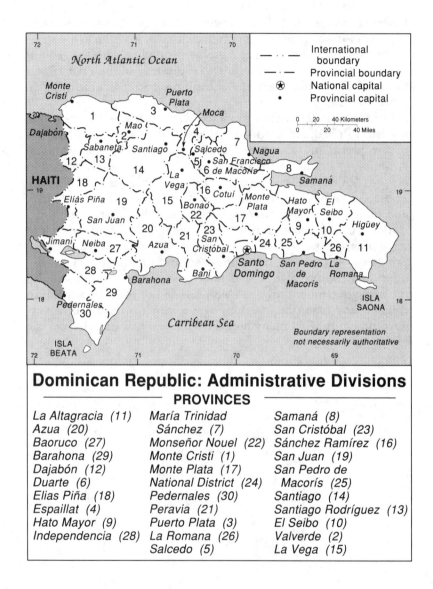

Dominican Republic: Administrative Divisions
PROVINCES

La Altagracia (11)	María Trinidad	Samaná (8)
Azua (20)	Sánchez (7)	San Cristóbal (23)
Baoruco (27)	Monseñor Nouel (22)	Sánchez Ramírez (16)
Barahona (29)	Monte Cristi (1)	San Juan (19)
Dajabón (12)	Monte Plata (17)	San Pedro de
Duarte (6)	National District (24)	Macorís (25)
Elias Piña (18)	Pedernales (30)	Santiago (14)
Espaillat (4)	Peravia (21)	Santiago Rodríguez (13)
Hato Mayor (9)	Puerto Plata (3)	El Seibo (10)
Independencia (28)	La Romana (26)	Valverde (2)
	Salcedo (5)	La Vega (15)

Figure 1. Dominican Republic: Administrative Divisions, 1989

Country Profile

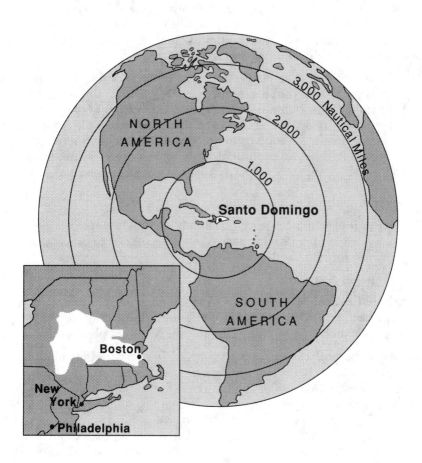

Country.

Formal Name: Dominican Republic.

Short Form: Dominican Republic.

Term for Citizens: Dominicans.

Capital: Santo Domingo.

Geography.

Size: Approximately 48,442 square kilometers.

Topography: Mountain ranges divide country into three regions: northern, central, and southwestern. Seven major drainage basins, most important that of Yaque del Norte River. Largest body of water Lago Enriquillo (Lake Enriquillo), in southwest. Highest mountain peak, Pico Duarte, rises in Cordillera Central (Central Range) to height of 3,087 meters.

Climate: Primarily tropical, with temperatures varying according to altitude. Seasons defined more by rainfall than by temperature. For most of country, rainy season runs roughly from May through November; dry season, from November through April. Rainfall not uniform throughout country because of mountain ranges. Tropical cyclones strike country on average of once every two years and usually have greatest impact along southern coast.

Society

Population: Annual rate of increase thought to be approximately 2.5 percent in mid-1980s. Projected total population to be just over 7 million by mid-1990.

Language: Spanish.

Ethnic Groups: Majority of mid-1980s population (approximately 73 percent) mulatto, a legacy of black slavery during colonial period. Approximately 16 percent of Dominicans white; 11 percent black.

Education and Literacy: An estimated 74 percent of population literate in 1986. Education system included six years of compulsory primary education, an additional six years of secondary education, and higher education at one of more than twenty-six postsecondary institutions. Major university and sole public institution was Autonomous University of Santo Domingo (Universidad Autónoma de Santo Domingo—UASD).

Health: State-funded health programs reached 78 to 89 percent of population. Facilities concentrated in Santo Domingo and Santiago de los Caballeros (Santiago); service in rural areas suffered accordingly. Main causes of death pulmonary circulatory diseases and intestinal diseases. Average life expectancy 62.6 years for 1980–84 period.

Religion: More than 90 percent Roman Catholic. Protestant groups also active; Evangelicals most successful in attracting converts.

Economy

Gross Domestic Product (GDP): Approximately US$5.6 billion in 1987, roughly US$800 per capita.

Agriculture: Accounted for about 15 percent of GDP, employed some 35 percent of labor force, and generated approximately half of all exports in 1988. Sugar traditionally the major crop, although its importance declined steadily during 1970s and 1980s. Coffee, cocoa, and tobacco also produced for export. Exports of nontraditional agricultural products, particularly pineapple and citrus fruit, expanded in 1980s.

Industry: Manufacturing, mining, and construction combined to contribute over 31 percent of GDP in 1988. These industries also employed almost 10 percent of labor force and accounted for two-thirds of country's exports. Assembly manufacturing subsector achieved fastest growth in 1980s as a result of government expansion of Industrial Free Zones throughout country. Major mineral exports gold, silver, bauxite, and nickel, all of which had low prices on world markets during 1980s. Construction benefited greatly from government public works projects and expansion of tourist industry.

Services: Tourism leading service industry; replaced sugar as country's leading foreign-exchange earner in 1984. Government supported development of tourist industry, but economic shortcomings such as inadequate water and energy supply and shortages of construction materials slowed expansion of facilities and adversely affected service to visitors. Financial services contributed 7 percent to GDP in 1988; transportation and communications accounted for additional 6 percent.

Currency: Dominican Republic peso (RD$), consisting of 100 centavos. Peso maintained on a par with United States dollar until 1985, when it was allowed to float against dollar. Value of peso plunged, reaching a low of US$1 = RD$8 in mid-1988, but had rebounded slightly to US$1 = RD$6.35 by 1989.

Imports: Approximately US$1.5 million in 1987, highest level ever recorded. Oil imports declined on a percentage basis from 1980 to 1987, but imports of intermediate goods, consumer goods, and capital goods increased over same period, contributing to negative trade balance.

Exports: Approximately US$718 million in 1987, a ten-year low. Decline in export value mainly attributable to low sugar prices on world market from 1984–87.

Balance of Payments: Overall deficit reached US$593 million in 1987, roughly 11 percent of GDP. Effect of deficit cushioned somewhat by cash remittances from Dominicans living abroad, tourism, a draw down of reserves, and rescheduling of country's foreign debt.

Fiscal year (FY): Calendar year, except in case of State Sugar Council (Consejo Estatal de Azúcar—CEA), which runs on cycle October 1 to September 30.

Fiscal Policy: Fiscal deficits mounted in 1980s, mainly as result of dwindling revenues. Revenues fell from 16 percent of GDP in 1970 to 10 percent in 1982, as Dominican governments provided tax incentives to business without securing sufficient alternate sources of revenue. Although not exorbitant relative to GDP, expenditures continued to rise throughout 1980s as government maintained subsidies on imported foodstuffs, gasoline, public utilities, and transportation in order to keep prices artificially low for low-income consumers. Debt service accounted for 22 percent of total expenditures in 1988 budget. Under President Joaquín Balaguer Ricardo, expanded public works programs boosted capital expenditures from 30 percent to over 40 percent of budget.

Transportation and Communications

Roads: Most common means of travel; in 1989 road network approxiately 17,000 kilometers, 70 percent of it paved.

Ports: As result of improvements to facilities during 1980s, Haina replaced Santo Domingo and Boca Chica as country's leading port. Other major shipping ports included Cabo Rojo and Barahona. Cruise ships stopped either at Santo Domingo or Puerto Plata.

Railroads: Rail system existed mainly to transport sugarcane. Its 1,725 kilometers of rail made it one of longest in Caribbean.

Airports: Four international airports. Major facilities Las Américas, near capital, and La Unión, near Puerto Plata. Smaller airports at La Romana and Santiago.

Telecommunications: Country boasted one of the most technologically advanced telecommunications industries in Latin America and Caribbean, offering wide range of services to consumers. Service concentrated in urban areas, however.

Government and Politics

Government: Republic with elected representative governmental system. Executive was dominant branch. Presidents served four-year terms and could be reelected. Legislature, known formally as Congress of the Republic, consisted of Senate and Chamber of Deputies. Judicial power exercised by Supreme Court of Justice and by other courts created by 1966 Constitution and by law. All judges chosen by Senate, not by president. Provincial (state) governors appointed by president; municipalities (counties) governed by elected mayors and municipal councils.

Politics: Following independence from Haiti in 1844, country characterized by political instability for almost a century. Dictator Rafael Leónidas Trujillo Molina took power in 1930 and ruled in repressive authoritarian fashion until his assassination in 1961. Brief civil war broke out in 1965 between liberal Constitutionalists—supporters of 1963 constitution promulgated during short-lived presidency of Juan Bosch Gaviño—and conservative Loyalist military factions. Conflict aborted by direct military intervention by United States. Subsequent elections brought Trujillo protégé Balaguer to presidency, an office he held for twelve years. Balaguer's attempt to nullify 1978 elections thwarted by pressure from Washington, allowing Silvestre Antonio Guzmán Fernández of social democratic Dominican Revolutionary Party (Partido Revolucionario Dominicano—PRD) to assume nation's leadership. PRD also won 1982 elections with lawyer Salvador Jorge Blanco as its standard bearer. Both PRD governments plagued by economic difficulties that forced them to institute austerity measures instead of social reforms they initially advocated. Declining popularity of Jorge government contributed to Balaguer's election for a fourth term beginning in 1986.

International Relations: Diplomatic activities concentrated on Caribbean, Latin America, United States, and Western Europe. Relations with neighboring Haiti traditionally strained, owing to numerous cultural divergences and long history of Dominicans and Haitians meddling in each other's affairs. Most important international relationship with United States, on which Dominican Republic has political, economic, and strategic dependence.

International Agreements and Membership: Signatory of Inter-American Treaty of Reciprocal Assistance (Rio Treaty) and all major inter-American conventions. Member of United Nations and its specialized agencies, Organization of American States, International Monetary Fund (see Glossary), Inter-American Development Bank, and other multilateral financial institutions. Also adhered to General Agreement on Tariffs and Trade.

National Security

Armed Forces: Dominican armed forces consisted of army, navy, and air force. Total personnel in 1989 about 20,800.

Organization: President constitutional commander in chief. Chain of command extended downward to secretary of state for the armed forces, then to deputy secretaries of state for individual branches of service, each of whom administered through a chief of staff and a general staff. Chiefs of staff exercised operational control, except in emergencies. Country divided into three defense zones: Southern Defense Zone, Western Defense Zone, and Northern Defense Zone.

Equipment: Army's equipment, mostly of United States manufacture, largely outmoded or poorly maintained. Dominican Navy in 1989 consisted of only one offshore and seventeen inshore vessels, mostly United States-made craft of World War II vintage. Dominican Air Force assets somewhat more modern and included Cessna A–37B Dragonfly jets and C–47 transports.

Police: National Police only police organization in country. Total manpower in 1989 about 10,000. Commanded by director general, subordinate to secretary of state for interior and police.

Chapter 1. Dominican Republic: Historical Setting

*Sketch of the landing at Hispaniola, reputedly drawn
by Christopher Columbus*

THE DOMINICAN REPUBLIC EXPERIENCED many setbacks on the road to the democratic system under which it functioned in the late 1980s. The nation did not enjoy full independence until 1844, when it emerged from twenty-two years of occupation by Haiti; this liberation came later than that of most Latin American countries. Reacceptance of Spanish rule from 1861 to 1865 demonstrated the republic's insecurity and dependence on larger powers to protect it and to define its status. Dominican vulnerability to intervention from abroad was also made evident by the United States military occupation of 1916–24 and by a more limited action by United States forces during a brief civil war in 1965.

Politically, Dominican history has been defined by an almost continuous competition for supremacy among caudillos of authoritarian ideological convictions. Political and regional competition overlapped to a great extent because mainly conservative leaders from the south and the east pitted themselves against generally more liberal figures from the northern part of the Valle del Cibao (the Cibao Valley, commonly called the Cibao). Traditions of personalism, militarism, and social and economic elitism locked the country into decades of debilitating wars, conspiracies, and despotism that drained its resources and undermined its efforts to establish liberal constitutional rule.

In the late 1980s, the republic was still struggling to emerge from the shadow of the ultimate Dominican caudillo, Rafael Leónidas Trujillo Molina (1930–61), who emerged from the military and held nearly absolute power throughout his rule. The apparent establishment of a democratic process in 1978 was a promising development; however, the survival of democracy appeared to be closely linked to the country's economic fortunes, which had declined steadily since the mid–1970s. As it had throughout its history, the republic continued to struggle with the nature of its domestic politics and with the definition of its economic and political role in the wider world.

The First Colony

The island of Hispaniola (La Isla Española) was the first New World colony settled by Spain. As such, it served as the logistical base for the conquest of most of the Western Hemisphere. Christopher Columbus first sighted the island in 1492 toward the end of his first voyage to "the Indies." Columbus and his crew

3

found the island inhabited by a large population of friendly Taino Indians (Arawaks), who made the explorers welcome. The land was fertile, but of greater importance to the Spaniards was the discovery that gold could be obtained either by barter with the natives, who adorned themselves with golden jewelry, or by extraction from alluvial deposits on the island.

After several attempts to plant colonies along the north coast of Hispaniola, Spain's first permanent settlement in the New World was established on the southern coast at the present site of Santo Domingo. Under Spanish sovereignty, the entire island bore the name Santo Domingo. Indications of the presence of gold—the life's blood of the nascent mercantilist system—and a population of tractable natives who could be used as laborers combined to attract many Spanish newcomers during the early years. Most were adventurers who, at least initially, were more interested in acquiring sudden wealth than they were in settling the land. Their relations with the Taino Indians, whom they ruthlessly maltreated, deteriorated from the beginning. Aroused by continued seizures of their food supplies, other exactions, and abuse of their women, the formerly peaceful Indians rebelled—only to be crushed decisively in 1495.

Columbus, who ruled the colony as royal governor until 1499, attempted to put an end to the more serious abuses to which the Indians were subjected by prohibiting foraging expeditions against them and by regulating the informal taxation imposed by the settlers. Being limited to this milder form of exploitation engendered active opposition among the settlers. To meet their demands, Columbus devised the *repartimiento* system of land settlement and native labor under which a settler, without assuming any obligation to the authorities, could be granted in perpetuity a large tract of land together with the services of the Indians living on it.

The *repartimiento* system did nothing to improve the lot of the Indians, and the Spanish crown changed it by instituting the system of *encomienda* in 1503. Under the *encomienda* system, all land became in theory the property of the crown, and the Indians thus were considered tenants on royal land. The crown's right to service from the tenants could be transferred in trust to individual Spanish settlers (*encomenderos*) by formal grant and the regular payment of tribute. The *encomenderos* were entitled to certain days of labor from the Indians, who became their charges. *Encomenderos* thus assumed the responsibility of providing for the physical wellbeing of the Indians and for their instruction in Christianity. An *encomienda* theoretically did not involve ownership of land; in practice, however, possession was gained through other means.

The hard work demanded of the Indians and the privations that they suffered demonstrated the unrealistic nature of the *encomienda* system, which effectively operated on an honor system as a result of the absence of enforcement efforts by Spanish authorities. The Indian population died off rapidly from exhaustion, starvation, disease, and other causes. By 1548 the Taino population, estimated at 1 million in 1492, had been reduced to approximately 500. The consequences were profound. The need for a new labor force to meet the growing demands of sugarcane cultivation prompted the importation of African slaves beginning in 1503. By 1520, black African labor was used almost exclusively.

The early grants of land without obligation under the *repartimiento* system resulted in a rapid decentralization of power. Each landowner possessed virtually sovereign authority. Power was diffused because of the tendency of the capital city, Santo Domingo (which also served as the seat of government for the entire Spanish Indies), to orient itself toward the continental Americas, which provided gold for the crown, and toward Spain, which provided administrators, supplies, and immigrants for the colonies. Local government was doomed to ineffectiveness because there was little contact between the capital and the hinterland; for practical purposes, the countryside fell under the sway of the large landowners. Throughout Dominican history, this sociopolitical order was a major factor in the development of some of the distinctive characteristics of the nation's political culture such as paternalism, personalism, and the tendency toward strong, even authoritarian, leadership (see The System of Dominican Politics, ch. 4).

As early as the 1490s, the landowners demonstrated their power by successfully conspiring against Columbus. His successor, Francisco de Bobadilla, was appointed chief justice and royal commissioner by the Spanish crown in 1499. Bobadilla sent Columbus back to Spain in irons, but Queen Isabella soon ordered him released. Bobadilla proved an inept administrator, and he was replaced in 1503 by the more efficient Nicolás de Ovando, who assumed the titles of governor and supreme justice. Because of his success in initiating reforms desired by the crown—the *encomienda* system among them—de Ovando received the title of Founder of Spain's Empire in the Indies.

In 1509 Columbus's son, Diego Columbus, was appointed governor of the colony of Santo Domingo. Diego's ambition and the splendid surroundings he provided for himself aroused the suspicions of the crown. As a result, in 1511 the crown established the *audiencia,* a new political institution intended to check the power of the governor. The first *audiencia* was simply a tribunal composed of three judges whose jurisdiction extended over all the West Indies. In this region, it formed the highest court of appeal. Employment of the *audiencia* eventually spread throughout Spanish America.

The tribunal's influence grew, and in 1524 it was designated the Royal Audiencia of Santo Domingo, with jurisdiction in the Caribbean, the Atlantic coast of Central America and Mexico, and the northern coast of South America, including all of what is now Venezuela and part of present-day Colombia. As a court representing the crown, the *audiencia* was given expanded powers that encompassed administrative, legislative, and consultative functions; the number of judges increased correspondingly. In criminal cases, the decisions of the *audiencia* were final, but important civil suits could be appealed to the Royal and Supreme Council of the Indies (Real y Supremo Consejo de las Indias) in Spain.

The Council of the Indies, created by Charles V in 1524, was the Spanish crown's main agency for directing colonial affairs. During most of its existence, the council exercised almost absolute power in making laws, administering justice, controlling finance and trade, supervising the church, and directing armies.

The arm of the Council of the Indies that dealt with all matters concerning commerce between Spain and its colonies in the Americas was the House of Trade (Casa de Contratación), organized in 1503. Control of commerce in general, and of tax collection in particular, was facilitated by the designation of monopoly seaports on either side of the Atlantic Ocean. During most of the colonial period, overseas trade consisted largely of annual convoys between monopoly ports. Trade between the colonies and countries other than Spain was prohibited. The crown also restricted trade among the colonies. These restrictions hampered economic activity in the New World and encouraged contraband traffic.

The Roman Catholic Church became the primary agent in spreading Spanish culture in the Americas. The ecclesiastical organization developed for Santo Domingo and later extended throughout Spanish America reflected a union of church and state actually closer than that prevailing in Spain itself. The Royal Patronage of the Indies (Real Patronato de las Indias, or, as it was called later, the Patronato Real) served as the organizational agent of this affiliation of the church and the Spanish crown.

Santo Domingo's prestige began to decline in the first part of the sixteenth century with the conquest of Mexico by Hernán Cortés in 1521 and the discovery there, and later in Peru, of great wealth in gold and silver. These events coincided with the exhaustion of the alluvial deposits of gold and the dying off of the Indian labor force in Santo Domingo. Large numbers of colonists left for Mexico and Peru; new immigrants from Spain largely bypassed Santo Domingo for the greater wealth to be found in lands to the west. The population of Santo Domingo dwindled, agriculture languished, and Spain soon became preoccupied with its richer and vaster mainland colonies.

The stagnation that prevailed in Santo Domingo for the next 250 years was interrupted on several occasions by armed engagements, as the French and the English attempted to weaken Spain's economic and political dominance in the New World. In 1586 the English admiral, Sir Francis Drake, captured the city of Santo Domingo and collected a ransom for its return to Spanish control. In 1655 Oliver Cromwell dispatched an English fleet, commanded by Sir William Penn, to take Santo Domingo. After meeting heavy resistance, the English sailed farther west and took Jamaica instead.

The withdrawal of the colonial government from the northern coastal region opened the way for French buccaneers, who had a base on Tortuga Island (Île de la Tortue), off the northwest coast of present-day Haiti, to settle on Hispaniola in the mid-seventeenth century. Although the Spanish destroyed the buccaneers' settlements several times, the determined French would not be deterred or expelled. The creation of the French West India Company in 1664 signalled France's intention to colonize western Hispaniola. Intermittent warfare went on between French and Spanish settlers over the next three decades; however, Spain, hard-pressed by warfare in Europe, could not maintain a garrison in Santo Domingo sufficient to secure the entire island against encroachment. In 1697, under the Treaty of Ryswick, Spain ceded the western third of the island to France. The exact boundary of this territory (Saint-Domingue—now Haiti) was not established at the time of cession and remained in question until 1929 (see fig. 1).

During the first years of the eighteenth century, landowners in the Spanish colony did little with their huge holdings, and the sugar plantations along the southern coast were abandoned because of harassment by pirates. Foreign trade all but ceased, and almost all domestic commerce took place in the capital city.

The Bourbon dynasty replaced the Habsburgs in Spain in 1700. The new regime introduced innovations—especially economic reforms—that gradually began to revive trade in Santo Domingo. The crown progressively relaxed the rigid controls and restrictions on commerce between the mother country and the colonies and among the colonies. The last convoys sailed in 1737; the monopoly port system was abolished shortly thereafter. By the middle of the century, both immigration and the importation of slaves had increased.

In 1765 the Caribbean islands received authorization for almost unlimited trade with Spanish ports; permission for the Spanish colonies in the Americas to trade among themselves followed in 1774. Duties on many commodities were greatly reduced or were removed altogether. By 1790 traders from any port in Spain could buy and sell anywhere in Spanish America, and by 1800 Spain had opened colonial trade to all neutral vessels.

As a result of the stimulus provided by the trade reforms, the population of the colony of Santo Domingo increased from about 6,000 in 1737 to approximately 125,000 in 1790. Of this number, about 40,000 were white landowners, about 25,000 were black or mulatto freedmen, and some 60,000 were slaves. The composition of Santo Domingo's population contrasted sharply with that of the neighboring French colony of Saint-Domingue, where some 30,000 whites and 27,000 freedmen extracted labor from at least 500,000 black slaves. To the Spanish colonists, Saint-Domingue represented a powder keg, the eventual explosion of which would echo throughout the island.

Haiti and Santo Domingo

Although they shared the island of Hispaniola, the colonies of Saint-Domingue and Santo Domingo followed disparate paths. Cultural differences explained the contrast to some extent, but the primary divergence was economic. Saint-Domingue was the most productive agricultural colony in the Western Hemisphere, and its output contributed heavily to the economy of France. By contrast, Santo Domingo was a small colony with little impact on the economy of Spain. Prosperous French plantation owners sought to maximize their gain through increased production for a growing world market. Thus, they imported great numbers of slaves from Africa and drove this captive work force ruthlessly.

Although by the end of the eighteenth century economic conditions were improving, landowners in Santo Domingo did not enjoy the same level of wealth attained by their French counterparts in Saint-Domingue. The absence of market-driven pressure to increase production enabled the domestic labor force to practice subsistence agriculture and to export at low levels. For this reason, Santo Domingo imported far fewer slaves than did Saint-Domingue. Spanish law also allowed a slave to purchase his freedom and that of his family for a relatively small sum. This contributed to the higher proportion of freedmen in the Spanish colony; by the turn of the century, freedmen actually constituted the majority of the population. Also in contrast to conditions in the French colony, this population profile contributed to a somewhat more egalitarian society, plagued much less by the schisms of race.

Stimulated to some degree by a revolution against the monarchy that was well underway in France, the inevitable explosion took place in Saint-Domingue in August 1791 (see The Slave Rebellion of 1791, ch. 6). The initial reaction of many Spanish colonists to news of the slaughter of Frenchmen by armies of rebellious black slaves was to flee Hispaniola entirely. Spain, however, saw in the unrest an opportunity to seize all, or part, of the western third of the island through an alliance of convenience with the British. These intentions, however, did not survive encounters in the field with forces led by the former slave, François-Dominique Toussaint Louverture (see Toussaint Louverture, ch. 6). In recognition of his leadership against the Spanish (under whose banner he had begun his military career), the British, and rebellious royalists and mulattoes, Toussaint was named governor general of Saint-Domingue by the French Republic in 1796. By the next year, Spain had surrendered the entire island to his rule. This action reflected not only Spain's growing disengagement from its colony, but also its setbacks in Europe and its relative decline as a world power.

Although France nominally enjoyed sovereignty over the entire island of Hispaniola, it was prevented from establishing an effective presence or administration in the east by continuing conflict between the indigenous forces led by Toussaint—and later by Jean-Jacques Dessalines—and an expeditionary force dispatched to Hispaniola by Napoléon Bonaparte in 1802 in an effort to bring the island more firmly under French control. Upon defeating the French, Dessalines and his followers established the independent nation of Haiti in January 1804. A small French presence, however, remained in the former Spanish colony. Dessalines attempted to take the city of Santo Domingo in March 1805, but he turned back after receiving reports of the approach of a French naval squadron.

By 1808 a number of émigré Spanish landowners had returned to Santo Domingo. These royalists had no intention of living under French rule, however, and they sought foreign assistance for a rebellion that would restore Spanish sovereignty. Help came from the Haitians, who provided arms, and from the British, who occupied Samaná and blockaded the port of Santo Domingo. The remaining French representatives fled the island in July 1809.

The 1809 restoration of Spanish rule ushered in an era referred to by some historians as España Boba (Foolish Spain). Under the despotic rule of Ferdinand VII, the colony's economy deteriorated severely. Some Dominicans began to wonder if their interests would not best be served by the sort of independence movement that was sweeping the South American colonies. In keeping with this sentiment, Spanish lieutenant governor José Núñez de Cáceres announced the colony's independence as the state of Spanish Haiti on November 30, 1821. Cáceres requested admission to the Republic of Gran Colombia (consisting of what later became Colombia, Ecuador, and Venezuela), recently proclaimed established by Simón Bolívar and his followers. While the request was in transit, however, the president of Haiti, Jean-Pierre Boyer, decided to invade Santo Domingo and to reunite the island under the Haitian flag.

The twenty-two years of Haitian occupation witnessed a steady economic decline and a growing resentment of Haiti among Dominicans. The agricultural pattern in the former Spanish colony came to resemble the one prevailing in all of Haiti at the time— that is, mainly subsistence cultivation with little or no production of export crops. Boyer attempted to enforce in the new territory the Rural Code (Code Rural) he had decreed in an effort to improve productivity among the Haitian yeomanry, but the Dominicans proved no more willing to adhere to its provisions than the Haitians had been (see Boyer: Expansion and Decline, ch. 6). Increasing numbers of Dominican landowners chose to flee the island rather than to live under Haitian rule; in many cases, Haitian administrators encouraged such emigration, confiscated the holdings of the émigrés, and redistributed them to Haitian officials. Aside from such bureaucratic machinations, most of the Dominicans' resentment of Haitian rule developed because Boyer, the ruler of an impoverished country, did not (or could not) provision his army. The occupying Haitian forces lived off the land in Santo Domingo, commandeering or confiscating what they needed to perform their duties or to fill their stomachs. Dominicans saw this as tribute demanded by petty conquerors, or as simple theft. Racial animosities also affected attitudes on both sides; black Haitian troops reacted with reflexive resentment against lighter-skinned Dominicans, while Dominicans came to associate the Haitians' dark skin with the oppression and the abuses of occupation.

Religious and cultural life also suffered under the Haitian occupation. The Haitians, who associated the Roman Catholic Church with the French colonists who had so cruelly exploited and abused them before independence, confiscated all church property in the east, deported all foreign clergy, and severed the ties of the remaining clergy to the Vatican. For Dominicans, who were much more strongly Roman Catholic and less oriented toward folk religion than the Haitians, such actions seemed insulting and nihilistic. In addition, upper-class Haitians considered French culture superior to

Spanish culture, while Haitian soldiers and others from the lower class simply disregarded Hispanic mores and customs.

The emigration of upper-class Dominicans served to forestall rebellion and to prolong the period of Haitian occupation because most Dominicans reflexively looked to the upper class for leadership. Scattered unrest and isolated confrontations between Haitians and Dominicans undoubtedly occurred; it was not until 1838, however, that any significant organized movement against Haitian domination began. Crucial to these stirrings was a twenty-year-old Dominican, of a prominent Santo Domingo family, who had returned home five years earlier after seven years of study in Europe. The young student's name was Juan Pablo Duarte.

Dominican history can in many ways be encompassed by a series of biographies. The personality and attributes of Duarte, however, ran counter to those of most of the country's caudillos. Duarte was an idealist, an ascetic, a genuine nationalist, a man of principle, and a romantic in a romantic age. Although he played no significant part in its rule, he is considered the father of his country. He certainly provided the inspiration and impetus for the achievement of independence from Haiti. Shocked, when he returned from Europe, by the deteriorated condition of Santo Domingo, the young student resolved to establish a resistance movement that would eventually throw off the Haitian yoke. He dubbed his movement La Trinitaria (The Trinity) because its original nine members had organized themselves into cells of three; the cells went on to recruit as separate organizations, maintaining strict secrecy, with little or no direct contact among themselves in order to minimize the possibility of detection or betrayal to the Haitian authorities. Young recruits flocked to Duarte's banner (almost literally, for it was Duarte who designed the modern Dominican flag) as a result of the pent-up resentment under Haitian rule. Despite its elaborate codes and clandestine procedures, La Trinitaria was eventually betrayed to the Haitians. It survived largely intact, however, emerging under the new designation, La Filantrópica, to continue its work of anti-Haitian agitation.

Despite their numbers and their base of popular support, the Trinitarios (as the rebels still referred to themselves) required a political disruption in Haiti proper to boost their movement toward its ultimate success. The overthrow of Boyer in the Revolution of 1843 provided a catalyst for the Dominican rebels. Charles Rivière-Hérard replaced Boyer as president of Haiti. Like most Haitian leaders, he required a transition period in which to deal with competitors and to solidify his rule. Rivière-Hérard apparently identified one disaffected Haitian faction in the administration of the eastern territory; his crackdown on this group extended to the Trinitarios as well, because apparently there had been some fruitless contacts between the Dominicans and some liberal Haitians. The increased pressure induced Duarte to leave the country temporarily in search of support in other Latin American states, mainly Colombia and Venezuela. In December 1843, a group of Duarte's followers urged him to return to Santo Domingo. They feared that their plans for an insurrection might be betrayed to the Haitians and had therefore resolved to carry them through quickly. Duarte sailed as far north from Caracas as the island of Curaçao, where he fell victim to a violent illness. When he had not arrived home by February 1844, the rebels, under the leadership of Francisco del Rosario Sánchez and Ramón Mella, agreed to launch their uprising without him.

On February 27, 1844—thereafter celebrated as Dominican Independence Day—the rebels seized the Ozama fortress in the capital. The Haitian garrison, taken by surprise and apparently betrayed by at least one of its sentries, retired in disarray. Within two days, all Haitian officials had left Santo Domingo. Mella headed the provisional governing junta of the new Dominican Republic. Duarte, finally recovered, returned to his country on March 14. The following day, he entered the capital amidst great adulation and celebration. As is so often the case in such circumstances, the optimism generated by revolutionary triumph would eventually give way to the disillusion caused by the struggle for power.

Santana and Báez: The Caudillos Take Charge

Two leaders dominated the period between 1844 and 1864: General Pedro Santana Familias and Buenaventura Báez Méndez. Dissimilar in appearance and temperament, the two alternated in power by means of force, factionalism, and repeated efforts to secure their country's protection or annexation by a foreign power. Their unprincipled, self-serving dominance did much to entrench the tradition of caudillo rule in the Dominican Republic.

The Infant Republic

Santana's power base lay in the military forces mustered to defend the infant republic against Haitian retaliation. Duarte, briefly a member of the governing junta, for a time commanded an armed force as well. He was temperamentally unsuited to generalship, however, and the junta eventually replaced him with General José María Imbert. Duarte assumed the post of governor of the Cibao, the northern farming region administered from the city of Santiago de los Caballeros, commonly known as Santiago (see fig. 1).

In July 1844, Mella and a throng of other Duarte supporters in Santiago urged him to take the title of president of the republic. Duarte agreed to do so, but only if free elections could be arranged. Santana, who felt that only the protection of a great power could assure Dominican safety against the Haitian threat, did not share Duarte's enthusiasm for the electoral process. His forces took Santo Domingo on July 12, 1844, and they proclaimed Santana ruler of the Dominican Republic. Mella, who attempted to mediate a compromise government including both Duarte and Santana, found himself imprisoned by the new dictator. Duarte and Sánchez followed Mella into prison and subsequently into exile.

Although in 1844 a constituent assembly drafted a constitution, based on the Haitian and the United States models, which established separation of powers and legislative checks on the executive, Santana proceeded to emasculate the document that same year by demanding the inclusion of Article 210, which granted him untrammeled power "during the current war" against Haiti.

As it turned out, the Dominicans repelled the Haitian forces, on both land and sea, by December 1845. Santana's dictatorial powers, however, continued throughout his first term (1844–48). He consolidated his power by executing anti-Santana conspirators, by rewarding his close associates with lucrative positions in government, and by printing paper money to cover the expenses of a large standing army, a policy that severely devalued the new nation's currency. Throughout his term, Santana also continued to explore the possibility of an association with a foreign power. The governments of the United States, France, and Spain all declined the offer.

Santana responded to general discontent, prompted mainly by the deteriorating currency and economy, by resigning from the presidency in February 1848 and retiring to his ranch in the province of El Seibo. The Council of Secretaries of State, made up of former cabinet members, selected minister of war Manuel Jiménez to replace Santana in August 1848. Jiménez displayed little enthusiasm and no aptitude as a ruler. His tenure, which would probably have been brief in any case, ended in May 1849. The violent sequence of events that culminated in Jiménez's departure began with a new invasion from Haiti, this time led by self-styled emperor Faustin Soulouque (see Decades of Instability, 1843–1915, ch. 6). Santana returned to prominence at the head of the army that checked the Haitian advance at Las Carreras in April 1849. As the Haitians retired, Santana pressed his advantage against Jiménez. After some brief skirmishes between his forces and those loyal to the president, Santana took control of Santo Domingo and the government on May 30, 1849.

13

Although Santana once again held the reins of power, he declined to formalize the situation by standing for office. Instead, he renounced the temporary mandate granted him by the legislature and called for an election—carried out under an electoral college system with limited suffrage—to select a new president. Santana favored Santiago Espaillat, who won a ballot in the Congress on July 5, 1849; Espaillat declined to accept the presidency, however, knowing that he would have to serve as a puppet so long as Santana controlled the army. This cleared the way for Báez, president of the legislature, to win a second ballot, which was held on August 18, 1849.

Báez made even more vigorous overtures to foreign powers to establish a Dominican protectorate. Both France (Báez's personal preference) and the United States, although still unwilling to annex the entire country, expressed interest in acquiring the bay and peninsula of Samaná as a naval or commercial port. Consequently, in order to preserve its lucrative trade with the island nation and to deny a strategic asset to its rivals, Britain became more actively involved in Dominican affairs. In 1850 the British signed a commercial and maritime treaty with the Dominicans. The following year, Britain mediated a peace treaty between the Dominican Republic and Haiti.

Báez's first term established the personal rivalry with Santana that dominated Dominican politics until the latter's death in 1864. President Báez purged Santana's followers (*santanistas*) from the government and installed his own sycophants (*baecistas*) in their place, pardoned a number of Santana's political opponents, reorganized the military in an effort to dilute Santana's power base, and apparently conceived a plan to create a militia that would serve as a counterforce to the army.

Seeing his influence clearly threatened, Santana returned to the political arena in February 1853, when he was elected to succeed Báez. The general moved quickly to deal with Báez, who had once been a colonel under his command. In a public address on July 3, 1853, Santana denounced Báez as a collaborator under the Haitian occupation (which was true) and a paid agent of influence for the Haitians after independence (which may have been true, although not to the extent that Santana declared). Publicly characterizing Báez's presence in the nation a threat to security, Santana exercised his authority under Article 210 of the constitution and expelled the former president from the Dominican Republic.

Although he enjoyed considerable popularity, Santana confronted several crises during his second term. In February 1854, a constituent assembly promulgated a new, liberal constitution that eliminated the dictatorial powers granted by Article 210. With his control over the army restored, however, Santana readily forced the adoption of a new constitution restoring most of the excised prerogatives of the executive. On the international front, renewed annexation talks between the Dominican and the United States governments aroused the concern of Haitian emperor Soulouque. Motivated, at least in part, by a desire to prevent the acquisition of any portion of Hispaniola by the slaveholding United States, Soulouque launched a new invasion in November 1855. However, Dominican forces decisively defeated the Haitians in a number of engagements and forced them back across the border by January 1856.

The final crisis of Santana's second term also originated in the foreign policy sphere. Shortly after the Haitian campaign, the Dominican and the United States governments signed a commercial treaty that provided for the lease of a small tract in Samaná for use as a coaling station. Although Santana delayed implementation of the lease, its negotiation provided his opponents—including *baecistas* and the government of Spain—with an opportunity to decry Yankee imperialism and to demand the president's ouster. Pressure built to such an extent that Santana felt compelled to resign on May 26, 1856, in favor of his vice president, Manuel de la Regla Mota.

Regla Mota's rule lasted almost five months. An empty treasury forced the new president to discharge most of the army. Thus deprived of the Dominican rulers' traditional source of power, his government all but invited the return of Báez. With the support of the Spanish, Báez was named vice president by Regla Mota, who then resigned in Báez's favor. Not a forgiving man by nature, Báez lost little time before denouncing ex-president Santana and expelling him from the country. Once again, Báez purged *santanistas* from the government and replaced them with his own men.

Báez had little time in which to savor his triumph over his rival, however. Reverting to the policies of his first term, the government flooded the country with what rapidly became all but worthless paper money. Farmers in the Cibao, who objected strongly to the purchase of their crops with this devalued currency, rose against Báez in what came to be known as the Revolution of 1857. Their standard-bearer, not surprisingly, was Santana.

Pardoned by a provisional government established at Santiago de los Caballeros, Santana returned in August 1857 to join the revolution. He raised his own personal army and soon dominated the movement. A year of bloody conflict between the governments of Santiago and Santo Domingo took a heavy toll in lives and money. Under the terms of a June 1857 armistice, Báez once again fled to Curaçao with all the government funds that he could carry. Santana proceeded to betray the aspirations of some of his liberal revolutionary followers by restoring the dictatorial constitution of 1854. *Santanismo* again replaced *baecismo;* only a small group of loyalists realized any benefit from the exchange, however. Politically, the country continued to walk a treadmill. Economically, conditions had become almost unbearable for many Dominicans. The general climate of despair ensured the inevitable success of Santana's renewed efforts to secure a protector for his country.

Annexation by Spain, 1861–65

On March 17, 1861, Santana announced the annexation of the Dominican Republic by Spain. A number of conditions had combined to bring about this reversion to colonialism. The Civil War in the United States had lessened the Spanish fear of retaliation from the north. In Spain itself, the ruling Liberal Union of General Leopoldo O'Donnell had been advocating renewed imperial expansion. And in the Dominican Republic, both the ruler and a portion of the ruled were sufficiently concerned about the possibility either of a renewed attack from Haiti or of domestic economic collapse to find the prospect of annexation attractive.

Support for annexation did not run as deep as Santana and his clique had represented to the Spanish, however. The first rebellion against Spanish rule broke out in May 1861, but it was quashed in short order. A better organized revolt, under the leadership of the *baecista,* General Sánchez, sprang up only a month later. Santana, now bearing the title of captain general of the Province of Santo Domingo, was forced to take to the field against his own countrymen as the representative of a foreign power. The wily Santana lured Sánchez into an ambush, where he was captured and executed. Despite this service, Santana found his personal power and his ability to dole out patronage to his followers greatly restricted under Spanish rule. In a fit of pique, he resigned the captaincy general in January 1862.

Resentment and rebellion continued, fed by racial tension, excessive taxation, the failure to stabilize the currency, the uncompensated requisition of supplies by the Spanish army, heavy-handed reform of local religious customs by an inflexible Spanish archbishop, and the restriction of trade to the benefit of the Spanish empire. The Spaniards quelled more uprisings in 1863, but guerrilla actions continued. In response to the continuing unrest, a state of siege was declared in February 1863.

Rebellious Dominicans set up a provisional government in Santiago, headed by General José Antonio Salcedo Ramírez, on

September 14, 1863. Their proclamation of an Act of Independence launched what is known as the War of Restoration. For their part, the Spanish once again turned to Santana, who received command of a force made up largely of mercenaries; however, this campaign was the last for the old caudillo. By this time, his popularity had all but disappeared. Indeed, the provisional government had denounced Santana and had condemned him to death for his actions against his countrymen. On June 14, 1864, a broken and despondent Santana saved the rebels the trouble of carrying out their sentence. The timing of his death lent credence to speculation that he had committed suicide, although this belief was never proven.

Meanwhile, the guerrilla war against the Spanish ground on. The rebels further formalized their provisional rule by replacing Salcedo (who had advocated the return of Báez to rule a restored republic) and by then holding a national convention on February 27, 1865, which enacted a new constitution and elected Pedro Antonio Pimentel Chamorro president.

Circumstances began to favor a Spanish withdrawal. The conclusion of its Civil War promised that the United States would make new efforts to enforce the Monroe Doctrine, which barred European powers from the Western Hemisphere. Spanish military forces, unable to contain the spread of the insurrection, lost even greater numbers of troops to disease than they did to the guerrillas. The O'Donnell government had fallen, taking with it any dreams of a renewed Spanish empire. On March 3, 1865, the Queen of Spain approved a decree repealing the annexation of Santo Domingo.

The Spanish left political chaos in their wake. A power struggle began between the conservative, cacique-dominated south and the more liberal Cibao, where the prevalence of medium-sized landholdings contributed to a more egalitarian social structure. The two camps eventually coalesced under the banners of separate political parties. The Cibaeños (residents of the Cibao) adhered to the National Liberal Party (Partido Nacional Liberal), which became known as the Blue Party (Partido Azul). The southerners rallied to the Red Party (Partido Rojo).

The conservative Reds effectively employed their numerical superiority in the capital to force the restoration of Báez, who returned triumphantly from exile and assumed the presidency on December 8, 1865. Never again, however, would he exercise the sort of dictatorial control over the republic that he and Santana had once alternately enjoyed. The country's institutions had changed. Regional forces mustered during the War of Restoration had replaced the national army that previously had done battle with the Haitians. Political power had likewise been diffused, particularly between the opposing poles of the Cibao and the south. Under these conditions, it was difficult, if not impossible, for one man to dominate the entire nation.

The Contest for Power, 1865–82

After a successful uprising that forced Báez to flee the country in May 1866, a triumvirate of Cibaeño military leaders, the most prominent of whom was Gregorio Luperón, assumed provisional power. General José María Cabral Luna, who had served briefly as president in 1865, was reelected to that post on September 29, 1866. The *baecistas,* however, were still a potent force in the republic; they forced Cabral out and reinstalled Báez on May 2, 1868. Once again, his rule was marked by peculation and efforts to sell or to lease portions of the country to foreign interests. These included an intermittent campaign to have the entire country annexed by the United States. He was once again overthrown by rebellious Blues in January 1874.

After a period of infighting among the Blues, backing from Luperón helped Ulises Francisco Espaillat Quiñones to win election as president on March 24, 1876. Espaillat, a political and economic liberal, apparently intended to broaden personal freedoms and to set the nation's economy on a firmer footing. He never had the opportunity to do either, however. Rebellions in the south and the east forced Espaillat to resign on December 20, 1876. Ever the opportunist, Báez returned once more to power. The most effective opposition to his rule came from guerrilla forces led by a politically active priest, Fernando Arturo de Meriño Ramírez. In February 1878, the unpopular Báez left his country for the last time; he died in exile in 1882.

Both Santana and Báez had now passed from the scene. They had helped to create a nation where violence prevailed in the quest for power, where economic growth and financial stability fell victim to a seemingly endless political contest, and where foreign interests still perceived parts of the national territory as available to the highest bidder. This divisive, chaotic situation invited the emergence of a Machiavellian figure who would "unite" the republic.

Ulises Heureaux, 1882–99

Ulises Heureaux, Luperón's lieutenant, stood out among his fellow Dominicans both physically and temperamentally. The illegitimate son of a Haitian father and a mother who was originally from the island of St. Thomas, he was distinguished by his blackness from most other contenders for power, with the exception of Luperón. As events were to demonstrate, he also possessed a singular thirst for power and a willingness to take any measures necessary to attain and to hold it.

During the four years between Báez's final withdrawal and Heureaux's ascension to the presidency, seven individuals held or claimed national, regional, or interim leadership. Among them were Ignacio María González Santín, who held the presidency from June to September 1878; Luperón, who governed from Puerto Plata as provisional president from October 1879 to August 1880; and Meriño, who assumed office in September 1880 after apparently fraudulent general elections. Heureaux served as interior minister under Meriño; his behind-the-scenes influence on the rest of the cabinet apparently exceeded that of the president. Although Meriño briefly suspended constitutional procedures in response to unrest fomented by some remaining *baecistas*, he abided by the two-year term established under Luperón and turned the reins of government over to Heureaux on September 1, 1882.

Heureaux's first term as president was not particularly noteworthy. The administrations of Luperón and Meriño had achieved some financial stability for the country; political conditions had settled down to the point that Heureaux needed to suppress only one major uprising during his two-year tenure. By 1884, however, no single potential successor, among the various caciques who constituted the republic's ruling group, enjoyed widespread support. Luperón, still the leader of the ruling Blue Party, supported General Segundo Imbert for the post, while Heureaux backed the candidacy of General Francisco Gregorio Billini. A consummate dissembler, Heureaux assured Luperón that he would support Imbert should he win the election, but Heureaux also had ballot boxes in critical precincts stuffed in order to assure Billini's election.

Inaugurated president on September 1, 1884, Billini resisted Heureaux's efforts to manipulate him. Thus denied de facto rule, Heureaux undermined Billini by spreading rumors to the effect that the president had decreed a political amnesty so that he could conspire with ex-president Cesáreo Guillermo Bastardo (February 27-December 6, 1879) against Luperón's leadership of the Blues. This precipitated a governmental crisis that resulted in Billini's resignation on May 16, 1885. Vice President Alejandro Woss y Gil succeeded Billini. Heureaux assumed a more prominent role under the new government; a number of his adherents were included in the cabinet, and the general himself assumed command of the national army in order to stem a rebellion led by Guillermo, whose suicide when he was faced with capture removed another potential rival for power and further endeared Heureaux to Luperón, a long-time enemy of Guillermo.

Luperón accordingly supported Heureaux in the 1886 presidential elections. Opposed by Casimiro de Moya, Heureaux relied on his considerable popularity and his demonstrated skill at electoral manipulation to carry the balloting. The blatancy of the fraud in some areas, particularly the capital, inspired Moya's followers to launch an armed rebellion. Heureaux again benefited from Luperón's support in this struggle; it delayed his inauguration by four months, but it further narrowed the field of political contenders. Having again achieved power, Heureaux maintained his grip on it for the rest of his life.

Several moves served to lay the groundwork for Heureaux's dictatorship. Constitutional amendments requested by the president and effected by the Congress extended the presidential term from two to four years and eliminated direct elections in favor of the formerly employed electoral college system. To expand his informal power base, Heureaux (who became popularly known as General Lilís, thanks to a common mispronunciation of his first name) incorporated both Reds and Blues into his government. The president also established an extensive network of secret police and informants in order to avert incipient rebellions. The press, previously unhampered, came under new restrictions.

In the face of impending dictatorship, concerned Dominican liberals turned to the only remaining figure of stature, Luperón. The elections of 1888 therefore pitted Heureaux against his political mentor. If the dictator felt any respect for his former commander, he did not demonstrate it during the campaign. Heureaux's agents attacked Luperón's campaigners and supporters, arresting and incarcerating considerable numbers of them. Recognizing the impossibility of a free election under such circumstances, Luperón withdrew his candidacy, declined the entreaties of those of his followers who urged armed rebellion, and fled into exile in Puerto Rico.

Although plots, intrigue, and abortive insurrections continued under his rule, Heureaux faced no serious challenges until his assassination in 1899. He continued to govern in mock-constitutional fashion, achieving reelection through institutionalized fraud. Despite his relatively secure position, his repression of dissent became more severe, and the number of political prisoners expanded along with the dictator's paranoia. Like Santana and Báez before him, Heureaux sought the protection of a foreign power, principally the United States. Although annexation was no longer an option, the dictator did offer to lease the Samaná Peninsula to the United States.

The deal was never consummated, however, because of opposition from the liberal wing of the Blue Party and a number of concerned European powers. In 1891 Washington and Santo Domingo did conclude a reciprocity treaty that allowed twenty-six United States products free entry into the Dominican market in exchange for similar duty-free access for certain Dominican goods. The governments of Germany, Britain, and France all filed official protests over the treaty, which they saw as detrimental to their most-favored-nation trading status.

Under Heureaux, the Dominican government considerably expanded its external debt. Although some improvements to infrastructure resulted, much of the money went to support the dictator's personal extravagances and the financial requirements of his police state. The failure to apply the funds productively exacerbated both domestic budget deficits and shortfalls in the external balance of payments. In an effort to head off complete bankruptcy, the government turned to the familiar expedient of printing paper money. The huge issuance of 1897, however, debased the currency to such an extent that even Dominicans refused to accept it.

Despite the dictator's comprehensive efforts to suppress opposition—his network of spies and agents extended even to foreign countries—a revolutionary organization eventually emerged. Established in Puerto Rico by Horacio Vásquez Lajara, a young adherent of Luperón, the group called itself the Young Revolutionary Junta (Junta Revolucionaria de Jóvenes). Other prominent members of the group included Federico Velásquez and Ramón Cáceres Vásquez. The three returned to their plantations in the Cibao and began to lay the groundwork for a coordinated rebellion against the widely detested Heureaux. The impetuous Cáceres, however, opted for a revolution at a single stroke when the dictator passed through the town of Moca on July 26, 1899. He shot Heureaux several times and left the longtime ruler fatally wounded amid a startled crowd. Cáceres escaped unharmed.

Renewed Conflict, 1899–1916

After a brief period of armed conflict, the revolutionaries prevailed. Vásquez headed a provisional government established in September 1899. Free, direct elections brought to the presidency Juan Isidro Jiménez Pereyra on November 15. The Jiménez administration faced a fiscal crisis when European creditors, led by the French, began to call in loans that had been contracted by Heureaux. Customs fees represented the only significant source of government revenue at that time. When the Jiménez government pledged 40 percent of its customs revenue to repay its foreign debt, it provoked the ire of the San Domingo Improvement Company. A United States-based firm, the Improvement Company had lent large sums to the Heureaux regime. As a result, it had not only received a considerable percentage of customs revenue, but also had been granted the right to administer Dominican customs in order to ensure regular repayment. Stung by the Jiménez government's resumption of control over its customs receipts, the directors of the Improvement Company protested to the United States Department of State. The review of the case prompted a renewed interest in Washington in Dominican affairs.

The death of Heureaux, however, had by no means ushered in an era of political tranquility. Jiménez's various financial negotiations with foreign powers had aroused opposition among nationalists, particularly in the Cibao, who suspected the president of bargaining away Dominican sovereignty in return for financial settlements. Government forces led by Vásquez put down some early uprisings. Eventually, however, personal and political competition between Jiménez and Vásquez brought them into more serious conflict. Vásquez's forces proclaimed a revolution on April 26, 1902; with no real base of support, Jiménez fled his office and his country a few days later. Although highly principled, Vásquez was not a strong leader. Squabbles among his followers and opposition to his government from local caciques grew into general unrest that culminated in the seizure of power by ex-president Woss y Gil in April 1903.

Dominican politics had once again polarized into two largely nonideological camps. Where once the Blues and the Reds had contended for power, now the *jimenistas* (supporters of Jiménez; sing., *jimenista*) and the *horacistas* (supporters of Vásquez and Cáceres; sing., *horacista*) vied for control. Woss y Gil, a *jimenista,* made the mistake of seeking supporters among the *horacista* camp and he was overthrown by the *jimenista* general, Carlos F. Morales Languasco, in December 1903. Rather than restore the country's leadership to Jiménez, however, Morales set up a provisional government and announced his own candidacy for the presidency—with Cáceres as his running mate. The renewed fraternization with the *horacistas* incited another *jimenista* rebellion. This uprising proved unsuccessful, and Morales and Cáceres were inaugurated on June 19, 1904.

Conflict within the Morales administration between supporters of the president and those of the vice president debilitated the government. By late 1905, it became clear that Morales had lost effective control to Cáceres and the cabinet. Morales resolved to lead a coup against his own government; his plan was discovered by the *horacistas,* however, and he was captured and dispatched into exile. Cáceres assumed the presidency on December 29, 1905.

The influence of the United States had increased considerably during the first few years of the twentieth century. United States military forces had intervened in a minor way to ensure the safety of United States citizens and to prevent the deployment of warships by European governments seeking immediate repayment of debt. By 1904 Washington had begun to take a greater interest in the stability of Caribbean nations, particularly those—like the Dominican Republic—situated along the approaches to the forthcoming Panama Canal. The administration of Theodore Roosevelt took a particular interest in resolving the republic's economic situation. It negotiated an agreement in June 1904 whereby the Dominican government bought out the holdings of the San Domingo Improvement Company. The Morales government also agreed to accept the appointment by the United States government of a financial agent to oversee the repayment of the outstanding debt to the Improvement Company from customs duties. This agreement was subsequently superseded by a financial accord signed between the two governments on February 7, 1905; under the provisions of this accord, the United States government assumed responsibility for all Dominican debt as well as for the collection of customs duties and the allocation of those revenues to the Dominican government and to the repayment of its domestic and foreign debt. Although parts of this agreement were rejected by the United States Senate, it formed the basis for the establishment in April 1905 of the General Customs Receivership, the office through which the United States government administered the finances of the Dominican Republic.

The Cáceres government became the financial beneficiary of this arrangement. Freed from the burden of dealing with creditors, Cáceres attempted to reform the political system. Constitutional reforms placed local *ayuntamientos* (town councils) under the power of the central government, extended the presidential term to six years, and eliminated the office of vice president. Cáceres also nationalized public utilities and established a bureau of public works to administer them. All of these actions engendered both opposition and support. The curtailment of local authority particularly irked those caciques who preferred to rule through compliant *ayuntamientos.* The continued financial sovereignty of the Yankees also outweighed the economic benefits of the receivership in the minds of many nationalistic Dominicans. Intrigues fomented in exile by Morales, Jiménez, and others beset Cáceres. On November 19,

1911, a small group headed by Luis Tejera assassinated Cáceres as he took his evening drive through the streets of Santo Domingo.

Occupation by the United States, 1916–24

The assassination of Cáceres turned out to be but the first act of a frenzied drama that culminated in the republic's occupation by the United States. The fiscal stability that had resulted from the 1905 receivership eroded under Cáceres's successor, Eladio Victoria y Victoria; most of the increased outlays went to support military campaigns against rebellious partisans, mainly in the Cibao. The continued violence and instability prompted the administration of President William H. Taft to dispatch a commission to Santo Domingo on September 24, 1912, to mediate among the warring factions. The presence of a 750-member force of United States marines apparently convinced the Dominicans of the seriousness of Washington's threats to intervene directly in the conflict; Victoria agreed to step down in favor of a neutral figure, Roman Catholic archbishop Adolfo Alejandro Nouel Bobadilla. The archbishop assumed office as provisional president on November 30.

Nouel proved unequal to the burden of national leadership. Unable to mediate successfully between the ambitions of rival *horacistas* and *jimenistas,* he stepped down on March 31, 1913. His successor, José Bordas Valdez, was equally unable to restrain the renewed outbreak of hostilities. Once again, Washington took a direct hand and mediated a resolution. The rebellious *horacistas* agreed to a ceasefire based on a pledge of United States oversight of elections for members of local *ayuntamientos* and a constituent assembly that would draft the procedures for presidential balloting. The process, however, was flagrantly manipulated and resulted in Bordas's reelection on June 15, 1914. Both *horacistas* and *jimenistas* took offense at this blatant maneuver and rose up against Bordas.

The United States government, this time under President Woodrow Wilson, again intervened. Where Taft had cajoled the combatants with a clear intimation of military action, Wilson delivered an ultimatum: elect a president or the United States will impose one. The Dominicans accordingly selected Ramón Báez Machado as provisional president on August 27, 1914. Comparatively fair presidential elections held on October 25 returned Jiménez to the presidency. Despite his victory, however, Jiménez felt impelled to appoint leaders and prominent members of the various political factions to positions in his government in an effort to broaden its support. The internecine conflicts that resulted had quite the opposite effect, weakening the government and the president and emboldening Secretary of War Desiderio Arias to take

Rafael Leónidas Trujillo Molina
Courtesy Library of Congress

Offices of the General Customs
Receivership, Santo
Domingo, 1907
Courtesy National Archives

control of both the armed forces and the Congress, which he compelled to impeach Jiménez for violation of the constitution and the
laws. Although the United States ambassador offered military support to his government, Jiménez opted to step down on May 7,
1916.

Arias never formally assumed the presidency. The United States
government had apparently tired of its recurring role as mediator
and had decided to take more direct action. United States forces
had already occupied Haiti by this time (see The United States
Occupation, 1915-34, ch. 6). The initial military administrator of
Haiti, Rear Admiral William Caperton, had actually forced Arias
to retreat from Santo Domingo by threatening the city with naval
bombardment on May 13. The first marines landed three days later.
Although they established effective control of the country within
two months, the United States forces did not proclaim a military
government until November. Most Dominican laws and institutions remained intact under military rule, although the shortage
of Dominicans willing to serve in the cabinet forced the military
governor, Rear Admiral Harry S. Knapp, to fill a number of portfolios with United States naval officers. The press and radio were
censored for most of the occupation, and public speech was limited.

The surface effects of the occupation were largely positive. The
marines restored order throughout most of the republic (with the
exception of the eastern region); the country's budget was balanced,
its debt was diminished, and economic growth resumed; infrastructure projects produced new roads that linked all the country's
regions for the first time in its history; a professional military organization, the Dominican Constabulary Guard, replaced the partisan forces that had waged a seemingly endless struggle for power
(see History and Development of the Armed Forces, ch. 5). Most
Dominicans, however, greatly resented the loss of their sovereignty
to foreigners, few of whom spoke Spanish or displayed much real
concern for the welfare of the republic.

The most intense opposition to the occupation arose in the eastern
provinces of El Seibo and San Pedro de Macorís. From 1917 to
1921, the United States forces battled a guerrilla movement in that
area known as the *gavilleros*. The guerrillas enjoyed considerable
support among the population, and they benefited from a superi-
or knowledge of the terrain. The movement survived the capture
and the execution of its leader, Vicente Evangelista, and some initially fierce encounters with the marines. However, the *gavilleros*
eventually yielded to the occupying forces' superior firepower, air
power (a squadron of six Curtis Jennies), and determined (often
brutal) counterinsurgent methods.

After World War I, public opinion in the United States began to run against the occupation. Warren G. Harding, who succeeded Wilson in March 1921, had campaigned against the occupations of both Haiti and the Dominican Republic. In June 1921, United States representatives presented a withdrawal proposal, known as the Harding Plan, which called for Dominican ratification of all acts of the military government, approval of a loan of US$2.5 million for public works and other expenses, the acceptance of United States officers for the constabulary—now known as the National Guard (Guardia Nacional)—and the holding of elections under United States supervision. Popular reaction to the plan was overwhelmingly negative. Moderate Dominican leaders, however, used the plan as the basis for further negotiations that resulted in an agreement allowing for the selection of a provisional president to rule until elections could be organized. Under the supervision of High Commissioner Sumner Welles, Juan Bautista Vicini Burgos assumed the provisional presidency on October 21, 1922. In the presidential election of March 15, 1924, Horacio Vásquez Lajara handily defeated Francisco J. Peynado. Vásquez's Alliance Party (Partido Alianza) also won a comfortable majority in both houses of Congress. With his inauguration on July 13, control of the republic returned to Dominican hands.

The Era of Trujillo

The Vásquez administration shines in Dominican history like a star amid a gathering storm. After the country's eight years of subjugation, Vásquez took care to respect the political and civil rights of the population. An upswing in the price of export commodities, combined with increased government borrowing, buoyed the economy. Public works projects proliferated. Santo Domingo expanded and modernized. This brief period of progress, however, ended in the resurgent maelstrom of Dominican political instability. The man who would come to occupy the eye of this political cyclone was Rafael Trujillo.

Although a principled man by Dominican standards, Vásquez was also a product of long years of political infighting. In an effort to undercut his primary rival, Federico Velásquez, and to preserve power for his own followers, the president agreed in 1927 to a prolongation of his term from four to six years. There was some debatable legal basis for the move, which was approved by the Congress, but its enactment effectively invalidated the constitution of 1924 that Vásquez had previously sworn to uphold. Once the president had demonstrated his willingness to disregard constitutional procedures in the pursuit of power, some ambitious opponents

27

decided that those procedures were no longer binding. Dominican politics returned to their pre-occupation status; the struggle
among competing caudillos resumed.

Trujillo occupied a strong position in this contest. The commander of the National Army (Ejército Nacional, the new designation of the armed force created under the occupation), Trujillo
came from a humble background. He had enlisted in the National
Police in 1918, a time when the upper-class Dominicans, who had
formerly filled the officer corps, largely refused to collaborate with
the occupying forces. Trujillo harbored no such scruples. He rose
quickly in the officer corps, while at the same time he built a network of allies and supporters. Unlike the more idealistic North
American sponsors of the constabulary, Trujillo saw the armed force
not for what it should have been—an apolitical domestic security
force—but for what it was: the main source of concentrated power
in the republic.

Having established his power base behind the scenes, Trujillo
was ready by 1930 to assume control of the country. Although elections were scheduled for May, Vásquez's extension in office cast
doubt on their potential fairness. (Vásquez had also eliminated from
the constitution the prohibition against presidential reelection.) This
uncertainty prompted Rafael Estrella Ureña, a political leader from
Santiago, to proclaim a revolution in February. Having already
struck a deal with Trujillo, Estrella marched on the capital; army
forces remained in their barracks as Trujillo declared his "neu-
trality" in the situation. The ailing Vásquez, a victim of duplicity
and betrayal, fled the capital. Estrella assumed the provisional presidency.

Part of the arrangement between Estrella and Trujillo apparently involved the army commander's candidacy for president in
the May elections. As events unfolded, it became clear that Trujillo
would be the only candidate that the army would permit to participate; army personnel harassed and intimidated electoral officials
and eliminated potential opponents. A dazed nation stood by as
the new dictator announced his election with 95 percent of the vote.
After his inauguration in August, and at his express request, the
Congress issued an official proclamation announcing the commence-
ment of "the Era of Trujillo."

The dictator proceeded to rule the country like a feudal lord for
thirty-one years. He held the office of president from 1930 to 1938
and from 1942 to 1952. During the interim periods, he exercised
absolute power, while leaving the ceremonial affairs of state to puppet presidents such as his brother, Héctor Bienvenido Trujillo Molina, who occupied the National Palace from 1952 to 1960, and

Joaquín Balaguer Ricardo, an intellectual and scholar who served from 1960 to 1961. Although cast in the mold of old-time caudillos such as Santana and Heureaux, Trujillo surpassed them in efficiency, rapacity, and utter ruthlessness. Like Heureaux, he maintained a highly effective secret police force that monitored (and eliminated, in some instances) opponents both at home and abroad. Like Santana, he relied on the military as his primary support. Armed forces personnel received generous pay and perquisites under his rule, and their ranks and equipment inventories expanded. Trujillo maintained control over the officer corps through fear, patronage, and the frequent rotation of assignments, which inhibited the development of strong personal followings (see History and Development of the Armed Forces, ch. 5). The other leading beneficiaries of the dictatorship—aside from Trujillo himself and his family—were those who associated themselves with the regime both politically and economically. The establishment of state monopolies over all major enterprises in the country brought riches to the Trujillos and their cronies through the manipulation of prices and inventories as well as the outright embezzlement of funds.

Generally speaking, the quality of life improved for the average Dominican under Trujillo. Poverty persisted, but the economy expanded, the foreign debt disappeared, the currency remained stable, and the middle class expanded. Public works projects enhanced the road system and improved port facilities; airports and public buildings were constructed, the public education system grew, and illiteracy declined. These advances might well have been achieved in even greater measure under a responsive democratic government, but to Dominicans, who had no experience with such a government, the results under Trujillo were impressive. Although he never tested his personal popularity in a free election, some observers feel that Trujillo could have won a majority of the popular vote up until the final years of his dictatorship.

Ideologically, Trujillo leaned toward fascism. The trappings of his personality cult (Santo Domingo was renamed Ciudad Trujillo under his rule), the size and architectural mediocrity of his building projects, and the level of repressive control exercised by the state all invited comparison with the style of his contemporaries, Hitler in Germany and Mussolini in Italy. Basically, however, Trujillo was not an ideologue, but a Dominican caudillo expanded to monstrous proportions by his absolute control of the nation's resources. His attitude toward communism tended toward peaceful coexistence until 1947, when the Cold War winds from Washington persuaded him to crack down and to outlaw the Dominican Communist Party (Partido Comunista Dominicano—PCD). As always, self-interest and the need to maintain his personal power guided Trujillo's actions.

Although conspiracies—both real and imagined—against his rule preoccupied Trujillo throughout his reign, it was his adventurous foreign policy that drew the ire of other governments and led directly to his downfall. Paradoxically, his most heinous action in this arena cost him the least in terms of influence and support. In October 1937, Trujillo ordered the massacre of Haitians living in the Dominican Republic in retaliation for the discovery and execution by the Haitian government of his most valued covert agents in that country. The Dominican army slaughtered as many as 20,000 largely unarmed men, women, and children, mostly in border areas, but also in the western Cibao. News of the atrocity filtered out of the country slowly; when it reached the previously supportive administration of President Franklin D. Roosevelt in the United States, Secretary of State Cordell Hull demanded internationally mediated negotiations for a settlement and indemnity. Trujillo finally agreed. The negotiations, however, fixed a ludicrously low indemnity of US$750,000, which was later reduced to US$525,000 by agreement between the two governments. Although the affair damaged Trujillo's international image, it did not result in any direct efforts by the United States or by other countries to force him from power.

In later years, the Trujillo regime became increasingly isolated from the governments of other nations. This isolation compounded the dictator's paranoia, prompting him to increase his foreign interventionism. To be sure, Trujillo did have cause to resent the leaders of certain foreign nations, such as Cuba's Fidel Castro Ruz, who aided a small, abortive invasion attempt by dissident Dominicans in 1959. Trujillo, however, expressed greater concern over Venezuela's President Rómulo Betancourt (1959–64). An established and outspoken opponent of Trujillo, Betancourt had been associated with some individual Dominicans who had plotted against the dictator. Trujillo developed an obsessive personal hatred of Betancourt and supported numerous plots of Venezuelan exiles to overthrow him. This pattern of intervention led the Venezuelan government to take its case against Trujillo to the Organization of American States (OAS). This development infuriated Trujillo, who ordered his foreign agents to assassinate Betancourt. The attempt, on June 24, 1960, injured, but did not kill, the Venezuelan president. The incident inflamed world opinion against Trujillo. The members of the OAS, expressing this outrage, voted unanimously to sever diplomatic relations and to impose economic sanctions on the Dominican Republic.

The firestorm surrounding the Betancourt incident provoked a review of United States policy toward the Dominican Republic by the administration of President Dwight D. Eisenhower. The United States had long tolerated Trujillo as a bulwark of stability in the Caribbean; some in Washington still saw him as a desirable counterforce to the Castro regime. Others, however, saw in Trujillo another Fulgencio Batista—the dictator Castro deposed in 1959—ripe for overthrow by radical, potentially communist, forces. Public opinion in the United States also began to run strongly against the Dominican dictatorship. In August 1960, the United States embassy in Santo Domingo was downgraded to consular level. According to journalist Bernard Diederich, Eisenhower also asked the National Security Council's Special Group (the organization responsible for approving covert operations) to consider the initiation of operations aimed at Trujillo's ouster. On May 30, 1961, Trujillo was assassinated. According to Diederich, the United States Central Intelligence Agency supplied the weapons used by the assassins.

The Post-Trujillo Era

Transition to Elected Government

At the time of his assassination, Trujillo was seventy years old. He had left no designated successor. It soon became clear that the conspirators had planned his assassination more thoroughly than the subsequent seizure of government, which never took place. Puppet President Balaguer remained in office, allowing the late dictator's son, Rafael Trujillo Lovatón (also called Rafael, Jr., or Ramfis), to return from Paris and assume de facto control. Ramfis lacked the dynamism of his father, however, and he eventually fell into a dispute with his two uncles over potential liberalization of the regime. The "wicked uncles"—Héctor and José Arismendi Trujillo Molina—returned to the republic from exile in November 1961. Ramfis, having little enthusiasm for a power struggle, fled the country.

Opposition from Washington, made very plain by the deployment of United States warships off the Dominican coast, blunted the ambitions of the uncles and forced them to resume their exile only days later. Balaguer retained the presidency. As a protégé of the fallen dictator, however, he had neither a power base nor a popular following. Popular unrest, punctuated by a general strike, forced Balaguer to share power with a seven-member Council of State, established on January 1, 1962. The council included Balaguer and the two surviving assassins of Trujillo, Antonio Imbert Barrera and Luis Amiama Tío (the others having been slain by Trujillo's security service). The council lasted only sixteen days, however, before air force general Pedro Rodríguez Echavarría overthrew it in a coup d'état. Rodríguez's attempt at rule also foundered on the rocks of popular protest and opposition from the United States. Less senior officers seized the general, deported him, and restored the council minus Balaguer, who had also been exiled.

The restored Council of State guided the country until elections could be organized. The leading candidates were Juan Bosch Gaviño, a scholar and poet, who had organized the opposition Dominican Revolutionary Party (Partido Revolucionario Dominicano—PRD) in exile, and Viriato Fiallo of the National Civic Union (Unión Cívica Nacional—UCN). In the balloting of December 20, 1962, the conservative image of the UCN and its association with the country's economic elite benefited Bosch, whose support came mainly from the urban lower class. Bosch won the election with 64 percent of the vote; the PRD also captured two-thirds majorities in both houses of the legislature.

The Bosch administration was very much an oddity in Dominican history up to that point: a freely elected, liberal, democratic government that expressed concern for the welfare of all Dominicans, particularly those of modest circumstances, those whose voices had never really been heard before in the National Palace. The 1963 constitution separated church and state, guaranteed civil and individual rights, and endorsed civilian control of the military. These and other changes, such as land reform, struck conservative landholders and military officers as radical and threatening, particularly when juxtaposed against three decades of somnolent authoritarianism under Trujillo. The hierarchy of the Roman Catholic Church also resented the secular nature of the new constitution, in particular its provision for legalized divorce. The hierarchy, along with the military leadership and the economic elite, also feared communist influence in the republic, and they warned of the potential for "another Cuba." The result of this concern and opposition was a military coup on September 25, 1963.

Civil War and United States Intervention, 1965

The coup effectively negated the 1962 elections by installing a civilian junta, known as the Triumvirate, dominated by the UCN. The initial head of the Triumvirate, Emilio de los Santos, resigned on December 23 and was replaced by Donald Reid Cabral. The Triumvirate never succeeded in establishing its authority over competing conservative factions both inside and outside the military;

it also never convinced the majority of the population of its legitimacy. The widespread dissatisfaction with Reid and his government, coupled with lingering loyalties to Bosch, produced a revolution in April 1965.

The vanguard of the 1965 revolution, the *perredeístas* (members of the PRD) and other supporters of Bosch, called themselves Constitutionalists (a reference to their support for the 1963 constitution). The movement counted some junior military officers among its ranks. A combination of reformist military and aroused civilian combatants took to the streets on April 24, seized the National Palace, and installed Rafael Molina Ureña as provisional president. The revolution took on the dimensions of a civil war when conservative military forces, led by army general Elías Wessín y Wessín, struck back against the Constitutionalists on April 25. These conservative forces called themselves Loyalists. Despite tank assaults and bombing runs by Loyalist forces, however, the Constitutionalists held their positions in the capital; they appeared poised to branch out and to secure control of the entire country.

On April 28, the United States intervened in the civil war. President Lyndon B. Johnson ordered in forces that eventually totaled 20,000, to secure Santo Domingo and to restore order. Johnson had acted in the stated belief that the Constitutionalists were dominated by communists and that they therefore could not be allowed to come to power. The intervention was subsequently granted some measure of hemispheric approval by the creation of an OAS-sponsored peace force, which supplemented the United States military presence in the republic. An initial interim government was headed by Trujillo assassin Imbert; Héctor García Godoy assumed a provisional presidency on September 3, 1965. Violent skirmishes between Loyalists and Constitutionalists went on sporadically as, once again, elections were organized.

Joaquín Balaguer, 1966–78

A fractious campaign ensued between the country's two leading political figures: Bosch and Balaguer. Bosch's appeal was tempered by fear; many Dominicans felt that his reelection would rekindle the violence of April 1965. This trepidation aided Balaguer, who also appealed to conservative voting sectors such as peasants, women (considered to be more religious than men), and businesspeople. Balaguer thus won handily, garnering 57 percent of the vote in balloting held July 1, 1966. His Reformist Party (Partido Reformista—PR) also captured majorities in the Congress.

Balaguer went on to serve as president for twelve years. A relative nonentity under Trujillo, he demonstrated, once in power, the astuteness with which he had studied the techniques of the late dictator. Even though as a conservative he theoretically was more secure against military machinations, he actively sought to head off opposition from the armed forces by rewarding officers loyal to him, purging those he suspected, and rotating everyone's assignments on a regular and frequent basis. He curtailed nonmilitary opposition through selective (compared to the Trujillo years) repression by the National Police. His reelection in 1970 and in 1974 was accomplished largely through intimidation. The PRD, the only viable, broad-based opposition party, boycotted both elections to safeguard the well-being of those who would have been their candidates.

The Dominican economy expanded at a record rate under Balaguer. Favorable international prices for sugar provided the basis for this so-called Dominican miracle. Foreign investment, foreign borrowing, foreign aid, the growth of tourism, and extensive public works programs also contributed to high levels of growth. By the late 1970s, however, the expansion had slowed considerably as sugar prices dipped and oil prices rose. Rising inflation and unemployment diminished support for the government, particularly among the middle class.

The PRD, feeling the mood of the population and sensing support from the administration of United States president Jimmy Carter, nominated Silvestre Antonio Guzmán Fernández to oppose Balaguer in the elections of May 16, 1978. A relatively heavy 70 percent turnout seemed to favor the PRD; early returns confirmed this as Guzmán built a sizable lead. Early in the morning of May 17, however, military units occupied the Central Electoral Board and impounded the ballots. Clearly, Balaguer was attempting to nullify the balloting or to falsify the results in his favor. Only forceful remonstrances by the Carter administration, backed up by a naval deployment, moved Balaguer to allow the resumption of the vote count. Two weeks later, Guzmán's victory was officially announced.

Antonio Guzmán, 1978–82

Guzmán's assumption of office on August 16, 1978, presented many political challenges to both him and the republic. Mindful of the fate of Juan Bosch sixteen years before, Guzmán determined to move slowly in the area of social and economic reforms and to deal as directly as possible with the threat of political pressure from the armed forces. He attacked the latter problem first with a program of military depoliticization that included the removal or the reassignment of general officers of questionable loyalty or professionalism, the promotion of younger and more apolitical officers than those who had held sway under Balaguer, and the institution of a formal training course for officers and enlisted personnel that stressed the nonpolitical role of the armed forces in a democratic society. This campaign was largely successful, and it constituted the major legacy left by Guzmán to his successor, Salvador Jorge Blanco.

Politically, Guzmán was restrained to some extent by the unusual outcome of the 1978 elections. Although the Central Electoral Board acknowledged the PRD's victories in the races for the presidency and the Chamber of Deputies (the lower house of Congress), it managed through some creative counting—apparently taking the number of ballots not used in some provinces and dividing them among the top two vote-getters—to give Balaguer's PR a sixteen-to-eleven majority in the Senate. This essentially granted the PR a legislative veto over any initiatives Guzmán might wish to launch, and it also became a factor in the president's cautious approach to reform.

Some observers felt that Guzmán's economic and social background—he was a wealthy cattle rancher from the Santiago area—influenced his economic policies as well. Despite his nationalization of public transportation and an increase in the minimum wage, more reform-minded politicians, even within his own party, criticized the president for his inadequate response to continued economic decline. Jorge was one of Guzmán's leading critics in this area; ironically, he too, would be confronted with the stark realities of the economy and the lack of acceptable options available to the president after his own election in 1982 (see Political Developments since 1978, ch. 4). Faced with the continually rising oil prices and declining sugar prices, Guzmán opted for politically unpopular austerity policies, including a steep increase in the retail price of gasoline. Compounding the general woes of a slowed economy was the extensive damage wreaked on the country by Hurricane David in August 1979.

In retrospect, the Guzmán administration represented a bridge between lingering post-Trujillo authoritarianism and a more liberal, democratic style of politics and government. Guzmán's professionalization of the military was a significant contribution to this process. Although the Dominican economic situation plagued him, Guzmán handled matters with sufficient competence to allow for the election of Jorge on the PRD ticket on May 16, 1982. (Guzmán had pledged not to seek reelection.) Jorge's leading opponents had been PR candidate Balaguer and Bosch, who had split from the PRD and had formed his own party, the Dominican Liberation

Party (Partido de la Liberación Dominicana—PLD). For reasons never fully explained, Guzmán committed suicide in July 1982; he was said to have been depressed by allegations of corruption and nepotism in his administration. His vice president, Jacobo Majluta Azar, served out the remainder of the term. Guzmán's suicide prevented what would have been a historic event—the peaceful transfer of power from one freely and fairly elected president to another. Jorge's administration also fell victim to corruption and the effects of economic austerity. With the election and peaceful return to power of Balaguer in 1986, a tradition of fair electoral competition appeared to be developing; democracy seemed to be taking root in the Dominican Republic (see Political Developments since 1978, ch. 4).

* * *

Works in English dealing with the Dominican Republic have been produced by political scientists more often than by historians. Consequently, the student of the country's history is limited to works such as Selden Rodman's *Quisqueya: A History of the Dominican Republic,* which provides good background, but little detail; Rayford Logan's short volume, titled *Haiti and the Dominican Republic;* or Sumner Welles's voluminous, but dated, *Naboth's Vineyard.* A sense of the republic's history can also be culled from a number of volumes oriented toward politics or foreign relations. Among these, Howard Wiarda's *The Dominican Republic: Nation in Transition* provides a good general introduction to the country. *The Dominican Republic: A Caribbean Crucible* and *The Politics of External Influence in the Dominican Republic,* by Howard Wiarda and Michael Kryzanek, chart the republic's further political and economic progress. Bruce J. Calder's *The Impact of Intervention* is an excellent study of the United States occupation and its effects. *Trujillo: The Life and Times of a Caribbean Dictator,* by Robert D. Crassweller, provides a vivid portrait of the dominant figure in the nation's twentieth-century history. A broader perspective can be obtained from G. Pope Atkins and Larman C. Wilson's *The United States and the Trujillo Regime. The Dominican Republic: Politics and Development in an Unsovereign State,* by Jan Knippers Black, deals effectively with the 1978 transition to democracy and subsequent developments. (For further information and complete citations, see Bibliography.)

Chapter 2. Dominican Republic:
The Society and Its Environment

A bohío, *or rural hut*

DOMINICAN SOCIETY OF THE LATE 1980s reflected the country's Spanish-Caribbean heritage. It manifested significant divisions along the lines of race and class. A small fraction of the populace controlled great wealth, while the vast majority struggled to get by. The middle stratum worked both to maintain and to extend its political and economic gains. Generally speaking, Dominican society offered relatively few avenues of advancement; most of those available allowed families of middling means to enhance or to consolidate their standing.

The majority of the population was mulatto, the offspring of Africans and Europeans. The indigenous Amerindian population had been virtually eliminated within half a century of initial contact. Immigrants—European, Middle Eastern, Asian, and Caribbean—arrived with each cycle of economic growth. In general, skin color followed the social hierarchy: lighter skin was associated with higher social and economic status. European immigrants and their offspring found more ready acceptance at the upper reaches of society than did darker-skinned Dominicans.

The decades following the end of the regime of Rafael Leónidas Trujillo Molina (1930–61) were a time of extensive changes as large-scale rural-urban and international migration blurred the gulf between city and countryside. Traditional attitudes persisted: peasants continued to regard urban dwellers with suspicion, and people in cities continued to think of rural Dominicans as unsophisticated and naive. Nonetheless, most families included several members who had migrated to the republic's larger cities or to the United States. Migration served to relieve some of the pressures of population growth. Moreover, cash remittances from abroad permitted families of moderate means to acquire assets and to maintain a standard of living far beyond what they might otherwise have enjoyed.

The alternatives available to poorer Dominicans were far more limited. Emigration required assets beyond the reach of most. Many rural dwellers migrated instead to one of the republic's cities. The financial resources and training of these newcomers, however, were far inferior to those among typical families of moderate means. For the vast majority of the republic's population, the twin constraints of limited land and limited employment opportunities defined the daily struggle for existence.

In the midst of far-reaching changes, the republic continued to be a profoundly family-oriented society. Dominicans of every social

39

stratum relied on family and kin for social identity and for inter-personal relationships of trust and confidence, particularly in the processes of migration and urbanization.

Geography

The Dominican Republic is located on the island of Hispaniola (La Isla Española), which it shares with Haiti to the west. The 388-kilometer border between the two was established in a series of treaties, the most recent of which was the 1936 Protocol of Revision of the Frontier Treaty (Tratado Fronterizo) of 1929. The country is shaped in the form of an irregular triangle. The short side of the triangle is 388 kilometers long, while the two long sides form 1,575 kilometers of coastline along the Atlantic Ocean, the Caribbean Sea, and the Mona Passage. The total area of the country is approximately 48,442 square kilometers. Although it boasts the highest elevations in the Antilles, it also has a saltwater lake below sea level (see fig. 2).

Natural Regions

The mountains and valleys of the Dominican Republic divide the country into the northern, the central, and the southwestern regions. The northern region, bordering the Atlantic Ocean, consists of the Atlantic coastal plain, the Cordillera Septentrional (or Northern Mountain Range), the Valle del Cibao (Cibao Valley), and the Samaná Peninsula. The Atlantic coastal plain is a narrow strip that extends from the northwestern coast at Monte Cristi to Nagua, northwest of the Samaná Peninsula. The Cordillera Septentrional is south of, and runs parallel to, the coastal plain. Its highest peaks rise to an elevation of over 1,000 meters. The Valle del Cibao lies south of the Cordillera Septentrional. It extends 240 kilometers from the northwest coast to the Bahía de Samaná in the east and ranges in width from 15 to 45 kilometers. To the west of the ridge lies the Valle de Santiago and to the east is the Valle de la Vega Real. The Samaná Peninsula is an eastward extension of the northern region, separated from the Cordillera Septentrional by an area of swampy lowlands. The peninsula is mountainous; its highest elevations reach 600 meters.

The central region is dominated by the Cordillera Central (Central Range); it runs eastward from the Haitian border and turns southward at the Valle de Constanza to end in the Caribbean Sea. This southward branch is known as the Sierra de Ocoa. The Cordillera Central is 2,000 meters high near the Haitian border and reaches a height of 3,087 meters at Pico Duarte, the highest point in the country. An eastern branch of the Cordillera Central extends through the Sierra de Yamasá to the Cordillera Oriental (Eastern Range). The main peaks of these two mountain groups are not higher than 880 meters. The Cordillera Oriental is also known as the Sierra de Seibo.

Another significant feature of the central region is the Caribbean coastal plain, which lies south of the foothills of the Sierra de Yamasá and the Cordillera Oriental. It extends 240 kilometers from the mouth of the Ocoa River to the extreme eastern end of the island. The Caribbean coastal plain is 10 to 40 kilometers wide and consists of a series of limestone terraces that gradually rise to a height of 100 to 120 meters at the northern edge of the coastal plains at the foothills of the Cordillera Oriental. Finally, the central region includes the Valle de San Juan in the western part of the country; the valley extends 100 kilometers from the Haitian border to the Bahía de Ocoa.

The southwestern region lies south of the Valle de San Juan. It encompasses the Sierra de Neiba, which extends 100 kilometers from the Haitian border to the Yaque del Sur River. The main peaks are roughly 2,000 meters high, while other peaks range from 1,000 to 1,500 meters. On the eastern side of the Yaque del Sur lies the Sierra de Martín García, which extends twenty-five kilometers from the river to the Llanura de Azua (Plain of Azua).

The Hoya de Enriquillo, a structural basin that lies south of the Sierra de Neiba, is also within the southwestern region. The basin extends ninety-five kilometers from the Haitian border to the Bahía de Neiba and twenty kilometers from the Sierra de Neiba to the Sierra de Baoruco. The Sierra de Baoruco extends seventy kilometers from the Haitian border to the Caribbean Sea. Its three major peaks surpass 2,000 meters in height. The Procurrente de Barahona (Cape of Barahona) extends southward from the Sierra de Baoruco and consists of a series of terraces.

Drainage

The Dominican Republic has seven major drainage basins. Five of these rise in the Cordillera Central and a sixth, in the Sierra de Yamasá. The seventh drainage system flows into the Lago Enriquillo (Lake Enriquillo) from the Sierra de Neiba to the north and from the Sierra de Baoruco to the south. In general, other rivers are either short or intermittent.

The Yaque del Norte is the most significant river in the country. Some 296 kilometers long, with a basin area of 7,044 square kilometers, it rises near Pico Duarte at an altitude of 2,580 meters in the Cordillera Central. It empties into the Bahía de Monte Cristi on the northwest coast, where it forms a delta. The Yaque del Sur

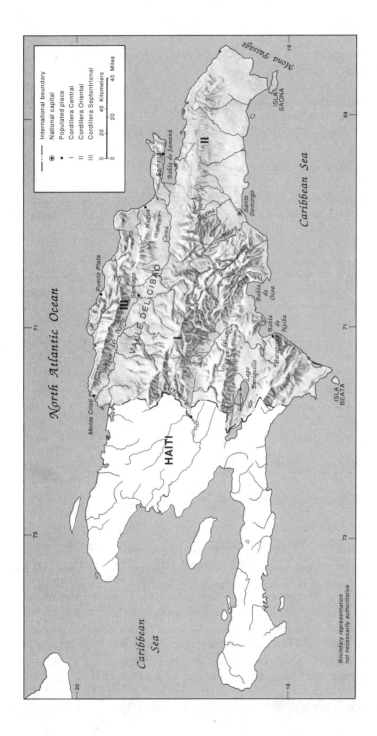

Figure 2. Dominican Republic: Topography and Drainage

is the most important river on the southern coast. It rises at an altitude of 2,707 meters in the southern slopes of the Cordillera Central. Its upper course through the mountains constitutes 75 percent of its total length of some 183 kilometers. The basin area is 4,972 square kilometers. The river forms a delta near its mouth in the Bahía de Neiba.

The Lago Enriquillo lies in the western part of the Hoya de Enriquillo. Its drainage basin includes ten minor river systems and covers an area of more than 3,000 square kilometers. The northern rivers of the system rise in the Sierra de Neiba and are perennial, while the southern rivers rise in the Sierra de Baoruco and are intermittent, flowing only after heavy rainfall. The Lago Enriquillo itself covers some 265 square kilometers. Its water level varies because of the high evaporation rate, yet on the average it is forty meters below sea level. The water in the lake is saline.

Climate

The Dominican Republic has primarily a tropical climate, with more diurnal and local variations in temperature than seasonal ones, and with seasonal variability in the abundance of rainfall. The average annual temperature is 25°C, ranging from 18°C at an altitude of over 1,200 meters to 28°C at an altitude of 10 meters. Highs of 40°C are common in protected valleys, as are lows of zero in mountainous areas. In general, August is the hottest month, and January and February are the coolest ones.

Seasons, however, vary more as a function of rainfall than of temperature. Along the northern coast, the rainy season lasts from November through January. In the rest of the country, it runs from May through November; May is the wettest month. The dry season lasts from November through April; March is the driest month. The average annual rainfall for the country as a whole is 1,500 millimeters. This varies, however, from region to region, and ranges from 350 millimeters in the Valle de Neiba to 2,740 millimeters in the Cordillera Oriental. In general, the western part of the country, including the interior valleys, receives the least rain.

Tropical cyclones—such as tropical depressions, tropical storms, and hurricanes—occur on the average of once every two years in the Dominican Republic. Over 65 percent of the storms strike the southern part of the country, especially along the Hoya de Enriquillo. The season for cyclones lasts from the beginning of June to the end of November; some cyclones occur in May and December, but most take place in September and October. Hurricanes usually occur from August through October. They may produce

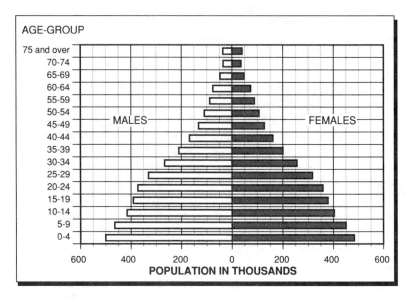

Source: Based on information from Dominican Republic, Oficina Nacional de Estadística,
La República Dominicana en Cifras, 1987, 14, Santo Domingo, 1987, 49, 51.

*Figure 3. Dominican Republic: Estimated Population Distribution by Age
and Sex, 1990*

winds greater than 200 kilometers per hour and rainfall greater
than 500 millimeters in a twenty-four-hour period.

Population

Size and Growth

It has been estimated that the country's total population in
mid-1990 will total slightly more than 7 million (see fig. 3). Growth
had been high since official census taking began in 1920. The rate
peaked during the 1950s at 3.6 percent per year. During the 1960s
and the 1970s, the population grew at 2.9 percent annually; by
the mid-1980s, the rate was thought to be roughly 2.5 percent.

The total fertility rate, although still relatively high, declined substantially in the 1970s. Official estimates indicated that half of all
married women used contraceptives. Both the Dominican Republic's continued high population growth rates and field studies be-
lied this figure, however.

The government began supporting family planning in 1967, but
clinics were concentrated in the cities and larger towns. Both the
Secretariat of State for Public Health and Social Welfare (Secretaría

de Estado de Salud Pública y Asistencia Social—SESPAS) and the National Population and Family Council (Consejo Nacional de Población y Familia—CNPF) offered family planning services. By the 1980s, both organizations were trying to make their programs more responsive to the needs of rural families.

Birth control encountered strong resistance from both sexes, especially in the countryside and the smaller cities. Although women did use a variety of substances believed to be contraceptives or abortifacients, there was considerable misinformation about family planning. Many men believed birth control threatened their masculinity; some women refused to use contraception because some methods produced nausea and other side effects. International migrants were more aware of the available options, and some women migrants did use modern contraceptives.

The traditional (non-administrative) subregions of the country included Valdesia and Yuma in the southeast, Enriquillo and Del Valle in the southwest, and the Central Cibao, the Eastern Cibao, and the Western Cibao in the north. The subregion of densest settlement was Valdesia on the southern coast, which contained the nation's capital and more than 40 percent of the population. Roughly one-third of all Dominicans lived in the National District. The other major area of settlement was the Central Cibao, which accounted for more than 20 percent of total population (see table 2, Appendix A).

Administrations had attempted to control both population growth and its distribution since the 1950s. The Trujillo regime fostered agricultural colonies scattered throughout the countryside and strung along the western frontier with Haiti. Some were coupled with irrigation projects.

Beginning in the late 1970s, the government also set up industrial free zones around the country. Although the desire to increase employment was the government's primary motivation, the establishment of free zones had as a secondary goal the dispersal of industrialization, and thus migration, away from Santo Domingo (see Manufacturing, ch. 3). Intercensal growth rates on the subregional and the provincial levels reflected these trends. Puerto Plata grew at more than twice the rate of the nation as a whole in the 1970s. The southeast, especially the National District, expanded much faster than most of the country, as did La Romana.

Migration

The Dominican Republic was a country of migrants in the late 1980s; according to the 1981 census, nearly one-quarter of the population was living in a province other than that in which they had

45

been born. Surveys in the mid-1970s found that nearly two-thirds of city dwellers and half of those in the countryside had migrated at least once. Rural areas in general, especially in the Central Cibao, have experienced significant levels of out-migration. The movement of peasants and the landless into the republic's growing cities accounted for the lion's share of migration. Indeed, Dominicans had even coined a new word, *campuno,* to describe the rural-urban campesino migrant. The principal destinations for migrants were the National District followed by the provinces of La Romana, Independencia, and San Pedro de Macorís (see fig. 1). In the National District, 46 percent of the inhabitants were migrants. The industrial free zones were the other major destinations for migrants in the 1970s.

Women predominated in both rural-urban and urban-rural migration. Men, however, were more likely than women to move from city to city or from one rural area to another. In general, migrants earned more than non-migrants, and they suffered lower rates of unemployment, although underemployment was pervasive. Urban-rural migrants had the highest incomes. This category, however, consisted of a select group of educated and skilled workers, mostly government officials, teachers, and the like, who moved from cities to assume specific jobs in rural areas. They received higher wages as a recompense for the lack of urban amenities in villages.

Migrants spoke of the migration chain (*cadena*) that tied them to other migrants and to their home communities. Kin served as the links in the chain. They cared for family, lands, and businesses left behind, or, if they had migrated earlier, assisted the new arrivals with employment and housing. The actual degree of support families could, or were willing to, give a migrant varied widely.

The process of rural-urban migration typically involved a series of steps. The migrant gradually abandoned agriculture and sought more non-agricultural sources of income. Migrants rarely arrived in the largest, fastest growing cities ''green'' from the countryside. They acquired training and experience in intermediate-sized cities and in temporary nonfarm jobs en route.

International migration played a significant role in the livelihood of many Dominicans. Anywhere from 8 to 15 percent of the total population resided abroad. Estimates of those living and working in the United States in the mid-1980s ranged from 300,000 to as high as 800,000. Roughly 200,000 more were in San Juan, Puerto Rico, many of them presumably waiting to get into the United States. Most migrants went to New York; but by the mid-1980s, their destinations also included other cities of the eastern seaboard.

A sizable minority (about one-third) emigrated because they were unemployed, but most did so to attain higher income, to continue their educations, or to join other family members. In the early 1980s, most emigrants were relatively better educated and more skilled than the Dominican populace as a whole. Most came from cities, but the middling to large farms of the overpopulated Cibao also sent large numbers. Working in the United States has become almost an expected part of the lives of Dominicans from families of moderate means.

Cash remittances from Dominicans living abroad have become an integral part of the national economy. Migrants' remittances constituted a significant percentage of the country's foreign exchange earnings (see Balance of Payments, ch. 3). Remittances were used to finance businesses, to purchase land, and to bolster the family's standard of living. Most migrants saw sending money as an obligation. Although some refused to provide assistance, they came under severe criticism from both fellow migrants and those who remained behind. The extent to which a migrant's earnings were committed to family and kin was sometimes striking. Anthropologist Patricia Pessar has described a Dominican man in New York who earned less than US$500 per month. He sent US$150 of this to his wife and children and another US$100 to his parents and unmarried siblings.

Money from abroad had a multiplier effect; it spawned a veritable construction boom in migrants' hometowns and neighborhoods in the mid-1970s. Migrants also contributed significant sums for the church back home. Many parish priests made annual fund-raising trips to New York to seek donations for local parish needs.

The impact of out-migration was widely felt; in one Cibao village, for example, 85 percent of the households had at least one member living in New York in the mid-1970s. Where migration was common, it altered a community's age pyramid: eighteen to forty-five-year olds (especially males) were essentially missing. Emigration also eliminated many of the natural choices for leadership roles in the home community.

Urbanization

For most of its history, the Dominican Republic was overwhelmingly rural; in 1920 over 80 percent of its populace lived in the countryside, and by 1950 more than 75 percent still did. Substantial urban expansion began in the 1950s, and it gained tremendous momentum in the 1960s and the 1970s. Urban growth rates far outdistanced those of the country as a whole. The urban population expanded at 6.1 percent annually during the 1950s, 5.7

percent annually during the 1960s–70s, and 4.7 percent annually through the mid-1980s.

In the early decades of the twentieth century, the country was not only largely rural, but the urban scene itself was dominated by smaller cities and provincial capitals. In 1920 nearly 80 percent of all city dwellers lived in cities with fewer than 20,000 inhabitants. Santo Domingo, with barely more than 30,000 residents, accounted for only 20 percent of those in cities. By contrast, in 1981 Santo Domingo alone accounted for nearly half of all city dwellers; it had more than double the total population of all cities of more than 20,000 inhabitants. Cities with fewer than 20,000 inhabitants—nearly 80 percent of the urban population in 1920—constituted less than 20 percent by 1981.

Santo Domingo approximately doubled its population every decade between 1920 and 1970. Its massive physical expansion, however, dated from the 1950s. The growth in industry and urban construction, coupled with Trujillo's expropriations of rural land, fueled rural-urban migration and the city's growth. The republic's second and third largest cities, Santiago de los Caballeros (Santiago) and La Romana, also experienced significant expansion in the 1960s and the 1970s. Santiago, the center of traditional Hispanic culture, drew migrants from the heavily populated Cibao. La Romana, in the southeast, grew as a center of employment in the sugar industry as well as a center of tourism and the site of the country's first industrial free zone (see Manufacturing, ch. 3).

Population growth and rural-urban migration strained cities' capacity to provide housing and amenities. Nevertheless, in 1981 nearly 80 percent of city dwellings had access to potable water; 90 percent had some type of sewage disposal; and roughly 90 percent had electricity. The proportion of homes with piped, or easy access to, potable water, however, actually declined by nearly ten percentage points in the 1970s. By the mid-1980s, there was an estimated housing deficit of some 400,000 units. The need was greatest in the National District. Squatter settlements grew in response to the scarcity of low-cost urban housing. In Santo Domingo these settlements were concentrated along the Ozama River and on the city's periphery.

Public housing initiatives dated from the late 1950s, when Trujillo built some housing for government employees of moderate means. Through the mid-1980s, a number of different government agencies played a role. The Technical Secretariat of the Presidency (Secretaría Técnica de la Presidencia) designed a variety of projects in Santo Domingo. The Aid and Housing Institute and the National Housing Institute bore primary responsibility for the

View of Altos de Chavón, near La Romana
Courtesy Mark Salyers

financing and the construction of housing. In general, public efforts had been hampered by extreme decentralization in planning, coupled with equally extreme concentration in decision making. The primary beneficiaries of public projects were usually from lower income groups, although they were not the poorest urban dwellers. Projects targeted those making at least the minimum wage, i.e., the lower middle sector or the more stable segments of the working class.

Racial and Ethnic Groups

Ethnic Heritage

The island's indigenous inhabitants were the Taino Indians (Arawaks) and a small settlement of Caribs around the Bahía de Samaná. These Indians, estimated to number perhaps 1 million at the time of their initial contact with Europeans, had died off by the 1550s. The importation of African slaves began in 1503. By the nineteenth century, the population was roughly 150,000: 40,000 of Spanish descent, an equal number of black slaves, and the remainder of freed blacks or mulattoes. In the mid-1980s, approximately 16 percent of the population was considered white and 11 percent black; the remainder were mulattoes.

Contemporary Dominican society and culture are overwhelmingly Spanish in origin. Taino influence is limited to cultigens and to a few vocabulary words, such as *huracán* (hurricane) and *hamaca* (hammock). African influence has been largely ignored, although certain religious brotherhoods with significant black membership incorporated some Afro-American elements. Observers also have noted the presence of African influence in popular dance and music.

49

There was a preference in Dominican society for light skin and "white" racial features. Blackness in itself, however, did not restrict a person to a lower status position. Upward mobility was possible for the dark-skinned person who managed to acquire education or wealth. Social characteristics, focusing on family background, education, and economic standing, were in fact more prominent means of identifying and classifying individuals. Darker-skinned persons were concentrated in the east and the south. The population of the Cibao, especially in the countryside, consisted mainly of whites or mulattoes.

Dominicans traditionally preferred to think of themselves as descendants of the island's Indians and the Spanish, ignoring their African heritage. Thus, phenotypical African characteristics were disparaged. Emigrants to the United States brought a new level of racial consciousness to the republic, however, when they returned. Those who came back during the 1960s and the 1970s had experienced both racial prejudice and the black pride movement in North America. Returning migrants brought back Afro hairstyles and a variety of other Afro-North Americanisms.

Modern Immigration

Although almost all migrants were assimilated into Dominican society (often with surprising speed and thoroughness), immigration had a pervasive influence on the ethnic and the racial configurations of the country. Within a generation or two, most immigrants were considered Dominican even though the family might well continue to maintain contact with relatives in the country of origin. Both the elite and the middle segments of society recruited new members with each economic expansion. The main impetus to immigration was the rise of sugar production in the late nineteenth and the early twentieth centuries. Nonetheless, some groups had earlier antecedents, while others arrived as late as the 1970s.

Nineteenth-century immigrants came from a number of places. Roughly 5,000 to 10,000 North American freedmen, principally Methodists, came in response to an offer of free land made during the period of Haitian domination (1822–44). Most, however, were city dwellers, and they quickly returned to the United States. A few small settlements remained around Santiago, Puerto Plata, and Samaná. They eventually were assimilated, although in the late 1980s English was still widely used in the region of Samaná. Sephardic Jews arrived from Curaçao in the late eighteenth century and, in greater numbers, following independence from Haiti in 1844. They were assimilated rapidly; both their economic assets and their white ancestry made them desirable additions from the point of view of the Dominican criollos. Canary Islanders arrived during the late colonial period as well, in response to the improved economic conditions of the 1880s. Spaniards settled during the period of renewed Spanish occupation (1861–65); many Spanish soldiers stayed after the War of Restoration (see Annexation by Spain, 1861–65, ch. 1). Germans established themselves—principally in Puerto Plata—primarily in the tobacco trade.

The expansion of the sugar industry in the late nineteenth century drew migrants from every social stratum. Cubans and Puerto Ricans, who began arriving in the 1870s, aided in the evolution of the sugar industry as well as in the country's intellectual development. In addition, significant numbers of laborers came from the British, the Dutch, and the Danish islands of the Caribbean. They also worked in railroad construction and on the docks. Initial reaction to their presence was negative, but their educational background (which was superior to that of most of the rural populace), their ability to speak English (which gave them an advantage in dealing with North American plantation owners), and their industriousness eventually won them a measure of acceptance. They founded Protestant churches, Masonic lodges, mutual aid societies, and a variety of other cultural organizations. Their descendants enjoyed a considerable measure of upward mobility through education and religion. They were well represented in the technical trades (especially those associated with the sugar industry) and on professional baseball teams.

Arabs—Lebanese and lesser numbers of Palestinians and Syrians—first arrived in the late nineteenth century, and they prospered. Their assimilation was slower, however, and many still maintained contacts with relatives in the Middle East. Italians, as well as a few South American immigrants, also arrived during this period and were assimilated rapidly. A few Chinese came from other Caribbean islands and established a reputation for diligence and industriousness. More followed with the United States occupation of the island (1916–24). They began as cooks and domestic servants; a number of their descendants were restaurateurs and hotel owners.

The most recent trickle of immigrants entered the country from the 1930s to the 1980s. Many founded agricultural colonies that suffered a high rate of attrition. Among the groups were German Jews (1930s), Japanese (after World War II), and Hungarians and Spaniards (both in the 1950s). More Chinese came from Taiwan and Hong Kong in the 1970s; by the 1980s, they were the second fastest growing immigrant group (Haitians being the first). Many had sufficient capital to set up manufacturing firms in the country's industrial free zones.

Haitians

Modern Haitian migration to the Dominican Republic dates from the late nineteenth century, when increasing North American capital boosted sugar production. Dominicans have never welcomed these immigrants. Their presence resulted from economic necessity borne of the reluctance of Dominicans to perform the menial task of cane cutting. The 1920 census listed slightly under 28,000 Haitian nationals in the Dominican Republic. Successive governments attempted to control the numbers of Haitians entering the country; the border was periodically closed in the 1910s and the 1920s. By 1935, however, the number had increased to more than 50,000. Trujillo ordered a general roundup of Haitians along the border in 1937, during which an estimated 20,000 Haitians were killed (see The Era of Trujillo, ch. 1).

Since the 1950s, a series of bilateral agreements has regulated legal Haitian immigration. In the late 1970s and the early 1980s, the government contracted for 10,000 to 20,000 temporary Haitian workers annually for the sugarcane harvest. Observers believed that an equal number of Haitians entered illegally. The 1960 census enumerated slightly under 30,000 Haitians. By 1980 estimates suggested the total number of Haitians residing permanently or semipermanently was on the order of 200,000, of whom 70,000 were workers.

During the 1970s and the early 1980s, some Haitians rose into higher positions in sugar production and in other areas of the economy. They continued to account for the vast majority of cane cutters, but roughly half of all labor recruiters and field inspectors also were Haitians. In addition, Haitians worked harvesting coffee, rice, and cocoa and in construction in Santo Domingo. By 1980 nearly 30 percent of the paid laborers in the coffee harvest were Haitian; in the border region, the proportion rose to 80 percent. A reasonably skilled coffee picker could nearly double the earnings of the average cane cutter. Overall, however, Haitians' earnings still lagged; their wages averaged less than 60 percent of those of Dominicans.

Urban Society

The Elite

The last 200 years transformed the composition and the configuration of the country's elite. Nonetheless, at the end of the 1980s, the Dominican Republic continued to be a country where a relatively small number of families controlled great wealth, while the

View of National Highway One (Duarte Highway) north of Santo Domingo
Courtesy Inter-American Development Bank

majority of the population lived in poverty. The middle stratum struggled (at its lower end) to maintain economic standing and to expand its political participation and (at its upper reaches) to gain greater social acceptance and economic prosperity. Hispanic-Mediterranean ideals about the proper mode of life and livelihood continued to be significant. The primary social division was between two polar groups: the elite (*la gente buena* or *la gente culta*) and the masses.

The first half of the nineteenth century saw the elimination of many of the noteworthy families of the colonial era. During the period of Haitian domination, many prominent landowners liquidated their holdings and left. The War of Restoration against Spain permitted some social and economic upward mobility to members of the lower classes who had enjoyed military success. An increase in sugarcane production brought immigrants of European extraction, who were assimilated rapidly. Poorer elite families saw a chance to improve their financial status through marriage to recently arrived and financially successful immigrants. Even more well-to-do families recognized the advantages of wedding their lineage and lands to the monied merchant-immigrant clans. Although the Chinese were generally excluded from this process, and the Arabs encountered resistance, virtually everyone else found ready acceptance.

This pattern has repeated itself over the years. Each political or economic wave has brought new families into the elite as it imperilled the economic standing of others. By the end of the 1980s, this privileged segment of society was hardly monolithic. The interests of the older elite families, whose wealth was based mostly on land (and whose prosperity diminished during the Trujillo years), did not always match those of families who had amassed their fortunes under Trujillo, or the interests of those whose money came from the expansion in industry during the 1960s and the 1970s. The 1965 civil war further polarized and fragmented many segments of the middle and the upper classes (see Civil War and United States Intervention, 1965, ch. 1).

Although rural elite families were relatively monolithic, in Santo Domingo and Santiago there was a further distinction between families of the first and the second ranks (*la gente de primera* and *la gente de segunda*). Those of the first rank could claim to be a part of the 100 families referred to locally as the *tutumpote* (totem pole— implying family worship and excessive concern with ancestry). Those of the second rank had less illustrious antecedents; they included the descendants of successful immigrants and the nouveaux riches who had managed to intermarry with more established families.

Family loyalties were paramount, and the family represented the primary source of social identity. Elite families relied on an extensive network of kin to maintain their assets. In difficult times, the family offered a haven; as the situation improved, it provided the vehicle whereby one secured political position and economic assets. Siblings, uncles, aunts, cousins, and in-laws comprised the pool from which one selected trusted business partners and loyal political allies. This process of networking pervaded every level of society. The elite, however, profited to a much greater degree from kinship-based networking than did members of the lower classes.

The number of potential kin grew as an individual's net worth increased. The successful were obliged, as a matter of course, to bestow favors on a widely extended group of kin and confreres. Individual success in the political arena brought with it a host of hangers-on whose fortunes rose and fell with those of their patron. The well-to-do tried to limit the demands of less illustrious kin and to secure alliances with families of equal or greater status. These ties permitted the extended family to diversify its social and economic capital.

The Middle Sector

The middle sector in the late 1980s represented roughly 30 to 35 percent of the population, concentrated in the ranks of salaried professionals in government and the private sector. Members of this group had virtually no independent sources of wealth, and so they were responsive to changes in the buying power of wages and to contractions in employment that accompanied economic cycles. The middle level followed the racial stratification of the society as a whole: generally lighter-skinned as one proceeded up the social scale. As a group, the middle sector differed in lifestyle, in marital stability, and in occupations from the poor urban masses. Those belonging to this sector firmly adhered to the Hispanic ideals of leisure and lifestyle espoused by the elite, and they considered themselves, at least in spirit, a part of *la gente buena*. As with the elite, economic expansion, based on the growth of sugar production in the late nineteenth century, broadened the middle reaches of the social ladder as well. Those of this new middle segment, however, were limited in their upward mobility by dark skin and/or limited finances. They were a diverse group, including small shopowners, teachers, clerical employees, and professionals. They lacked a class identity based on any sense of common social or economic interests; moreover, any sense of mutual interest was undermined by the pervasiveness of the patron-client system. Individuals improved their status by linking up with a more privileged protector, not by joint political action for a shared goal.

The life strategy of middle-class families was similar to that of the elite. Their goals were to diversify their economic assets and to extend their network of political and social influence. As with the elite, the middle-level family solidified its position through patronage. An influential family could offer jobs to loyal followers and supporters. People expected that those with power would use it for their own ends and for the advancement of their own and their family's interests. Ties to government were particularly important because the government was the source of many coveted jobs (see Public Administration, ch. 4).

The Urban Poor

The limited availability of adequately paid and steady employment defined life for most urban Dominicans. Unemployment in the 1980s ranged between 20 and 25 percent of the economically active population. In addition, another 25 percent of the work force was considered underemployed. In Santo Domingo and Santiago, the two largest cities, roughly 48 percent of the self-employed, more than half of those paid piece rates, and 85 percent of temporary workers were underemployed. A late 1970s survey of five working-class neighborhoods in Santo Domingo found that 60 percent of household heads had no regular employment (see Labor, ch. 3). Under such conditions, those workers having regular employment constituted a relatively privileged segment of the urban populace.

Rural-urban migration made the situation of the urban poor even more desperate; however, the chances of earning a living were slightly better in cities than in rural areas, although the advantages of an urban job had to be weighed against the higher cost of foodstuffs. Landless, or nearly landless, agricultural laborers might find it difficult to work even a garden plot, but the rural family could generally get by on its own food production. For the urban poor, however, the struggle to eat was relentless.

Under conditions of chronically high unemployment, workers enjoyed little power or leverage. Protective labor laws were typically limited in their coverage to workers in private companies with more than ten employees. Organized labor made significant gains in the early 1960s, but by the late 1980s only a scant 12 to 15 percent of the labor force was unionized (see Labor, ch. 3). The legal code prohibited nearly half of all workers (public employees and utility workers) from strikes and job actions (see Interest Groups, ch. 4).

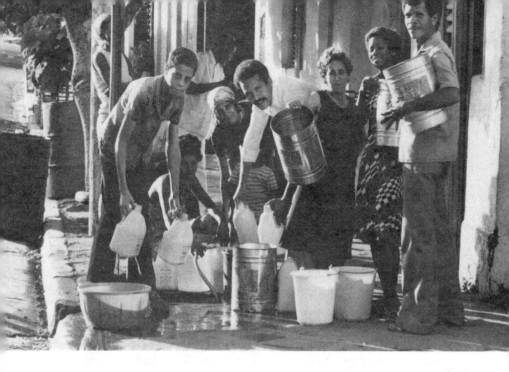

Residents fetching water from a broken pipe, Barrio
San Juan Bosco, Santo Domingo
Courtesy Inter-American Development Bank

Roughly one-quarter of urban households surveyed in the mid-1970s were headed by women. Even in families with a male breadwinner, a woman was frequently the more consistent income earner among poorer city dwellers. Women's economic activities were diverse—if poorly remunerated. They took in washing and ironing, and they did domestic work. The more prosperous sewed. Some bought cheap or used items and raffled them off. A few who could muster the necessary capital ran stalls selling groceries, cigarettes, and candy, but their trade was minimal. In smaller towns, women also performed a variety of agricultural processing tasks: grinding coffee, husking garlic, winnowing beans, and washing pig intestines.

Like more well-to-do city families, the poor tried, wherever possible, to maintain ties with their kin in the countryside. Aid and assistance flowed both ways. Farmers with relatives in the city stayed with them on trips to town and repaid this hospitality with foodstuffs from their fields. New rural-urban migrants were assisted by kin who had already made the transition. The poor were handicapped in these exchanges because they typically had fewer kin in a position to help. Nonetheless, the obligation to help was deeply felt. Women who migrated to cities returned to their families in the countryside as economic conditions and family needs dictated.

The small urban neighborhood functioned as the center of social life. Most sharing, mutual aid, and cooperative activity took place within the confines of a narrow circle of neighbors and kin. Most Dominicans shared a general belief that neighbors should assist each other in times of need.

Rural Society

Most small rural neighborhoods and villages were settled originally by one or two families. Extensive ties of kinship, intermarriage, and *compadrazgo* (coparenthood) developed among the descendants of the original settlers (see Family and Kin, this ch.). Most villagers married their near neighbors. First cousins frequently married, despite the formal legal prohibitions against this practice. The social life of the countryside likewise focused on near neighbors, who were frequently direct blood relations. The bonds of trust and cooperation among these relatives formed at an early age. Children wandered among the households of extended kin at will. Peasants distrusted those from beyond their own neighborhoods, and they were therefore leery of economic relations with outsiders. The development of community-wide activities and organizations was handicapped by this widespread distrust. People commonly assumed deceit in others, in the absence of strong, incontrovertible proof to the contrary.

Until the latter twentieth century, most joint activities were kin-based: a few related extended families joined together for whatever needed attention. The *junta* was the traditional cooperative work group. Friends, neighbors, and relatives gathered at a farmer's house for a day's work. There was no strict accounting of days given and received. As wage labor became more common, the *junta* gave way to smaller cooperative work groups, or it fell into disuse entirely.

In small towns, social life focused on the central park, or the plaza; in rural neighborhoods most social interaction among nonkin took place in the stores, the bars, and the pool rooms where men gathered to gossip. Six-day workweeks left little time for recreation or socializing. Many farm families came to town on Sundays to shop and to attend Mass. The women and children generally returned home earlier than the men to prepare Sunday dinner; the men stayed to visit, or to enjoy an afternoon cockfight or an important baseball or volleyball game.

Landholding in the late 1980s was both concentrated among large holders and fragmented at the lower end of the socioeconomic scale.

All but the largest producers faced some constraints in terms of land and money. Indeed, a national survey conducted in 1985 found extensive rural poverty. More than 40 percent of the households surveyed owned no land; another 25 percent had less than half a hectare. Roughly 70 percent of all families relied on wage labor.

Land reform legislation had had little overall impact on landholding both because the reforms contained few provisions for land redistribution and because they were poorly enforced. Redistribution began in the 1960s with land accumulated by Trujillo and acquired by the state after his death. By the early 1980s, irrigated rice farms, which had been left intact and had been farmed collectively, were slated for division into small, privately owned plots. All told, by 1980 the Dominican Agrarian Institute (Instituto Agrario Dominicano—IAD) had distributed state land to approximately 67,000 families—less than 15 percent of the rural population.

Population growth over the past century had virtually eliminated the land reserves. Parents usually gave children plots of land as they reached maturity, so that they could marry and begin their own families. Over the generations, the process had led to extreme land fragmentation. Contemporary practices adapted to these constraints. Educating children, setting them up in business, or bankrolling their emigration limited the number of heirs competing for the family holdings and assured that the next generation would be able to maintain its standard of living. One or two siblings (usually the oldest and the youngest) remained with the parents and inherited the farm. In other cases, siblings and their spouses stayed on the parental lands; each couple farmed its own plot of land, but they pooled their labor for many agricultural and domestic tasks.

Migration served as a safety valve (see Migration, this ch.). Migrants' remittances represented an essential component in many household budgets. These timely infusions of cash permitted medium-sized landholders to meet expenses during the months before harvest; they also allowed families to purchase more land. In communities with a history of fifteen to twenty years of high levels of emigration, such emigration had an inflationary impact on the local land market. For those relying on wage labor to earn a living, the impact was more ambiguous. In some communities, the increase in migration meant more casual work was available as more family members migrated. In other instances, migrants' families switched to livestock raising to limit labor requirements, or they hired an overseer to handle the agricultural work. Both these practices limited the overall demand for casual labor.

The vast majority (84 percent) of farm women contributed to the family's earnings. Women devised means of earning income that meshed with their domestic tasks: they cultivated garden plots, raised small livestock, and/or helped to tend the family's fields. In addition, many rural women worked at diverse cottage industries and vending. They sold everything from lottery tickets to homemade sweets.

In the mid-1980s, approximately 20 percent of rural households were headed by women. The lack of services in rural areas increased women's working days with physically demanding and time-consuming domestic tasks. Single women were further handicapped by the traditional exclusion of women from mechanized or skilled agricultural work. Women worked during the labor-intensive phases of harvesting and processed crops like cotton, coffee, tobacco, and tomatoes. They usually earned piece rates rather than daily wages, and their earnings lagged behind those of male agricultural laborers.

Sugar Plantations

Most sugar mills and cane fields were concentrated in the southeast coastal plains. Three large groups owned 75 percent of the land: the State Sugar Council (Consejo Estatal del Azúcar— CEA), Casa Vicini (a family operation), and Central Romana (formerly owned by Gulf and Western Corporation). The government created CEA in 1966, largely from lands and facilities formerly held by the Trujillo family.

In the mid-1980s, there were roughly 4,500 *colonos* (sugar planters) who owned some 62,500 hectares. These small to middle-sized landholders were independent growers who sold their harvested cane to the sugar mills. Although the level of prosperity of the *colonos* varied significantly, some were prosperous enough to hire laborers to cut their cane and to buy cane from smaller producers. Their actual number fluctuated widely in response to the market for cane. There were only 3,200 in 1970; this number had more than doubled by 1980, but it had then declined by mid-decade.

Some *colonos* were descendants of former small mill owners driven out of business during the expansion of sugar production in the late nineteenth to the early twentieth century. The parents, or grandparents, of others were either subsistence farmers, who had switched to cane cultivation in response to rising demand for sugar, or successful field workers. Like virtually all Dominican farmers, *colonos* faced land fragmentation that increased geometrically with each generation.

Sugar mills continued to be a major source of work for rural Dominicans, although direct employment peaked at a high of

Vendors selling ice and oranges
Courtesy Mark Salyers

roughly 100,000 workers in the early 1970s. By the mid-1980s, the mills employed approximately 65,000 workers. The sugar industry generated considerable indirect employment as well; some observers estimated that as much as 30 percent of the population was directly or indirectly affected by sugar production (see Crops, ch. 3). The 40,000 to 50,000 cane cutters constituted the bulk of the work force. Most were immigrant Haitians or their descendants (see Haitians, this ch.). In the sugar industry's highly stratified work force, there were clear divisions among cane cutters, more skilled workers (largely Dominicans), clerical staff, and managers. Workers' settlements (*bateyes*) dotted the mill and the surrounding fields; they usually included stores, schools, and a number of other facilities.

Mixed Farming

Landholding was less concentrated in the north and the west; mixed crop and livestock raising dominated agricultural production. Much production was geared to subsistence, but growers also produced a number of cash crops such as cocoa, tobacco, coffee, and vegetables. The twin constraints of land and money affected the various strata of rural society differently, depending on the precise configuration of resources a family could command, but hardship was widespread.

Those without land were the most hard pressed. Agricultural laborers rarely enjoyed opportunities for permanent employment. Most worked only sporadically throughout the year. During periods of high demand for labor, contractors formed semipermanent work groups that contracted their services out to farmers. As in much of social life, the individual stood a better chance if he could couch his request for work in terms of a personal link of kinship with the prospective employer.

Families that depended on wage labor had very limited resources at their disposal. Their diet lacked greens and protein; eggs and meat were luxury items. Such fare as boiled plantains, noodles, and broth often substituted for the staple beans and rice. Keeping children in school was difficult because their labor was needed to supplement the family's earnings.

Those with very little land (less than one hectare) also faced very severe constraints. Although members of this group had enough land to meet some of their families' subsistence needs and even sold crops occasionally, they also needed to resort to wage labor to make ends meet. Like wage laborers, smallholders had trouble leaving children in school. The children's prospects were extremely limited, moreover, because their parents could neither give them land nor educate them. The daily need for food also limited farmers' ability to work their own land. Those who were both land-poor and cash-poor faced a dilemma: they could not work their lands effectively because to do so meant foregoing wage labor needed to feed their families. A variety of sharecropping arrangements supplemented wage labor for those smallholders able to muster some cash or credit. These were of little use to the landless; only those who had land or money to finance a crop entered into these schemes. Smallholders and the landless lived enmeshed in a web of dependent relationships: they depended on their neighbors and kin for help and assistance, on store owners for credit, and on larger landholders for employment.

Families with middle-sized holdings (from one to three hectares) faced slightly different problems. They often had enough land and financial resources to meet most of their families' food needs and to earn cash from the sale of crops or livestock. They did not usually need to work for hire, and sometimes they could hire laborers themselves. They usually ate better than smallholders, and their children stayed in school longer. However, although middle holders earned more, they also had greater needs for cash during the year, particularly if they hired laborers before harvest.

Even relatively large holders faced seasonal shortages of cash. Their production costs—especially for hired labor—were typically higher. Their standard of living was notably higher than that of people with less land. They generally ate better and could afford meat or fish more frequently. Although their holdings supported their generation adequately, subdivision among the family's offspring would typically leave no heir with more than a hectare or two. Faced with this prospect, these farmers often encouraged their children to pursue nonagricultural careers and helped support them financially during their student years.

Almost all farmers depended to varying degrees on credit from local storekeepers. The landless and the land-poor needed credit simply to feed their families. Middling landholders used it to tide them over the lean months before harvest. Prevailing interest rates varied considerably, but the poorest farmers—those who could not offer a harvest as collateral and who usually needed short-term credit—generally paid the highest rates.

Farmers often depended on storekeepers to market their crops because they were usually unable to accumulate sufficient produce to make direct marketing a viable option. Most farmers committed their crops to their merchant-creditor long before harvest. Store owners could not legally require that someone who owed them money sell his or her crops to them. Nonetheless, for the farm family, the possibility of being denied necessary credit at a time of future need acted as a powerful incentive. The cycle of debt, repayment, and renewed debt was constant for most.

Traditionally, the local storekeeper aided farmers in ways beyond the extension of credit. He often established a paternalistic relationship with his customers; farmers consulted him on matters ranging from land purchases to conflicts with neighbors. Such patronage carried a hefty price tag, however; farmers found it difficult to haggle about terms with a storekeeper who was also a friend or a relative. Studies of coffee growers in the mid-1970s found that the cost of credit could easily take one-third to one-half of a middling landholder's profits.

Cooperatives sometimes offered an alternative. The most successful drew their membership from groups of kin and neighbors already linked by ties of trust. Cooperatives provided a solution for farmers vexed by the problem of cash shortfalls. Consumer and savings and loan cooperatives thus expanded the options for some rural families. Cooperatives have not ameliorated appreciably the plight of the poorest rural dwellers, however. Cooperative loans were predicated on a family's ability to pay, which effectively excluded the landless and the land-poor.

Family and Kin

The family was the fundamental social unit. It provided a bulwark in the midst of political upheavals and economic reversals. People emphasized the trust, the assistance, and the solidarity that kin owed to one another. Family loyalty was an ingrained and unquestioned virtue; from early childhood, individuals learned that relatives were to be trusted and relied on, while those outside the family were, implicitly at least, suspect. In all areas of life and at every level of society, a person looked to family and kin for both social identity and succor.

Formal organizations succeeded best where they were able to mesh with pre-existing ties of kinship. Indeed, until the 1960s and the 1970s, most community activities were kin-based: a few related extended families joined together for joint endeavors. In the countryside, the core of extensively related families remained pivotal, despite large-scale migration and urbanization. If anything, the ties among kin extended more widely in contemporary society because modern transportation and communications allowed families to maintain ties over long distances and during lengthy absences.

In general, the extent to which families interacted, and the people with whom they interacted, depended on their degree of prosperity. Families with relatively equal resources shared and

Rural family
Courtesy Inter-American Development Bank

cooperated. Where there was marked disparity in families' wealth, the more prosperous branches tried to limit the demands made by the poorer ones. On the one hand, generosity was held in high esteem, and failure to care for kin in need was disparaged; but on the other hand, families wished to help their immediate relatives and to give favors to those who could reciprocate.

A needy relative might receive the loan of a piece of land, some wage labor, or occasional gifts of food. Another type of assistance was a form of adoption, by which poorer families gave a child to more affluent relatives to raise. The adopting family was expected to care for the child and to see that he or she received a proper upbringing. The children were frequently little better than unpaid domestic help. Implicit in the arrangement was the understanding that the child's biological family, too, would receive assistance from the adopting family.

Kinship served as a metaphor for relations of trust in general. Where a kin tie was lacking, or where individuals wished to reinforce one, a relationship of *compadrazgo* would often be established. Those so linked are *compadres* (co-parents or godparents). In common with much of Latin America, strong emotional bonds linked *compadres*. *Compadres* used the formal *usted* instead of *tú* in addressing one another, even if they were kinsmen. Sexual relations between *compadres* were regarded as incestuous. *Compadres* were commonly chosen at baptism and marriage, but the relationship extended to the two sets of parents. The tie between the two sets of parents was expected to be strong and enduring. Any breach of trust merited the strongest community censure.

There were three accepted forms of marriage: civil, religious, and free unions. Both serial monogamy and polygamous unions were socially accepted. Annulment was difficult to obtain through the Roman Catholic Church; this fact, in addition to the expense involved, made couples reluctant to undertake a religious marriage. Civil marriage was relatively common. Divorce in this case was relatively easy and uncomplicated. Marriage forms also reflected the individual's life cycle. Most opted for free unions when they were younger, then settled into more formal marriages as they grew older and enjoyed more economic security. Class also played a role: religious marriage was favored by middle-class and upper-class groups, and it thus indicated higher socioeconomic status. The ideal marriage involved a formal engagement and a religious wedding followed by an elaborate fiesta.

No shame accrued to the man who fathered many children and maintained several women as concubines. Public disapproval followed only if the man failed to assume the role of "head of the family" and to support his children. When a free union dissolved, a woman typically received only the house she and her mate inhabited. The children received support only if they had been legally recognized by their father.

Families were usually more stable in the countryside. Since the partners were usually residing in the midst of their kin, a man could not desert his wife without disrupting his work relationship with her family. A woman enjoyed greater leverage when she could rely on her family to assist if a union failed or when she owned her own land and thus had a measure of financial independence.

In keeping with the doctrine of machismo, males usually played a dominant role within the family, and they received the deference due to the head of the household. There was wide variation in practice, however. Where a man was absent, had limited economic assets, or was simply unassertive, a woman would assume the role of head of the family.

Sex role differentiation began early: boys were allowed to run about unclothed, while girls were much more carefully groomed and dressed. Bands of boys played unwatched; girls were carefully chaperoned. Girls were expected to be quiet and helpful; boys enjoyed much greater freedom, and they were given considerable latitude in their behavior. Boys and men were expected to have premarital and extramarital sexual adventures. Men expected, however, that their brides would be virgins. Parents went to considerable lengths to shelter their daughters in order to protect their chances of making a favorable marriage.

Parent-child relationships were markedly different depending on the sex of the parent. Mothers openly displayed affection for their children; the mother-child tie was virtually inviolate. Informal polls of money changers in the 1970s indicated that remittances sent from the United States for Mother's Day exceeded even those sent at Christmas. Father-child relationships covered a broader spectrum. Ideally, the father was an authority figure to be obeyed and respected; however, fathers were typically more removed from daily family affairs than mothers.

Religion

More than 90 percent of Dominicans were professed Roman Catholics. In the late 1980s, the church organization included 1 archdiocese, 8 dioceses, and 250 parishes. There were over 500 clergy, more than 70 percent of whom belonged to religious orders. This number yielded a ratio of nominal Roman Catholics to priests of more than 10,000 to 1. Among Latin American countries only Cuba, Honduras, and El Salvador had higher ratios in the late 1980s.

Roman Catholicism is the official religion of the Dominican Republic, established by a Concordat with the Vatican. For most of the populace, however, religious practice was limited and formalistic. Few actually attended Mass regularly. Popular religious practices were frequently far removed from Roman Catholic orthodoxy. What little religious instruction most Dominicans traditionally received came in the form of rote memorization of the catechism. Many people felt that they could best approach God through intermediaries—the clergy, the saints, witches (*brujos*), and curers (*curanderos*). The saints played an important role in popular devotion. *Curanderos* consulted the saints to ascertain which herbs, roots, and various home cures to employ. *Brujos* also cured by driving out possessive spirits that sometimes seized an individual.

Many Dominicans viewed the Roman Catholic clergy with ambivalence. People respected the advice of their local priest, or their bishop, with regard to religious matters; however, they often rejected the advice of clergy on other matters on the assumption that priests had little understanding of secular affairs. Activist priests committed to social reform were not always well-received because their direct involvement with parishioners ran counter to the traditional reserve usually displayed by the Roman Catholic clergy.

Villagers often criticized this social involvement. Nonetheless, the priest was generally the only person outside their kinship group that people trusted and confided in. As such, the parish priest often served as an advocate in rural Dominicans' dealings with larger society.

Foreigners predominated among the clergy. The clergy itself was split between the traditional, conservative hierarchy and more liberal parish priests. At the parish level, some priests engaged in community development projects and in efforts to form *comunidades de base* (grass-roots Christian communities), designed to help people organize and work together more effectively.

The Roman Catholic Church was apolitical during much of the Trujillo era, although a pastoral letter protested the mass arrests of government opponents in 1960. This action so incensed Trujillo that he ordered a campaign of harassment against the Church. Only the dictator's assassination prevented his planned imprisonment of the country's bishops. The papal nuncio attempted to administer humanitarian aid during the 1965 civil war. The bishops also issued various statements throughout the 1970s and the 1980s, calling for respect for human rights and an improved standard of living for the majority. In the 1970s, Bishop Juan Antonio Flores of La Vega campaigned for indemnification for peasants displaced by the expansion of the Pueblo Viejo mine. Bishop Juan F. Pepen and Bishop Hugo Polanco Brito both supported the efforts of peasants and sugar *colonos* to organize.

Protestants first came as migrants from North America in the 1820s. West Indian laborers added to their numbers in the late nineteenth and the early twentieth centuries. By the 1920s, the various Protestant groups had organized nationally and had established links with North American Evangelical groups. The main Evangelical groups included the Seventh Day Adventists, the Dominican Evangelical Church, and the Assemblies of God. Protestant groups expanded, mainly in the rural areas, during the 1960s and the 1970s; Pentecostals made considerable inroads in some regions. With minor exceptions, relations between Protestants and the Roman Catholic majority were cordial.

Most Haitian immigrants and their descendants adhered to voodoo, and practiced it in secret because the government and the general population regarded the folk religion as pagan and African. In Haiti voodoo encompassed a well-defined system of hierology and ceremonialism (see Voodoo, ch. 7).

Social Welfare

Education

Formal education included the primary, the secondary, and higher education levels. The six-year primary cycle was compulsory. Three years of preschool were offered in some areas, but not on a compulsory basis. There were several types of secondary school; most students (90 percent) attended the six-year *liceo,* which awarded the *bachillerato* certificate upon completion and was geared toward university admission. Other secondary programs included teacher training schools, polytechnics, and vocational schools. All primary and secondary schools were under the formal jurisdiction of the Secretariat of State for Education and Culture (Secretaría de Estado de Educación y Cultura). In 1984 there were an estimated 5,684 primary schools and 1,664 secondary schools.

Despite the compulsory nature of primary education, only 17 percent of rural schools offered all six grades. This explained to some degree the lower levels of secondary enrollment. For those who did go on to the secondary level, academic standards were low, the drop-out rate reportedly was high, and all but the poorest students had to buy their textbooks—another disincentive to enrollment for many.

The government decreed major curriculum reforms at the primary and secondary levels in the 1970s in an effort to render schooling more relevant to students' lives and needs. Expanded vocational training in rural schools was called for as part of the reforms. Few changes had been fully implemented by the early 1980s, however. Primary-school teachers were trained in specialized secondary schools; the universities trained secondary-school teachers. In 1982, however, roughly half of all teachers lacked the required academic background. A chronic shortage of teachers was attributable to low pay (especially in rural areas), the relatively low status of teaching as a career, and an apparent reluctance among men to enter the profession.

Education expanded at every level in the post-Trujillo era. Enrollment as a proportion of the primary school-aged population grew by more than twenty percentage points between the mid-1960s and the mid-1980s, and that of the secondary school-aged population nearly quadrupled. By the mid-1980s, the primary school population was virtually fully enrolled, but only 45 percent of those of secondary school age were enrolled.

Problems accompanied educational expansion. Teaching materials and well-maintained facilities were lacking at every level. Salaries and operational expenses took up most of the education budget, leaving little surplus for additional investment and growth. In addition, although an estimated 74 percent of the population was literate in 1986, the expansion of educational programs and facilities left a sizable backlog of illiterates largely untouched. Although there were some programs in adult literacy, in 1981 fully one-third of the population over twenty-five years of age had

69

never attended school; in some rural areas the proportion rose to half (see table 3, Appendix A).

Higher education enjoyed the most spectacular growth. At Trujillo's death there was one university, the University of Santo Domingo (Universidad de Santo Domingo), with roughly 3,500 students. By the late 1980s, there were more than twenty-six institutions of higher education with a total enrollment of over 120,000 students. Legislation created the National Council of Higher Education (Consejo Nacional de Educación Superior—CONES) in 1983 to deal with issues surrounding accreditation, the awarding of degrees, and the coordination of programs on a national level.

The sole public institution was the Autonomous University of Santo Domingo (Universidad Autónoma de Santo Domingo—UASD). The UASD traced its lineage directly to the Universitas Santi Dominici, established in 1538. Although the university's administration was autonomous, the government provided all of its funding. This enabled the UASD to offer courses free of charge to all enrolled students. The student body reached approximately 100,000 in 1984. The leading private institutions were the Catholic University Mother and Teacher (Universidad Católica Madre y Maestra—UCMM), located in Santiago and administered by the Roman Catholic Church, and the Pedro Henríquez Ureña National University (Universidad Nacional Pedro Henríquez Ureña—UNPHU) in Santo Domingo. In the early 1980s, UCMM had a student body of approximately 5,000, while UNPHU enrolled approximately 10,000.

Enrollment in private schools also expanded during the post-Trujillo era. Private schools, most of them operated by the Roman Catholic Church, enjoyed a reputation for academic superiority to public schools. By the 1970s, they appeared to be the preferred educational option for the urban middle class.

Health and Social Security

Programs offered through the Secretariat of State for Public Health and Social Welfare (Secretaría de Estado de Salud Pública y Asistencia Social—SESPAS) covered 70 to 80 percent of the population in the late 1980s. The Dominican Social Security Institute (Instituto Dominicano de Seguro Social) covered another 5 percent (or 13 percent of the economically active population), and the medical facilities of the armed forces reached an additional 3 to 4 percent. SESPAS had a regionally based, five-tiered health care system designed to bring primary care to the whole population. The services ranged from specialized hospitals in the National District to rural clinics scattered throughout the countryside.

Student in computer science class, Santo Domingo
Courtesy Inter-American Development Bank

Both personnel and facilities were concentrated in the two largest cities (see table 4, Appendix A). There were roughly 3,700 inhabitants per physician nationally, for example, but this figure ranged from about 1,650 in the National District to roughly 5,000 in some southeast provinces and in the south-central provinces. Similarly, more than half of all hospital beds were in the National District and the central Cibao.

SESPAS began a major effort to improve rural health care in the mid-1970s. By the early 1980s, the government had set up more than 5,000 rural health clinics, health subcenters, and satellite clinics. Doctors, performing their required year of social services, as well as a variety of locally hired and trained auxiliary personnel staffed the facilities. Critics charged that lack of coordination and inadequate management hampered the program's effectiveness, however. Preventive services offered through local health workers (who were often poorly trained in disease prevention and in basic sanitation) were not coordinated with curative services. In addition, absenteeism was high, and supplies were lacking. In 1982 there were approximately 2,500 physicians in the country (a ratio of one physician to 2,600 inhabitants) and 516 dentists.

Life expectancy at birth was 62.6 years for the 1980–84 period, 60.9 years for males and 63.4 for females. The crude mortality rate was 4.7 per 1,000 population in 1981. The infant mortality rate was 31.7 per 1,000 live births in 1982—down from 43.5 per 1,000 in 1975. Early childhood mortality declined from 5.9 per 1,000 in 1970 to 3.2 in 1980. The main causes of death in the population as a whole were pulmonary circulatory diseases and intestinal diseases (see table 5, Appendix A). Enteritis, diarrheal diseases, and protein energy malnutrition were the major causes of death in those under four. Maternal mortality in 1980 was 1.66 deaths per 1,000 live births. The main causes were toxemia, hemorrhages, and sepsis associated with birth or abortion. Roughly 60 percent of births were attended by medical personnel. As of late 1988, the Dominican Republic had reported 701 cases of acquired immune deficiency syndrome (AIDS); of these, 65 had died. Studies of the human immunodeficiency virus conducted in 1986 among sample groups of Dominican homosexual and bisexual males indicated an infection rate of 8.3 percent, much lower than the rate detected in some similar sample groups in the United States.

Social security coverage included old-age pensions, disability pensions, survivors' and maternity benefits, and compensation for work injuries. General tax revenues supplemented employer and employee contributions. Wage earners, government employees (under special provisions), and domestic and agricultural workers were eligible, although the benefits that most domestic and farm workers received were quite limited. Permanent workers whose salaries exceeded 122 Dominican Republic pesos (RD$—for value of the peso, see Glossary) per week and the self-employed were excluded. In the early 1980s, more than 200,000 workers were enrolled. They represented only about 13 percent of the economically active population, or approximately 22 percent of wage earners. Most of those enrolled were in manufacturing, commerce, and construction.

Although the level of government services exceeded that of the republic's impoverished neighbor, Haiti, limited resources, inefficiency, and a lagging economy circumscribed the overall impact of these programs. In 1985 some 8.8 percent of the national budget supported health services and an additional 6.9 percent funded social security and welfare programs. From the perspective of the late 1980s, there appeared little prospect for major improvement in the quality of life for most Dominicans by the end of the twentieth century.

* * *

There is a wealth of information on rural life and the changing rural-urban context in the Dominican Republic. Kenneth Sharpe's *Peasant Politics,* Glenn Hendricks's *The Dominican Diaspora,* Patricia R. Pessar's works, and Malcolm T. Walker's *Politics and the Power Structure,* all give a sense of the constraints most Dominicans must deal with. Jan Knippers Black's *The Dominican Republic: Politics and Development in an Unsovereign State* and H. Hoetink's *The Dominican People* are both valuable background reading. Sherri Grasmuck's "Migration within the Periphery: Haitian Labor in the Dominican Sugar and Coffee Industries" details the contemporary situation of Haitians in the Dominican Republic. José del Castillo and Martin F. Murphy describe the broad outlines of emigration and immigration in "Migration, National Identity, and Cultural Policy in the Dominican Republic." "Agricultural Development, the Economic Crisis, and Rural Women in the Dominican Republic," by Belkis Mones and Lydia Grant, describes the ways in which rural women earn a living. (For further information and complete citations, see Bibliography.)

Chapter 3. Dominican Republic:
The Economy

The Plaza del Mercado, Puerto Plata, ca. 1873

LONG DEPENDENT ON SUGAR, the Dominican Republic diversified its economy during the 1970s and the 1980s to include mining, assembly manufacturing, and tourism. In 1987 the country's gross domestic product (GDP—see Glossary) was approximately US$5.6 billion, or roughly US$800 per capita, which made the island nation the third poorest state in Latin America. A lower-middle-income country by World Bank (see Glossary) standards, the Dominican Republic depended on imported oil and, despite diversification, retained its historical vulnerability to price fluctuations in the world sugar market. Although poverty continued to be acute for many rural citizens in the 1980s, the economy had progressed significantly since the 1960s.

Beginning in the late 1960s, the Dominican economy began the arduous task of diversifying away from sugar. By 1980 the mining industry had become a major foreign exchange earner; exports of gold, silver, ferronickel, and bauxite constituted 38 percent of the country's total foreign sales. In the 1980s, the assembly manufacturing industry, centered in Industrial Free Zones (see Glossary), began to dominate industrial activity. During this decade, the number of people employed in assembly manufacturing rose from 16,000 to nearly 100,000, and that sector's share of exports jumped from 11 percent to more than 33 percent. Tourism experienced a similarly dramatic expansion during the 1980s, when the number of hotel rooms quadrupled. Revenues from tourism surpassed sugar earnings for the first time in 1984, and by 1989 total foreign exchange earnings from tourism nearly matched earnings from all merchandise exports.

Despite indisputable advances, by 1990 the country also faced serious inflation, chronic balance-of-payments deficits, and a large foreign debt. More important, whereas the Dominican Republic had made great strides since the dictatorial rule of Rafael Leónidas Trujillo Molina (1930–61), the nation's political economy continued to be strongly influenced by patronage, graft, and a lingering lack of political will to confront the traditional institutions that continued to restrain economic performance.

Growth and Structure of the Economy

Only three decades after their arrival on Hispaniola (La Isla Española) in 1492, Spanish mercantilists largely abandoned the island in favor of the gold and silver fortunes of Mexico and Peru (see The First Colony, ch. 1). The remaining Spanish settlers briefly established an economic structure of Indian labor tied to land under the systems of *repartimiento* (grants of land and Indian labor) and *encomienda* (grants of Indian labor in return for tribute to the crown). The rapid decline of the Indian population ended the *encomienda* system by the mid-1500s, however. Little productive economic activity occurred in Eastern Hispaniola (the approximate site of the present-day Dominican Republic). The French assumed control of the western third of the island in 1697, establishing Saint-Domingue (modern-day Haiti), which developed into a productive agricultural center on the basis of black slave labor. In the eastern part of the island, cattle ranching was common, but farming was limited to comparatively small crops of sugar, coffee, and cocoa.

The Spanish side of Hispaniola slowly developed a plantation economy during the nineteenth century, much later than the rest of the West Indies. For much of the century, political unrest disrupted normal economic activity and hindered development. Corrupt and inefficient government, by occupying Haitian forces and by self-serving Dominican caudillos, served mainly to increase the country's foreign debt. After failing to achieve independence from Spain in the Ten Years' War (1868–78), Cuban planters fled their homeland and settled in Hispaniola's fertile Cibao region, where they grew tobacco and later cocoa. When tobacco prices fell in the late nineteenth century, United States companies began to invest heavily in the large-scale cultivation of sugar, a crop that dominated the Dominican economy for most of the twentieth century.

The rise of the sugar industry represented only one aspect of growing United States influence on the island in the early twentieth century. In 1904 United States authorities established a receivership over Dominican customs to administer the repayment of the country's commercial debt to foreign holders of Dominican bonds. United States forces occupied the Dominican Republic from 1916 to 1924, for the purposes of restoring order and limiting European (primarily German) influence. Although security interests motivated the occupation, the United States also reaped commercial benefits. Dominican tobacco, cocoa, and sugar, previously exported to French, German, and British markets, were shipped instead to the United States. The powerful United States sugar companies came to dominate banking and transportation, and they benefited from the partition of former communal lands, which allowed the companies to augment their holdings. Although politically unpopular, the United States presence helped stabilize Dominican finances and greatly improved the physical infrastructure, as roads, sanitation systems, ports, and schools were built. The United States Marines left in 1924, but United States economic advisers remained to manage customs revenues until 1932, two years into the thirty-one-year Trujillo dictatorship.

For more than three decades, the Trujillo regime invested heavily in infrastructure, but the bulk of economic benefits accrued to the dictator, his family, and his associates. Trujillo's primary means of self-enrichment was the national sugar industry, which he rapidly expanded in the 1950s despite a depressed international market. In the process of establishing his enormous wealth, he forced peasants off their land, looted the national treasury, and built a personal fiefdom similar to those of the Somoza and the Duvalier families in Nicaragua and Haiti, respectively. Before his assassination in 1961, Trujillo and his coterie reputedly possessed more than 600,000 hectares of improved land and 60 percent of the nation's sugar, cement, tobacco, and shipping assets. This immense wealth encompassed eighty-seven enterprises, including twelve of the country's fifteen sugar mills. Although the economy experienced steady growth under Trujillo, roughly 6 percent a year in the 1950s, the unequal distribution of that growth impoverished rural Dominicans as thoroughly as were any of their counterparts elsewhere in the Western Hemisphere.

The period between Trujillo's assassination and the 1965 civil war was chaotic economically as well as politically. Instability prompted capital flight. While demands on spending increased—mainly as a result of social programs instituted under the presidency of Juan Bosch Gaviño (February-September, 1963)—bureaucratic upheaval hampered the collection of needed revenue. The country's economy was buoyed to some extent by infusions of cash from abroad in the forms of foreign aid (mainly from the United States) and loans.

During the presidency of Joaquín Balaguer Ricardo (1966–78), the country experienced a period of sustained economic growth characterized by relative political unity, economic diversification, the establishment of a developmental role for the state, and a more equitable distribution of the benefits of growth among the citizenry. During its peak growth period, from 1966 to 1976, the economy expanded at a rate of nearly 8 percent a year, one of the highest growth rates in the world at the time. With the formation of the National Planning Council in 1966, the national government assumed a developmental role after centuries of neglect. The Balaguer administration increased spending on social services, introduced the Industrial Incentive Law (Law 299) to protect domestic manufacturing and to spur more import substitution (see Glossary) industries, and promoted mining, assembly manufacturing, construction, and tourism. Mining in particular took on a greater role as that sector's share of exports grew from an insignificant level in 1970 to 38 percent by 1980. Land reform programs helped rural dwellers to improve their economic status somewhat, but government pricing policies and the trend toward urbanization inhibited growth in rural areas. The country's physical infrastructure—roads, ports, and airfields—also expanded.

The apex of the Dominican economic "miracle" came in 1975 when sugar prices peaked, other commodity prices were high, and gold exports became significant. Despite these fortuitous circumstances, the country still failed to register a trade surplus that year, an indication of structural problems in the economy. Economic growth slowed by the late 1970s as sugar prices fluctuated and the quadrupling of oil prices that began in 1973 turned the country's terms of trade (see Glossary) sharply negative. Growing balance-of-payments shortfalls, declining government revenues resulting from widespread tax exemptions, and growing expenditures on state-operated companies rapidly increased the country's debt. The symbolic, if not the real, end of the Dominican economic "miracle" arrived in the form of Hurricane David and Hurricane Frederick in 1979. The two storms killed more than 1,000 Dominicans, and they caused an estimated US$1 billion in damage.

In the early 1980s, oil prices jumped again, international recession stifled the local economy, sugar prices hit a forty-year low, and unprecedentedly high interest rates on foreign loans spiraled the economy into a cycle of balance-of-payments deficits and growing external debt. Because economic growth averaged slightly above 1 percent per annum during the first half of the decade, per capita income declined. Another devastating blow was dealt in the 1980s by reduced United States sugar quotas, in response to the lobbying efforts of domestic producers, which served to cut the volume of Dominican sugar exports to the United States by 70 percent between 1981 and 1987.

The unstable economic situation prompted the administration of Salvador Jorge Blanco (1982–86) to enter into a series of negotiations with the International Monetary Fund (IMF—see Glossary) and to begin to restructure government economic policies. In 1983 the Jorge government signed a three-year Extended Fund Facility with the IMF that called for lower fiscal deficits, tighter credit policies, and other austerity measures. This paved the way for the first in a series of rescheduling agreements with foreign creditors. Although the reschedulings slowed the pace of repayment, the higher consumer prices that resulted from the agreements sparked food riots. The administration consequently suspended the agreements. In 1985 the Jorge government signed a one-year IMF

Sugarcane fields
Courtesy Inter-American Foundation
Loading rail cars with sugarcane
Courtesy Mark Salyers

81

Standby Agreement that included more austerity measures and the floating of the Dominican Republic peso (RD$; for value of the peso—see Glossary) in relation to the dollar for the first time in decades. Serious differences of opinion over the pace of reforms again ended the agreement prematurely, and the electorate ousted Jorge's Dominican Revolutionary Party (Partido Revolucionario Dominicano—PRD) in 1986 in favor of former president Balaguer, who evoked memories of the economic growth of the 1970s (see Political Developments since 1978, ch. 4).

In contrast to Jorge, the Balaguer administration, refusing to negotiate with the IMF, sought to avoid the austere economic conditions that IMF agreements usually entailed. The economy expanded rapidly in 1987, but then contracted sharply in 1988, largely in response to government spending patterns. Balaguer's continued devaluation of the peso maintained the country's burgeoning export sector and tourist trade, but eroded the quality of life of poorer Dominicans earning fixed salaries. The administration's expansionary fiscal policies also fueled unprecedented inflation (prices rose 60 percent in 1988 alone), which worsened economic conditions for poor people. By the close of the decade, the country's foreign debt had reached nearly US$4 billion, roughly double the 1980 figure.

High levels of inflation, increasing debt, and persistent deficits masked several positive trends during the 1980s. The most positive development was the country's rapid diversification away from its dependence on sugar. New jobs in assembly manufacturing offset many of the lost jobs in the cane fields. Employment in assembly operations grew from 16,000 in 1980 to nearly 100,000 by 1989. This represented the world's fastest growth in free-zone employment during the 1980s. By 1987 the value of assembly exports surpassed that of traditional agricultural exports. The Dominican Republic also enjoyed the Caribbean's fastest growth in tourism during the 1980s. Although the mining industry suffered from low prices and labor disputes, it contributed a significant percentage of foreign exchange as well. The agricultural sector also diversified to a limited degree with a new emphasis on the export of nontraditional items such as tropical fruits (particularly pineapple), citrus, and ornamental plants to the United States under the Caribbean Basin Initiative (CBI—see Appendix B).

Economic Policy

Fiscal Policy

The Budget Office within the Technical Secretariat of the Presidency

(Secretaría Técnica de la Presidencia) administered fiscal policies. The fiscal year (FY—see Glossary) concurred with the calendar year throughout the government, except in the case of the State Sugar Council (Consejo Estatal de Azúcar—CEA), which ran on the cycle October 1 to September 30. Fiscal authorities traditionally pursued rather conservative policies, allowing for small deficits and occasional surpluses. Fiscal deficits grew in the 1980s, however, as the result of dwindling revenues and increasing losses from price and exchange-rate subsidies to state-owned enterprises. Revenues, as a percentage of GDP, fell from 16 percent in 1970 to a low of 10 percent by 1982, placing the Dominican Republic below virtually every Latin American country in this category. Liberal incentive laws enacted to spur industrialization during the 1960s and the 1970s were the main cause of the erosion of the revenue base. Beginning with the Jorge administration, officials began to increase taxes on an ad hoc basis, assessing mainly international trade. A moderate expansion of revenues resulted. Nonetheless, fiscal deficits averaged roughly 5 percent of GDP a year in the mid-1980s to the late 1980s. The shortfalls were financed by the printing of more pesos, a policy that accelerated inflation. Successive governments demonstrated a lack of political will to address the structural deficiencies on both the expenditure and the revenue sides of the national budget.

The execution of fiscal policies was influenced by personal and political custom. For example, many businesses illegally received tax-exempt status because of political contacts, while other qualified firms did not. Tax evasion among wealthier Dominicans was common. Government corruption, particularly among the parastatals, was believed to be similarly commonplace. The 1989 conviction of former president Jorge on charges that he and military leaders embezzled large sums on military contracts illustrated the extent of official corruption. The lack of competitive bidding on government construction contracts also contributed to perceptions of fiscal mismanagement. Despite Balaguer's anticorruption drive of the 1980s, institutionalized graft prevailed.

Expenditures

Government expenditures, as a percentage of GDP, reached 21 percent by 1987, up from an earlier low of 15 percent; both figures were low by the standards of most developing countries. These data indicated that, with the exception of the enterprises inherited from Trujillo's holdings, the government's role in the economy was relatively limited. The ratio of total spending had also declined, beginning in the 1970s, because of the decline in revenues as a percentage of total output. Falling revenues dictated a corresponding decrease in the percentage of spending on social services, which worsened the position of poorer Dominicans. Ironically, a major drain of fiscal resources in the 1980s was the result of the low prices of goods and services provided by government-subsidized enterprises, such as utility companies, many of which were created to cater to lower-income citizens. These subsidies began in the 1970s, at a time of greater government resources; by the 1980s, however, they had created serious price distortions between government and market prices. Politicians were reluctant to cut price subsidies to the poor in the late 1980s, as the economy weakened and popular expectations for continued government support remained high.

Government spending was divided between current and capital expenditures. Current expenditures averaged nearly 70 percent of total expenditures during most years, and they were divided among the categories of social services, general services, and financial services. Social services received 30 percent of the national budget in 1988, some 13 percent of which was dedicated to education and 8 percent, to public health. As recently as 1984, social expenditures had accounted for 47 percent of the total. General services constituted 21 percent of spending: about 7 percent of this was allocated to defense; 5 percent, to judiciary and police; and 9 percent, to government operations. The 1988 budget also allocated 22 percent of expenditures under the designation of financial services to debt servicing; this percentage was lower than it had been in previous years, as a result of debt rescheduling. During most of the 1980s, capital expenditures (referred to as economic services in the budget) represented at least 30 percent of total government expenditures, a relatively high proportion. As the Balaguer administration initiated major public-works projects in the late 1980s, the budget share dedicated to capital expenditures increased to more than 40 percent.

Revenues

The core of the government's fiscal problems lay on the revenue side. Starting in 1970, revenues, as a percentage of GDP, steadily declined. These revenues hit a low in 1982, as the result of generous tax exemptions for industry. Many economists criticized the role of fiscal exemptions in the island's industrialization because the government thereby forfeited badly needed revenues in favor of job creation. In 1983 the government introduced a 6-percent value-added tax and initiated a number of ad hoc taxes on international trade, licensing, luxury items, and foreign exchange transactions. These new taxes, however, did not make up for the loss of revenue that had resulted from the low rates of taxation on income and business profits.

A fundamental feature of the nation's tax system was the low level of taxes on income and profits. In 1985 income taxes represented only 0.6 percent of GDP, well below the average of 2 percent of GDP for all developing countries. Furthermore, the income tax was effectively regressive because it utilized a flat rate and allowed numerous exemptions. Most new corporations, generally the most dynamic, benefited from at least one of the many fiscal incentives, and these enterprises therefore added little to the public coffers. In 1987 taxes on income and profits accounted for 19 percent of total tax revenue. Because of the political strength of the local and the foreign business communities, major reforms in this section of the tax law were unlikely (see Interest Groups, ch. 4).

In addition to personal and corporate income taxes, goods and services and international trade were also taxed. Taxes on goods and services equalled 36 percent of all taxes in 1987, whereas those on international trade had reached 43 percent, a relatively high share. Steep import tariffs and export taxes on principal commodities constituted the bulk of taxes on trade. Dominican authorities found taxes on imports and exports far easier to legislate and to collect than domestic taxes, despite the fact that they created numerous economic disincentives. Non-tax revenues, such as government income from property and other equity, provided 12 percent of total revenues in 1987.

Monetary and Exchange-Rate Policies

The Monetary Board of the Dominican Central Bank (Banco Central de la República Dominicana—BCRD) determined monetary policy and oversaw the nation's financial system. The BCRD performed typical central bank functions: it controlled the money supply, allocated credit, sought to restrain inflation, managed the national debt, allocated foreign exchange, and issued currency. The currency since 1948 had been the Dominican Republic peso, which was divided into 100 centavos and was issued in bank note denominations similar to those of the United States.

The BCRD successfully controlled prices in the Dominican Republic until the 1980s. During most of the 1970s, inflation remained below 10 percent, with the exception of 1974 and 1979, when oil prices increased substantially. During the 1980s, however, inflation afflicted the economy, eroding real wages, weakening the peso, and straining the financial system. As measured by the Dominican consumer price index, inflation had jumped from 5 percent in 1980 to 38 percent by 1985. The inflation rate reached 60 percent in 1988. Although the BCRD attempted to restrict the money supply in order to slow inflation, the central government's expansionary fiscal policies and chronic balance-of-payments deficits continued to push prices upward as the decade came to a close. The BCRD favored the use of reserve ratios, as its monetary policy tool of choice, during the 1980s. By regulating the amount in liquid reserves that financial institutions had to keep on their premises, this policy provided a check on the growth of credit. As inflation worsened in 1987, the BCRD temporarily instituted a 100 percent reserve requirement on all new loans. Credit was also restricted by regulation of the interest rate, but the BCRD fixed the rate by the imposition of legal ceilings rather than by letting rates float at market levels. High reserve ratios in the late 1980s squeezed the private sector's access to long-term credit even as its share of the credit market increased in relation to the public sector's share. As a consequence of the swift rise in the price index, real interest rates were often negative in the mid-1980s to the late 1980s as the BCRD's fixed rates failed to keep pace with inflation.

Of major concern to policy makers was the rising cost of basic consumer goods. Many prices were set by the government's National Price Stabilization Institute (Instituto Nacional de Estabilización de Precios—Inespre). Despite Inespre's efforts, food prices rose faster than all other prices during the 1980s. Inespre's pricing policies responded more to political concerns than to economic realities. Prices of basic foodstuffs were maintained at unrealistically low levels, in part because urban violence often resulted from efforts to bring these prices more in line with the free market. Keeping urban consumer prices low necessitated the purchase of staple crops from Dominican farmers at less than fair value, a practice that depressed the income and the living standard of rural Dominicans.

The Dominican peso, officially on par with the United States dollar for decades, underwent a slow process of devaluation on the black market from 1963 until the government enacted a series of official devaluations during the 1980s. In 1978 a Dominican law actually required that the peso be equal in value to the dollar, but as economic conditions worsened, authorities abandoned this policy. The most important change in Dominican exchange policy came in 1985 when the Jorge government, acting in accordance with the terms of an IMF stabilization program, floated the national currency in relation to the dollar, thereby temporarily wiping out the previously extensive black market. The floating peso fell to a level of US$1 = RD$3.12, an official devaluation of over 300 percent that proved to be a major shock to the economy. Preferential exchange

rates, however, remained in force for oil imports and parastatal transactions. The devaluation caused higher domestic prices and bur-
dened many poorer citizens, while it boosted the country's export
sector through newly competitive prices. Rising inflation, balance-
of-payments deficits, and foreign debt compelled further devaluations after 1985. The peso stabilized somewhat at US$1 = RD$6.35
by 1989, after bottoming out at nearly US$1 = RD$8 in mid-1988.
As a result of these fluctuations, the Monetary Board experiment-
ed during the 1980s with a multi-tier fixed exchange rate, a floating exchange rate, and other systems until by 1988 it had settled
on a fixed rate subject to change based on the country's export competitiveness and domestic inflation. An important provision of the
exchange-rate policy of 1988 prohibited currency transactions at the
country's exchange banks and channeled all foreign currency transactions into the commercial banks under BCRD supervision.

Labor

Formal Sector

According to official statistics, the Dominican labor force had
grown to 2.8 million by 1988. The labor force equaled about 74
percent of the nation's 3.8 million economically active citizens, a
group that included all those between the ages of 15 and 64. Official
unemployment stood at 26 percent, but like many of the country's
labor statistics, this measure was only an approximation. More than
80,000 workers entered the job market annually in the 1980s. Unemployment declined slightly in the late 1980s, and it was expected
to continue to drop because of the explosive growth of free-zone
manufacturing jobs. The seasonal nature of jobs in agriculture and
tourism, however, created patterns of structural underemployment
that affected a quarter of the labor force. Half of the economically
active population suffered from either unemployment or underemployment.

The structure of the labor force had changed significantly during the post-Trujillo era as agriculture's share of output diminished.
In 1950 agriculture had employed 73 percent of Dominican labor,
but by the end of the 1980s it accounted for as little as 35 percent.
Industry and services had incorporated approximately 20 percent
and 45 percent, respectively, of displaced agricultural labor. As
a consequence of gaps in the labor statistics, official estimates of
the female segment of the economically active population varied
widely, from 15 to 30 percent of the labor force. Whatever the total figures, the role of women, particularly in the urban economy,
was growing by the late 1980s. Seventy percent of the employees

in free zones were women; as greater numbers of free zones opened in the late 1980s, the rate of employment for females more than doubled the rate of employment for males. This shift represented a major transformation in the labor force; previously, the percentage of women in the Dominican work force had been lower than that for any other Latin American country. Men continued to dominate agricultural jobs in the late 1980s. These were among the lowest-paid jobs in the country. The highest salaries were earned in mining, private utilities, financial services, and commerce. The distribution of income among workers was highly skewed; the top 10 percent earned 39 percent of national income, while the bottom 50 percent garnered only 19 percent.

Dominican labor laws dated back to the Labor Code of 1951. Among the many matters on which the code ruled were the maximum number of foreigners that could be employed in a workplace, guidelines for labor unions, child labor practices, the minimum wage, the length of the workweek, vacations, holiday pay, Christmas bonuses, overtime, social security, and other benefits. No government agency enforced labor legislation, however, which reduced the actual power of most workers vis-à-vis management.

In the 1980s, the most controversial labor law was the one governing the national minimum wage. Although the Congress of the Republic increased minimum wages on several occasions throughout the decade, unusually high inflation usually outpaced these increases, which reduced the real wages of workers. General strikes or other confrontations between labor and government frequently resulted. Government officials were reluctant to grant frequent raises in the minimum wage, in part, because they felt the need to keep Dominican wages competitive with those of other developing countries. Dominican wages did indeed remain lower than those in other Caribbean Basin countries, with the exception of impoverished Haiti.

Organized labor represented between 12 percent and 15 percent of the labor force in the late 1980s. The number of active union members ranged somewhere between the government's estimate of 250,000 and labor's figure of more than 500,000. Thousands of unions were syndicated into eight major labor confederations; nearly 100,000 Dominicans also belonged to independent unions. Scores of peasant-based movements and organizations were also active. Thirty-two percent of the eight labor confederations' member unions were affiliated with the International Confederation of Free Trade Unions, 16 percent with the World Confederation of Labor, and slightly more than half with international communist unions. Unions appeared only after the Trujillo era, and in the 1980s they were still young, weak, poorly financed, and politically divided. The issues most important to Dominican labor included rising prices, the declining real minimum wage, and collective bargaining. Industrial disputes increased noticeably in the late 1980s. In particular, these took the form of general strikes and intensified activism among professionals. Organized labor had begun to establish a foothold in the free zones, and disputes over unionization in these areas loomed as the fundamental labor issue of the future.

Informal Sector

Many Dominicans escaped formal government data collection, but nonetheless played a major economic role, particularly in the urban economy. Estimates of the size of the informal urban economy in the late 1980s ranged from 20 percent to 50 percent of the total urban labor force. Workers in the informal sector included self-employed people, unpaid family workers, domestic servants, and very small businesses or "microenterprises" of only a few workers in manufacturing and assorted services. Although little reliable data existed on the country's informal sector, many in that sector received economic assistance from the United States Agency for International Development (AID), the Inter-American Foundation, and other development agencies to promote their expansion into the formal sector. Some observers believed that the growth of the informal sector was a response to the complex legal framework for business, restrictive exchange-rate controls, widespread informal financial markets, pricing and tax policies, and the often-cited Dominican preference for highly personal relations.

Agriculture

Agriculture, the backbone of the Dominican economy for centuries, declined in significance during the 1970s and the 1980s, as manufacturing, mining, and tourism began to play more important roles in the country's development. During the 1960s, the agricultural sector employed close to 60 percent of the labor force, contributed one-quarter of GDP, and provided between 80 and 90 percent of exports. By 1988, however, agriculture employed only 35 percent of the labor force, accounted for 15 percent of GDP, and generated approximately half of all exports. The declining importance of sugar, the principal source of economic activity for nearly a century, was even more dramatic. Sugar's share of total exports fell from 63 percent in 1975 to under 20 percent by the late 1980s.

The transformation in agriculture paralleled the country's demographic trends. In 1960, some 70 percent of the country's population was rural; by the 1990s, upwards of 70 percent was expected to be urban. Government policies accelerated urbanization through development strategies that favored urban industries over agriculture in terms of access to capital, tariff and tax exemptions, and pricing policies. As a consequence, the production of major food crops either stagnated, or declined, in per capita terms from the mid-1970s to the late 1980s. Lower world prices for traditional cash crops and reductions in the United States sugar quota also depressed the production of export crops in the 1980s.

Land Tenure and Land Policy

The uneven distribution of arable land continued to be a fundamental obstacle to the economic development of the Dominican Republic in the 1980s. Despite active attempts to reform land tenure patterns, the basic dichotomy of latifundio and *minifundio* continued to be the predominant feature of rural life. According to the 1981 agricultural census, 2 percent of the nation's farms occupied 55 percent of total farmland. By contrast, landholdings averaging under 20 hectares, which represented 82 percent of all farms (314,665 units), covered only 12 percent of the land under cultivation. Land distribution on both extremes was notably worse. Some 161 farms, 0.1 percent of all farms, occupied 23 percent of all productive land, whereas tens of thousands of peasants possessed only a few *tareas.* (The *tarea,* the most common measurement of land on the island, equalled one-sixteenth of a hectare.)

The government was the largest landholder. The CEA and the Dominican Agrarian Institute (Instituto Agrario Dominicano— IAD), the national land reform agency, controlled the overwhelming share of public-sector land, most of which was derived from Trujillo's estate. The two major sugar producers in the private sector, Central Romana and Casa Vicini, along with several large cattle ranches, represented the largest private landholdings.

Data from the 1981 census displayed a land tenure structure that was essentially the same as that reflected in the 1971 census. The total number of farms in the 1981 survey was 385,000, up from 305,000 a decade earlier. While the number of farms had increased substantially, the amount of cultivated land had actually decreased slightly, from 2.74 million hectares in 1971 to 2.67 million hectares in 1981. The greater number of farms had resulted from agrarian reform measures and population growth, whereas the decrease in land cultivated had been caused by erosion, development, urbanization, the decline of the sugar market, and other factors. The size of the average farm shrank from 1,439 hectares in 1971 to 698 hectares in 1981, an indication of some minor success in land reform. Types of ownership were not so well documented, but government surveys indicated that individuals owned 66 percent of all farms, families owned 16 percent, and other types of tenure, such as cooperative ownership, sharecropping, and renting, accounted for the remaining 18 percent.

The concentration of land in the Dominican Republic, although it could trace its roots back to Christopher Columbus's parceling of land, had resulted principally from the "latifundization" of land with the advent of commercial sugarcane production in the late nineteenth century. The concentration of arable land ownership increased after 1948, when Trujillo intensified his involvement in the sugar industry. Trujillo doubled the amount of land dedicated to sugarcane, in a little over a decade. The dictator and his cronies seized as much as 60 percent of the nation's arable land through colonization schemes, the physical eviction of peasants from their land, and the purchase of land through spurious means. In the aftermath of Trujillo's assassination in 1961, the government expropriated his family's landholdings by means of Decree 6988, thus setting the stage for contemporary land policy.

In 1962 the post-Trujillo Council of State created the IAD, to centralize agrarian reform and land policy, with a mandate to redistribute the ruler's former holdings to peasants. Agrarian reform was hindered by the country's stormy political transitions in the 1960s, but it was strengthened in 1972 by legislation that authorized the government to expropriate unused farms in excess of 31.4 hectares under certain conditions. During the 1970s and the 1980s, however, the IAD made slow and uneven progress in dividing up the government's huge new properties. IAD reforms provided individuals, cooperatives, and settlements (*asentamientos*) with parcels of land. A range of support services, including land-clearing, road construction, irrigation, agricultural extension services, and credit, usually were also provided. By the end of 1987, the IAD and its predecessor agencies had redistributed more than 409,000 hectares of land. The redistribution included 454 projects that benefited 75,000 families, or 460,000 citizens. In the late 1980s, IAD-sponsored land yielded 40 percent of the national output of rice, 75 percent of tomatoes, 31 percent of corn, and 39 percent of bananas and plantains.

Despite the broad mandate for land reform, a cause strongly advocated by the Balaguer administration in the late 1980s, many criticized the IAD's overall lack of progress since 1962. The greatest progress on land reform occurred from 1966 to 1978, when the government redistributed approximately 174,000 hectares. Reform slowed considerably from 1978 to 1986, when only 66,000 hectares were redistributed. Making land available, however, is only one component of successful reform. Peasants criticized the IAD's sluggish performance in transferring land titles, its providing mainly marginal agricultural land, and the generally inadequate level of support services caused by the lack of funding and the ineffectual management of the IAD. Only 38 percent of IAD land was actually devoted to the cultivation of crops in the late 1980s; 9 percent was devoted to livestock and 53 percent to forestry or to other uses.

After decades of wrangling, the Dominican Republic completed the 1980s with the issue of land largely unresolved from the perspectives of both peasants and commercial farmers, a failure most evident in data demonstrating an ongoing pattern of skewed land ownership. Frequent spontaneous land seizures and invasions by peasants of underused land throughout the 1980s epitomized rural frustrations. On one end of the economic spectrum, numerous rural associations, disconcerted by the pace and the quality of land reform, participated in land seizures, demanding "land for those who work it," an approach that forced the land reform issue into the judiciary rather than into the legislature. On the other end of this spectrum, agribusinesses complained of the government's inconsistent policies with regard to the expropriation of land. Some analysts viewed such inconsistencies as a deterrent to new investment in agriculture and therefore as counterproductive to the republic's efforts to diversify its economy away from sugar. Poverty continued to be a largely rural phenomenon and land a sensitive political subject, indicating that agrarian reform would persist as an issue.

Land Use

An estimated 27,452 square kilometers, or 57 percent of the Dominican Republic's total territory of 48,442 square kilometers, was devoted to agriculture-related activities in the late 1980s. According to a soil survey conducted in 1985, 43 percent of the country's total area was moderately suited, or well-suited, for cultivation. The Cibao and the Vega Real regions, north and northeast of Santo Domingo, respectively, contained the republic's richest agricultural lands and produced most of the nation's food and cash crops, with the exception of sugar. Sugarcane cultivation centered on the coastal plains of the south and the east.

Farming Technology

In the 1980s, Dominican farmers still suffered from the legacies of Trujillo's neglect and industrial strategies that placed little emphasis on agricultural development outside the sugar industry. As a result,

*Aerial shot along Dominican-Haitian border contrasts
denuded hillsides of Haiti (on left) with forested hillsides
of the Dominican Republic (on right).
Courtesy James P. Blair ©1987, National Geographic Society*

the average farmer used far fewer purchased inputs, such as fertilizers, tractors, and irrigation, than his counterparts in many other Latin American countries.

Some progress had been made in irrigation systems by the late 1980s. The poor distribution of the country's generally adequate rainfall necessitated the development of irrigation under the management of the governmental National Water Resources Institute (Instituto Nacional de Recursos Hidráulicos—INDRHI). The amount of irrigated land increased rapidly with the construction of several dams, such as Tavera Dam and Sabana Yegua Dam, in the 1970s and the 1980s. By the late 1980s, however, only about 139,000 hectares, less than 15 percent of arable land, benefited from irrigation. Further expansion of irrigation was a key to reaching self-sufficiency, particularly in rice production. INDRHI pursued ambitious plans for future irrigation; it was projected that more than 200,000 hectares of land would be functionally irrigated by the early 1990s.

The Secretariat of State for Agriculture (Secretaria de Estado para la Agricultura—SEA) attempted to improve farming technology through its extension service and a series of agricultural research centers. The greatest constraints were money and training. The Superior Institute of Agriculture, established in 1962 and affiliated with the Catholic University Mother and Teacher (Universidad Católica Madre y Maestra—UCMM) in Santiago, successfully trained scores of agronomists; it also achieved crop innovations, the most important of which, in the late 1980s, concerned sorghum and African palm oil. Several regional, and generally crop-specific, institutes also conducted agricultural research.

Crops

Cash Crops

Despite ongoing diversification efforts, in the late 1980s the Dominican Republic continued to be the world's fourth largest producer of sugarcane. The sugar industry influenced all sectors of the economy and epitomized the nation's vulnerability to outside forces. Fluctuating world prices, adjustments to United States sugar quotas, and the actions of United States sugar companies (such as Gulf and Western Corporation's sale of all its Dominican holdings in 1985) all could determine the pace of economic development for decades.

Columbus introduced sugarcane to Hispaniola, but sugar plantations did not flourish in the Dominican Republic until the 1870s, much later than on most Caribbean islands. Investment by United

States sugar companies, such as the United States South Porto Rico Company and the Cuban-Dominican Sugar Company, rapidly transformed the Dominican economy. These companies had established themselves by the 1890s, and between 1896 and 1905 sugar output tripled. During the United States occupation (1916–24), the sugar industry expanded further, acquiring control of major banking and transportation enterprises.

Trujillo constructed a string of sugar mills, many of which he owned personally, beginning in 1948. The elimination of United States sugar quotas for Cuba after the Cuban Revolution of 1959 further enhanced the economic role of sugar, as the Dominican Republic assumed Cuba's former status as the main supplier under the quota system.

Heavy reliance on sugar created a number of economic difficulties. The harvest of sugarcane, the *zafra,* is arduous, labor-intensive, and seasonal, and it leaves many unemployed during the *tiempo muerto,* or dead season. Haitian laborers have harvested most of the Dominican cane crop since the late nineteenth century, by agreement between Hispaniola's two governments. Although Haitian cane cutters lived under conditions of virtual slavery (see Haitians, ch. 2; Migration, ch. 7), two factors continued to draw them across the border: depressed economic conditions in Haiti and the reluctance of Dominicans to perform the backbreaking, poorly regarded work of cane cutting.

After the death of Trujillo, Dominican policy makers faced the sensitive issue of how best to manage the dictator's economic legacy, which on the one hand was the rightful property of the people, but on the other hand represented more of a drain on national finances than a catalyst to development. These contradictions played themselves out within the CEA, an entrenched, politicized, and inefficient parastatal.

The role of sugar changed markedly in the 1980s as external conditions forced the national economy to diversify. Sugar prices had reached unprecedented highs in 1975 and again in 1979. The international recession of the early 1980s, however, pushed prices to their lowest level in forty years. Lower world prices hurt the Dominican economy, but the reduction of sales to the United States market, as a result of quota reductions that began in 1981, was even more costly because of the preferential price the United States paid under the quota system. The international market continued to be unpromising in the late 1980s. The market had been glutted by over-production, caused principally by European beet growers; major soft-drink manufacturers had also begun to turn to high-fructose corn sweeteners and away from cane sugar.

In the late 1980s, the CEA continued to control about 60 percent of national sugar output through the ownership of twelve of the country's sixteen sugar mills, employment of a work force of 35,000, and possession of 233,000 hectares of land, only 100,000 hectares of which were sown with sugarcane. Governed by a board—the members of which were drawn from the public sector, labor, and the private sector—the CEA operated at a financial loss and at lower productivity than the two major private sugar companies, Casa Vicini and Central Romana. Besides these major producers, thousands of small farmers (*colonos*) also grew cane. Sugar from all properties covered an estimated 240,000 hectares in 1987, and it yielded 816,000 tons, well below the 1.25 million tons harvested in 1976, the year of peak volume. Worse yet, lower prices kept 1987 sales at less than one-third of what was realized in 1975, when sugar export revenues peaked at US$577 million. The Dominican Republic still exported about half its sugar to the United States in the late 1980s (but, unlike in the past, not all under the quota system with its preferential prices). The Soviet Union became the second largest purchaser of Dominican sugar, following the signing of a three-year bilateral agreement in 1987.

Coffee, the second leading cash crop, was also subject to varying market conditions in the 1980s. Introduced as early as 1715, coffee continued to be a leading crop among small hillside farmers in the late 1980s; it covered 152,000 hectares throughout various mountain ranges. Coffee farming, like sugar growing, was seasonal, and it entailed a labor-intensive harvest involving as many as 250,000 workers, some of whom were Haitians. The preponderance of small holdings among Dominican coffee farmers, however, caused the coffee industry to be inefficient, and yields fell far below the island's potential. Output of coffee fluctuated with world prices, which reached an eight-year low in 1989. Another problem was the coffee bushes' vulnerability to the hurricanes that periodically ravaged the island.

The Dominican coffee industry faced not only national problems, but also international ones, which resulted mainly from the failure of the International Coffee Organization (ICO) to agree on quotas through its International Coffee Agreement (ICA). As a consequence, the Dominicans' ICA quota dropped several times late in the decade, hitting a low of 425,187 sixty-kilogram bags by 1988. Although Dominicans consumed much of their own coffee, they were increasingly forced to find new foreign markets because of the ICO's difficulties. As was true of many Dominican commodities, middlemen often smuggled coffee into Haiti for re-export overseas. Official coffee exports in 1987 were US$63 million, down from US$86 million in 1985 and US$113 million in 1986.

Cocoa endured as another principal cash crop, occasionally surpassing coffee as a source of export revenue. The Dominican cocoa industry emerged in the 1880s as a competing peasant crop, when tobacco underwent a steep price decline. Although overshadowed by sugar, cocoa agriculture enjoyed slow, but steady, growth until a period of rapid expansion in the 1970s. In response to higher world prices, the area covered with cacao trees grew from 65,000 hectares in 1971 to 117,000 hectares by 1980. Small farmers cultivated the most cocoa, producing some 40,000 tons on approximately 134,000 hectares in 1987. This crop was enough to make the Dominican Republic the largest producer of cocoa in the Caribbean. Cocoa exports in 1987 reached US$66 million. Despite the brisk growth in the crop, the Dominican cocoa industry suffered from low yields and from increasing quality-control problems. In addition, three exporters controlled 75 percent of all cocoa, thus limiting competition. The country also forfeited greater foreign-exchange earnings because only a small portion of the crop was processed before export.

Tobacco enjoyed a renaissance in the 1960s, with the introduction of new varieties and an increase in prices. Sales revenues peaked in 1978, but they declined considerably in the 1980s because of lower prices, disease, and inadequate marketing. In 1987, 23,000 hectares yielded 23,000 tons of tobacco. Black tobacco of the "dark air-cured and sun-cured" variety represented 88 percent of national production in the late 1980s. Manufactured into cigars for export, black tobacco was the foremost foreign-exchange earner among the various strains of the crop grown in the Dominican Republic.

Numerous companies participated in the export of black tobacco. Sales to Spain, the United States, the Federal Republic of Germany (West Germany), and France totaled US$14 million in 1987. A growing number of cigar companies operated out of the country's burgeoning free zones, registering US$26 million in sales in 1987.

Declining prices and structural changes in the international market for the Dominican Republic's traditional cash crops of sugar, coffee, cocoa, and tobacco forced the government to consider opportunities for nontraditional agricultural exports during the 1980s. This new emphasis on nontraditional exports also coincided with the implementation of the Caribbean Basin Initiative (CBI), which afforded the country reduced-tariff access to the United States market. The main categories of nontraditional exports that the government promoted included ornamental plants, winter vegetables

(vegetables not grown in the United States during winter months), citrus, tropical fruits, spices, nuts, and certain types of produce popular among the growing Hispanic and Caribbean populations in the United States. However, new investments in agribusiness during the 1980s were less successful than anticipated, particularly in comparison to the dramatic success of assembly manufacturing and tourism. Nonetheless, officials apparently had succeeded in broadening the options of farmers and investors from a few crops to a diverse range of products. The government spearheaded agricultural diversification through an export promotion agency, the Dominican Center for the Promotion of Exports (Centro Dominicano de Promoción de Exportaciones—Cedopex), and through cooperation with a nongovernmental organization, the Joint Agricultural Consultative Committee, which promoted agribusiness investment in the republic. By 1989 some successes had been achieved with citrus and pineapples, but quicker growth in nontraditional agricultural exports was hindered by the slow pace of the CEA's diversification program, which had scheduled portions of the fertile sugar plains for conversion to nontraditional crop production.

Food Crops

As part of the national dish of rice and beans, rice was the Dominican Republic's most important food crop in the late 1980s. Rice production expanded significantly in the post-Trujillo era, and by late 1979 the country had achieved self-sufficiency for the first time. Rice production, however, waned in the 1980s, forcing renewed imports. In 1987 about 112,000 hectares yielded 320,000 tons of rice, an amount inadequate to meet national demand, but well above the level of 210,000 tons in 1970.

Declines in production were related to a series of economic factors. Rice subsidies to the urban poor, who enjoyed less than two kilograms of rice a week as part of Inespre's food basket, or *canasta popular,* were generally at odds with the goal of increased output. The government's land reform measures also may have had a negative impact on rice yields; IAD's rice holdings, which rendered 40 percent of the nation's rice, were noticeably less productive than private rice holdings. In the late 1980s, the government continued to involve itself extensively in the rice industry by supplying irrigation systems to over 50 percent of rice farmers as well as technical support through the Rice Research Center in Juma, near Bonao. The government also moved to increase the efficiency of local distribution in 1987, when it transferred rice marketing operations from Inespre to the Agricultural Bank of the Dominican Republic

(Banco Agrícola de la República Dominicana—Bagricola) and then to the private sector.

The other principal grains and cereals consumed in the Dominican Republic included corn (or maize), sorghum, and imported wheat. Corn, native to the island, performed better than many food crops in the 1980s because of the robust growth of the poultry industry, which used 95 percent of the corn crop as animal feed. The strong demand for feed notwithstanding, Inespre's low prices for corn and other distortions in the local market caused by donated food from foreign sources decreased incentives for farmers and reduced output during the late 1970s and the early 1980s. As of 1987, corn covered 28,000 hectares, and it supplied 43,000 tons, an amount far below domestic needs. The cultivation of sorghum, a drought-resistant crop also used as a feed, expanded rapidly in the 1980s because of sorghum's suitability as a rotation crop on winter vegetable farms and as a new crop on newly idle cane fields. An estimated 16,000 hectares yielded 49,000 tons of sorghum in 1987, more than double 1980's output of 23,000 tons. Wheat was another increasingly important cereal because Dominicans were consuming ever-greater quantities of the commodity, donated primarily by the United States and France. As a result, the country's two mills were functioning at full capacity in the late 1980s. The government was reluctant to do something about Dominicans' preference for the heavily subsidized wheat over local cereals for fear of violent protests by poorer consumers.

Other major food crops included starchy staples such as plantains and an assortment of tubers. Dominicans consumed large quantities of plantains, usually fried, because of their abundance, sweet taste, and low cost. An estimated 31,000 hectares of trees produced 251,000 tons of plantain in 1987. Peasants routinely cultivated and consumed root crops, such as cassava, taro, sweet potatoes, and yams because they were cheap and easy to cultivate. Production of these basic food crops did not fare well in the late 1970s and the 1980s because of low government prices and the exodus of population to the cities. Some 17,000 hectares sown with cassava, the most common tuber, produced approximately 98,000 tons of that crop in the late 1980s.

Beans, a dietary staple and the chief source of protein for many Dominicans, were grown throughout the countryside. Although the country was generally self-sufficient in the universally popular red bean, shifts in output created the need to import some beans during the 1980s. Red beans covered 57,000 hectares, yielding 39,000 tons, whereas black beans were grown on only 9,000 hectares, yielding only 4,000 tons. Other varieties generated even smaller harvests.

Dominicans also grew an assortment of fruits, vegetables, spices, and other foods. These included bananas, peanuts, guava, tamarind, passion fruit, soursop, coconut, tomatoes, carrots, lettuce, cabbage, scallions, coriander, onions, and garlic.

Livestock

The raising of livestock, the basis of the economy during colonial times, continued to be a common practice in the 1980s, despite the country's warm climate and hilly interior. The predominant livestock on the island were beef and dairy cattle, chickens, and pigs. The country was essentially self-sufficient in its production of basic meats. Cattle-raising was still the primary livestock activity in the late 1980s, and the Dominican stock exceeded 2 million head, the great majority of which were beef cattle, raised mostly on medium-to-large ranches in the east. The annual output of slaughtered beef surpassed 80,000 tons annually, by the late 1980s, over 10 percent of which was processed by five specially certified slaughterhouses and was exported to the United States. Ranchers also smuggled out much beef to circumvent export duties. The country also contained an undetermined, but dwindling, number of dairy cows. The decline in the dairy cow population was the direct result of years of low government prices for milk. Implemented in an effort to keep milk prices low, this policy dramatically increased milk imports, and it created serious milk shortages. Many private milk pasteurizers consequently closed their businesses in the 1980s. By the late 1980s, only four pasteurizing plants, including one owned by Inespre, processed local milk and reconstituted imported powdered milk.

The poultry industry, in contrast to the dairy industry, enjoyed strong growth in the 1980s. A few large producers supplied the nation with 90,000 tons of broilers a year and with hundreds of millions of eggs. As in other developing countries, the cost of feed continued to play a major role in the pace of the poultry industry's expansion in the 1980s. The pork industry had also rebounded by the mid-1980s, after suffering the virtual eradication of its stock from 1978 to 1982 because of an epidemic of African Swine Fever (ASF; see Livestock and Fishing, ch. 8). Afterward, the Dominican Republic established an increasingly modern and well-organized pork industry. By the late 1980s, the national stock exceeded 500,000. This number was well below 1979's peak figure of 750,000, however. The government succeeded in restocking the pig population very rapidly after 1982, but higher feed prices and slack consumer demand for pork, previously a traditional Dominican favorite, in response to high prices had slowed that effort by 1989.

Forestry and Fishing

Pine, hardwood, and other tree cover, once ample, covered only 15 percent of the land by 1989. To offset losses caused by the indiscriminate felling of trees and the prevalence of slash-and-burn agriculture, the government outlawed commercial tree cutting in 1967. Since then, there had been some limited development of commercial plantation forestry, but the nation continued to import more than US$30 million in wood products each year. Although not so drastic as in Haiti, deforestation and the erosion that it caused posed serious environmental concerns for the country's watersheds into the 1990s and beyond. Reforestation efforts drew funding from a number of international development agencies during the 1980s.

The fishing industry also was underdeveloped. Undercapitalized, it consisted of only small coastal fishermen with modest nonrefrigerated boats, who barely exploited the 1,600 kilometers of coastline. The government did not place much emphasis on the industry and, therefore, provided little financial or other assistance to fishermen.

Industry

Manufacturing

Manufacturing, particularly assembly operations in free zones, constituted one of the most dynamic sectors of the Dominican economy in the 1980s. As had been true of mining, the growing role of manufacturing accelerated the industrialization and the diversification processes affecting the island's economy. Manufacturing in 1988 contributed about 17 percent of GDP, employed 8 percent of the labor force, and generated about one-third of exports, although assembly exports did not appear in normal trade data because of their free-zone origins. The sector consisted of traditional manufacturing, with large roles for both the public and the private sectors, and free-zone manufacturing, consisting mainly of assembly operations with some agro-processing as well. Growth in manufacturing during the 1980s centered on the free zones; their projected employment of as many as 180,000 workers by 1991, when compared with a total of only 16,000 workers in 1980, was expected to represent the most dramatic increase in assembly labor in the world during that ten-year period. Manufacturing's export performance was equally dramatic. Manufactured goods went from 11 percent of total exports in 1980 to 31 percent by 1987.

Traditional Manufacturing

During the Trujillo era, manufacturing grew more slowly than it did in other Latin American and Caribbean countries because of the dictatorship's disproportionate emphasis on sugar production. In 1968 the Balaguer government introduced the Industrial Incentive Law (Law 299). For the first time, domestic manufacturers received substantial tariff protection from foreign competition. In the same year, the government signalled the beginning of industrial diversification in the post-Trujillo era by establishing the Industrial Development Board to oversee industrial policy. Although these incentives stimulated an array of domestic industries, created jobs, and helped to diversify the country's industrial base, Dominican industries failed to develop a capacity to compete internationally. Although envisioned largely in terms of import substitution, most Dominican industries depended heavily on foreign inputs. In addition, because they were generally capital-intensive, these industries failed to provide adequate employment for a burgeoning population.

Local manufacturing was both inefficient and inequitable. The application of tariff and income tax exemptions became a politicized process whereby benefits accrued to individual firms rather than to specific industries. The Jorge government, which itself manipulated incentives regulations to its political advantage, introduced in 1983 the Democratizing Law 299, purportedly to standardize industrial incentives for all producers.

In the late 1980s, more than 5,000 traditional manufacturing firms existed in the republic. Food-processing activities were dominant, representing over 50 percent of manufacturing activity, followed by chemicals, 12 percent; textiles, 9 percent; and nonmetallic minerals, 6 percent. Some 3 percent of all firms accounted for nearly 50 percent of all industrial output; these firms, however, employed only 23 percent of the manufacturing labor force, indicating the capital-intensive nature of larger companies. By contrast, 85 percent of the smallest firms registered only 30 percent of industrial production, while employing 50 percent of Dominican workers.

The Dominican government generally abstained from involvement in new manufacturing operations, but twenty-five industrial enterprises, part of the Trujillo "legacy," remained in the government's portfolio in the late 1980s. Most of these parastatals were under the control of a state holding company, the Dominican State Enterprises Corporation (Corporación Dominicana de Empresas Estatales—Corde). Initially converted into state-owned enterprises

Workroom of a microenterprise shoe factory, Santiago
Courtesy Inter-American Foundation
Industrial Free Zone
Courtesy United States Agency for International Development

as the "inheritance of the people," Dominican parastatals endured in the late 1980s because of their role in the political patronage system (see Public Administration, ch. 4). Corde's holdings were diverse, ranging from a five-man auto parts firm to a 1,600-employee cigarette factory. Although the Balaguer administration considered privatizing some state-owned enterprises to improve its fiscal position, that prospect remained unlikely because of the political value of such firms.

Free-Zone Manufacturing

There was no economic process more dynamic in the Dominican Republic during the 1980s than the rapid growth of free zones. Although the Dominican government established the legal framework for free zones in 1955, it was not until 1969 that the Gulf and Western Corporation opened the country's first such zone in La Romana. Free-zone development progressed modestly in the 1970s, but it accelerated rapidly during the 1980s as the result of domestic incentives, such as Free-Zone Law 145 of 1983 and the United States CBI of 1984. Free-Zone Law 145, a special provision of the Industrial Incentive Law, offered very liberal incentives for free-zone investment, including total exemption from import duties, income taxes, and other taxes for up to twenty years. By the close of the decade, the results of free-zone development were dramatically clear. From 1985 to 1989, the number of free zones had more than doubled, from six to fifteen; employment had jumped from 36,000 to nearly 100,000. The number of companies operating in free zones had increased from 146 to more than 220. In 1989 six more free zones were being developed, and three more had been approved. These zones were projected to bring the total to twenty-four by the mid-1990s. Demand nonetheless outpaced growth, forcing some companies to wait as long as a year to acquire new factory space.

The country's free zones varied widely in terms of size, ownership, production methods, and location. The size of free zones ranged from only a few hectares to more than 100 hectares. Private companies operated nine of the country's fifteen free zones in 1989, but only four of those were managed as for-profit ventures. The government administered six zones, including the Puerto Plata free zone, the only mixed public-private venture. Most companies in the free zones, 66 percent in 1989, were from the United States. Dominicans owned 11 percent of the firms, and the remaining enterprises had originated in Puerto Rico, Taiwan, Hong Kong, Panama, the Republic of Korea (South Korea), Canada, Italy, and Liberia. Most free zones hosted an assortment of producers, while a few focused on a limited number of subsectors, such as garments, electronics, or information services. Other free-zone products included footwear, apparel, jewelry, velcro, furniture, aromatics, and pharmaceuticals. Most operations were performed under short-term subcontracting arrangements. The government also afforded free-zone benefits to certain agro-businesses, dubbed special free zones, which were physically located outside the free zones themselves, thus causing some agro-processing to fall under the free-zone export category. Among the most innovative activities in the free zones were information services, such as data entry, Spanish-English translation, computer software development, and even toll-free telephone services for Spanish-speakers in the United States; all of these services were available because of the island's advanced telecommunications infrastructure (see Communications, this ch.). By 1989 nearly every region of the country was home to at least one free zone; the greatest concentration was found in the south and southeast.

Apart from the incentives of Free-Zone Law 145 and other domestic legislation, a growing number of foreign companies chose the Dominican Republic as an investment site because of the twin plant scheme (see Glossary), or 936 scheme, with Puerto Rico under the CBI. The twin-plant concept allowed companies to benefit both from the exemption of United States import duties under the CBI and from the income tax exemptions granted to firms in Puerto Rico under Section 936 of the United States tax code, while also taking advantage of the Dominican Republic's low labor costs. As the Spanish-speaking country closest to Puerto Rico and the most prolific developer of free zones in the region, the Dominican Republic hosted over 50 percent of the seventy twin-plant investments that had been recorded by 1989.

The National Council for Free Zones (Consejo Nacional de Zonas Francas—CNZF), within the Secretariat of State for Industry and Commerce, spearheaded free-zone development. A major justification for the development of free zones was the levels of employment that the generally labor-intensive work stimulated. Also, free zones provided hard currency, mostly in the form of wages, rent, utilities, and supplies, for a nation hungry for foreign exchange. By the late 1980s, however, jobs in the free zones were only beginning to make a dent in the country's chronically high unemployment, which had averaged about 25 percent for more than a decade.

Based on the export success of Southeast Asian nations, free-zone development had a proven economic value, but it was not without policy trade-offs. Although the strategy provided numerous

105

jobs, the new jobs that it created offered limited opportunity for advancement. Similarly, with the exception of information services and agro-processing, free-zone enterprises entailed limited technology transfer for longer-term development. Free-zone development also forged few economic links with the local economy because of the limited value added by assembly operations. Besides labor and utilities, few local inputs became part of the manufacturing process, mostly because of insufficient local supply, uneven quality, and certain government regulations. The rapid growth of free-zone construction also created some nationwide bottlenecks in cement production, the generation of electricity, and other basic services. Finally, the liberal tax and tariff exemptions extended to free-zone manufacturers reduced the potential revenue base of the government and forced domestic businesses and individuals to assume a greater portion of the tax burden.

Mining

Like the economy at large, the mining industry enjoyed extraordinary growth in the 1970s, when the country's major ferronickel and *doré* (gold and silver nugget) operations were inaugurated. Mining's contribution to GDP rose from 1.5 percent in 1970 to 5.3 percent by 1980, where it remained in the late 1980s. Although the mining sector employed only about 1 percent of the labor force throughout this period, it became a major foreign-exchange earner, increasing from an insignificant portion of exports in 1970 to as much as 38 percent by 1980, then leveling off at approximately 34 percent in 1987. Nonetheless, mining companies struggled in the 1980s because of low international prices for the island's key minerals—gold, silver, bauxite, and nickel. In the late 1980s, the government strove to tap new resources and to strengthen export diversification by actively seeking foreign investment in mining (see table 6).

Gold and silver *doré,* which occur naturally in the Dominican Republic, played a central role in the rapid emergence of mining. Although the Spanish mined gold on the island as early as the 1520s, gold production in the Dominican Republic was insignificant until 1975, when the private firm Rosario Dominicano opened the Pueblo Viejo mine, the largest open-pit gold mine in the Western Hemisphere. In 1979 the Dominican government, then owner of 46 percent of the shares of Rosario Dominicano, purchased the remaining equity from Rosario Resources, Inc., a New York-based company, thereby creating the largest Dominican-owned company in the country. Rosario's huge mining infrastructure, with an annual capacity of 1.7 million troy ounces of gold and silver, impelled by rapidly increasing international prices for gold, had nearly succeeded in pushing *doré* past sugar as the country's leading source of export revenue by 1980. From 1975 to 1980, gold and silver skyrocketed from 0 percent of exports to 27 percent. Declining prices for gold and silver during the 1980s, however, curtailed the extraordinary growth trend of the 1970s, and by 1987 *doré* exports represented only 17 percent of total exports (one percentage point above ferronickel exports, and one percentage point below sugar exports). Declining reserves also limited *doré* production. Japanese and United States companies actively explored new gold reserves on the island, but gold mining was shifting away from the search for oxide ores, supplies of which were dwindling, toward the more expensive process of exploiting sulphide ores. There were some alluvial gold deposits as well.

Ferronickel also contributed to the mining prosperity of the 1970s. From 1918 to 1956, the United States Geological Survey performed a series of mineral studies in the Dominican Republic. These studies encouraged the Canadian firm Falconbridge to undertake its own nickel testing starting at the end of that period. Falconbridge successfully opened a pilot nickel plant in 1968, and by 1972 the company had begun full-scale ferronickel mining in the town of Bonao. In the late 1980s, the Bonao ferronickel mine was the second largest in the world. Buoyed by high international prices, nickel exports rose from 11 percent of total exports in 1975 to 14 percent by 1979. Although nickel exports, as a percentage of total exports, continued to climb in the 1980s, reaching 16 percent by 1987, lower world prices for nickel and a lengthy dispute between the government and Falconbridge over tax payments hampered output throughout the decade. Unlike gold, nickel had been proven to exist in large reserves in the Dominican Republic, which meant bright prospects for mining.

The Aluminum Company of America (Alcoa) began bauxite mining in the southwest province of Barahona in 1958. Bauxite output peaked in 1974 when Alcoa surface-mined nearly 1.2 million tons; exports totaled as much as US$22 million as late as 1979. As with other minerals, however, the international recession of the early 1980s caused bauxite prices to topple, as world supply outpaced demand. Alcoa closed its Dominican bauxite operations in 1982 and its small limestone mine in 1985. The Barahona mine remained closed until 1987, when the government purchased Alcoa's facilities and recommenced bauxite mining, selling the red ore to Alcoa for processing in Suriname.

The Dominican Republic also produced varying amounts of iron, limestone, copper, gypsum, mercury, salt, sulfur, marble, onyx, travertine, and a variety of industrial minerals, mainly for the construction industry. In the late 1980s, the National Marble Company was a profitable, but outmoded, government monopoly that mined marble, onyx, and travertine for the local construction industry. Corde's Minas de Sal y Yeso extracted salt and gypsum, generally at a loss. Salt mining was primitive, and its product was destined solely for the local market. The private sector mined and exported limestone, some of which went to the United States.

The government increasingly favored greater participation by the private sector in mining, so that the state's resources might be combined with the technology and the capital of foreign firms. Mining's promoters also sought to diversify the economy's export basis and to improve its international credit worthiness. Through Decree 900 of March 1983, the Jorge government further defined and limited the role of government in mining, by providing broader incentives for private involvement. Nonetheless, the state retained exclusive rights to mine gold, gypsum, and marble. United States, Japanese, Australian, and European firms explored Dominican soils after 1987, when the government opened up areas previously closed to foreign investors.

Construction

The construction industry had a major effect on the economy during the 1970s and the 1980s, as government-funded public works provided thousands of jobs and improved the physical infrastructure. In 1987 the sector contributed nearly 9 percent of GDP, a relatively high figure for a developing country. Construction activity boomed in the early 1970s, increasing at a rate of 16 percent annually from 1970 to 1975, faster than any other sector during that period, with the exception of mining. Public-works projects such as dams, roads, bridges, hospitals, low-income housing, and schools transformed the national infrastructure during the 1970s. The sector's rapid growth continued in the 1980s, but it was very uneven because of fluctuations in annual government spending. Private-sector construction, particularly of free-zone facilities and hotels, also boosted industry performance.

Construction firms, like many other Dominican businesses, relied heavily on personal contacts. For example, in the late 1980s the government awarded only about 15 percent of its construction contracts through a competitive bidding process. Government authorities, up to and including the president, negotiated or offered the remaining contracts as if they were personal spoils. The Balaguer administration's emphasis on construction in the late 1980s focused primarily on renovations in Santo Domingo, and it included the construction of museums, a lighthouse, and a new suburb, all in preparation for 1992's observance of the five-hundredth anniversary of Columbus's arrival in the New World.

The construction sector generally was self-sufficient; less than one-third of all construction materials was imported. Domestically produced materials included gravel, sand, clay, tiles, cables, piping, metals, paint, and cement. Although the main indicators of construction materials output generally rose in the 1980s, the rapid expansion of activity during the decade caused a serious shortage of cement that slowed the progress of some projects. The Dominican government built cement factories in Santiago and San Pedro de Macorís in 1977 in joint ventures, with private investors, to complement its major plant in Santo Domingo, but the new capacity quickly became insufficient, and the country was forced to begin importing cement by the mid-1980s. By the late 1980s, cement factories were operating at full capacity, a rarity among developing countries such as the Dominican Republic. Besides materials, the industry encompassed ten major construction firms as well as several design and civil engineering companies, which handled all but the most complex projects. The construction sector was a major employer of unskilled labor, which constituted 65 percent of that industry's work force.

Energy

The cost and the availability of energy became major impediments to development in the 1970s and the 1980s. An oil importing nation, the Dominican Republic saw its import bill for petroleum multiply tenfold in absolute terms during the 1970s. Although oil prices eased during the 1980s, the country faced a new energy crisis as a result of a critical shortage of electrical-generating capacity. Inadequate supplies of electricity resulted by the late 1980s in frequent power outages, frustrated consumers, and disrupted productive activities.

The country's aggregate consumption of energy was low, even by Latin American standards. For example, Costa Rica consumed more than half again the amount that the Dominican Republic did on a per capita basis in the 1980s. The energy consumed by the nation came from a variety of sources: petroleum and petroleum products (49 percent), wood (26 percent), biomass (20 percent), hydropower (3 percent), and coal (2 percent). The country continued to be dependent on imported crude oil and related petroleum products, and its narrow domestic energy resource base satisfied barely half the nation's energy demand. The potential supply of hydropower, the most promising resource, was estimated at 1,800 megawatts (MW), but less than a quarter of that amount was being tapped in 1989. Wood and charcoal use was constrained by the small size of the country's remaining forests. Biomass, mostly bagasse from sugarcane residue, was getting more use but had limited potential as a fuel. Deposits of lignite (brown coal) were known to exist in the Samaná Peninsula in undetermined amounts, but exploitation of this resource was considered unprofitable in the late 1980s. Nontraditional energy resources, such as geothermal and solar power, were also being considered, but they, too, promised little return on potential investment in the 1980s.

United States, Venezuelan, and Canadian oil companies began prospecting for oil in Dominican soil in the early twentieth century; these efforts met with little success, however. Only small deposits were known to exist at Charco Largo in the 1980s, and the prospect of new oil finds appeared poor. Consequently, the country imported crude oil and certain special petroleum products that could not be refined locally. Mexico and Venezuela, under the San José Accord (see Glossary), met about one-third of the country's oil needs at concessional rates. Under pressure from urban consumers, the government traditionally had subsidized gasoline prices; sudden price increases, like those of 1984 and 1989, often triggered unrest.

The Dominican Electric Company (Corporación Dominicana de Electricidad—CDE), a parastatal that replaced a private company in 1955, operated the country's national electrical system in 1989. The CDE supplied two-thirds of the country's 1,573 MW electrical capacity in 1986. Private and public production—used to power mines, sugar mills, cement factories, other industries, and residences—accounted for the balance. Oil-based thermal plants generated most of the nation's electricity (62 percent). Smaller amounts were produced by gas turbines (14 percent), hydroelectric dams (14 percent), and other sources (10 percent). Residences consumed the most electricity (41 percent), followed by industry (28 percent), the public sector (19 percent), and commercial users (12 percent). Prices ranged from the low subsidized rates afforded households to the much higher tariffs the CDE charged its large commercial customers. Only 38 percent of Dominican homes had electricity in the late 1980s, a low percentage by Latin American standards; for example, 54 percent of Jamaicans had such access.

Generally dilapidated and outdated, the CDE's facilities suffered from inadequate maintenance and inefficient, politicized financial management. For example, approximately one-third of all electricity generated in 1988 was lost because of maintenance problems or unauthorized use. Not surprisingly, by the late 1980s the country was facing a huge deficit in electrical capacity that was substantially

The Tavera Dam
Courtesy Inter-American Development Bank

hindering economic development. Some areas suffered as many as 500 hours of outages a year, which often caused damage to appliances because of drops in voltage and other irregularities. Because of this unreliable service, many businesses, especially in free zones, ran their own generators. With assistance from the World Bank and the Japanese government, the CDE attempted to improve efficiency by increasing tariffs, upgrading infrastructure, and expanding capacity. The Balaguer administration in the late 1980s considered privatizing portions of the CDE's operations. Nevertheless, demand was expected to outpace supply for years to come.

Services

Tourism

The Dominican tourist industry grew tremendously during the 1970s and the 1980s, and by 1989 it boasted more than 18,000 hotel rooms—more than any other location in the Caribbean. Foreign-exchange earnings from tourism also multiplied dramatically, during the 1980s, from US$100 million in 1980 to US$570 million by 1987, or the equivalent of 80 percent of all merchandise exports. In 1984 tourism replaced sugar as the country's leading foreign-exchange earner, exemplifying the growing diversity of the Dominican

111

economy. The number of tourists visiting the island increased from 278,000 in 1975 to 792,000 in 1985, and in 1987 the number of vacationers surpassed 1 million for the first time. This total surpassed those of traditional resort locations like Bermuda and Barbados, and it made the Dominican Republic the fifth largest earner of tourism dollars in the Caribbean, behind the Bahamas, Puerto Rico, Jamaica, and the United States Virgin Islands.

Government promotion of tourism did not begin in earnest until the passage in 1971 of the Tourist Incentive Law (Law 153). Law 153 created certain "tourist poles" to promote the industry's growth, and, more important, it provided investors in tourism a ten-year tax holiday and an exemption from tariffs on imports not available locally. The law also created a special arm of the central bank to co-finance new investments in the sector. In 1979 the administration of Silvestre Antonio Guzmán Fernández (1978–82) elevated the director of the country's tourism development efforts to cabinet level, a further indication of official interest and commitment.

The Dominican Republic offered a number of attractions to tourists, not least among them, its bargain rates and liberal divorce laws. As a consequence of numerous devaluations of the peso in the 1980s, the country was the least expensive Caribbean resort. The republic also benefited from a general upswing in Caribbean tourism in the 1980s, associated with the strong United States economy. Each year during the decade, the United States accounted for more than 50 percent of the visitors to the Dominican Republic. Other vacationers came mainly from Canada, Italy, Spain, West Germany, and the Scandinavian countries. As the island offered more "all-inclusive" package vacations to visitors, the average tourist expenditure and length of stay also increased, indicating the gradual maturation of the trade. Levels of hotel occupancy generally were very high, between 80 percent and 90 percent. Traditionally, the most popular resorts had been in La Romana, Puerto Plata, and Santo Domingo, but new beach hotels in the southwest, the east, and the north all promised to be major attractions in the future.

Despite its successes, the tourist industry was still relatively young, and it faced a series of problems related to its rapid growth. For example, inadequate supplies of clean water and electricity, combined with slow construction caused by shortages of materials, forced some vacationers to leave early because of unsuitable accommodations. Although workers were drawn by tourism's higher wages and the access that it provided to foreign currencies, the rapid development of the industry ensured that qualified labor continued to be in short supply. Tellingly, the industry's return rate for visitors was low, by Caribbean standards.

Banking and Financial Services

The Dominican Republic had a diversified, dynamic financial system in the 1980s, which had undergone rapid expansion throughout the post-Trujillo era. In the late 1980s, more than 400 financial enterprises, representing 17 types of institutions, made up the country's financial services sector, which contributed 7 percent of GDP in 1988. The financial system in the 1980s included the Dominican Central Bank (Banco Central de la República Dominicana—BCRD); see Monetary and Exchange-Rate Policies, this ch.), commercial banks, savings and loan institutions, private development finance companies (or *financieras*), mortgage banks, state banks, and assorted other establishments.

The financial system grew rapidly after 1961, as the private sector gained greater access to credit, new forms of finance became available, and Dominicans created new institutions to meet their growing credit needs. The number of formally regulated financial institutions rose from 7 in 1960 to 31 in 1970, and to 78 by 1985. These institutions had a total of 263 branch offices. Much of the growth in the 1970s and the 1980s involved consumer finance companies and larger *financieras*, which underwrote medium-term and long-term loans for priority economic sectors. The financial sector experienced a crisis in the first half of the 1980s because of the poor macroeconomic climate, but increased government regulation as part of a 1985 stabilization program eased some of the system's problems. Despite high inflation and unusually high interest rates, many new commercial banks and related services were founded in the late 1980s.

Twenty-four commercial banks made up the core of the private financial system in 1989. Commercial banks controlled about 64 percent of the financial system's total assets, and over 40 percent of commercial bank funds were deposited in one bank, the Reserve Bank (Banco de Reservas de la República Dominicana). Although it served as the main fiscal agent of the government, the Reserve Bank also operated as a commercial bank. Banks were largely Dominican-owned, especially after several foreign banks sold most of their portfolios to local banks in 1984 and 1985 because of the unfavorable economic climate. Nonetheless, Chase Manhattan and Citibank, from the United States, and the Bank of Nova Scotia, from Canada, maintained local operations in the late 1980s. Banks provided a full range of services, and they were the only institutions offering checking accounts. The Superintendency of Banks, within the Secretariat of State for Finance, regulated the banks in conjunction with the Central Bank.

Commercial bank loans to productive sectors favored manufacturing, which received 34 percent of bank credit in 1987; followed by agriculture, 19 percent; services, 8 percent; and construction, 6 percent. The remainder financed exports, imports, and consumer purchases.

The growth in investment in the priority areas of assembly manufacturing and tourism increased the private-sector share of total domestic credit, beginning in 1984, despite tight credit conditions. Large corporations dominated access to bank credit, often irrespective of their credit worthiness or need for credit, mainly because of their superior ''connections.'' Besides their assets in the domestic banking system, Dominicans held an estimated US$1 billion in accounts overseas, mainly in the United States.

Savings and loan associations and mortgage banks were the main sources of household finance. Seventeen savings and loan associations served the nation in 1989, up from only twelve in 1970. These associations, established since 1962, contained 19 percent of the financial system's assets and catered mostly to middle-income homebuyers, but they also offered passbook savings, certificates of deposit, and collateralized loans. The National Housing Bank (Banco Nacional de la Vivienda—BNV) regulated the savings and loan institutions by imposing per-family lending ceilings. Fourteen mortgage banks, holding about 10 percent of the financial system's assets, served mostly upper-income homeowners. The most prominent of these institutions was the Dominican Mortgage Bank (Banco Hipotecario Dominicano—BHD). Unlike the savings and loans, however, mortgage banks also financed the short-term needs of builders and medium-term and long-term commercial construction. Both the Central Bank and the BNV regulated mortgage banks, but they imposed less stringent regulations than those applied to the savings and loan associations. Lower-income homebuyers obtained credit via the National Housing Institute and household finance companies (*sociedades inmobiliarias*).

The very popular *financieras*, the equivalent of private development finance companies, controlled 6 percent of national assets, and they were an important vehicle for the financing of medium-term and long-term investment in priority sectors. The number of *financieras* had grown from eight in 1970 to twenty-five by 1989. Established in 1966, *financieras* issued stocks and funded bonds, guaranteed by government financial institutions, to mobilize capital in major development projects in agribusiness, industry, transportation, and tourism. In addition, they supplied technical assistance to borrowers, and they served as guarantors of the liabilities of others. As many as 300 consumer finance companies, also called *financieras,* providing short-term consumer credit throughout the countryside, were largely unregulated. Increased government regulation of the small *financieras,* particularly in the area of currency speculation, forced many to close in the late 1980s.

Three state banks played a relatively minor role in the financial system. These included the BNV, which provided some housing-related finance, and the Industrial Finance Corporation, which played a smaller role than its name suggested. The Agricultural Bank of the Dominican Republic (Banco Agrícola de la República Dominicana—Bagricola), by contrast, was an important creditor. Through its thirty branch offices, Bagricola covered most of the countryside in an attempt to serve small farmers. It faced an uphill battle, as both public sector and private sector credit policies favored urban activities. The bank declined in importance during the early 1980s because of a high level of unpaid debt, but it rebounded in the late 1980s as it became more autonomous and, for the first time, mobilized capital through savings accounts.

A wide range of other financial enterprises, providing a broad array of financial services, also existed in the Dominican Republic. Many of these organizations served the large informal sector. The Dominican Development Foundation and the Association for Microenterprise Development were successful lenders to microenterprises and unincorporated businesses. Rural credit unions, in existence for decades, also served rural borrowers and savers. Money lenders abounded as well. Monetary authorities closed down some seventy exchange banks in 1988 as part of foreign exchange reforms; it remained unclear in 1989 whether that was to be a permanent policy. Fifty insurance companies, half of which were locally owned, underwrote policies in the late 1980s, under the supervision of the Superintendency of Insurance.

Transportation

The Dominican Republic's relatively advanced transportation infrastructure had experienced sustained expansion since the 1950s. Transportation, along with communications, accounted for approximately 6 percent of GDP in 1988, and that share was growing because of the booming tourist industry. Roads were the most common medium of travel. The national road network, which totaled more than 17,000 kilometers in 1989, was extensive by Caribbean standards. One-quarter of all roads were highways (see fig. 4). Seventy percent of the highways were paved, and they received some maintenance. Poor conditions were extremely common, and

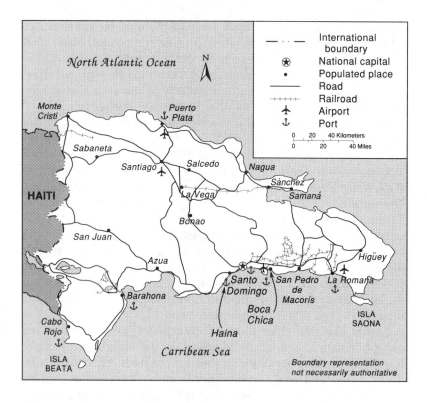

Figure 4. Dominican Republic: Transportation System, 1989

80 percent of all feeder roads were badly deteriorated by the mid-1980s. Moreover, most roadways were narrow and flooded easily. The Directorate for Highway Maintenance of the Secretariat of State for Public Works and Communications provided poor up-keep services, largely because of an insufficient budget. The World Bank and the Inter-American Development Bank (IDB) financed programs in the late 1980s that would upgrade roads and develop better maintenance systems. An estimated 60,000 registered freight vehicles and 10,000 unregulated, inter-urban jitneys constituted the republic's commercial transportation fleet.

The country's 325-kilometer railroad system was one of the longest in the Caribbean. The CEA owned 60 percent of the railroad, which primarily served the sugar industry. Over half of all sugar-cane traveled from the fields to the mills by rail. Central Romana also operated a railroad for its private sugar interests. The other owners of railroads included the state-operated salt mining and bauxite companies, Dominican Agrarian Institute (Instituto Agrario

Dominicano—IAD), and Falconbridge. Falconbridge also operated nearly all of the country's pipelines, seventy-four kilometers of which supplied oil to the Canadian firm's ferronickel smelting plant in Bonao.

Fifteen seaports were in operation in the late 1980s. Nine were engaged in international commerce, while six were limited to commerce among Dominican ports; however, only four were considered major ports. Shipping was the leading form of international commerce. The country's major seaport was Haina, located on the Caribbean coast just west of Santo Domingo. New container equipment that it received during the 1980s made Haina one of the most modern ports in the Caribbean. As a consequence, Haina replaced Santo Domingo and Boca Chica as the Dominican Republic's central shipping facility. The government funded renovation of the port of Santo Domingo in the late 1980s, however, converting it into one the region's major berths for cruise ships. Most other seaports were specialized as well: Boca Chica handled sugar exports; Cabo Rojo and Barahona shipped minerals; and Puerto Plata also catered to cruise ships. The Dominican Port Authority regulated only the capital's ports in the late 1980s, but by law it was given responsibility for the eventual administration of all the country's wharves. Foreign lines dominated shipping, despite a Dominican law that required 40 percent of all vessels to fly Dominican flags. Domestic undercapacity, however, rendered that law unenforceable. Many rivers traversed the island, but few were commercially navigable.

Four international airports accommodated the nation's growing numbers of travelers. The two major airports were Las Américas, near Santo Domingo, and the newer La Unión, near Puerto Plata, both of which handled wide-bodied jets. Las Américas traditionally received more than two-thirds of all air passengers and most air cargo, but La Unión's share of air passengers grew steadily after its completion in the 1970s as a result of the burgeoning tourist industry on the north coast. A French construction company renovated the Las Américas airport in 1989, so that it could more effectively manage the growing influx of passengers. The smaller international airports at La Romana and Santiago accommodated mainly chartered flights. Fourteen carriers scheduled regular flights within the Dominican Republic in 1989. Four of these carriers also offered direct daily flights to the United States. Dominican Airlines (Compañía Dominicana de Aviación—CDA, also known as Dominicana) was the country's national airline; traditionally, it had served 35 percent of all passengers. The parastatal's heavy financial losses in the 1980s forced it to cancel many flights, however, which reduced its market share. By 1989 the government had decided to sell 49 percent of CDA's stock to a foreign airline in a bid to bolster its finances. A local company, Alas del Caribe, flew domestic flights.

The Dominican side of Hispaniola also contained an estimated 120 clandestine airstrips. Many of these were used by international drug traffickers during the 1980s to transit the island en route to the United States (see Crime, ch. 5).

Communications

One of the most modern and dynamic sectors of the Dominican economy was the telecommunications industry, which surpassed its counterparts in every Latin American and Caribbean nation in terms of technology. Telecommunications services, however, were largely concentrated in urban areas.

The most impressive and technologically advanced component of the nation's telecommunications network was its phone system. Codetel, a wholly owned subsidiary of the United States company GTE, operated approximately 90 percent of the 250,000-unit national phone system under the regulatory authority of the General Directorate for Telecommunications of the Secretariat of State for Public Works and Communications. Codetel planned to double the number of phones in the country by the mid-1990s. Some of the advanced features of the phone system included direct domestic and international dialing, toll-free access to the United States through "800" numbers, incoming toll-free or WATS service, high-speed data transmission capabilities, fiber-optic cables, digital switching, and a full range of services usually available only to consumers in the United States. In 1987 the Dominican Republic became the second Latin American country to boast cellular mobile telephones, and it was the only developing country in the hemisphere to offer this service to the public on a national basis. Codetel and other companies also offered telex, electronic mail, telenet, and facsimile services to the public. A member of the International Telecommunications Satellite Organization (Intelsat), the country possessed a satellite earth station, submarine cable to the United States Virgin Islands, and microwave stations. In 1989 a fiber-optic cable to Puerto Rico was completed to expedite sophisticated data transmission to the United States.

The Dominican Republic's unique advantage in terms of telecommunications technology allowed the creation of new industries derived from the growing field of information technology. For example, four free zones in the Dominican Republic served information industries, and the free zone in San Isidro was a teleport with direct links to United States telecommunications networks. These new information industries provided a wide range of innovative services that were creating a comparative advantage for the republic by the late 1980s. These services included data entry, telemarketing support for United States companies, response to toll-free service calls for Hispanic consumers in the United States, computer graphics services, computer software development, and Spanish-English translation services. Potentially, any computer-based service available in the United States that could be transmitted via satellite or through fiber-optic cables could be handled in the Dominican Republic.

Foreign Economic Relations

Foreign Trade

According to official figures, exports in 1987 dipped to US$718 million, a ten-year low. Diminished exports, in combination with the country's largest import bill ever (US$1.5 billion), caused the nation's merchandise trade deficit to reach the unprecedented and precarious level of US$832 million. Traditional exports suffered a steady decline from 1984 to 1987 because of a steep drop in sugar revenues.

This negative data on overall exports, however, masked positive patterns in exports at the sectoral level, as the economy continued to diversify away from sugar. For example, the structure of Dominican exports changed dramatically from 1981 to 1987 as the share of traditional exports (sugar, coffee, cocoa, and tobacco) dropped from 62 percent to 43 percent, while minerals as a percentage of exports went from 28 percent to 34 percent, and nontraditionals jumped from 10 to 23 percent. These data, however, excluded free-zone exports, which technically were not recorded as merchandise trade. Free-zone exports swelled from the equivalent of 10 percent of total exports to 31 percent of total exports from 1981 to 1987, and in 1987 free-zone export revenues surpassed those derived from traditional agricultural exports for the first time (see table 7, Appendix A).

The novel composition of Dominican exports also caused a redirection of the country's goods and services toward the United States market and those of developed countries in general. The United States share of Dominican exports, after peaking at 83 percent in 1970, fell to 52 percent by 1980, but then leaped to 87 percent by 1987, indicating a somewhat risky dependence on a single export market. Puerto Rico's share of the country's exports, which were included in the United States figures, steadily increased during the 1980s, and it exceeded 7 percent by 1987. Less developed countries received only 3 percent of Dominican exports in 1987; only 2 percent of all foreign sales went to Latin America. The Soviet Union, which first contracted to purchase Dominican sugar in the mid-1980s, accounted for 2 percent of exports, a figure that was expected to increase. European markets, particularly Spain, Switzerland, and Belgium, received the balance. An unknown, but presumably large, amount of exports was smuggled out of the Dominican Republic, especially to Haiti, to circumvent international agreements, exchange controls, and export taxes.

The government supported the diversification of exports through the Dominican Center for Export Promotion (Centro Dominicano de Promoción de Exportaciones—Cedopex). Although established in 1971, Cedopex had a minimal economic role until the 1980s, when the country began to move from import substitution toward export promotion. An important foundation of that policy was the Export Incentive Law of 1979 (Law 69), which afforded duty-free entry of imported inputs for exporters and provided certain foreign-exchange benefits. In the first five years that Cedopex administered Law 69, businesses exported 275 new products as a result of the legislation. This number rose considerably after 1984 with the passage of the CBI, the signing of bilateral textile agreements with the United States, and the designation of a series of new free zones. Cedopex also extended conventional investment promotion services, such as market research, overseas promotion of new products, and investor guidance to government regulations. Despite these advances in export promotion, some economists pointed to the continued use of export taxes and the outright prohibition of certain exports, mainly staple foods, as disincentives to improved export performance.

Dominican imports reached an unprecedented US$1.55 billion in 1987. Even more alarming than the country's unparalleled trade deficit, however, was its inability to reduce import demand even as oil prices fell during the late 1980s. Oil's share of total imports, as high as 61 percent in 1980 after the disruptions of the 1970s, declined to a manageable 24 percent by 1987. Non-oil imports mounted, however, thereby ravaging the country's balance of payments and leaving the nation vulnerable in the event of another oil price increase. In order of importance, other imports included intermediate, consumer, and capital goods. A large percentage of increased imports in the late 1980s was dedicated to public sector projects pursued for both economic and political reasons. The country drew an increasing share of its total imports from developed countries; this figure grew from 62 percent in 1981 to 78 percent

Unloading lumber, port of Haina
Courtesy Inter-American Development Bank

in 1987. The United States was the major supplier, providing 55 percent of imports, followed by Japan with 11 percent, and West Germany and Canada with 2 percent each. Developing countries contributed only 22 percent. This consisted primarily of oil imports originating in Venezuela and Mexico.

The government's import policies in the 1980s continued to endorse steep tariff protection for local industry, and only limited import liberalization was achieved. In the late 1980s, the country banned more than 100 imports, mostly agro-industrial products, and some tariffs reached 350 percent. Moreover, successive Dominican governments used import tariffs as a political tool to reward powerful constituents. Excessive public sector imports and exchange-rate subsidies for certain parastatals exacerbated the import crisis in the late 1980s.

The republic's other trade policies consisted of securing markets for traditional and nontraditional exports through bilateral agreements, such as the United States sugar quota agreement, the United States General System of Preferences, the CBI, and the 807 program (see Glossary), as well as international agreements for coffee, cocoa, and other products. For many years, the Dominican Republic unsuccessfully attempted to become a member of the Caribbean Community and Common Market (Caricom) and the

121

Lomé Convention (see Glossary) of the European Economic Community. Although the country had achieved observer status in both, full participation continued to be unlikely because Dominican exports competed directly with those of other members.

Balance of Payments

Poor trade performance and a heavy debt burden caused the country's balance of payments to register severe deficits during the 1980s. In 1987 the overall deficit reached US$593 million, or roughly 11 percent of GDP. This deficit was financed by a draw down in reserves and a rollover of the oil debt owed to Venezuela and Mexico.

The nation's current account was chronically negative; it had not registered an annual surplus for decades. Large merchandise trade deficits were the prime cause of current account deficits. After 1981, however, increased revenues from "invisibles" (tourism and remittances from abroad) reduced the current account deficit, which by 1987 stood at 6 percent of GDP. Remittances—cash transfers sent from the nearly 1 million Dominicans residing in the United States—were an increasingly important source of foreign exchange. In 1987 they were estimated to range from US$300 to US$800 million a year. Reduced interest payments on the country's foreign debt because of debt rescheduling also lowered the service debit on the current account.

The country's capital account, like that of most Latin American countries in the 1980s, suffered from capital outflows precipitated by the debt crisis. This crisis essentially precluded new commercial bank lending to the Dominican Republic during the decade. Most new capital flows were registered in the form of official multilateral and bilateral aid and as foreign investment. The United States Department of Commerce estimated cumulative foreign investment at US$400 million in 1987, approximately half of which came from the United States. The nation was increasingly dependent on foreign assistance to stabilize its balance of payments, and its continued drawing on negative reserves placed it in a tenuous financial position as the decade came to a close.

Foreign Debt

The Dominican Republic's foreign debt had grown to nearly US$4 billion by 1989, about double the 1980 total. The country's debt skyrocketed during the 1970s, barely more than a decade after Trujillo had paid it off, an event he had proclaimed as the "financial emancipation of the nation." Subsequent indebtedness was incurred in the context of a tenfold increase in the oil import bill, increasingly unfavorable terms of trade, and volatile sugar prices. Persistent balance-of-payment shortfalls, relatively easy access to loans from foreign commercial banks, and the demand for funds occasioned by ambitious public sector projects rapidly indebted the country; from 1975 to 1980, the national debt surged from US$700 million to nearly US$2 billion. Further deterioration in the country's terms of trade, unprecedentedly high interest rates, and international recession increased the country's foreign debt in the 1980s, even in the absence of new commercial lending.

In 1988, 63 percent of the public sector external debt was owed to public institutions, including 20 percent to multilateral organizations and 43 percent to bilateral creditors; 23 percent was owed to 90 commercial banks, with the remainder classified under other categories, such as oil credits owed to Mexico and Venezuela. The structure of the country's debt, which remained rather stable during the decade, differed from the debt structure of Latin America as a whole, in that so much more of the region's foreign liabilities (57 percent) were commercial. From 1983 to 1988, Dominican debt as a percentage of GDP grew from 48 percent to 94 percent, signaling that debt was swiftly outpacing economic output. As a result of frequent rescheduling, however, debt repayments as a percentage of total exports declined from 23 percent in 1983 to 15 percent in 1988.

The BCRD, the central bank, took an activist approach to managing foreign debt. The major tool was rescheduling. Beginning with a rescheduling of US$500 million of its commercial debt in 1983, the country embarked on a series of debt negotiations that entailed a Paris Club (see Glossary) rescheduling agreement of US$270 million in 1985, another commercial bank deal of US$787 million in 1986, and a rollover of Venezuelan and Mexican oil debt in 1987. Although debt rescheduling eased the short-term debt burden and improved the government's cash flow, it did not establish long-term solvency. In an effort to reduce its actual debt, the government experimented with debt-equity swaps, a process by which investors purchased the country's United States-denominated debt at a discounted level in local currency, which was then applied to investments in the republic. In 1988 the Debt Conversion Unit of the BCRD's Monetary Board approved the concept of debt-equity conversions, and in 1989 the first such swap converted US$9 million in debt into a free-zone investment at a discount of 35 percent. Investors provided the BCRD with more than US$650 million in other proposals for investments in tourism, free zones, agro-industries, utilities, and mining. To restrain expansion of the money supply, the BCRD consented to a maximum of US$50 million in conversions annually. Even under the best circumstances, however, debt-equity swaps would only partially reduce the debt. As of late 1989, the government and its creditors had not agreed on a comprehensive debt strategy.

Foreign Assistance

The IMF, the World Bank, and the IDB were the major multilateral donors in the Dominican Republic. The IMF, the lender of last resort and for purposes of economic stabilization, had a long and controversial history in the country. The Jorge government had signed agreements with the IMF in 1983 and 1985, but both ended prematurely because of disagreements over the pace and the extent of economic reforms. Austerity measures mandated under the 1985 IMF agreement were met with widespread rioting and other violence. The Balaguer administration (1986–90) had yet to sign an IMF agreement as of 1989, and it often lambasted the international institution over its unpopular economic remedies. In the absence of an IMF agreement, World Bank lending was limited to about US$15 million a year, mainly in support of road construction, energy, financial sector reform, and other technical assistance. The IDB had assisted the island since the early 1960s; in the 1980s it provided funding for projects in irrigation, education, hurricane assistance, and highways.

The United States was the major bilateral donor in the Dominican Republic, furnishing between one-quarter and one-half of bilateral assistance. The level of United States assistance since the 1940s had fluctuated widely in response to economic and political trends. The Dominican Republic became one of the top recipients of United States aid in 1966, when US$100 million in economic assistance was provided in the aftermath of the United States occupation. Assistance slowed during the 1970s, averaging only US$21 million a year. The United States Agency for International Development (AID) strengthened its presence in the 1980s, and from 1984 to 1987, United States assistance averaged US$115 million a year, the highest level since 1966. The composition of United States assistance changed markedly during the 1980s, from an emphasis on development assistance—which constituted 56 percent of total aid in 1979 but only 25 percent in 1987—to greater use of Economic Support Funds (mainly balance-of-payments support), which, although they had not existed in 1979, accounted for approximately 55 percent of aid in 1985. The level of food aid under the Public Law 480 (Food for Peace) program remained fairly constant, about 45 percent of total aid. The focus of AID's interventions in the republic also shifted dramatically, from basic human needs—education, health, and family planning in the 1970s—to short-term economic stabilization, privatization, export promotion, economic policy reform, natural resource management, and small business development. Besides AID, other United States bilateral agencies, such as the Peace Corps and the Overseas Private Investment Corporation actively assisted development.

Japanese, European, and Canadian bilateral development agencies also had representatives on the island. Private nongovernmental development groups, both local and international, were numerous in the Dominican Republic; they provided hurricane relief, food donations, and project support to multilateral and bilateral donors.

Although privation and poverty persisted, especially in rural areas, the economy appeared in the late 1980s to be moving toward a new phase of development, based on export promotion and new, innovative service industries. Reliance on the United States as a customer, supplier, and aid donor was crucial to this process. Long-term prospects for diversification and growth were encouraging, providing the government was able to deal effectively with negative trends in trade and the balance of payments. The problem of the foreign debt appeared intractable, partially for political reasons. As in other areas, however, the Dominican economy in 1989 contrasted dramatically with the sugar-dominated fiefdom left behind by Trujillo in 1961.

* * *

The works that best describe the Dominican economy in the 1980s include Claudio Vedovato's *Politics, Foreign Trade, and Economic Development: A Study of the Dominican Republic,* Howard J. Wiarda and Michael J. Kryzanek's *The Politics of External Influence in the Dominican Republic,* and Jan Knippers Black's *The Dominican Republic: Politics and Development in an Unsovereign State.* The annual *Dominican Republic: Investors Handbook,* published by the American Chamber of Commerce of the Dominican Republic, provides a useful guide to economic developments. As of 1989, however, there was no definitive book-length study detailing the economy's shift from sugar toward free-zone manufacturing, tourism, and other nontraditional activities. The World Bank, the International Monetary Fund, the United States Agency for International Development, and the United States Department of Agriculture issue the most important field-based studies on the Dominican Republic available on a regular basis. The United Nations Economic Commission for Latin America and the Caribbean and the Economist Intelligence Unit also publish helpful annual reports on the Dominican economy. On the island, the Dominican Central Bank, the Technical Secretariat of State of the Presidency, the Investment Promotion Council, the State Sugar Council, and the Dominican Center for the Promotion of Exports, all generate essential data and studies on local economic activity. (For further information and complete citations, see Bibliography.)

Chapter 4. Dominican Republic: Government and Politics

View of the Alcázar de Colón, the home of the Spanish governor, Diego Columbus

THE ROOTS OF DEMOCRACY were not deep in the Dominican Republic. The country traditionally had been mostly poor, rural, and underdeveloped. It had a weak economy, largely based on sugar exports, and it lacked the social and the political infrastructures—political parties, interest groups, and effective government institutions—necessary for democratic rule. Thus, for most of their history the people of the Dominican Republic had lived under authoritarian governments.

In addition, the international climate had not favored democracy and development. The Dominican Republic, a small, dependent nation, poor in resources, shared the island of Hispaniola (La Isla Española) with more populous but even poorer Haiti. Tensions between the two nations could be traced back to the nineteenth century, when Haiti controlled the entire island (1822–44), or, farther back, to the era of colonial rule by the Spaniards. The Dominican Republic's economy, historically oriented toward the export of primary products for the world market, was dependent on fluctuating world market prices for those products, or on the quotas set by major importers—factors beyond the Dominican Republic's control. Moreover, the country's strategic location in the Caribbean, astride all the major sea lanes linking North America and South America and leading into the Panama Canal, exposed the country to the buffeting winds of international politics, or led to its occupation by major powers such as Spain, Britain, France, the Netherlands, and, most recently, the United States. The nation's almost inevitable entanglement in international conflicts afforded it little opportunity to develop autonomously.

Beginning in the early 1960s, however, many things began to change in the Dominican Republic. Per capita income in the late 1980s was four times what it had been in 1960. The country's population was approximately 70 percent urban (the corresponding figure in 1960 was 30 percent), more literate (in about the same proportion), and more middle class. Political institutions had developed and had become more consolidated. The country's international debt continued to be a major problem and a severe drain on the economy, but in general the Dominican Republic's economic position within the international community was more stable than it had been in past decades. These changed conditions made the climate more conducive to democracy than it had been at any previous time.

In 1961 assassins ended the thirty-one-year dictatorship of Rafael Leónidas Trujillo Molina. There followed five years of instability that witnessed a short-lived democratic regime under Juan Bosch Gaviño, the military overthrow of Bosch, a Bosch-led revolution in 1965, civil war, United States intervention, and the restoration of stability in 1966 under a former Trujillo puppet, Joaquín Balaguer Ricardo. Balaguer governed for the next twelve years, until forced to bow to the electorate's desire for change in 1978. That year Silvestre Antonio Guzmán Fernández, of Bosch's party, the Dominican Revolutionary Party (Partido Revolucionario Dominicano—PRD), won the presidency. Guzmán was succeeded by another PRD leader, Salvador Jorge Blanco (1982–86). In 1986 the shrewd, but aging, Balaguer won four more years as president in another fair and free election.

There was, therefore, a democratic breakthrough in the Dominican Republic in the early 1960s that led to instability, conflict, intervention, and eventually an authoritarian restoration. In 1978, however, a new democratic opening occurred. Whether this new democracy would be more permanent than other frustrated efforts in the past, or the Dominican Republic would again revert to instability and authoritarianism, remained to be seen.

The System of Government
Constitutional Development

By 1989 the Dominican Republic had gone through 29 constitutions in less than 150 years of independence. This statistic is a somewhat deceiving indicator of political stability, however, because of the Dominican practice of promulgating a new constitution whenever an amendment was ratified. Although technically different from each other in some particular provisions, most new constitutions contained in reality only minor modifications of those previously in effect. Sweeping constitutional innovations were actually relatively rare.

The large number of constitutions does, however, reflect a basic lack of consensus on the rules that should govern the national political life. Most Dominican governments felt compelled upon taking office to write new constitutions that changed the rules to fit their own wishes. Not only did successive governments often strenuously disagree with the policies and the programs of their predecessors, but they often rejected completely the institutional framework within which their predecessors had operated. Constitutionalism—loyalty to a stable set of governing principles and laws rather than to the person who promulgates them—became a matter of overriding importance in the Dominican Republic only after the death of Trujillo.

Dominicans historically had agreed that government should be representative and vaguely democratic, that there should be civil and political rights, separation of powers, and checks and balances. Beyond that, however, consensus broke down. The country actually had been alternately dominated throughout its history by two constitutional traditions, one relatively democratic and the other authoritarian. Rarely were there attempts to bridge the gap between these diametric opposites.

The first Dominican constitution was promulgated in 1844, immediately after the nation achieved independence from Haiti. It was a liberal document with many familiar elements—separation of powers, checks and balances, and a long list of basic rights. However, an authoritarian government replaced the country's liberal, democratic government during its first year. The new regime proceeded to write its own constitution. This second constitution considerably strengthened the executive, weakened the legislative and the judicial branches, and gave the president widespread emergency powers, including the power to suspend basic rights and to rule by decree. Thereafter, governance of the country often alternated between liberal and authoritarian constitutional systems.

Even the dictator Rafael Trujillo always took care to operate under the banner of constitutionalism. Under Trujillo, however, the legislature was simply a rubber stamp; the courts were not independent; and basic rights all but ceased to exist. He governed as a tyrant, unfettered by constitutional restrictions.

After Trujillo's death in 1961, the constitution was amended to provide for new elections and to allow the transfer of power to an interim Council of State. Although promulgated as a new document, the 1962 constitution was actually a continuation of the Trujillo constitution, and it was thus unpopular.

In 1963, Bosch's freely elected, social-democratic government drafted a new and far more liberal constitution. It separated church and state, put severe limits on the political activities of the armed forces, established a wide range of civil liberties, and restricted the rights of property relative to individual rights. These provisions frightened the more conservative elements in Dominican society, which banded together to oust Bosch and his constitution in September 1963. Subsequently, the more conservative 1962 constitution was restored. In the name of constitutionalism, Bosch and his followers launched a revolution in 1965, the objective of which was restoration of the liberal 1963 constitution.

131

Largely as a result of the United States military intervention of April 1965, the civil war had died down by 1966. With Balaguer and his party in control, the Dominicans wrote still another constitution. This one was intended to avert the conflicts and polarization of the past by combining features from both the liberal and the conservative traditions. The 1966 Constitution incorporated a long list of basic rights, and it provided for a strengthened legislature; however, it also gave extensive powers to the executive, including emergency powers. In this way, the country sought to bridge the gap between its democratic and its authoritarian constitutions, by compromising their differences. Although the 1966 Constitution had been amended several times afterwards, it was this document under which the Dominican Republic continued to operate in 1989 (see fig. 5).

The Executive

The executive had long been the dominant branch in the Dominican governmental system. The president's powers derived from his supreme authority over national administration, the armed forces, and all public affairs. In addition, the president was the beneficiary of the worldwide trends toward centralized decision making and increased executive dominance. Television and other forms of modern mass communications also focused greater attention on the president. The political culture of the Dominican Republic, with its emphasis on machismo and strong leadership, reinforced this tendency to make the president the focal point of the political system. Not surprisingly, Dominican presidents traditionally had been dominant, charismatic, forceful personalities.

The Constitution vests executive power in a president who is elected by direct popular vote and whose term of office is four years. There is no prohibition against a president's seeking reelection, but since the electoral defeat of Balaguer in 1978, presidents had limited themselves to one term. The Constitution requires that presidential candidates be Dominican citizens by birth or origin, at least thirty years old, and in possession of all political and civil rights. A candidate cannot have been a member of the military, or the police, for at least one year prior to his election. Vice presidential candidates must meet the same qualifications.

The vice president may assume the office of president when the chief executive is ill, outside the country, or otherwise unable to perform his duties. If the president dies, or becomes permanently unable to carry out the functions of his office, the vice president serves until the next scheduled election. If the vice president is also unable to fill the office, the president of the Supreme Court of Justice (who is chosen by the Senate) serves temporarily. Within fifteen days, he must convene the National Assembly (which consists of both houses of the Congress of the Republic), which must then select a substitute to fill out the term.

The Dominican Constitution takes twenty-seven paragraphs to spell out the president's extensive powers. Among the most important are those that grant him authority over virtually all appointments and removals of public officials; empower him to promulgate the laws passed by Congress; direct him to engage in diplomatic relations; and empower him to command, to deploy, and to make appointments in, the armed forces. The president also has vast emergency powers to suspend basic rights in times of emergency, to prorogue the Congress, to declare a state of siege, and to rule by decree. Historically, the exercise of these emergency powers usually had been the prelude to dictatorship.

The few limitations the Constitution places on presidential authority focus primarily on the requirement to secure congressional consent to certain appointments, treaty negotiations, entry into certain contracts, and the exercise of emergency powers. These provisions put no more than a limited check on presidential authority, however, because the Dominican voting system almost automatically guarantees the president a majority of his followers in Congress. The Dominican courts also offer little impediment to the exercise of executive power, mainly because they lack the power of judicial review.

The 1966 Constitution provides for ministers and subcabinet ministers to assist in public administration. These officials must be Dominican citizens, at least twenty-five years of age, with full civil and political rights. The powers of the ministers are determined by law; they are not set forth in the Constitution. However, the president is constitutionally responsible for the actions of his ministers. Ministers serve at the president's discretion, can be removed by him, and function both as administrators of their ministries and as agents of presidential authority.

In a system as heavily weighted toward the executive as the Dominican one, the force of a president's personality can do much to determine his relative success or failure in office. Trujillo, the dictator, was tough and forceful; Bosch, the democrat, was weak and ineffectual. Balaguer, although he appeared meek in public, proved to be a very shrewd politician.

The Legislature

The 1966 Constitution confers all legislative powers on the Congress of the Republic, which consists of a Senate and a Chamber

133

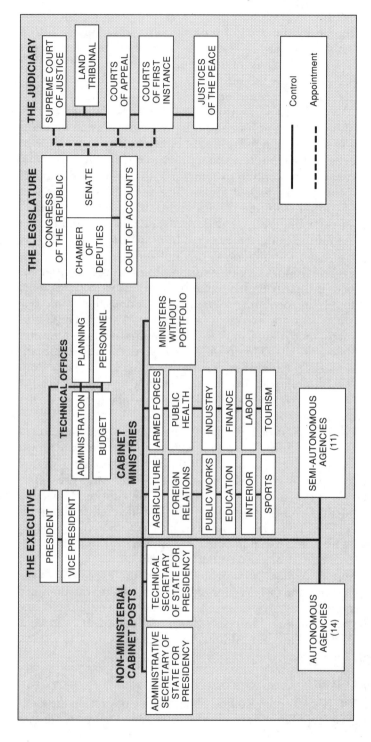

Figure 5. Dominican Republic: Structure of the Government, 1989

of Deputies. The election of senators and deputies is by direct vote every four years. Congressional terms, therefore, are coterminous with presidential terms, which greatly increases the possibility that the president's party will enjoy a majority in the legislature.

One senator is elected from each of the country's provinces and from the National District (Santo Domingo) (see fig. 1). In 1989 the Dominican Senate had thirty members. Deputies also represent provinces, but their seats are apportioned on the basis of population; thus, the more populous provinces and the National District have larger delegations. In 1989 there were 120 representatives in the Chamber of Deputies.

Deputies and senators must be Dominican citizens, at least twenty-five years old, with full civil and political rights. They must have been natives, or residents for at least five years, of the province they wish to represent. Naturalized citizens are eligible to run for Congress if they have been Dominican citizens for ten years. Congressmen are not allowed to hold another public office concurrently.

The Senate and the Chamber of Deputies may meet together as the National Assembly on certain specific occasions cited by the Constitution—for example, when both the president and the vice president are unable to complete their terms of office and a successor must be designated. By a three-fourths vote, the Chamber of Deputies may bring accusations—against public officials—before the Senate, but it has no other exclusive powers. In contrast, the Senate has several exclusive powers: selecting members of the Supreme Court and other lower courts, choosing the president and the members of the Central Electoral Board, approving diplomatic appointments made by the president, and hearing cases of public misconduct brought before it by the Chamber of Deputies.

The Congress has broad powers to levy taxes, to change the country's political subdivisions, to declare a state of emergency, to regulate immigration, to approve or to reject extraordinary expenditures requested by the executive, to legislate on all matters concerning the public debt, to examine annually all the acts of the executive, to interrogate cabinet ministers (a bow to parliamentary government), and to legislate on all matters not within the constitutional mandate of other branches of government or contrary to the Constitution.

For more than a century, the Congress remained a submissive, even somnolent, branch. For many years, under one or another of the country's many dictators, it did not meet at all. Beginning in the 1960s, however, the Congress began to assert itself. President Bosch sometimes had trouble with members of his own party in the Congress; and, although Balaguer ruled as a strong leader from 1966 to 1978, his Congress did not always function as a rubber stamp either.

The real breakthrough came with the restoration of full democracy in 1978. Even though, under presidents Guzmán and Jorge, the majority in Congress belonged to the president's party, that did not stop the Congress from dissenting on various bills, frustrating presidential initiatives in certain particulars, and serving as an increasingly important check on the executive. Although not yet coequal with the executive as a branch of government, the Congress had grown as an independent body, and its ability to check presidential power could no longer be easily dismissed.

The Judiciary

Judicial power is exercised by the Supreme Court of Justice and by other courts created by the Constitution and by law. The Constitution establishes courts of first instance in each province as well as a land tribunal and courts of appeal. Justices of the peace exist in each municipality and in the National District. The Constitution also mandates a court of accounts, which examines the country's finances and reports to the Congress.

Centralized and hierarchical, the Dominican legal system is patterned after the French system. It employs a code-law legal system rather than a common law system, such as the one used in the United States. Detailed and comprehensive, the codes leave little room for United States-style judicial activism or citation of precedent. Legal reasoning is deductive (from the codes), rather than inductive, or based on past cases.

The Constitution calls for a Supreme Court consisting of nine judges. Judges are chosen by the Senate, not by the president, ostensibly to limit executive power. The Senate also selects the judges for the lower courts. Supreme Court justices must be Dominican citizens by birth or parentage, at least thirty-five years old, with full political and civil rights. They are required to have law degrees and to have practiced law, or held judicial office, for at least twelve years. These requirements become progressively less strict for lower-court justices.

The Supreme Court has the exclusive power to assume jurisdiction in matters affecting the president and other high officials, to act as a court of cassation, to serve as a court of last instance in matters forwarded from appellate courts, to exercise final disciplinary action over other members of the judiciary, and to transfer justices from one jurisdiction to another. The Supreme Court does not have the formal power to review the constitutionality of laws, decrees, or resolutions put into effect by the president or the Congress, although a movement began in the late 1970s toward limited judicial oversight of government acts.

The courts in the Dominican Republic historically have been subservient to the government in power. Moreover, politics has frequently dominated court proceedings, and the entire judicial system may be subject to outside pressures and, at times, even intimidation. Nevertheless, since the early 1960s the court system has become stronger, and the judiciary has become a more independent, if not a coequal, branch of government.

Public Administration

The fall of the Trujillo dictatorship in 1961 did not produce a corresponding disruption of the traditions and practices characteristic of the government service. Corruption, nepotism, wholesale dismissals for purely political reasons, loyalty checks, patronage, and the sowing of distrust and suspicion had become ingrained habits which, unlike Trujillo, did not disappear overnight. However, the old habits were challenged by new pressures: demands that the bureaucracy provide real goods and services, that public functions be carried out honestly and efficiently, and that the government respond to the pent-up needs and demands of the population. The clash between the traditional patterns of bureaucratic behavior and new demands for public services, such as health care, education, water supplies, and electricity, contributed significantly to the political instability of the post-Trujillo period.

No effective law existed to protect Dominican public officials in their jobs. From the cabinet level to the lowest ranks, virtually all civil servants were appointed, served, and could be removed largely at the will of the president. The result was a patronage-dominated system in which public sector jobs were given out in return for loyalty and service.

Merit, achievement, and competence, therefore, were not always the main criteria guiding government appointments. The public bureaucracy was often characterized by genuine incompetence, even at the highest levels. Nepotism and corruption—defined as a favor in return for a favor, the granting of special governmental privileges to favored persons, private enrichment stemming from public service, or outright bribery—were also widespread. Those who tried to be honest were scorned; they were considered foolish by their colleagues. Indeed, government service was thought of, not so much as an honored career, but as a brief opportunity to indulge oneself at the public trough. The frequent failure of government programs could often be attributed directly to the corruption and incompetence of

137

the bureaucracy. Patronage and related activities were often tolerated at lower levels, so long as they were kept within reasonable bounds; however, when the corruption became blatant, as it did under President Jorge, the government was likely to suffer at the polls.

Under the president were a number of technical offices—administration, planning, budget, personnel—designed to help him perform his job more effectively. These offices generally did not function well, however, and most Dominican presidents continued to operate as personalistic and patronage leaders.

The size of the cabinet could vary; in 1989 it consisted of sixteen secretaries of state, three without ministerial portfolio. There were also an administrative secretary of state for the presidency, a technical secretary of state for the presidency, and twelve additional secretaries of state administering various ministries. The cabinet did not function as an independent arm of, nor very often as an advisory body for, the presidency (although some of its individual members might); rather, it was a loose collection of administrators, operating almost entirely according to the wishes of the president.

In addition to the cabinet ministries, there were in 1989 fourteen autonomous agencies and eleven semiautonomous agencies. The autonomous and semiautonomous agencies were established in the early 1960s to administer new public programs as well as the vast properties and enterprises inherited by the state after the death of Trujillo, who in addition to his political power had vast economic holdings. These agencies administered an array of programs and enterprises, ranging from farm loans to cooperatives and vast sugar lands. The largest of these were the State Sugar Council (Consejo Estatal de Azúcar—CEA), the 85,000 employees of which made it the largest employer in the country, and the State Enterprises Corporation (Corporación Dominicana de Empresas Estatales—Corde), into which a number of smaller state-owned enterprises had been consolidated.

Dominated by patronage considerations and plagued by corruption, the autonomous and semiautonomous agencies were frequently mismanaged. Some officials, believing that these agencies could be run more efficiently by the private sector, periodically proposed putting them up for sale. The usual reactions to such efforts included objections from nationalists about selling out the national patrimony; from politicians, seeking to preserve patronage opportunities; and from the employees of the state-run agencies, who feared layoffs under private sector management.

Local Government

The Dominican system of local government, like the Dominican legal system, was based on the French system of top-down rule and strong central authority. The country was divided into twenty-nine provinces, plus the National District (Santo Domingo). The provinces, in turn, were subdivided into a total of seventy-seven municipalities (or counties). Each province was administered by a civil governor appointed by the president. A governor had to be a Dominican citizen, at least twenty-five years old, and in full possession of his civil and political rights. The powers and duties of governors are set by law. The Constitution establishes the structure of local government; its specific functions are enumerated in the municipal code.

The municipalities and the National District were governed by mayors and municipal councils, both popularly elected to four-year terms. The size of the councils depended on the size of the municipality, but each was required to have at least five members. The qualifications of local officials as well as the powers and duties of mayors and councils were set by law. Naturalized citizens could hold municipal office, provided they had lived in the community at least ten years.

Neither provinces nor municipalities had any independent power to levy taxes, so few services could be initiated at the local level. There were no local police departments, only a single national force. Policy and programs with regard to education, social services, roads, electricity, and public works were similarly administered at the national level, rather than at the provincial or the municipal level. Local government was therefore weak and ineffective, not only because it lacked taxing authority, but also because, in the Dominican system, the central government set virtually all policy.

Starting in the early 1960s, various efforts were made to strengthen Dominican local government. A new municipal league came into existence in 1962, and efforts were made to develop community spirit, local initiative, and self-help projects. These projects were not wholly successful, in large part because of the traditional arrangement under which virtually all power flowed downward from the central government. In the late 1980s, Santo Domingo remained the focus of the country's affairs, the source of power and largesse.

The Electoral System

The electoral system in place as of 1989 could trace its roots to the death of Trujillo. Following the dictator's assassination in 1961, the Dominican government asked the Organization of American

States (OAS) to send a technical advisory mission to the country to help set up a system of free elections. Upon the mission's recommendation, the country established a hierarchy of electoral boards. The Central Electoral Board, consisting of three members appointed by the Senate, was the highest of these bodies.

Members of the Central Electoral Board were appointed to serve twelve-year terms. The Board chose the members of the provincial and municipal boards, who served at its pleasure. The Board issued regulations to ensure free and honest elections; directed the distribution of ballots, equipment, and voting materials; and supervised the functioning of the lower-level electoral boards.

The Central Electoral Board was given responsibility for printing ballots for each Dominican political party. To facilitate voting by those unable to read, each party's ballot was printed a different color. The ballots also bore the emblems of the parties participating, as an additional aid to nonreaders. Election day was a national holiday; alcoholic beverages could not be sold that day, and the polls were open from 6:00 A.M. to 6:00 P.M.

Voting was free, secret, and obligatory for both men and women. Suffrage was granted to everyone eighteen years old or older and to every married person regardless of age. Members of the police or the armed forces were ineligible to vote, as were those who had lost their political and civil rights, such as incarcerated criminals. Elections were regulated by law, and they were administered by the Central Electoral Board.

Dominican elections could be breathtaking affairs. In 1978 losing candidate Balaguer impounded the ballot boxes and seemed about to steal the election; pressure from the United States forced a resumption of the vote count, which led to Guzmán's victory. The 1986 presidential election also produced controversy. This time Balaguer won, but the losing candidate of the PRD Jacobo Majluta Azar, claimed fraud and refused to concede. Majluta demanded a recount and threatened that violence might result otherwise. In this case, an independent electoral commission headed by the archbishop of Santo Domingo intervened in the dispute, verified the Balaguer victory, and persuaded Majluta to accept its independent vote tally.

Since 1978, elections had gained legitimacy as a means of choosing the president and other leaders. The elections of 1982 and 1986 had generally been fair, honest, competitive, and free, but elections still represented only one of several possible means to power in the Dominican Republic, the others being a skillfully executed coup d'état or a heroic revolution. Moreover, Dominican elections did not necessarily bestow the definitive legitimacy usually accorded an elected government in more developed democratic nations.

Political Dynamics

The System of Dominican Politics

The Dominican Republic's long history of political instability had included many revolutions, coups d'état, barracks revolts, and *pronunciamientos* (insurrections accompanied by declarations of disagreement with the existing government), as well as social and political breakdowns. Coups and revolutions are among the easiest political phenomena to measure systematically. When a country has had so many, one must conclude that they are a regular, normal part of the political process. Therefore, it is not the case that Dominican politics are unsystematic.

Politics in the Dominican Republic functions on a smaller and less formal scale than politics in the United States. Sometimes it seems that everyone in the Dominican Republic who counts politically knows everyone else who counts; many in this group are also interrelated by blood or marriage. It is a small country, with only one main city. Politics is therefore more like old-fashioned United States county politics. In this context, family and clan networks, patronage systems, close friendships, the bonds of kinship, personal ties, and extended family, ethnic, or other personal connections are as important as the more formal and impersonal institutions of a larger political system. The Dominican Republic has large-scale organizations, such as political parties, interest groups, professional associations, and bureacratic organizations, but often the informal networks are at least as important. They are, in addition, the features that are the most difficult for outsiders to penetrate and to understand.

To comprehend Dominican politics, therefore, one must understand first of all the family networks: who is related to whom, and how and what (if anything) these family ties mean. One must also understand the social and the racial hierarchies, who speaks to whom and in what tone of voice, who sees whom socially, and what these social ties imply politically. One must know about past business deals and associations, whether they were clean or "dirty," and what each family or individual knows or thinks about associates. One must understand where the different families "fit" in the Dominican system, whether they are old rich or new rich, their bloodlines, what they share politically, and what pulls them apart. Many of these family and clan associations and rivalries go back for generations.

141

Family and personalistic associations overlap and interact with the institutions of a more modern political system in all sorts of complex ways. For example, what goes by the name of a political party actually may turn out to be the personalistic apparatus of a single politician or family; or a certain office within the government bureaucracy may turn out to be the private preserve of a single family or clan. In order to understand Dominican politics, one must comprehend these complex overlaps of traditional and modern institutions and practices, of family and clan-based politics, and of modern political organizations.

Political Developments since 1978

The contemporary political system of the Dominican Republic dates from 1978. That year Balaguer, who had governed the country in an authoritarian and paternalistic manner for the preceding twelve years, was forced, because of domestic and international pressures, to yield the presidency to Guzmán, a wealthy rancher and candidate of the PRD, who had clearly won the election. Guzmán governed democratically and with full respect for human rights, but he committed suicide in 1982, apparently because of evidence of corruption reaching into his own family. The vice president, Majluta, took over temporarily until a new government, which actually had been elected before Guzmán's suicide, could be inaugurated.

The 1982 election was fair, honest, and competitive. It was won by Jorge, a lawyer who, like Guzmán, was a member of the PRD. But whereas Guzmán had represented the conservative wing of the party, Jorge represented its centrist, or social democratic, wing.

President Jorge continued, like Guzmán, to govern in a democratic matter. His government respected civil liberties and honored human rights. Jorge had promised to expand the democratic reforms begun by his predecessor in the areas of agrarian reform, social justice, and modernization. He campaigned on the slogan, and entered office with the intention of bringing, "economic democracy" to the country to go with its now flourishing political democracy.

But 1982, the year of Jorge's inauguration, was the year the bottom dropped out of the Dominican economy. The country began to feel the full impact of the second oil price rise, induced by the Organization of Petroleum Exporting Countries (OPEC); recession in the United States and Western Europe dried up the market for Dominican exports; and the international debt crisis also hit home strongly. These conditions forced Jorge to abandon his ambitious reform agenda in favor of severe austerity, belt-tightening, and a cutback in services. The nation witnessed the wrenching dilemma of a reform democrat, a socialist, who had to give up his entire social democratic program in order to impose severely restrictive economic policies, the burden of which, as usual, fell most heavily on the shoulders of the poor—precisely those people who had been Jorge's main constituency. Jorge's popularity plummeted, and in 1985 riots broke out in response to his austerity measures, riots that the police put down with considerable loss of civilian life.

To his credit, Jorge succeeded in putting in place a sorely needed budget-balancing program that offered hope of getting the country out of its severe economic troubles. The steep decline in the president's popularity, however, prompted even members of his own party in the Congress and elsewhere to turn against him. In addition, increasing evidence of corruption in the public bureaucracy began to surface; as the austerity measures pinched, there was little extra money in the system, and the low-level patronage that had always existed began to be perceived as blatant, high-level graft. As Jorge's popularity declined, so did that of his entire government and his party.

New elections were held in 1986. President Jorge's deeply divided PRD eventually nominated Majluta, Guzmán's vice president, who four years earlier had served a short stint as interim president. Majluta was of Lebanese background, a long-time PRD stalwart, and a businessman who was tainted with the corruption of the previous administrations. He was opposed by Balaguer, who, though old and legally blind, still enjoyed widespread popularity. Many associated Balaguer with the economic boom of the 1970s; in addition, he was widely admired as a shrewd, resourceful, and skilled politician. In a very closely contested election, Balaguer won with 41 percent of the vote to Majluta's 39 percent. Another former president, Bosch, candidate of the leftist Dominican Liberation Party (Partido de la Liberación Dominicana—PLD), garnered 18 percent.

In office, Balaguer proved as adept as before, although now slowed by age and infirmity. He juggled assignments within the armed forces to ensure its loyalty and support; followed policies that pleased the economic elites, while at the same time doling out land and patronage to the peasants; and fostered greater contact with Cuba, while simultaneously keeping United States support. He listened to advice from all quarters, but kept his own counsel, kept his subordinates off guard and insecure so they could not develop a base from which to challenge the president himself, and refused to designate a successor while keeping all his own options open. Balaguer delegated some limited power and patronage to subordinates, but he kept most of the reins of power in his own hands; he let cabinet and autonomous agency heads have a bit of responsibility, while he maintained control of the all-important jobs—patronage, money, and military matters. Whatever one thinks of his policies, Balaguer must be considered one of the cleverest presidents in Dominican history.

Interest Groups

The Dominican Republic did not have the large number of interest groups and the intensely competitive pluralism found in larger, more advanced nations. In the 1970s and the 1980s, a growing number of private associations started to fill the organizational vacuum that many Dominicans held primarily responsible for their nation's history of instability. That process remained incomplete, however, and the *falta de organización* (lack of organization) was still the bane of national life.

The Armed Forces

The armed forces (army, navy, air force, and National Police) were among the best organized and the most powerful groups in Dominican national life. The military was more than a simple interest group, however. Stemming historically from the medieval Spanish system, the military constituted an integral part of the political regime, but one only nominally subordinate to civilian authority.

The modern Dominican armed forces were a product of the Trujillo era and of the often corrupt and brutal practices of that regime. Trujillo built up the armed forces enormously and gave them modern equipment, but he also encouraged graft, rake-offs, and political interference (see History and Development of the Armed Forces, ch. 5).

Since Trujillo, various efforts had been made to reform, to modernize, and to professionalize the armed forces. These efforts had been only partially successful. In the late 1980s, the armed forces undoubtedly were better trained, better educated, and better equipped than before, but military personnel also tended to use their positions to augment their salaries, to acquire wealth and land, and to exercise political as well as military power, sometimes on a grand scale. At the same time, civilian political interference in the military (promotions, commands, favoritism, etc.) occurred at least as often as military interference in political affairs.

Since the mid-1970s, the pressures to reform the armed forces and to make them definitively apolitical and subordinate to civilian authority had intensified. Evidence of the success of this subordination

144

President Joaquín Balaguer Ricardo visits a military
installation during his first term
Courtesy United States Department of Defense

is that, in various crises (for example, the electoral crises of 1978 and 1986 and the riots of 1985), the military behaved quite professionally and made no effort to seize the government. Nevertheless, no one is really certain how the armed forces would react in the face of endemic unrest, a popular guerrilla movement, economic collapse, or the possibility of a leftist electoral victory.

The Roman Catholic Church

The Dominican Republic remained over 90 percent Roman Catholic in the late 1980s, despite major gains by Protestant groups, especially evangelical, charismatic, and spiritualist sects (see Religion, ch. 2). The Dominican Roman Catholic Church was historically conservative and traditionalist; in general it supported the status quo and the existing power structure. The Roman Catholic Church was weak institutionally, however, with little land, few educational or social institutions, and little influence over the daily lives of most Dominicans.

Since the 1960s, the Roman Catholic Church had ceased to identify wholly with the status quo. Rather, it tended to stand for moderate change. It organized mainstream Catholic political parties, trade

145

unions, student groups, peasant leagues, and businessmen's associations.

Liberation theology (see Glossary) had made few inroads in the Dominican Republic. A few priests espoused liberationist ideas, but they were not considered to be in the mainstream of the clergy. Nor had there been calls by church officials for an alliance with Marxist groups, let alone calls for guerrilla struggles or other militant action against the system.

As the Dominican Republic modernized and secularized, the church lost some of its influence. The country had legalized divorce in 1963 and had instituted government-sponsored family planning in 1967, two measures the church had opposed. The church seldom succeeded in mobilizing voters in support of its favored programs. With only about 10 percent of the population engaged as active, practicing Catholics, and with Protestant groups continuing to grow rapidly, political scientists estimated that the church had gone from being one of the top three most influential interest groups, in past decades, to about the sixth or the seventh by the late 1980s.

Economic Elites

If the Roman Catholic Church had been gradually losing political strength, the power of the economic elites had been steadily growing. Most Dominicans considered a strong economy essential to the successful development efforts of any government in power; only the country's economic entrepreneurs had the wherewithal and the expertise to promote economic growth. Therefore, economic importance also implied political importance.

By the 1980s, the Dominican Republic's economy was no longer almost exclusively agrarian. Trade, tourism, commerce, industry, banking, real estate, and services had also become important sectors of the economy. These economic changes also meant that the Association of Landowners and Agriculturists (Asociación de Hacendados y Agricultores), once the preeminent political interest group, had relinquished some of its influence to the Chamber of Commerce, the associations of industry and of exporters, various professional associations, and other economic groups. The enormous economic power of these groups allowed them to wield political power as well.

Although many observers considered the armed forces to be the ultimate arbiter of Dominican national affairs, on an everyday basis the economic elites wielded far more power. They constituted the primary source of cabinet and other high-level government appointees—regardless of which government was in power. They often enjoyed direct access to government decision making and decision makers. They were the people who knew how to get things done at home and abroad for the country, and the government depended on them for advice and often for financing. Under these circumstances, the economic elites were indispensable to the effective functioning, not just of the economy, but of the country.

Trade Unions

As of 1989, trade unions had not played the consistently strong role in the political system that the economic elites had. Only a small percentage (5 to 7 percent) of the population (12 to 15 percent of the labor force) belonged to labor unions in the late 1980s, and the unions themselves tended to be internally fragmented and weak.

The trade unions were also inclined to be highly political; most were associated with the major political parties. There were a Christian Democratic trade union group, a communist labor organization, a group of unions associated with the PRD, an organization for government workers, a teachers' union, and one relatively nonpartisan group. The several union groups conflicted as often with each other as with management.

Since most Dominicans earned very low salaries, the unions could not support themselves, or very many of their activities, on the basis of union dues. Several of the major groups received funding from outside the country. In addition, because the country typically had high rates of unemployment and underemployment and a surplus of unskilled labor, employers often replaced workers who tried to organize. Sometimes employers engaged in what could be described as union-breaking activities, including the summoning of the police to put down union activities. These and other conditions both weakened and politicized the labor movement. Although collective bargaining had gained popularity and legitimacy, political action was still more widely used by the unions to satisfy their demands. Political action might take the form of street demonstrations, violence, marches to the National Palace, and general strikes—all meant to put pressure on the government to side with the workers in labor disputes. In extreme cases, a general strike might be called in an effort to topple a government or a labor minister deemed insufficiently receptive to labor's demands.

Student Politics

The Dominican Republic had some 80,000 students enrolled in institutions of post-secondary education in the late 1980s. The largest institution, the Autonomous University of Santo Domingo

147

(Universidad Autónoma de Santo Domingo—UASD), had its main campus in the capital city and several branches in different areas of the country. The Catholic University Mother and Teacher (Universidad Católica Madre y Maestra—UCMM) was located in the second largest city, Santiago de los Caballeros (Santiago); another private university, the Pedro Henríquez Ureña National University (Universidad Nacional Pedro Henríquez Ureña—UNPHU), competed with the public university in the capital, as did a branch of the Catholic University. Several private research centers and technical institutes provided specialized post-secondary education (see Education, ch. 2).

The Autonomous University was highly politicized. The student body sometimes devoted whole weeks, or even semesters, to political activities. Most of the activist groups were composed of people who espoused leftist ideologies: old-line communists, Trotskyites, independent revolutionaries, Marxist-Leninists, sympathizers of Juan Bosch and his PLD, sympathizers of the PRD, and radical Christian organizations accounted for most of the membership of student political groups. The private universities were less politicized. Even in the public universities, however, the level of politicization varied according to the faculty: arts and letters as well as law tended to be more political; medicine and the sciences tended to be less so.

University students were important political actors, although as a group they did not appear to have the ability to topple a government by themselves. However, because education (especially higher education) was so rare in the Dominican Republic, the students formed an intellectual elite in the eyes of those less educated than they. Hence, in alliance with the trade unions and the urban unemployed, the students had the potential to provide a moral leadership that would expand their political reach and power.

Peasants

Traditionally the forgotten sector of Dominican society, the peasants were largely illiterate, unorganized, and politically inarticulate. Although numerically the largest group in Dominican society, politically they were the weakest.

By the late 1980s, however, vast changes had begun to occur, even in the Dominican countryside. For example, in 1960 the country was 70 percent rural and 30 percent urban, but as 1990 approached those percentages had been reversed. In the intervening decades, millions of peasants had left the harsh life of the countryside behind for the somewhat more promising life of the cities; many others had emigrated, mainly to Puerto Rico and the United States.

In addition, mobilization and organization had begun in the countryside. The requirement that voters be literate had been struck down in 1962. Peasants voted regularly and in high numbers, usually splitting their votes between liberal and conservative candidates. Beginning in the early 1960s, Peace Corps volunteers, political party officials, community organizers, students, missionaries, and government officials had been fanning out into the countryside organizing the peasants, soliciting their votes, and generally mobilizing them. Modern communications—radio, even television—also reached the countryside, and, along with numerous farm-to-market roads, they had helped ease the isolation of rural life.

Numerous peasant cooperatives and associations had also sprung up. Like the unions and the student groups, most of these were associated with the main political parties: Bosch's PLD, the PRD, and the Social Christian Reformist Party (Partido Reformista Social Cristiano—PRSC; also referred to as the Christian Democrats). Balaguer also attracted widespread support among the peasants because they associated his rule with peace, stability, and prosperity. In highly paternalistic fashion, and with great publicity, Balaguer also made a point of handing out land titles to peasants for lands formerly belonging to Trujillo. Despite the upswing in their political activities, however, the peasants were still not effectively organized, and they seldom managed to influence national policy making.

Middle Class

By the 1980s, Dominican society no longer consisted of a small landed elite at the top and a huge mass of peasants at the bottom, with almost no one in between. In large part, as a result of the economic development and modernization that had occurred since the end of the Great Depression, a sizable middle class, constituting 30 to 35 percent of the population, had emerged (see Urban Society, ch. 2).

The middle class consisted of shopkeepers, government officials, clerks, military personnel, white-collar workers of all kinds, teachers, professionals, and the better paid members of the working class. Most of the middle class resided in Santo Domingo, but secondary cities like Santiago, Barahona, Monte Cristi, La Romana, San Francisco de Macorís, and San Pedro de Macorís had also developed sizable middle-class populations.

The middle class, not the oligarchy, had come to predominate within the country's major political institutions: the Roman Catholic Church, the military officer corps, the government service, the political parties, interest groups, and even the trade union leadership.

However, the middle class was often divided on social and political issues. Generally, its members advocated peace, order, stability, and economic progress. It backed Balaguer in the late 1960s and the early 1970s because he was thought to stand for those things that the middle class wanted; later it supported the PRD governments of Guzmán and Jorge for the same reason.

The middle class used to support authoritarian governments because it thought they would best protect its interests; in the 1980s, however, the middle-class consensus generally supported democracy as the best way to preserve stability and to sustain development.

The Bureaucracy

Its large ministries, autonomous agencies, and public corporations made the Dominican government by far the largest employer in the country. By dint of numbers and its location in the capital city, the bureaucracy constituted a major interest group in its own right.

The Dominican Republic's ineffectual civil service laws left government employees subject to wholesale turnovers with virtually every change of government. The system worked more on the basis of patronage—with government positions given out in return for personal and political loyalty and service—than on the basis of merit.

In an effort to protect themselves, government workers had formed unions. However, their activities and effectiveness were generally severely circumscribed by the country's antiquated civil service laws. Some unions, such as those for teachers and employees of the state-run sugar industry, had themselves become highly politicized, usually in a leftist direction. Frequent clashes occurred between these unions and the police.

Dominated by patronage and rife with corruption, the public service was neither efficient nor responsive. Various efforts had been made over the years to reform this vast, cumbersome bureaucracy. Yet politicians often hesitated to tamper with it because the patronage positions provided by the bureaucracy constituted one of the main sources of their power. For the same reason, they resisted the privatization of the many inefficient and cumbersome state-owned enterprises. Political leaders recognized the inefficiencies of these bloated enterprises, but they also appreciated the effectiveness of buying the loyalty of friends, allies, and even political foes, by putting them on the public payroll.

Outside Actors

The Dominican Republic is a relatively small and weak country, heavily dependent on the outside world economically and strategically, and located in the center of one of the world's most important areas of East-West and North-South conflict—the volatile Caribbean. For these reasons, various outside actors have long exercised a significant degree of influence in the island nation's internal politics.

In the early nineteenth century, the principal outside actors were Spain, France, and Britain; toward the end of the century, Germany and the United States had also become involved in Dominican affairs. Because the Dominican Republic shares the island of Hispaniola with Haiti, and because Haiti represented a constant threat to the Dominican Republic, both before and after the Haitian occupation of 1822–44, Haiti also exerted significant influence (see Haiti and Santo Domingo, ch. 1).

A variety of transnational actors have played a significant role in Dominican politics. Transnational actors had no single national identity; they transcended national boundaries, but had local influence nonetheless. They included multinational corporations, the Socialist International (the international grouping of social democratic parties highly involved in Dominican affairs during the 1970s and the 1980s), the Vatican, the Chamber of Commerce, and the Christian Democratic International, among others.

Many of these agencies, or the embassies of such countries as the United States or Haiti, played a role not only in Dominican international affairs, but in the country's internal affairs as well. Some of them tried to influence national politics; they maintained programs (scholarships, travel awards, etc.) to attract and to influence young people, labor leaders, and government officials. In many ways, they functioned almost like domestic interest groups. In a small, weak, and dependent country like the Dominican Republic, the influence of outside actors was often considerable.

Political Parties

Political parties and a political party system in the modern sense had a very short history in the Dominican Republic, dating back only to the early 1960s. Most parties were weakly organized, had weak and inexperienced political leadership, were neither very ideological nor programmatic, and were generally based on personalistic followings rather than on concrete programs.

Beginning in the mid-1960s, two main parties, or movements, had dominated Dominican politics. These were the PRD and the Reformist Party (Partido Reformista—PR). Both these parties had gone through several reorganizations.

The PRD had been founded in 1939 by exiles from the Trujillo dictatorship. It functioned as an exiled organization for twenty-two years, before returning to the Dominican Republic in 1961 after Trujillo's assassination.

In the late 1980s, the PRD was a left-of-center, democratic political party. Strongly oriented toward social justice, it sought to assist peasants and workers. Although nationalistic, the PRD belonged to the Socialist International. Its platform supported both political and economic democracy. A strongly reformist party, the PRD nonetheless was committed to implementing change through democratic means.

On the strength of this program, the PRD, led by the charismatic Juan Bosch, had won the 1962 election, the freest in the country's history, by a two-to-one margin. Bosch was overthrown, however, after only seven months in office. The PRD organized a constitutionalist revolt, in 1965, aimed at restoring democratic government, but the revolution was put down militarily by the United States, an action that made Bosch and many PRD leaders bitterly resentful of the United States. Perceived as a symbol of instability and revolution, Bosch lost the 1966 election to Balaguer. For the next twelve years, the PRD went into eclipse; it functioned primarily as the Dominican Republic's largest opposition party. After a major split, Bosch left to form his own, more radical, PLD.

In 1978, under Guzmán, and again in 1982 under Jorge, the PRD won the national elections. It governed moderately and without the rancor of the past, but as it tried to put its social program into effect, it ran up against the constraints of austerity.

The PRD had a clear ideological program and was the best-organized political party in the country; however, it was torn by personal and ideological differences. Pitted against each other were its right wing, led by Majluta; its center, led by Jorge; and its left wing, led by José Francisco Peña Gómez. These differences became even more pronounced in 1989. Former president Jorge was indicted for corruption, and hence his popularity plummeted; Majluta was neither trusted nor respected by many in the party and the nation; and Peña Gómez was reportedly contemplating the launching of his own independent movement, which would further split the PRD. A number of younger leaders, such as Jorge protégé Hatuey de Camps Jiménez, also rose to prominence within the party in the 1980s. When unified, the PRD was usually strong enough to win elections, but when divided it usually lost. After the death of Trujillo, the PRD was divided more often than it was unified.

The other major party was the PR, the personal machine of President Balaguer. More conservative than the PRD, the PR lacked a clear-cut program. It consisted of officeholders, job seekers, and persons loyal to Balaguer. The PR functioned more as a patronage mechanism than as a party with an identifiable ideology. Balaguer used this political machine to win elections in 1966, 1970, and 1974. The PR dispensed jobs and favors and, in general, helped him to govern.

In 1985 Balaguer promoted a union between the PR and the Revolutionary Social Christian Party (Partido Revolucionario Social Cristiano—PRSC). The PRSC was the established Christian Democratic party in the country; it was widely respected, but it had little electoral strength. Balaguer gave the PRSC the leadership and the electoral support that it had lacked. The PRSC, in turn, gave Balaguer the support of its trade union, student, and peasant organizations; its legitimacy as a serious Christian Democratic party; and its connections with the Christian Democratic International. The new party designated itself the Social Christian Reformist Party (Partido Reformista Social Cristiano—PRSC), changing its name slightly, but retaining the old initials. The PRSC won the 1986 election by a slim margin over the PRD.

The third major party, Bosch's PLD, won 18 percent of the vote in 1986. It was more radical than the PRD and more anti-United States. Its program called for the establishment of a "revolutionary dictatorship" and for close relations with Cuba and the Soviet Union. The PLD appealed to young people and to those whose disaffection with the prevailing social, political, and economic system in the Dominican Republic had reached an extreme degree; it gained popular support during the 1980s as a result of the country's manifold economic and political problems.

Balaguer and Bosch had long been personal, as well as political and ideological, rivals. Indeed, by 1989 these two men had been jousting with each other politically for some fifty years. In 1989 both were in their eighties. They were the two main protagonists, the two rival caudillos, of modern Dominican politics. Their rivalry delineated the overlap between traditional personalism and modern party politics.

The Dominican Republic's several minor parties were weakly organized, and they usually represented the personal followings of individual caudillos. In the 1986 election, none of these parties received as much as 1 percent of the vote, which made their eligibility to compete in future elections questionable. Several of these personal machines were simply testing the political waters in 1986, and they might come back in reorganized form in future elections. Another possibility was that their leaders might try to merge their organizations with the larger parties, or perhaps themselves become the candidates of the larger parties. These relations illustrated

153

the fluidity and the lack of institutionalization of the Dominican party system.

The extreme-left and communist parties never had much of a popular following. Bosch's formation of the PLD further undermined the potential support of the extreme left. Many Dominican peasants were conservative rather than radical, and the weak unions were increasingly oriented toward "bread-and-butter" issues rather than revolutionary action. In addition, the close ties of the Dominican Republic to the United States and the absence of widespread class conflict among Dominicans—Haitians formed the cane-cutting "proletariat" in the countryside, and, therefore, the potential for class conflict was sapped by racial, cultural, and nationalistic considerations—further diminished the possibility of a strong communist movement.

The two main far-left parties were the Dominican Communist Party (Partido Comunista Dominicano—PCD) and the Socialist Bloc (Bloque Socialista—BS). These two parties chose not to field candidates in the 1986 election, in part because doing so would have revealed their weak electoral appeal. The Moscow-line PCD did enter the 1986 election, and it received only 4,756 votes—considerably less than 1 percent of the total. Nevertheless, all the far-left parties actively criticized the PRD and the PRSC and publicly presented their own points of view. The communist parties had little popular following in their own right, but by attaching themselves to the nationalistic Bosch and the PLD they could conceivably wield influence out of proportion to their numbers.

Some signs indicated that a basic and more stable two-party system, consisting of the left-of-center PRD and the right-of-center PRSC, might be evolving in the Dominican Republic in the late 1980s. A two-and-a-half party system, with the PLD joining these other two, represented another possibility. Nevertheless, the political system continued to be quite fluid; personalities still counted at least as much as parties. Other routes to power existed besides party activism and elections; therefore, the consolidation of a stable, functioning party system could not yet be taken for granted.

The Mass Media

Beginning in the early 1960s, the Dominican Republic experienced a communications revolution. The spread of radio, television, and newspapers awakened the previously isolated countryside, stimulated rapid urbanization, and led to the political mobilization of millions of people who had never participated in politics before. In addition, since Trujillo's death in 1961, the Dominican media had been among the freest of all those in Latin America.

There were 123 radio stations—115 commercial and 8 government-sponsored—operating in the country in 1989. Of these, thirty-four stations operated in the capital city alone, and half that number broadcast from the second city, Santiago. Most other secondary cities had several radio stations. All stations were government-licensed. The Dominican Republic's large number of stations ensured that every part of the island was accessible to radio broadcasting.

The advent of cheap transistor radios in the early 1960s ushered in the communications revolution. Even poor peasants, eking out a subsistence living, could afford such a radio. Transistor radios brought in the political news from the capital city and thus helped to integrate rural elements into the national political life for the first time. Just as important, they also exposed Dominicans to the culture, the behavior, and the music of the outside world.

There were eighteen television channels, operated by six companies in 1989; two channels were government-owned, and sixteen were private. All were government-licensed. Although most Dominicans could not afford a set of their own, those who did not own one often watched at neighbors' houses or in public places, such as bars or shops. Thanks to relay stations, television broadcasts originating in Santo Domingo could be transmitted to the interior.

The main newspapers were *El Caribe* and *Listín Diario*. Both were dailies, published in the capital city, and both had circulations over 30,000. *El Caribe* was moderate and nationalistic; it was, for a long time, the main newspaper in the country. *Listín Diario,* founded in 1889 and published intermittently thereafter, was most recently revived in 1964. It was more reformist and more critical of the government. It established a reputation as a crusading paper and soon matched *El Caribe* in circulation.

Other major Santo Domingo newspapers were *El Tiempo, El Nacional,* and *Última Hora. El Tiempo* was conservative, *El Nacional* was more crusading and nationalistic, and *Última Hora* had been launched by *Listín Diario* as an afternoon newspaper to challenge *El Nacional.* In Santiago there were two main newspapers: *La Información,* a conservative afternoon paper, and *El Sol,* a moderate morning paper. Other cities had smaller papers, focused mainly on local news. The big circulation dailies all received the major wire services—Associated Press (AP), United Press International (UPI), Reuters, and others. As a result, their international coverage was often quite extensive.

The largest weekly newsmagazine in the country was *Ahora,* which was owned by *Nacional.*

Each main political party published its own small newspaper and aired its own radio program. The major trade unions, profession-al associations, and interest groups also produced their own newspapers, although they often published sporadically, and some maintained public relations offices. The armed forces operated its own radio station, and the Roman Catholic Church owned and operated several radio stations and small newspapers. The Voice of America was widely listened to; Radio Havana and Radio Mos-cow also beamed broadcasts that could be heard throughout the country.

Although the coverage of news stories was not always entirely professional, and although there had been attempts by government and the military over the years to intimidate, or even to close down, some papers and stations, by and large the Dominican media had been remarkably free, independent, and diverse since 1961. They performed an important educational function in the country, and they exerted an important influence in mobilizing the country po-litically. In fact, the mass media had become one of the most im-portant bulwarks of Dominican democracy.

Foreign Relations

The Dominican Republic maintained very limited relations with most of the countries of Africa, Asia, the Middle East, and Eastern Europe. It had little commerce, tourist trade, or diplomatic con-tact with most of these nations, and hence little reason for an em-bassy or mission. The Dominican Republic was not a global power with global responsibilities; nor, as a poor country, could it afford to maintain widespread diplomatic representation.

The Dominican Republic concentrated its diplomatic activities in four critical arenas: the circum-Caribbean, Latin America, the United States, and Western Europe. It belonged to the Organiza-tion of American States (OAS), the United Nations (UN), and other international bodies.

Although the Dominican Republic shares the island of Hispaniola with Haiti, traditionally relations between the two countries have seldom been good. In the nineteenth century, Haiti repeatedly invad-ed, plundered, and occupied the Dominican Republic. In addition, Dominicans tended to see Haiti as black, African, and uncivilized, in contrast to their own country, which they considered Hispanic and European.

When political troubles flared up in Haiti, Dominican govern-ments usually mobilized the armed forces and put them on alert.

Haitian political exiles often settled in Santo Domingo, which they used as a springboard for their partisan activities. Numerous Dominican governments had also tried to influence political events in Haiti. The border between the two countries had been closed on a number of occasions.

Over the years, higher salaries and better living conditions had induced many Haitians to settle in the Dominican Republic (see Migration, ch. 7). Dominicans would express resentment of this Haitianization, but at the same time they depended on Haitian labor. This was particularly true during the cane-cutting season, when thousands of Haitians were trucked in, kept in miserable labor camps, and then trucked back (although some remained behind, melding into the local population). The practice commonly gave rise to human rights abuses, and the term "slavery" was sometimes used when charges were raised in some international bodies.

Little trade or commerce existed between the Dominican Republic and Haiti. Each eyed the other's politics warily and often tried to influence the outcome. Because of the complex racial, cultural, and social disparities between the two nations, it seemed doubtful that relations between the two countries would ever be friendly.

Dominican relations with the nearby island of Puerto Rico were quite good. A considerable amount of commercial trade, tourism, and investment activity took place between the two islands. Many Dominicans emigrated to Puerto Rico, where they generally enjoyed better jobs, salaries, and benefits. A lively—and dangerous—traffic existed in small boats that traversed the Mona Passage, by night, carrying illegal Dominican émigrés to Puerto Rican shores. Puerto Rico's links to the United States through its commonwealth status also facilitated the migration of Dominicans to the United States mainland.

Many Puerto Ricans had invested in the Dominican Republic or owned weekend cottages there. At the same time, the large Dominican population in Puerto Rico was used by some as evidence to support the charge that Dominicans were taking jobs away from Puerto Ricans.

Despite a few minor points of contention, relations between the Dominican Republic and Puerto Rico were generally stable and amiable. In contrast, the Dominicans had an uneasy, and still largely informal, relationship with Cuba. The Dominican Republic had broken diplomatic relations with Cuba in 1962; on several subsequent occasions, Cuba sought to promote revolution in the Dominican Republic. With the growth of the Dominican economy in the 1970s, however, the Dominican Republic surpassed Cuba in per capita gross domestic product (GDP—see Glossary), reversing the two nations' traditional relative positions. By the late 1980s, the Dominicans dealt with Cuba from a position of strength rather than weakness, but they remained wary of Cuban military strength and the possibilities of Cuban subversion.

During the 1980s, the contacts between Cuba and the Dominican Republic increased: there were both sports and cultural exchanges. Most of these contacts were informal, but some official contacts between government representatives of the two countries also took place. For Cuba these exchanges formed part of its hemispheric-wide efforts to break out of the relative diplomatic and commercial isolation in which it existed after 1962 and to overcome the United States economic blockade. For the Dominican Republic, a flirtation with Cuba served to keep the domestic left from criticizing the government; it also put pressure on the United States, which in the 1980s did not favor normalization of relations with Cuba. One major impediment to closer ties was the competition of the two island nations in world sugar markets, a situation hardly calculated to encourage cooperation.

By 1989 the Dominican Republic had become more closely involved in the larger political and economic developments of the circum-Caribbean. It maintained close relations with Venezuela, with which it had important trade links. Its relations with the smaller, formerly British, Caribbean islands (including Jamaica) were also closer than they had been previously, and they included observer status in the Caribbean Community and Common Market (Caricom).

The Dominican Republic avoided too deep an involvement in the Central American imbroglios. It had offered its good offices and had served as an intermediary and peacemaker in some facets of the conflict. Not wanting to jeopardize its relations with Mexico, the Central American nations, or the United States, however, it had stayed aloof from the more controversial aspects of the various Central American conflicts. Dominicans were resentful when Nicaragua used its Soviet, East European, and "non-aligned" connections to beat out the Dominican Republic for a non-permanent seat on the UN Security Council.

The Dominican Republic's most important relations were with the United States. Politically, economically, and strategically, the Dominican Republic was more dependent on the United States than it was on any other nation. The United States maintained the largest embassy, by far, in Santo Domingo, and the Dominican embassy in Washington was the country's most important.

Dominicans sometimes resented the large United States presence in their country and the condescending and patronizing attitudes of some Americans. They also resented United States intervention in their internal affairs, particularly the military intervention of 1965. But most Dominicans strongly liked and admired the United States, wanted to travel or emigrate there, and had gotten used to the influence of the United States embassy in their country. Although Dominicans did not appreciate United States interference, they also feared United States inaction in regional affairs. Over the years, most Dominican politicians had determined that the prudent course was to make accommodations with the United States. In recent years, however, this relationship of dependence had become more one of bilateral interdependence.

The Dominican Republic maintained good relations with the nations of Western Europe and tried to increase trade with that region as a way of diversifying its economic relations. Cultural and political links were also important. The leading West European nations with interests in the Dominican Republic were the Federal Republic of Germany (West Germany), which significantly increased its exchange programs during the 1980s; Spain, for reasons of culture and language, as well as the Spaniards' generally more visible and active foreign policy in Latin America; and France, because of cultural and economic relations.

Among Asian nations, Japan had become a significant commercial presence in the 1980s, but it had little interest in political or strategic matters. The Republic of China (Taiwan) had extensive commercial and diplomatic relations. Similarly, Israel had provided aid and technical assistance and maintained some commercial, cultural, and diplomatic ties. In return, the Israelis often counted on the Dominican Republic to support their positions in international fora.

The Dominican Republic was a signatory to the Charter of the OAS, the Inter-American Treaty of Reciprocal Assistance (the Rio Treaty), the Pact of Bogotá, and all major inter-American conventions. Historically, its ties to, and involvement in, the OAS had been stronger than its relations with the UN.

The Dominican Republic was a member of the UN, its Economic Commission for Latin America (ECLA), and its Educational, Scientific, and Cultural Organization (UNESCO), the International Labour Organisation (ILO), the World Health Organization (WHO), and the International Court of Justice. It subscribed to the International Monetary Fund (IMF—see Glossary), the World Bank (see Glossary), the International Finance Corporation (IFC), the Inter-American Development Bank (IDB), and the International Development Association (IDA). It was a participant in the International Civil Aviation Organization (ICAO), the Universal

Postal Union (UPU), and the International Telecommunications Union (ITU). It was also a member of the World Meteorological Organization (WMO), the Postal Union of the Americas and Spain, and the International Atomic Energy Agency (IAEA).

In the 1980s, the Dominicans have actively sought leadership roles in international organizations. This trend, along with the establishment of new diplomatic and economic ties, prompted debate throughout the country on issues of foreign policy and strategic relations. Such an awareness of world affairs was understandable in a country the identity, development, and direction of which were, in considerable measure, the result of external influences.

* * *

An abundance of good books is available on the government and politics of the Dominican Republic. On the formative Trujillo era, see Jesús de Galíndez, *The Era of Trujillo;* the excellent biography by Robert Crassweller entitled *Trujillo;* and Howard J. Wiarda, *Dictatorship and Development: The Methods of Control in Trujillo's Dominican Republic.* Post-Trujillo developments are treated in detail in John Bartlow Martin, *Overtaken by Events,* and Howard J. Wiarda, *Dictatorship, Development, and Disintegration: Politics and Social Change in the Dominican Republic* (3 vols.), as well as Wiarda's briefer *The Dominican Republic: Nation in Transition.* The 1965 revolution and United States intervention are well covered in Piero Gleijeses, *The Dominican Crisis;* Dan Kurzman, *Santo Domingo: Revolt of the Damned;* Abraham Lowenthal, *The Dominican Intervention;* and Jerome Slater, *Intervention and Negotiation: The United States and the Dominican Republic.*

For the Balaguer era of the 1960s and the 1970s, see G. Pope Atkins, *Arms and Politics in the Dominican Republic;* Ian Bell, *The Dominican Republic;* and Howard J. Wiarda and Michael J. Kryzanek, *The Dominican Republic: A Caribbean Crucible.* More recent developments are analyzed in Jan Knippers Black, *The Dominican Republic: Politics and Development in an Unsovereign State,* and in Michael J. Kryzanek and Howard J. Wiarda, *The Politics of External Influence in the Dominican Republic.* (For further information and complete citations, see Bibliography.)

Chapter 5. Dominican Republic: National Security

The Torre del Homenaje, Santo Domingo

BY TRADITION, THE DOMINICAN REPUBLIC'S armed forces had been active participants in the competition for national political power and often had functioned as a praetorian guard for the government holding power. The military continued to play these parts as the 1990s neared; however, it appeared that, during the 1970s and the 1980s, successive governments had been able to reduce the military's former role in national political life (most evident in the early 1960s) as self-appointed final arbiter of public policy.

The armed forces' reduced stature was made evident in the late 1980s by their transformation into an interest group—albeit an important one—competing with other such groups for power and influence within the nation's increasingly pluralistic political system. It would be premature, however, to conclude that the goal of developing an institutionalized and apolitical military establishment had been completely realized by 1989. Individual military officers continued to exert considerable political influence, and armed forces units continued to be employed overtly during political campaigns. Nonetheless, the military's explicit support of civilian governments during the 1980s suggested that the armed forces had accepted the principle of civilian control.

As of mid-1989, the nation faced no credible external threat and only a negligible insurgent threat. As a result, the armed forces were principally employed in working with the National Police to maintain domestic order, chiefly by helping to control demonstrations, riots, and other large-scale threats to public order. Most such disturbances during the mid-1980s and the late 1980s received their impetus from domestic austerity programs inaugurated because of adverse international economic conditions. Public discontent over the concomitant deterioration of living conditions for ordinary citizens, as well as a decline in the level and the quality of public services, occasionally manifested itself in widespread, and sometimes violent, outbreaks that resulted in the intervention of the armed forces and police. The security forces were also called out on several occasions to deal with violence associated with political campaigning and elections.

National economic constraints during the mid-1980s and the late 1980s were reflected in defense budgets, as spending on weapons replacement and modernization was virtually eliminated. The military leadership apparently acquiesced in this policy, despite its serious effects on readiness. This acquiescence may have occurred because the armed forces' pay and benefits were largely shielded from the cuts.

For administrative purposes, the armed forces were under the jurisdiction of the secretary of state for the armed forces. Operational command of the approximately 21,000-member military was exercised through the deputy secretaries of state for the army, the navy, and the air force. The army was the largest and the most influential of the three services, and it was equipped mainly as a light infantry force. The navy was a coastal patrol force that included a battalion of marines. The air force flew transport planes and helicopters, and it had a small number of Cessna A–37B Dragonfly counterinsurgency aircraft used mainly for patrol purposes.

The National Police was the principal agency charged with maintaining public order. In addition to its paramilitary activities, it was organized to perform routine patrols and other crime prevention and control functions. Approximately half the members of the National Police were stationed in the capital. The rest were assigned to posts throughout the remainder of the country.

Criminal justice was the responsibility of the national government. The national judiciary, headed by the Supreme Court of Justice, administered the country's criminal courts, and the attorney general oversaw the system of government prosecutors. All penal and procedural statutes were issued by the central government.

History and Development of the Armed Forces

Spanish colonial militias were the first organized military forces in what is now the Dominican Republic. These forces maintained law and order over the entire island of Hispaniola (La Isla Española), which from 1496 was ruled from Santo Domingo, the center of Spanish colonial administration in the New World (see The First Colony, ch. 1). By the mid-1500s, when Spain's interests shifted to the richer colonies of Mexico and Peru, the Dominican colony had a well-established hierarchical social system that was based on authoritarian rule by a small white elite. The colony also included a large black slave population (see Ethnic Heritage, ch. 2).

The shift in Spain's colonial interests and the consequent withdrawal of most of Spain's military from the Dominican colony was followed by a long period of economic and political decay, during which domestic order deteriorated. The colony was threatened by pirates along the coast as well as by periodic encroachment by the forces of France and England, which were competing with each other and with Spain for territory and power in the New World.

As a result of this competition, Spain was forced in 1697 to cede the western third of Hispaniola to France. Tension over the boundary and continued international competition between France and Spain manifested itself in border disputes, and by 1797 France had prevailed on Spain to cede the rest of the island.

Before French rule became established in the Dominican colony, however, a slave revolt broke out in the western portion of the island, which came to be known as Haiti. In what proved to be the first in a series of Haitian incursions into Dominican territory, the rebellious Haitians invaded the poor and less populous eastern side of the island in 1801. Haitian forces were repulsed, but the rebellion within Haiti continued, and the French were forced to withdraw from the island by 1804. In 1809, helped by Britain, Spain regained control of the Dominican portion of the island. Spain ruled only until 1821, however, when the Dominican colonists revolted. Independence lasted just a few weeks before Haiti invaded in 1822. The Dominicans were not able to expel the Haitian forces until 1844 (see Haiti and Santo Domingo, ch. 1).

The long-delayed achievement of independence did not bring peace to the new Dominican Republic, nor did it improve public order. Political power was extremely decentralized, and competition among factions of the landowning white elite produced a level of national disunity that had disastrous effects on public safety. Although the central government had established a national army, this force essentially consisted of a small group of officers who were interested chiefly in personal enrichment and whose duties were largely ceremonial. The national army was far outnumbered by armed militias that were organized and maintained by local caudillos, who had set themselves up as provincial governors. Using these militias, the caudillos waged bloody civil wars as they contended for regional and national power. National political life was characterized by repeated coups and military uprisings against whichever caudillo—usually self-promoted to general-officer status—had gathered enough power to grab the presidency.

The continuous civil war, political upheaval, and misrule that characterized the republic's early years were punctuated by repeated Haitian attempts to invade. During such periods of danger, forces larger than the small national army were needed to defend the nation. These forces, hastily raised and poorly equipped, were essentially conglomerations of regional militias that had been filled out by poor farmers or landless plantation workers who had been impressed into service. Once the threat had subsided and Haitian forces had been repulsed, the militias would return to advancing the cause of particular regional leaders. The impressed troops would return home, where some would contribute to the general state of disorder by taking up banditry.

During its first thirty years of independence, the Dominican Republic was run directly, or indirectly, by General Pedro Santana Familias and General Buenaventura Báez Méndez, whose bitter rivalry was played out in civil wars that resulted in alternating Santana and Báez regimes (see Santana and Báez: The Caudillos Take Charge, ch. 1). Each of the two generals used his position to enrich himself, his relatives, and his followers at public expense. In order to deal with the national bankruptcy caused by civil war, corruption, and mismanagement, Santana called on Spain in 1861 to restore colonial rule. Nationalistic rebellions during 1861–65, however, forced the Spanish out.

General Ulises Heureaux took over the presidency in 1882. During his rule, political factionalism was repressed, and the nation enjoyed relative internal peace. Heureaux ruled in an increasingly brutal, autocratic, and corrupt manner, however, employing a network of spies and assassins. After he was himself assassinated in 1899, political factions again warred for power and for access to the national treasury. By 1904 the economy was a shambles, and foreign governments were threatening to use force to collect defaulted loans. Citing the need to avert European intervention, the United States assumed control of the management of Dominican customs receipts in 1905. During the next decade, a growing contingent of United States marines and other American officials attempted to establish internal order. Their limited efforts were apparently unsuccessful. The marines were authorized by President Woodrow Wilson to take full control of the Dominican government in 1916 (see Occupation by the United States, 1916–24, ch. 1).

The marines disbanded the regional militias, and they ruled the nation directly for eight years, acting as police in cities and in rural areas. As part of its effort to build effective institutions of government in the Dominican Republic, the United States formed a new Dominican Constabulary Guard to replace the old national army. Up to this time, both the civilian and the military elites had been drawn from the same wealthy landowning class. Intense resentment, among the elite, against the United States presence made it impossible to find recruits for the new constabulary among the landowning class. The ranks became filled by the lower strata of Dominican society, and, as a result, the new force had neither ties nor debts to the traditional elite. The most notable representative of the new military leadership was Rafael Leónidas Trujillo Molina, who entered the Dominican Constabulary Guard in 1919 as a second lieutenant.

In 1924, after the Dominican Republic had adopted a new constitution and had elected a civilian president, the United States forces withdrew. The same year, the guard was renamed the Dominican National Police, a somewhat misleading title for what had become more a military entity than a law enforcement organization. By that time, Trujillo had risen to the rank of major and had assumed one of the nation's two field commands. He had also emerged as one of the most influential voices within the force, increasingly able to mold its development to suit his personal ambitions. In 1928, when the National Police was renamed the National Army (Ejército Nacional), Trujillo became a lieutenant colonel and army chief of staff. As head of the nation's only centralized military force, Trujillo was the most powerful individual in the nation, even before his election to the presidency in 1930 (see The Era of Trujillo, ch. 1).

By 1930 the new Dominican military establishment had developed into a centrally controlled and well-disciplined force that was both larger and far better equipped than any previous Dominican military force. The unified, apolitical, and professional force that had been envisioned by the United States military government had not been realized, however. Instead, traditional Dominican patterns of military service persisted, including factionalism, politicization, and the perception that position entitled one to personal enrichment. Trujillo encouraged and strengthened these patterns, and he used them both to retain the support of the armed forces and to control them. Military officers became an elite national class, gaining wealth, favors, prestige, and power, and developing an ésprit de corps that Trujillo carefully nurtured. Under these conditions, a career in the military came to be esteemed as an avenue of upward mobility. The services themselves were built up, large quantities of arms were imported, and a defense industry was established.

Trujillo rationalized maintenance of a large military by citing the purported need for vigilance against Haiti and, particularly after the Cuban Revolution of 1959, against communism. For the most part, however, Trujillo used the large and powerful military establishment to maintain internal control over the nation. The army and the navy intelligence services were among the numerous agencies Trujillo employed to maintain close surveillance and rigid control over the population. In 1957 the intelligence and the secret police organizations were unified into the State Security Secretariat. With a personnel strength of 5,000, this new organization was larger than either the regular National Police, the air force, or the navy.

Trujillo did not rely solely on rewards to keep control over the military. From the time of his election in 1930 until he was assassinated in 1961, he maintained personal command of all aspects of military organization, including promotions, logistics, assignments, and discipline. He constantly shuffled personnel from assignment to assignment, and he prevented any potential rival from gaining an independent power base. Trujillo also used the tactic of frequent inspection, sometimes in person and sometimes by undercover operatives, to keep tabs on both men and operations. In addition, he brought many of his relatives and supporters into the armed forces, promoting them rapidly as a reward for loyalty.

As part of his effort to keep control over the armed forces, Trujillo also built up the air force as a political counterbalance to the army, and he encouraged factionalism in all the services. During a major expansion of the military after World War II, Trujillo acquired armored fighting vehicles from Sweden and formed a full armored battalion at San Isidro Air Base outside Santo Domingo. This battalion, which was directly subordinate to the Ministry of Defense, essentially constituted a fourth armed force, further splintering power within the military.

After Trujillo was assassinated in 1961, the military, as the nation's most powerful and best-organized interest group, claimed a major role in the political competition that followed. It soon became clear, however, that the factionalism encouraged by Trujillo prevented the military from acting as a unified institution. Instead, elements in the armed services allied with various civilian politicians. After Juan Bosch Gaviño of the center-left (or social democratic) Dominican Revolutionary Party (Partido Revolucionario Dominicano—PRD) won the presidential election in 1962, portions of the military became alarmed over his reforms and his tolerance of leftists and legal communist parties. In 1963 armed forces officers, led by Elías Wessín y Wessín (a colonel at the time), overthrew Bosch and replaced him with a civilian junta. Another military faction made up principally of army officers who called themselves Constitutionalists favored the return of Bosch. In 1965 this faction overthrew the civilian junta. In the following days, civil war erupted as the armed forces split into warring camps. The majority within the armed forces united behind Wessín y Wessín (who by this time had become a general) and attacked the new government with armored and air support. The Constitutionalists armed their civilian supporters in order to defend the capital (see Civil War and United States Intervention, 1965, ch. 1).

United States intervention in the conflict halted the fighting, but subsequent efforts to reunify the armed forces were only partly successful. The agreement to reintegrate those officers who had supported Bosch was never fully implemented, and only a few gained readmission. Politically, the outlook of the officer corps as a whole remained right of center after the civil war.

Although the armed forces continued to be a significant factor, their influence on national political life steadily declined. This decline began during the administration of Joaquín Balaguer Ricardo, who made effective use of some of the same tactics employed by Trujillo to maintain control over the military, including the encouragement and the manipulation of factionalism within the officer corps and the frequent shuffling of top assignments. At the same time, Balaguer gave senior officers a stake in his regime by appointing many to positions in government and in state-run enterprises. He also increased the number of general officers from six in 1966 to forty-eight by 1978.

The process of reining in the military advanced significantly during the terms of Balaguer's successors, Silvestre Antonio Guzmán Fernández (1978–82) and Salvador Jorge Blanco (1982–86), each of whom made a determined effort to institutionalize the armed forces and to remove the powerful group of officers who had supported Trujillo and Balaguer. The partial success of their efforts was demonstrated in 1984 to 1985, when the armed forces' leadership repeatedly and publicly supported Jorge's government in the face of social unrest provoked by adverse economic conditions. Although Jorge had not been the military's preferred candidate in the 1982 elections, the leadership chose to support him as constitutional head of state rather than to take power itself.

Military capability in the years after the 1965 civil war declined to an even greater extent than did the armed forces' national political role. After that time, each administration faced increasingly difficult national economic constraints that forced stringent limits on defense spending. Although force levels and personnel budgets were generally left untouched, aging equipment was not replaced. As a result, equipment in all three services was outmoded, in short supply, and in poor repair as of 1989.

The Role of the Military in Public Life

The 1966 Constitution describes the armed forces as "essentially obedient and nonpolitical and without the right to deliberate. The purpose of their creation is to defend the independence and integrity of the republic, to maintain public order, and to uphold the Constitution and the laws." By law, members of the armed forces are denied the right to vote and the right to participate in the activities of political parties and organized labor.

Although by 1989 the political influence of the armed forces had declined relative to the early 1960s, the characterization of the military as a nonpolitical body was still an ideal rather than a reality (see Interest Groups, ch. 4). The armed forces continued to be an organized force available for use against a regime's opposition, and military personnel and equipment were employed overtly to support candidates favored by the armed forces. Individual officers also competed for national political and economic power and privilege.

The practice of appointing military officers to positions in the civil administration had lessened somewhat by 1989, although, as was traditional, military officers continued to hold a significant number of government positions, serving either while in uniform or after temporary or permanent retirement. The appointment of military personnel to civilian positions occurred in part because officers possessed proven managerial and administrative skills that were frequently in short supply. The practice also provided a source of largess that gave powerful officers a stake in the current regime and a reward for loyalty to it. Many officers in such positions achieved levels of wealth not attainable in the purely military sphere.

Missions

The Dominican Republic faced no serious external military threat during the 1980s, and as of 1989, it appeared unlikely that the armed forces would be required to undertake an external defense mission during the 1990s. Nonetheless, military posture continued to focus on the potential security threats represented by Haiti and Cuba.

The nation's traditional enmity toward Haiti made security along the common border a matter of concern, and army troops and observation posts were located along the length of the 388-kilometer frontier. The Dominican armed forces did not view defense against a possible Haitian invasion as a particularly high priority, however. Border defense commanded relatively few military resources, in part because Haitian military capability was clearly unequal to that of Dominican forces. Despite these factors, the Dominicans showed no signs of forgetting Haiti's historically proven ability to raise large armies on short notice. Practically speaking, however, continuing political upheaval in Haiti represented a more serious concern than did a potential invasion. Several hundred thousand illegal Haitian immigrants were working in the nation as agricultural laborers, and the Dominicans feared that the number could grow if the economic situation in Haiti continued to deteriorate. Continuing border disputes between the two nations were also a source of concern (see Foreign Relations, ch. 4).

After Fidel Castro Ruz's assumption of power in 1959, the Dominican Republic also viewed Cuba as a potential external threat.

This stance was rooted in the anticommunist sentiments first espoused by Trujillo and still felt by most military officers as the 1980s ended. It also had a basis in a 1959 Cuban-based invasion attempt by anti-Trujillo Dominicans. Cuba itself had never taken overt military action against the nation, however, and security concerns usually focused on the prevention of Cuban-sponsored insurgency. Critics of the armed forces charged that the military justified attacks on political groups and on political and labor activists by falsely accusing them of having ties with Cuba.

In practice, the primary mission of the armed forces was to maintain internal security and public order in the nation. Until the mid-1970s, the military occasionally conducted operations against limited insurgencies, but by the late 1970s, the country was relatively free of insurgent groups. Those still in existence in 1989 were small underground groups confined mainly to remote mountain areas. These groups rarely presented a threat to public peace.

As part of its mission to assist the police in maintaining public order, the military kept close watch on political groups that it deemed possible sources of instability, including legal opposition parties. The armed forces were also frequently called out to augment police efforts to control demonstrations and riots. On several occasions during the 1980s, such disturbances resulted in injuries and loss of life, leading critics to charge that the armed forces had used unnecessarily harsh tactics to restore order.

Article 93 of the Constitution states that an objective of the creation of the armed forces is to pursue civic action programs and, at the direction of the executive branch, to participate in projects that promote national social and economic development. As a result, the armed forces maintained an active civic action program. Units of the armed forces dug wells, constructed roads, built houses and schools, and provided educational and sports equipment to rural schools. Military medical and dental teams made visits around the country. As part of its civic action mission, the army was largely responsible for protecting and replanting the nation's forests. It supervised the Directorate General of Forestry, through which the army helped to protect against forest fires and worked to publicize the need for forest conservation. The air force transported medicine, doctors, and food to areas damaged by hurricanes or other natural disasters, and flew the injured to hospitals. Navy schools trained most of the nation's diesel mechanics, and the navy played a large role in transporting the nation's stock of fuel oil. Critics of the armed forces asserted that these contributions, although varied, were sometimes limited in scope and were not nearly so important to national development as claimed in armed forces public relations statements.

Manpower

The combined strength of the three armed forces in 1989 was 20,800. This figure represented a ratio of 3.3 military personnel for every 1,000 citizens, which was below the average for other Latin American states.

Although the armed forces no longer had the strength and the military potential they enjoyed under Trujillo, the military continued to be a popular career. Although the Constitution provides for compulsory military service for all males between the ages of eighteen and fifty-four, the ranks were easily filled by volunteers, and the military did not present a drain on national manpower. Officers, noncommissioned officers (NCOs), and many enlisted personnel, as well, looked on the military as a long-term career. As a result, all three services consisted largely of experienced and well-trained professionals.

Entry into the armed forces was competitive, and most entrants were drawn from the middle and the lower-middle classes. Most enlisted personnel came from rural areas. There was a very small number of females in the military; most served in positions traditionally reserved for women, such as nursing. Women first gained admittance to positions traditionally held only by men in 1981, when a few female personnel were commissioned as medical officers.

Pay and conditions of service compared well with opportunities available in civilian fields. Larger installations maintained a number of commissaries and exchanges, and each of the three services operated officer and enlisted clubs. Military personnel also benefited from free medical service. Under the armed forces' generous benefit program, all members who had served thirty years were entitled to receive a pension based on 75 percent of their active-duty pay at the time of retirement. Certain officers, such as pilots and naval engineers, could receive a full pension after twenty years of service.

Defense Spending

The military budget for 1987 was US$64 million. This amount represented approximately 11 percent of central government expenditures, well in keeping with the levels maintained over the 1975 to 1987 period, which ranged between 7.8 and 11.7 percent. Defense expenditures, as a percentage of gross national product (GNP— see Glossary), averaged between 1.2 and 1.9 percent over the 1975 to 1987 period. In comparison with other Latin American countries, the nation spent a lower than average proportion of GNP for defense.

The value of military spending in Dominican currency rose steadily during the late 1970s; it held at relatively constant rates during the early 1980s and then rose rapidly in the late 1980s. These trends reflected the effects of inflation more than any real increase in military funding, however. When adjusted for inflation, the value of military spending actually fell at least 20 percent during the 1980s. The effects of shrinking financial resources on military readiness were exacerbated by a severe decline in the value of the peso. This resulted in a 40-percent drop in the United States dollar value of defense spending from 1983 to 1987, which greatly weakened the nation's ability to finance the arms imports necessary for modernization, not to mention replacements and spare parts.

This problem was made even more acute by the fact that most of the military budget was allocated to current operations. In 1986, for instance, capital expenditures accounted for only 3.3 percent of total military spending. The low proportion of the budget devoted to funding capital improvements was reflected in the following statistic: during the 1980s, military equipment never accounted for more than 0.7 percent of total imports. Until the early 1980s, the Dominicans imported most of their arms from the United States. Although the United States continued to be an important source of military equipment, the nation's principal arms supplier during the 1982–87 period was France.

Trujillo had established the nation's defense industry just after World War II. By the late 1950s, the Dominican Republic had the capacity to be nearly self-sufficient in small weapons. Although that capability had deteriorated by 1989, the nation still had a modest arms manufacturing industry, limited mainly to producing small vessels, ordnance, uniforms, and personal equipment. The arsenal at San Cristóbal, twenty-four kilometers west of Santo Domingo, could produce carbines, machine guns, mortars, and antitank guns, and could also rebuild heavier weapons and manufacture munitions. The nation produced military equipment for domestic use only, and it did not export any arms.

The United States government provided the Dominicans with military assistance on a continuing basis. During the 1958 to 1988 period, assistance totalled more than US$15.6 billion. A portion of these funds defrayed military training for 5,391 of the nation's uniformed personnel during the same period. During the 1970s and the early 1980s, this assistance focused mainly on improving counterinsurgency capability. After that time, United States security assistance increasingly sought to foster bilateral cooperation, especially in antinarcotics programs. As part of an overall decline in security assistance worldwide, United States military assistance to the nation fell sharply during the mid-1980s. Foreign military sales credits were phased out in 1986, and funds provided under the military assistance program were eliminated in 1988. Proposed United States security assistance for fiscal year (FY—see Glossary) 1990 consisted mainly of economic support funds that were intended to help build a stable political climate, foster economic growth, and strengthen democratic institutions. Funds were also allocated to provide military training for ninety-two members of the Domini-can armed forces, many in United States military schools.

Armed Forces Organization, Training, and Equipment

Under the Constitution, the president of the republic is the com-mander in chief of the armed forces. The chain of command ex-tended from the president to the secretary of state for the armed forces and then to deputy secretaries of state for the army, the navy, and the air force (see fig. 6). The secretary and the three deputies were all military personnel. The secretary, usually an army lieu-tenant general, was appointed by the president; the secretary also served as chief of the armed forces general staff. The deputies were appointed by the secretary with the approval of the president.

Each of the deputies controlled his service through a chief of staff and a general staff. Each general staff had five principal sections: personnel, intelligence, operations, logistics, and public relations. In addition, there was an administrative judge advocate section for each service to handle military legal matters. Except in emer-gencies, the chiefs of staff exercised operational control over the three services of the armed forces. In the late 1980s, the chiefs of staff consisted of an army lieutenant general, an air force major gen-eral, and a navy vice admiral.

The country was divided into three defense zones. The Southern Defense Zone was headquartered in Santo Domingo. It comprised the provinces of Peravia, San Cristóbal, Monte Plata, Hato Mayor, El Seibo, San Pedro de Marcorís, La Romana, La Altagracia, and the National District of Santo Domingo. The Northern Defense Zone, headquartered in Santiago de los Caballeros (Santiago), co-vered the provinces of Puerto Plata, Santiago, La Vega, Valver-de, Monseñor Nouel, Espaillat, Salcedo, Duarte, Sánchez Ramírez, María Trinidad Sánchez, and Samaná. The Western Defense Zone had its headquarters in Barahona. It covered Azua, Dajabón, Monte Cristi, Santiago Rodríguez, Elías Piña, San Juan, Baoruco, In-dependencia, Pedernales, and Barahona provinces (see fig. 1).

The Southern Defense Zone contained approximately half of the army's effective assets.

The armed forces secretariat operated several schools, including the three military academies. The secretariat also ran the General Juan Pablo Duarte Advanced School of the Armed Forces, which was located in Santo Domingo and provided a one-year command and staff course for senior officers. The school graduated its first class in 1984. In addition to these schools, which offered purely military curricula, the secretariat also administered the Vocational School of the Armed Forces and Police. The school was established in Baní in 1966, and other branches were later set up throughout the nation. The school trained enlisted personnel in trades that could be used in the armed forces as well as in civilian life. Its programs provided high-quality training in technical specialties to service members, police personnel, and selected civilians.

The armed forces maintained an integrated judicial system for courts-martial for officers, and each branch conducted courts for minor offenses. All persons subject to military jurisdiction who committed a crime or a misdemeanor while on military duty were accountable to military authorities. Those not on military duty were liable to prosecution by civilian authorities.

Although United States military aid and the number of United States military representatives in the nation diminished during the 1980s, the armed forces continued to maintain their closest foreign military relations with the United States. Under a 1962 bilateral military assistance agreement with the United States, Dominican officers attended advanced training programs run by the United States.

As of 1989, the Dominican Republic was a partner in several multilateral defense agreements and organizations designed to assure regional security. These included the Act of Chapultepec, the Inter-American Defense Board, the Inter-American Treaty of Reciprocal Assistance (Rio Treaty), and the Treaty on the Prohibition of Nuclear Weapons in Latin America (Tlatelolco Treaty). The country was also a signatory to the Biological Weapons Convention, the Limited Test Ban Treaty, the Treaty on the Non-Proliferation of Nuclear Weapons, and the Treaty on the Control of Arms on the Seabed.

The Army

As of 1989, the Dominican army had a strength of approximately 13,000. Army headquarters was located in Santo Domingo. The army consisted of infantry, armor, artillery, communications, engineer, medical, military police, transport, and war matériel units. The army had no airborne or air assets.

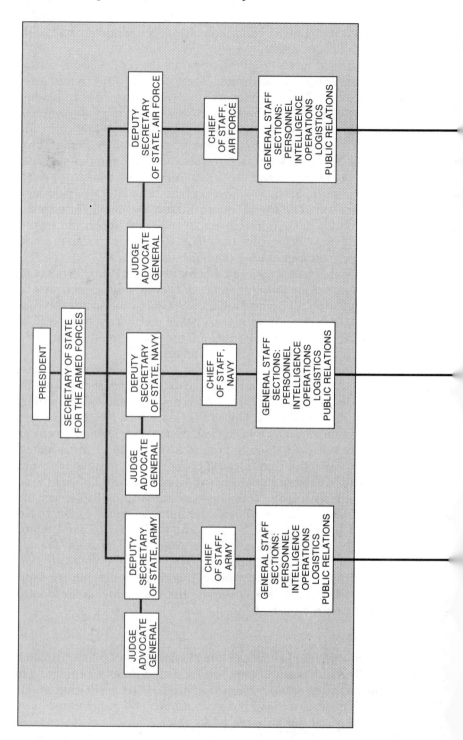

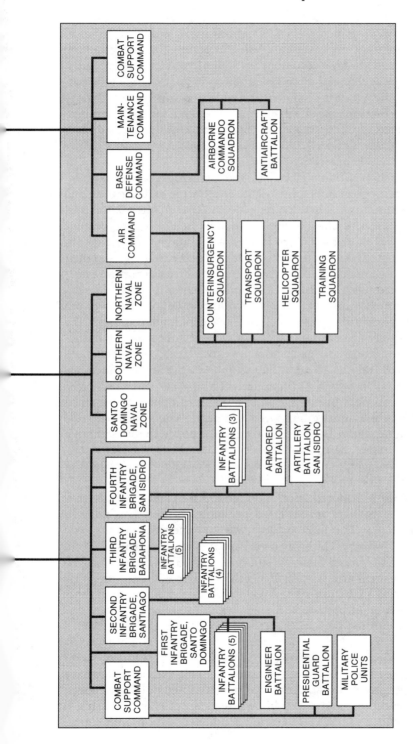

Figure 6. Dominican Republic: Organization of the Armed Forces, 1989

The army's principal tactical organizations were four infantry regimental-type organizations called brigades. Each brigade had three to five infantry battalions, as well as various support units. There were seventeen infantry battalions in all. Several of the battalions assigned outside the capital area performed constabulary functions that included involvement in local political and administrative matters. Other major combat elements included one artillery battalion, one armored battalion, one presidential guard battalion, and one engineer battalion.

Stationed near Santo Domingo, the First Brigade was traditionally the most powerful of the brigades, by virtue of its location and military resources. The First Brigade had five infantry battalions, as well as the nation's only engineer battalion. The Second Brigade and the Third Brigade were located at Santiago and Barahona, respectively. Their assets were spread across the country, and their units focused mainly on local problems. The Fourth Brigade, sometimes called the Armed Forces Training Center because of its extensive training mission, was located at San Isidro, just over ten kilometers east of the capital. The Fourth Brigade controlled the nation's only armored battalion, as well as three infantry battalions. The Fourth Brigade also provided basic, advanced, and specialized training. Also at San Isidro was the army's single artillery battalion, which was organized as a separate command under the general staff. Another separate and very powerful organization was the Combat Support Command, which included the presidential guard battalion and military police units. Although formally under the control of specific commands, the army's armored, engineer, and artillery assets were usually detached as support units to each of the four brigades.

As of 1989, armored assets included fourteen light tanks, twenty armored cars, and ten armored personnel carriers (see table 8, Appendix A). The field artillery was equipped with twenty-two 105mm howitzers. The army used United States 81mm and 120mm mortars and United States M40 106mm recoilless launchers. The principal small arm was the Federal Republic of Germany (West German) G3 7.62mm rifle. Much of the army's equipment was outmoded or in poor repair.

Army enlisted personnel received basic training at the Armed Forces Training Center near San Isidro. Advanced and specialized training was also provided to relevant units. Officer candidates were required to have graduated from high school and to have met strict physical requirements. Once accepted as officer cadets, they attended the four-year Military Academy at Haina, which had been founded in 1921. The army conducted a six-month course for infantry captains and lieutenants—a basic course designed to prepare the students to function efficiently as company commanders. Senior officers attended the armed forces staff college in Santo Domingo in preparation for battalion-level and higher commands.

The Navy

A Dominican navy was first established in 1873, when the country acquired a gunboat built in Scotland. By the time the navy was disbanded in 1916, during the United States Marine occupation, the fleet had acquired only two more gunboats and four armed launches. Several elements of the navy were incorporated into the Dominican Constabulary Guard in 1917 to function as a small coast guard. The navy remained an element of the National Army until 1943, when the Dominican National Navy was formally established as a separate service. During the next year, the navy began activities at the naval base at Las Calderas; in 1948 a separate naval school opened there.

The navy expanded greatly after World War II, acquiring vessels from Canada and the United States. By 1950 the Dominican navy had become the most powerful in the Caribbean. Its personnel numbered 3,000, including one marine battalion. Naval capability remained relatively constant up to the time of the 1965 civil war, when naval units participated in the bombardment of Constitutionalist positions in Santo Domingo. After 1965, aging vessels were not replaced, and the naval inventory steadily declined.

As of 1989, the navy had approximately 4,300 personnel. These included one battalion of marines. Navy headquarters was located at the 27 de Febrero Naval Base in Santo Domingo. Other main naval bases were located at Las Calderas and at Haina, both of which had dockyard facilities.

The navy chief of staff supervised the operations of three geographical commands. The Santo Domingo Naval Zone administered the naval headquarters and the various naval organizations located in the capital. The Northern Naval Zone, at Puerto Plata, was responsible for the coast from the northern border with Haiti to the Mona Passage at the eastern tip of the country. The Southern Naval Zone, headquartered at Barahona, covered the territory from the Mona Passage to the southern border with Haiti.

National economic constraints had reduced the Dominican fleet, by 1989, to one offshore vessel and seventeen inshore vessels (see table 9, Appendix A). Almost all were World War II-vintage craft of United States origin. The sole offshore vessel was a frigate modified

179

for use as a presidential yacht and cadet training vessel. The frigate had been acquired from Canada in the late 1940s, and it was the only vessel in the fleet not of United States origin. The navy's inshore vessels consisted of five corvettes used for patrol duties, eleven large patrol craft, and one amphibious landing craft. Support vessels included two tankers, ten tugs, and one floating dock.

Naval enlisted personnel received instruction at the training center at Las Calderas. The Naval Academy at Las Calderas offered a four-year course to officer cadets.

The Air Force

The air force traced its origins to 1928, when the government, inspired by the use of air power in World War I, authorized the creation of an aviation school. The nation's first military aviation element was established in 1932 as an arm of the National Army. As the Military Aviation Corps, the air force became an independent service in 1948. It underwent several name changes during the 1950s, being known as the Dominican National Aviation during 1952–55 and 1957–62 and as the Dominican Air Force during 1955–57. In 1962 it again became known as the Dominican Air Force, the name still in use as of 1989.

After World War II, Trujillo greatly expanded the air force, in part to form a counterweight to the army. By the mid-1950s, the air force had some 240 aircraft and approximately 3,500 personnel. After Trujillo's assassination, however, funds were not allocated for the replacement of aging aircraft, and the air force's air inventory dwindled rapidly.

Air force headquarters was located at San Isidro Air Base. Most aircraft were based at San Isidro as well. Other military air bases were located at Azua, Barahona, La Romana, La Vega, Monte Cristi, Puerto Plata, and San Cristóbal. The air force administered the general military medical center located in San Isidro. The air force also ran the nation's civil aeronautics directorate, and air force officers oversaw the operation of the nation's airports.

The air force, numbering some 3,800 personnel in 1989, was organized into four commands, all headquartered at San Isidro. The Air Command was responsible for the direction of all flight operations. It was made up of one counterinsurgency squadron equipped with eight Cessna A–37B Dragonflies, one transport squadron equipped with six C–47 Douglas Dakotas and seven other assorted aircraft, one helicopter squadron (consisting of thirteen aircraft) used for sea and air rescue and for transport, and one training squadron equipped with ten Beech T–34B Mentors and seven Beech T–41D Mescaleros (see table 10, Appendix A).

The Base Defense Command provided security for all bases and aircraft. It included an airborne commando squadron and an antiaircraft battalion, which was equipped with ten Bofors 40mm antiaircraft guns. The Maintenance Command was responsible for maintenance and repair. The Combat Support Command controlled all base services.

Air force cadets were trained at the Naval Academy at Las Calderas. All other ranks received their training at the Military Aviation School at Haina.

Ranks, Uniforms, and Insignia

The rank structure of the armed forces followed traditional lines and largely conformed to the pattern of the United States services, with minor variations reflecting the disparity in force levels. The army had eight enlisted ranks, six company and field-grade ranks, and three ranks for general officers (see fig. 7; fig. 8). The air force had seven enlisted ranks. Its officer ranks were identical to those of the army. Naval enlisted personnel were separated into six ranks; officers, into six; and flag-rank officers (admirals), into three. The highest rank attainable was lieutenant general (army or air force) or vice admiral (navy).

Uniforms resembled those of United States counterparts in cut, design, and material. The ground forces wore olive green uniforms; the air force, blue; and the navy, either navy blue or white. All branches also had khaki uniforms. The three categories of uniform included full dress, dress, and daily. The dress uniform was worn off-duty as well as on semiformal occasions. The basic uniform for officers consisted of a short-sleeve or a long-sleeve shirt, tie, trousers, belt, and black shoes. The basic uniform for army and air force enlisted personnel was an olive green fatigue uniform with combat boots. Navy enlisted personnel wore denim shirts and dungarees for work and middy blouse and trousers when off-duty.

Army and air force company-grade officers wore one, two, or three silver laurel leaves as their insignia of rank. For field-grade officers, rank insignia consisted of one to three gold stars. Brigadier, major, and lieutenant generals wore one, two, and three silver stars, respectively. Naval officer ranks were indicated by gold bands worn on the lower sleeve of the uniform jacket. Army and air force enlisted personnel wore green chevrons on the upper sleeve; navy enlisted personnel wore red chevrons.

Internal Security and Public Order

A domestic austerity program, begun in the mid-1980s, and falling prices for agricultural commodities, principally sugar, combined

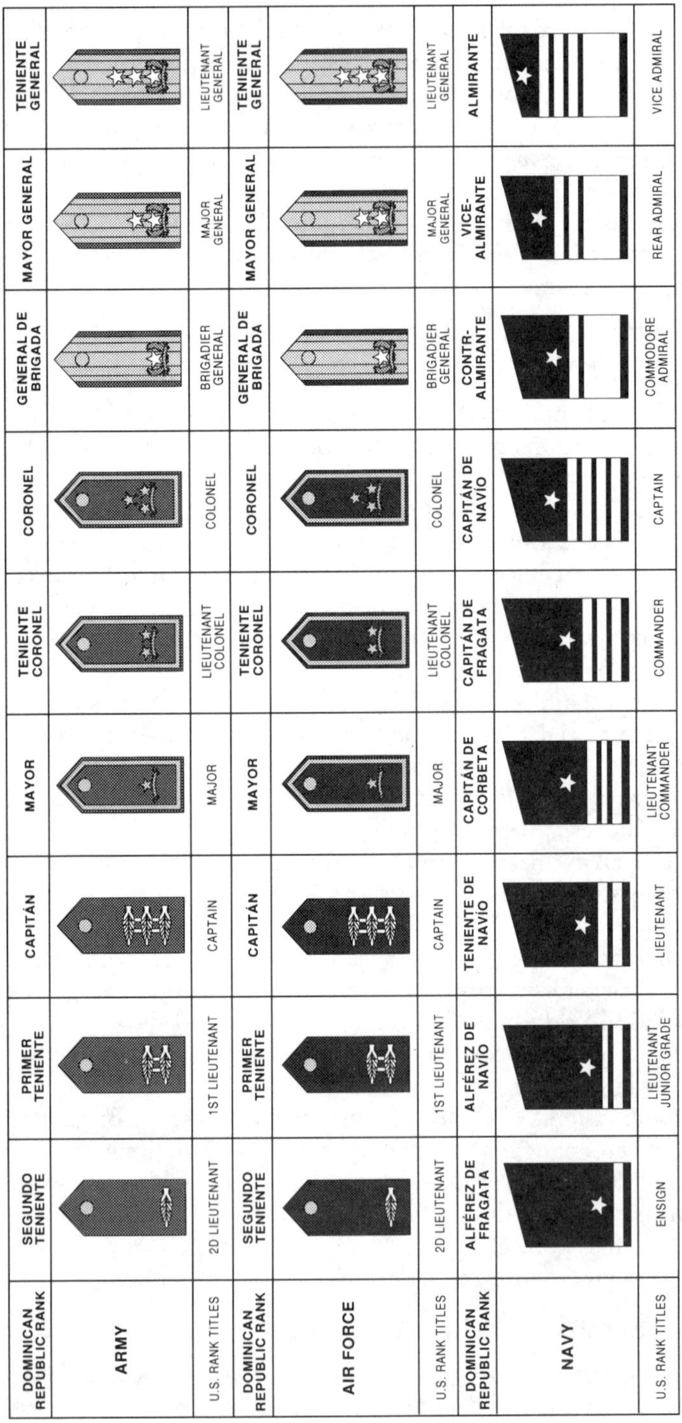

	DOMINICAN REPUBLIC RANK		U.S. RANK TITLES
ARMY	SEGUNDO TENIENTE		2D LIEUTENANT
	PRIMER TENIENTE		1ST LIEUTENANT
	CAPITÁN		CAPTAIN
	MAYOR		MAJOR
	TENIENTE CORONEL		LIEUTENANT COLONEL
	CORONEL		COLONEL
	GENERAL DE BRIGADA		BRIGADIER GENERAL
	MAYOR GENERAL		MAJOR GENERAL
	TENIENTE GENERAL		LIEUTENANT GENERAL

	DOMINICAN REPUBLIC RANK		U.S. RANK TITLES
AIR FORCE	SEGUNDO TENIENTE		2D LIEUTENANT
	PRIMER TENIENTE		1ST LIEUTENANT
	CAPITÁN		CAPTAIN
	MAYOR		MAJOR
	TENIENTE CORONEL		LIEUTENANT COLONEL
	CORONEL		COLONEL
	GENERAL DE BRIGADA		BRIGADIER GENERAL
	MAYOR GENERAL		MAJOR GENERAL
	TENIENTE GENERAL		LIEUTENANT GENERAL

	DOMINICAN REPUBLIC RANK		U.S. RANK TITLES
NAVY	ALFÉREZ DE FRAGATA		ENSIGN
	ALFÉREZ DE NAVÍO		LIEUTENANT JUNIOR GRADE
	TENIENTE DE NAVÍO		LIEUTENANT
	CAPITÁN DE CORBETA		LIEUTENANT COMMANDER
	CAPITÁN DE FRAGATA		COMMANDER
	CAPITÁN DE NAVÍO		CAPTAIN
	CONTR-ALMIRANTE		COMMODORE ADMIRAL
	VICE-ALMIRANTE		REAR ADMIRAL
	ALMIRANTE		VICE ADMIRAL

Figure 7. Dominican Republic: Officer Ranks and Insignia, 1989

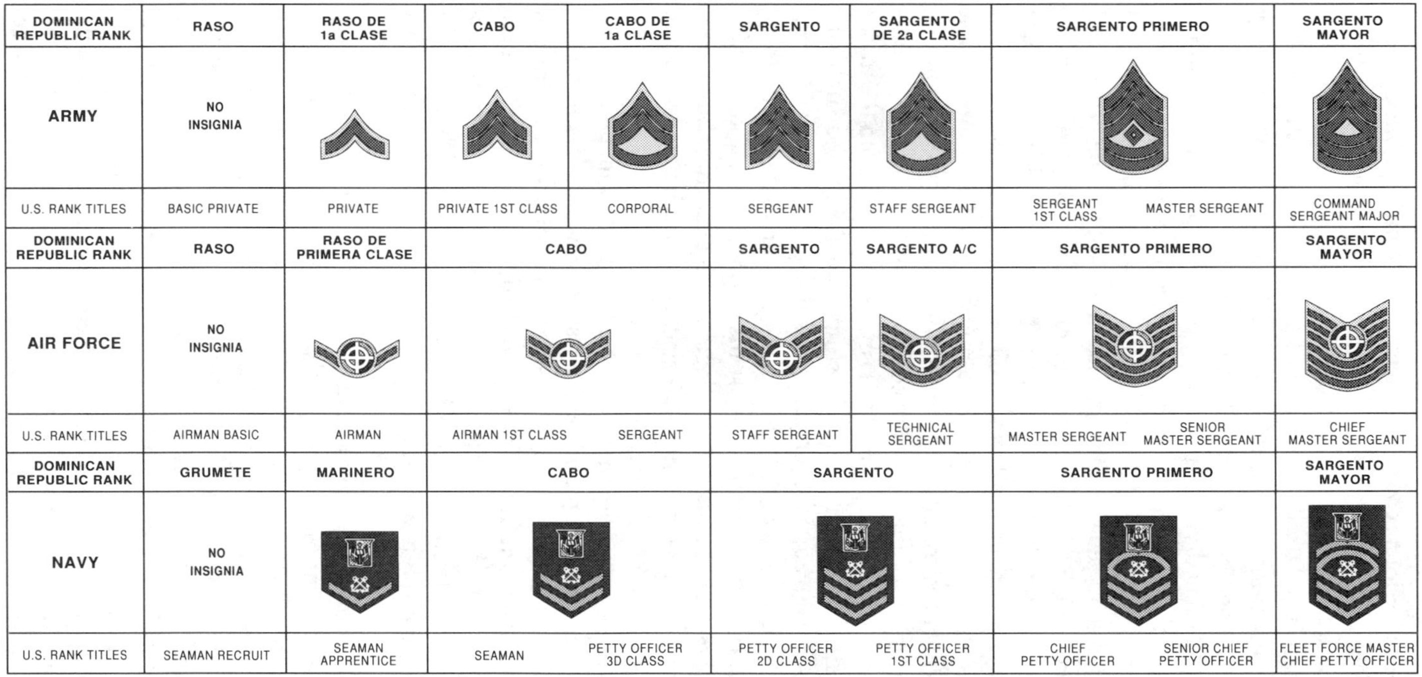

DOMINICAN REPUBLIC RANK	RASO	RASO DE 1a CLASE	CABO	CABO DE 1a CLASE	SARGENTO	SARGENTO DE 2a CLASE	SARGENTO PRIMERO	SARGENTO MAYOR
ARMY	NO INSIGNIA							
U.S. RANK TITLES	BASIC PRIVATE	PRIVATE	PRIVATE 1ST CLASS	CORPORAL	SERGEANT	STAFF SERGEANT	SERGEANT 1ST CLASS / MASTER SERGEANT	COMMAND SERGEANT MAJOR
DOMINICAN REPUBLIC RANK	RASO	RASO DE PRIMERA CLASE	CABO		SARGENTO	SARGENTO A/C	SARGENTO PRIMERO	SARGENTO MAYOR
AIR FORCE	NO INSIGNIA							
U.S. RANK TITLES	AIRMAN BASIC	AIRMAN	AIRMAN 1ST CLASS	SERGEANT	STAFF SERGEANT	TECHNICAL SERGEANT	MASTER SERGEANT / SENIOR MASTER SERGEANT	CHIEF MASTER SERGEANT
DOMINICAN REPUBLIC RANK	GRUMETE	MARINERO	CABO		SARGENTO	SARGENTO	SARGENTO PRIMERO	SARGENTO MAYOR
NAVY	NO INSIGNIA							
U.S. RANK TITLES	SEAMAN RECRUIT	SEAMAN APPRENTICE	SEAMAN	PETTY OFFICER 3D CLASS	PETTY OFFICER 2D CLASS	PETTY OFFICER 1ST CLASS	CHIEF PETTY OFFICER / SENIOR CHIEF PETTY OFFICER	FLEET FORCE MASTER CHIEF PETTY OFFICER / CHIEF PETTY OFFICER

Figure 8. Dominican Republic: Enlisted Ranks and Insignia, 1989

183

to produce a serious economic downturn in which unemployment rose steadily and wages failed to keep pace with inflation (see Growth and Structure of the Economy, ch. 3). As living standards declined, unrest manifested itself in the form of demonstrations, strikes, and illegal occupations of publicly owned lands. Most marches, mass assemblies, and demonstrations were relatively peaceful, but a few such events turned violent, resulting in numerous arrests and injuries and in a number of deaths. The decade's most violent protest took place in April 1984, when at least sixty people were killed in riots that followed the announcement of austerity measures and price increases for basic foodstuffs and fuel. Another series of riots, provoked by further price increases, left four dead and more than fifty injured in February 1985.

Among the groups most frequently involved in protests that turned violent were Marxist and radical leftist parties, populist agrarian organizations, organized labor, and students. Dominican Marxist parties, illegal under Trujillo, emerged from the underground after his death, and they supported Bosch and the Constitutionalists during the civil war. After Balaguer was elected president in 1966, several of the leftist parties unsuccessfully attempted to launch guerrilla warfare against his regime. During the 1980s, most of these groups operated as legal political parties. Some contested both the 1982 and the 1986 elections, but they failed to win any seats in the legislature.

Communist party organizations were badly fragmented by dissension over leadership and policy issues. The oldest and largest of the Marxist parties was the pro-Soviet Dominican Communist Party (Partido Comunista Dominicano—PCD). As of 1988, there were fifteen to twenty additional Marxist organizations in the nation, their orientations ranging from Maoist to pro-Cuban, to pro-Albanian, to pro-Soviet; some of these parties had fewer than twenty members.

Despite being weak, divided, and poorly supported, Marxist and leftist parties continued to be closely scrutinized by the police and the military. The government regularly detained members of such groups, as well as members of labor organizations and populist groups, who were believed to be preparing to instigate public disturbances. Such detentions were particularly prevalent during political campaigns. For instance, in May 1986 police detained four PCD candidates; their arrests brought to some 6,000 the number of communist militants detained during the campaigns. Those detained were usually released within forty-eight hours, which by law was the maximum period a person could be held without charge.

Organized labor and populist agrarian organizations staged several strikes, demonstrations, and other work-related actions during the late 1980s. These were generally peaceful events, designed to protest social conditions, low wages, and deteriorating public services. There were a few exceptions, however. Labor officials, for example, called a one-day nationwide general strike in July 1987; violence was isolated, but one man was killed during clashes between police and protesters in the capital.

Students frequently staged demonstrations in support of labor protests, or they joined directly in those protests. Student groups also mounted demonstrations concerning purely educational issues; some of these protests ended violently. In March 1985, for instance, students called for demonstrations to support increased funding for a university in the capital; these resulted in clashes with police that left one student dead. Students protesting the United States attack on Libya in April 1986 also clashed violently with police, forcing suspension of university classes for several days.

Political violence associated with campaigning and voting also broke out at times during the 1980s. Campaigning was for the most part free, open, and peaceful, but on a few occasions when rival political groups held competing campaign events, violence resulted. In November 1985, factionalism in the then-ruling PRD degenerated into violence as supporters of rival candidates for the party's presidential nomination engaged in confrontations that left two dead and caused the PRD convention tally to be delayed several weeks. In the months that followed, there were thirteen additional deaths related to the May 1986 elections; these occurred at polling places and during demonstrations over vote counting. Many of these deaths were caused by members of the security forces, who fired on demonstrators. Nine officers were either retired or dismissed as a result of one incident.

The treatment of Haitians living illegally in the Dominican Republic was a subject of controversy. Several Haitians were killed in 1985 during disturbances at a sugar plantation. The exact circumstances of the deaths were unclear, but it appeared that the incident was triggered by Haitian frustration over delays in the repatriation of cane cutters who had come to the Dominican Republic on temporary contract. After 1985 the government halted the practice of contracting for Haitian cane cutters, but this did not end the problem. The Roman Catholic Church, several political parties, labor groups, and several human rights groups charged that the government had forced illegal Haitian residents to engage in cane cutting by picking them up and giving them the choice of cutting cane or being forcibly repatriated. The government denied such charges, as well as allegations that some Haitians were forcibly removed from their homes and involuntarily repatriated.

Crime

The government did not publish statistics on the national incidence of crime, but the daily newspapers of Santo Domingo regularly reported criminal acts. The crimes enumerated ran the gamut from murder, rape, and robbery to fraud, counterfeiting, and extortion. According to the newspapers, rural crime accounted for only a small portion of the total. Crime in urban areas was believed to have risen during the 1980s as a result of growing unemployment, pervasive underemployment, and migration from rural to urban areas (see Urbanization, ch. 2; Labor, ch. 3). One manifestation of urban crime was criminal activity by juvenile street gangs. This problem was deemed sufficiently serious in 1988 to merit a campaign that targeted juvenile delinquents for detention.

Crimes associated with narcotics presented a growing problem in the 1980s, as drug traffickers attempted to use the Dominican Republic as a transshipment point between various Latin American countries and the United States. The police were on the front line of the war against drugs, but elements of the military took part as well. The navy, for instance, intercepted several boats carrying cocaine and marijuana during the late 1970s, and air force patrols were given the task of spotting seaborne drug traffickers. In 1988 the government created the National Economic Council for the Control of Drugs to coordinate domestic and international narcotics programs and to integrate the efforts of all police and military elements involved in antinarcotics activities.

Corruption among government officials was another problem given special attention by the government, as well as by the press. This attention reflected a widespread public perception, buttressed by documented accounts in the press, that corruption was pervasive in several spheres of official life. Successive governments had stated their intention to bring offenders to trial. Although several such proceedings had resulted, the perception persisted that corruption continued unabated.

The government's prosecution of some former officials had itself been tainted by charges that political persecution, not a desire for justice, was behind certain indictments. Such charges were made most forcefully in 1987, when former president Jorge and several top members of the armed forces leadership in his administration were charged with fraud in connection with weapons purchases. Jorge, in the United States for medical treatment at the time, was sentenced in absentia to twenty years in prison and was fined several million pesos. He returned to the nation in late 1988 to appeal his conviction. His trial was still underway as of mid-1989.

The National Police

The country's first police organization was a municipal force set up in 1844 in Santo Domingo. Beginning in 1847, other towns formed similar organizations. Eventually, there were independent police forces in every province. These forces were largely controlled by local caudillos, and the national executive branch had only nominal influence over them. These local forces were disbanded in 1916 during the United States occupation; the United States Marines, and later members of the Dominican Constabulary Guard, assumed police duties. The National Police was created in 1936. After that time, police activities in the nation were completely centralized, and no independent provincial or municipal forces existed.

In 1989 police personnel numbered some 10,000; the strength of the police had remained relatively constant since the 1950s. The director general of the National Police was a police major general, who was directly subordinate to the secretary of state of interior and police (see fig. 9). The police maintained a close relationship with the armed forces, and until the 1980s, the chief of the National Police was quite often a senior officer from one of the armed services. The director general was assisted by a deputy director and two sections: internal affairs and planning, and special operations. Three sections, each headed by an assistant director general, carried out the administration and operation of the National Police. These were the Administration and Support Section, the Police Operations Section, and the Special Operations Section.

The Administration and Support Section supervised personnel, police education and training, and finances. It was responsible for the logistical system, communications, transportation, records, the police radio station, the police laboratory, and the data processing center. This section administered the police academy at Hatillo in San Cristóbal Province. The Police Operations Section oversaw normal police operations. It was segmented into several functional departments, including robbery investigation, homicide investigation, felonies and misdemeanors against private property, highway patrol, and narcotics and dangerous drugs. Police patrolled on foot, on horseback, and by motorcycle and automobile. The customs and harbor police employed a small number of boats.

The deputy director of police functioned as the immediate superior of five regional directors. These officers, usually police brigadier generals, were responsible for five territorial zones: the Northeastern Zone (headquartered at San Francisco de Macorís),

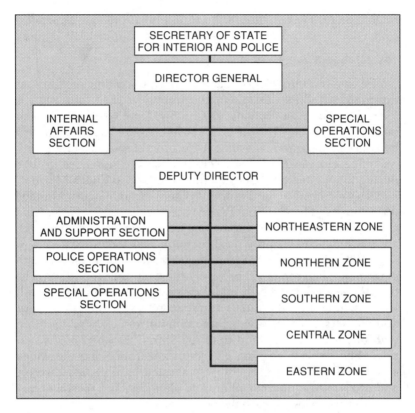

SECRETARY OF STATE
FOR INTERIOR AND POLICE

DIRECTOR GENERAL

INTERNAL
AFFAIRS
SECTION

SPECIAL
OPERATIONS
SECTION

DEPUTY DIRECTOR

ADMINISTRATION
AND SUPPORT SECTION

NORTHEASTERN ZONE

POLICE OPERATIONS
SECTION

NORTHERN ZONE

SPECIAL OPERATIONS
SECTION

SOUTHERN ZONE

CENTRAL ZONE

EASTERN ZONE

*Figure 9. Dominican Republic: Organization of the National
Police, 1989*

the Northern Zone (Santiago), the Southern Zone (Barahona), the
Central Zone (San Cristóbal), and the Eastern Zone (San Pedro
de Marcorís). The police regions each covered several provinces;
forces within the regions were broken down into provincial, company, detachment, and local police post divisions.

The Special Operations Section was responsible for the administration of the secret service, which in 1989 was headed by a police
brigadier general. The secret service performed undercover surveillance of domestic political groups and foreigners suspected of
espionage or of inciting political or economic disorder. In this capacity, the secret service coordinated its efforts with the National
Department of Investigations (Departamento Nacional de In-
vestigaciones—DNI), which was under the direct control of the
president. Created in 1962, the DNI was authorized to ''investigate any act committed by persons, groups, or associations that
conflict with the Constitution, laws, or state institutions, or that

attempt to establish any totalitarian form of government." The DNI was an investigative body and, unlike the police, it did not generally have arrest authority. The functions of the DNI were closely coordinated with those of the armed forces' intelligence units, as well as with the functions of the police. In 1989 the DNI was commanded by a retired army general.

Approximately half of all police personnel were stationed in the capital area, both because Santo Domingo was by far the nation's largest city and because police headquarters, as well as several special police units, were located there. Among the special units garrisoned in the capital was a paramilitary special operations battalion with some 1,000 personnel. The unit was used for riot-control in Santo Domingo, although elements could also be deployed rapidly to any section of the country. Other specialized police units included a specialized bank guard corps and a sappers corps that performed firefighting and civil defense duties.

Like the armed forces, the police participated actively in civic action projects. Police medical and dental teams provided services for poor residents throughout the country. The police also made donations to organizations set up to assist the poor.

The public image of the police had improved since the 1970s, but excesses on the part of police personnel, including beatings of suspects, continued to receive media publicity. Both government and police officials had announced their intent to monitor such activities and to take corrective measures, but complaints about such abuses continued to surface during the late 1980s. The role of the police in quelling disturbances and in supporting the government's political agenda also continued to spark controversy.

The Criminal Justice System

The Dominican criminal justice system was basically an inquisitorial arrangement in which a court and its staff took general charge of a criminal case, and the judge gathered evidence to supplement that produced by the prosecution and the defense. Evidence was largely committed to writing, and the final stage of the proceedings consisted of the judge's examining all the combined written material and then deciding whether or not he was convinced, beyond doubt, of the guilt of the accused. The nation's criminal courts did not, therefore, operate under a system of trial by jury.

The 1966 Constitution guarantees several basic legal rights to all citizens. These include the rights to due process, to public trial, and to habeas corpus protection. An accused person is also guaranteed protection against double jeopardy and self-incrimination. A written order from a competent judicial authority is required,

189

if any person is to be detained more than forty-eight hours or if an individual's home or property is to be searched. In practice, the police and other officials generally honored these guarantees during the 1980s.

In addition to the Supreme Court of Justice, the Constitution establishes four basic types of courts: courts of appeal, the Lands Tribunal, courts of first instance, and justice of the peace courts. Criminal cases were tried in all courts except the Lands Tribunal. There were also a few special courts that heard criminal cases, including one for minors. Most misdemeanor offenses were tried by the justice of the peace courts, of which there were about 100 in 1989, one in each municipality or township. The courts of first instance had original jurisdiction for criminal felony cases. There were twenty-nine of these, one for each province. Decisions could be, and regularly were, appealed to one of the nation's seven courts of appeal. These courts also had original jurisdiction over cases against judges of courts of first instance, government attorneys, provincial governors, and other specified officials.

The Supreme Court served as the nation's ultimate court of appeal. It exercised original jurisdiction in cases involving the president, the vice president, members of the cabinet and Congress, and judges and prosecutors of the higher courts (see The Judiciary, ch. 4). The court consisted of nine members, one of whom was designated president of the Supreme Court. The court also administered all of the nation's lower courts. The attorney general, who had the same rank as the president of the Supreme Court, represented the government's case and oversaw the system of government prosecutors. An accused person was entitled to be represented by an attorney. Indigent persons under accusation generally were provided free counsel in felony cases.

Although the judiciary was organizationally a separate branch of government, several observers have noted that the constitutional provisions governing the appointment and the tenure of judges in practice undermined judicial independence. All judges, from the Supreme Court to the justice of the peace courts, were appointed by the Senate, and they served four-year terms concurrent with the terms of elected officials. This system effectively made a judge's continued service subject to the approval of the dominant party in the Senate. Critics both inside and outside the government asserted that this arrangement subjected judges to undue political influence. This method of appointment and replacement also frequently resulted in a wholesale turnover of judicial personnel, especially when control of the Senate changed hands. Such turnovers affected the consistency of the judiciary's application and interpretation of the law.

The Constitution requires all judges to have law degrees, and judges at each level of the judiciary are required to have practiced law for a specified number of years. Supreme Court justices, for instance, must have a minimum of twelve years of experience, and judges of the courts of first instance are required to have two years of experience. Justices of the peace are also required to have a law degree; exceptions were permitted, however, in rural areas where it might be impossible to appoint a trained lawyer. Despite these requirements, during the mid-1980s the government admitted that the poor quality of some personnel, as well as corruption within the judiciary, affected public attitudes toward the justice system as a whole. In 1985 the president of the national bar association and the attorney general's office led a campaign against the low wages and the poor working conditions that, they claimed, greatly contributed to the poor quality of judges and to the practice, by some, of accepting money or preferential treatment in return for a favorable decision. The government responded to the campaign, which included cancelled hearings and demonstrations, by raising wages and by declaring its determination to rid the judiciary of corrupt judges.

One other factor that undermined public confidence in the criminal justice system was the prolonged delay before trial that characterized virtually every case. Preventive detention was legal, and it was commonly employed. A 1987 study revealed that over 85 percent of the nation's prison population was still awaiting trial. Many of these prisoners had been in jail for years.

Penal Law and Procedure

After independence the country adopted the French penal and criminal proceedings codes that had been in use during the Haitian occupation. Spanish translations were mandated by law in 1867. As of 1989, the most recent codes, adaptations of the original French documents to local traditions, had been adopted in 1884.

The 1884 Penal Code was composed of four books containing 487 articles. The first book dealt with penalties for crimes and provided for exile, imprisonment, temporary confinement, loss of civil rights, and assessment of fines. The death penalty—carried out by firing squad—was abolished in 1924 in favor of a maximum penalty of thirty years' imprisonment at forced labor. The second book dealt with criminal responsibility and liability, addressing such issues as mental competence, self-defense, and the ages at which perpetrators incur adult liability. The third book dealt with various felonies and misdemeanors, and it established punishments for each. The fourth book covered infractions of police regulations and their penalties.

The Code of Criminal Procedure consisted of two books. The first set forth rules governing the role of the police in judicial proceedings. The second established various practices for dealing with accused criminals; it provided for the involvement of different judicial bodies, according to the severity of the crime.

The Prison System

The code of criminal procedure also covered the operations of the nation's prison system. The law required each judicial district, or province, to maintain one prison for convicted offenders and another for accused individuals awaiting trial. Provincial governors bore responsibility for the maintenance of these prisons and for their security. The national penitentiary was La Victoria Penitentiary in Santo Domingo; all individuals sentenced to more than two years of imprisonment served their sentences in La Victoria. This penitentiary had shoe, carpenter, tailor, and barber shops, as well as other facilities where convicts could be taught a useful trade. Prisoners able to take advantage of such opportunities received wages for their labor. Police officers ran the nation's prisons. In the late 1980s, the head of La Victoria Penitentiary was a police brigadier general.

In practice, the corrections system received inadequate financing, and it suffered from unsanitary conditions and overcrowding. The government publicly acknowledged this problem in 1988 and announced its intention to develop a solution. As a first step, badly needed repairs were begun on La Victoria. These long overdue measures were prompted in part by a riot at the prison in June 1988 in which two inmates were killed. Reports in the local press cited two conflicting causes of the riot. One version held that the prisoners rioted to protest a move to limit visiting hours. The second explanation, offered by the government, suggested that the violence was instigated by drug traffickers angered by government's pressure on the narcotics trade.

Although the Dominican Republic's domestic situation was much more stable in the late 1980s than that of neighboring Haiti, the potential existed for localized, or even generalized, disturbances. Economic conditions—inflation, devaluation, food shortages— usually underlay most riots or demonstrations. Marxist and other radical leftist groups, however, often sought to exacerbate such upheavals in order to discredit the government. This situation placed considerable pressure on the police and the armed forces to respond to civil unrest in a professional manner and to minimize attendant injuries to civilians. Furthermore, this role as the institutional bulwark of elected civilian government was one that the leadership of the police and the armed forces took very seriously, particularly because it constituted their primary mission in the late twentieth century.

* * *

As of mid-1989, no definitive studies dealing comprehensively with national security matters in the contemporary Dominican Republic had been published. A general treatment of modern Dominican political life, touching on the military and its place in national life, can be found in G. Pope Atkins's *Arms and Politics in the Dominican Republic.* The most complete coverage of the history and development of the armed forces is contained in the section on the Dominican Republic in Adrian English's *Armed Forces of Latin America.* For developments since the early 1980s, the reader must search through issues of the *Latin American Report,* prepared by the Joint Publications Research Service, and the *Daily Report: Latin Report,* put out by the Foreign Broadcast Information Service. Current order of battle data are available in the International Institute of Strategic Studies' excellent annual, *The Military Balance.* The best overview of conditions of public order is contained in the section on the Dominican Republic in *Country Reports on Human Rights Practices,* a report submitted annually by the United States Department of State to the United States Congress. (For further information and complete citations, see Bibliography.)

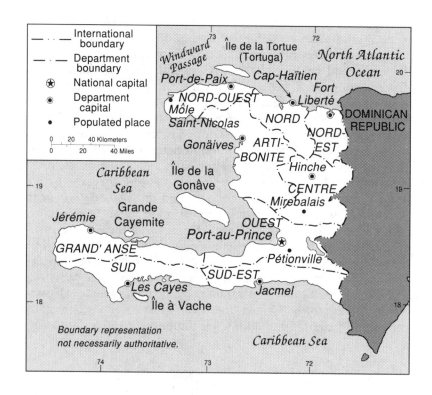

— ·· —	International boundary
— · —	Department boundary
✪	National capital
◉	Department capital
•	Populated place

0   20   40 Kilometers
0   20   40 Miles

Windward Passage   Île de la Tortue (Tortuga)   *North Atlantic Ocean*

Port-de-Paix   Cap-Haïtien

NORD-OUEST   Fort Liberté

Môle   Saint-Nicolas   NORD   DOMINICAN REPUBLIC

Gonäives   ARTI-BONITE   NORD-EST

Hinche

Caribbean Sea   Île de la Gonâve   CENTRE

Mirebalais

Jérémie   Grande Cayemite   OUEST

GRAND' ANSE   Port-au-Prince

SUD   Pétionville

SUD-EST

Les Cayes   Jacmel

Île à Vache

Boundary representation not necessarily authoritative.   *Caribbean Sea*

Figure 10. Haiti: Administrative Divisions, 1989

194

Country Profile

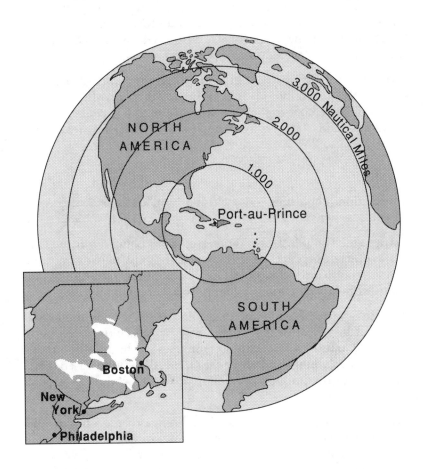

Country

Formal Name: Republic of Haiti (République d'Haïti).

Short Form: Haiti.

Term for Citizens: Haitians.

Capital: Port-au-Prince.

Geography

Size: Approximately 28,000 square kilometers.

Topography: Defined by five mountain ranges, dividing country into three regions: northern, central, and southern. Highest peak, the Morne de la Selle, located in the south, reaches an altitude of 2,715 meters. No navigable rivers. Largest lake is Étang Saumâtre, salt-water body located in southern region.

Climate: Tropical climate influenced by northeast trade winds. Wet season generally lasts from February through May, dry season from November to January. Rainfall pattern irregular because of mountainous topography. Temperature in lowland areas varies from 15°C to 25°C in winter, 25°C to 35°C in summer.

Society

Population: Population estimated at 6.1 million in 1969. Estimated growth averaged 1.4 percent annually from 1971 to 1982.

Language: The 1987 Constitution recognizes both French and Creole as official languages. Two languages linguistically distinct and not mutually comprehensible. Creole more widely spoken, but facility with French connotes higher social status.

Ethnic Groups: Population almost entirely black and mulatto as result of historical origin as slaveholding agricultural colony of France. Country's powerful economic and political elite mainly mulatto. Only ethnic minority the "Arabs"—Syrian, Lebanese, and Palestinian immigrants—most of whom worked in export-import sector.

Religion: Roman Catholicism official religion according to 1860 Concordat with Vatican. Voodoo more widely practiced than Catholicism and could be considered national religion. Much overlap between believers in both religions, with most voodooists considering themselves members of Roman Catholic Church. Although church joined in several antivoodoo campaigns in course of Haiti's history, its opposition to folk religion more sporadic and ambivalent than that of Protestant missionaries, who condemned voodoo as diabolical in nature.

Education and Literacy: As of 1982, 65 percent of population over age ten had received no education. Literacy rate estimated at 23 percent in 1987, but increasing as result of higher enrollments, beginning in late 1970s. Private schools overtook public schools in primary school enrollment in early 1980s. Chronic shortage of qualified teachers, mainly because of low pay. University of Haiti major institution of higher education.

Health: Malnutrition widespread, especially among children. Prenatal and postnatal care inadequate, contributing to high infant mortality rate of 124 per 1,000 live births in 1983. Most child deaths attributed to infectious diseases (especially diarrheal ailments), malnutrition, and acute respiratory illness. Most adult deaths from malaria, tuberculosis, parasitic diseases, and typhoid.

Economy

Gross Domestic Product (GDP): Approximately US$1.95 billion in 1987, or about US$330 per capita, lowest in Western Hemisphere. Economy contracted during most of 1980s.

Agriculture: Employed 65 percent of labor force and accounted for 35 percent of GDP and 24 percent of exports in late 1980s. Production suffered from severe deforestation and erosion, primitive techniques, land fragmentation, and lack of public and private investment. Coffee leading export, but production consistently fell below country's export quota as determined by International Coffee Organization. Other cash crops included sugar, cocoa, sisal, and cotton. Real per capita production of food crops declined during 1980s, necessitating high levels of basic grains imports.

Industry: Accounted for 23 percent of GDP in 1988, for 53 percent of exports, and for 6 percent of labor force. Most dynamic subsector was assembly manufacturing, mainly for United States market. Industry suffered in late 1980s because of political instability, country's failure to compete effectively with other Caribbean and Central American beneficiaries of Caribbean Basin Initiative (see Appendix B), high utility rates, infrastructure deficiencies, and shortage of skilled labor.

Services: Accounted for 42 percent of GDP in 1987, 23 percent of labor force in 1983. Banking and financial services major sectoral contributor. Transportation and communications systems inadequate; tourism dropped off substantially during 1980s.

Currency: Gourde (G). Official exchange rate maintained at G5 to US$1 since 1919. Black market trading began in early 1980s in response to high inflation and fiscal shortfalls. United States dollar also accepted as legal tender.

Imports: Approximately US$308 million in 1987. Foodstuffs leading import item, followed by machinery and transport equipment, manufacturing inputs, and petroleum.

Exports: Approximately US$198 million in 1987. Manufactured goods accounted for more than 50 percent of total, followed by coffee and handicraft items.

Fiscal Year (FY): October 1 through September 30.

Balance of Payments: Current account deficits throughout 1980s, although increased foreign aid flows compensated to some extent in FY 1986 and FY 1987. Following renewed political instability after unsuccessful elections in November 1987, capital flight and aid cutbacks exacerbated the balance of payments situation.

Fiscal Policy: Tradition of balanced budgets broken by expansion of public sector under Jean-Claude Duvalier (1971–86). Public sector deficit reached 10.6 percent of GDP in FY 1985, reduced slightly to 7 percent of GDP in FY 1987.

Transportation and Communications

Ports: Port-au-Prince leading commercial port, followed by Cap-Haïtien, which handled most cruise ship traffic. Lesser ports include Miragoâne, Les Cayes, Fort Liberté, Gonaïves, and Jérémie.

Railroads: Only rail line used for transporting sugarcane. No passenger rail service.

Roads: Over 3,700 kilometers of roads in 1989, 17 percent paved, 27 percent gravel or otherwise improved, and 56 percent unimproved dirt roads. Two paved highways linked northern and southern regions.

Airports: One international airport at Port-au-Prince. Eleven other airfields of varying quality.

Telecommunications: Telephone service highly concentrated in Port-au-Prince; extremely limited service in rural areas. Some 400 telex lines functioning in late 1980s.

Government and Politics

Government: Dynastic dictatorship of the Duvalier family ended in February 1986, when Jean-Claude Duvalier fled in face of popular revolt. He was succeeded by five-member National Council of Government (Conseil National de Gouvernement—CNG), made up of two military officers and three civilians. Members of constituent assembly, elected by popular vote in October 1986, produced new constitution ratified by plebiscite on March 29, 1987. Presidential

198

elections held on November 29, 1987, disrupted by violent attacks perpetrated mainly by former members of Duvalier's paramilitary organization, the *tonton makouts*. Armed forces administered subsequent presidential balloting on January 17, 1988. In balloting marked by nonparticipation by major candidates and low voter turnout, Leslie F. Manigat elected president. Manigat overthrown on June 20, 1988, by military coup led by Lieutenant General Henri Namphy, who had headed CNG. Namphy suspended 1987 Constitution and ruled as dictator. Lieutenant General Prosper Avril, backed by significant faction of noncommissioned officer corps, overthrew Namphy on September 17, 1988. Avril partially reinstated 1987 Constitution in March 1989 and survived coup attempt in April 1989 by officers with Duvalierist ties. Avril promised elections and paid lip service to democracy but essentially ruled as a military dictator.

Politics: Long history of rule by military leaders and dictators. François Duvalier, elected September 1957 in fairest direct elections in country's history, went on to establish dictatorship based on terror, manipulation, and co-optation of citizenry mainly through mechanism of the *tonton makouts*. After Duvalier's death in 1971, power passed to his son, Jean-Claude, whose excessive corruption and cronyism drained country's resources. Riots beginning in October 1985 overwhelmed the indecisive Duvalier and prompted military conspirators to demand his resignation and flight into exile in February 1986. Post-Duvalier instability attributable to weakness of nation's institutions and to complete inexperience with pluralistic democratic government.

International Relations: Focused mainly on United States, country's leading trade partner and (traditionally) major source of foreign aid, and neighboring Dominican Republic. International condemnation of Duvalier regime isolated country during 1960s and 1970s. Jean-Claude's economic policies, calculated to attract foreign investment and tourism, relieved this isolation to some extent. Relations with other Latin American and Caribbean countries limited by linguistic and cultural disparities.

International Agreements and Membership: Party to Inter-American Treaty of Reciprocal Assistance (Rio Treaty). Also member of United Nations, Organization of American States, Inter-American Development Bank, World Bank (see Glossary), International Monetary Fund (see Glossary), and General Agreement on Tariffs and Trade.

National Security

Armed Forces: Haitian Armed Forces (Forces Armées d'Haïti—FAd'H) include army, navy, air corps, and some police forces. Total armed forces and police strength approximately 8,000.

Organization: FAd'H military arm of Ministry of Interior and National Defense. Commander in chief appointed by president (Avril held both offices in late 1989). Chain of command runs through assistant commander in chief to geographical and functional commands. Two of three major army units—Dessalines Battalion and Leopards Corps—disbanded after April 1989 coup attempt, leaving Presidential Guard (Garde Présidentelle) as dominant force in capital. Administratively, country divided into nine military departments and three military regions.

Equipment: All branches, especially navy and air corps, ill-equipped. Army fielded antiquated weaponry of United States manufacture, although some units equipped with more modern small arms. Navy consisted of one armed tug, nine small patrol craft, and presidential yacht. Air corps totalled seventeen fixed-wing aircraft, thirteen trainers, and eight helicopters.

Police: Port-au-Prince police, with approximately 1,000 members, only functioning police force in late 1989. Armed forces personnel performed internal security functions in rural areas.

Chapter 6. Haiti: Historical Setting

Figure from a painting by Prosper Pierrelouis

HAITI FORMALLY RENOUNCED its colonial bond with France in January 1804, as the result of the only successful slave rebellion in world history. The country's longevity as an independent nation in the Western Hemisphere is second only to that of the United States. Over this span of almost two centuries, however, the country has never known a period free of tyranny, repression, political conflict, racial animosity, and economic hardship.

Haiti, the first black republic in modern times, sprang directly to self-governance from French colonialism, a system that had a profound impact on the nation. Haiti's colonial origins had demonstrated that an illiterate and impoverished majority could be ruled by a repressive elite. The slaveholding system had established the efficacy of violence and coercion in controlling others, and the racial prejudice inherent in the colonial system survived under the black republic. A light-skinned elite assumed a disproportionate share of political and economic power.

The chaotic and personalistic nature of Haitian political culture combined with chronic underdevelopment to provide fertile ground for a succession of despots, strongmen, and dictators. Even the few national leaders whose election apparently reflected popular sentiment, such as Dumarsais Estimé (1946–50) and François Duvalier (1957–71), rejected constitutional procedures in favor of retaining personal power. The popular revolt that deposed President For Life Jean-Claude Duvalier (1971–86) demonstrated the Haitian people's rejection of parasitic despotism. At the same time, however, the revolt reaffirmed another lesson of Haitian history: violence has often been the only effective route to change.

Spanish Discovery and Colonization

The island of Hispaniola (La Isla Española), which today is occupied by the nations of Haiti and the Dominican Republic, was one of several landfalls Christopher Columbus made during his first voyage to the New World in 1492. Columbus established a makeshift settlement on the north coast, which he dubbed Navidad (Christmas), after his flagship, the *Santa María,* struck a coral reef and foundered near the site of present-day Cap-Haïtien.

The Taino Indian (or Arawak) inhabitants referred to their homeland by many names, but they most commonly used *Ayti,* or *Hayti* (mountainous). Initially hospitable toward the Spaniards, these natives responded violently to the newcomers' intolerance and abuse. When Columbus returned to Hispaniola on his second voyage in 1493, he found that Navidad had been razed and its inhabitants, slain. But the Old World's interest in expansion and its drive to spread Roman Catholicism were not easily deterred; Columbus established a second settlement, Isabela, farther to the east.

Hispaniola, or Santo Domingo, as it became known under Spanish dominion, became the first outpost of the Spanish Empire. The initial expectations of plentiful and easily accessible gold reserves proved unfounded, but the island still became important as a seat of colonial administration, a starting point for conquests of other lands, and a laboratory to develop policies for governing new possessions. It was in Santo Domingo that the Spanish crown introduced the system of *repartimiento,* whereby *peninsulares* (Spanish-born persons residing in the New World) received large grants of land and the right to compel labor from the Indians who inhabited that land.

Columbus, Santo Domingo's first administrator, and his brother Bartolomé Columbus fell out of favor with the majority of the colony's settlers, as a result of jealousy and avarice, and then also with the crown because of their failure to maintain order. In 1500 a royal investigator ordered both to be imprisoned briefly in a Spanish prison. The colony's new governor, Nicolás de Ovando, laid the groundwork for the island's development. During his tenure, the *repartimiento* system gave way to the *encomienda* system (see Glossary) under which all land was considered the property of the crown. The system also granted stewardship of tracts to *encomenderos,* who were entitled to employ (or, in practice, to enslave) Indian labor.

The Taino Indian population of Santo Domingo fared poorly under colonial rule. The exact size of the island's indigenous population in 1492 has never been determined, but observers at the time produced estimates that ranged from several thousand to several million. An estimate of 3 million, which is almost certainly an exaggeration, has been attributed to Bishop Bartolomé de Las Casas. According to all accounts, however, there were hundreds of thousands of indigenous people on the island. By 1550 only 150 Indians lived on the island. Forced labor, abuse, diseases against which the Indians had no immunity, and the growth of the mestizo (mixed European and Indian) population all contributed to the elimination of the Taino and their culture.

Several years before the Taino were gone, Santo Domingo had lost its position as the preeminent Spanish colony in the New World. Its lack of mineral riches condemned it to neglect by the mother country, especially after the conquest of New Spain (Mexico). In 1535 the Viceroyalty of New Spain, which included Mexico and the Central American isthmus, incorporated Santo Domingo, the status of which dwindled still further after the conquest of the rich kingdom of the Incas in Peru. Agriculture became the mainstay of the island's economy, but the disorganized nature of agricultural production did not approach the kind of intense productivity that was to characterize the colony under French rule.

French Colonialism

Although Hispaniola never realized its economic potential under Spanish rule, it remained strategically important as the gateway to the Caribbean. The Caribbean region provided the opportunity for seafarers from England, France, and the Netherlands to impede Spanish shipping, to waylay galleons crammed with gold, and to establish a foothold in a hemisphere parceled by papal decree between the Roman Catholic kingdoms of Spain and Portugal. This competition was carried on throughout the Caribbean, but nowhere as intensely as on Hispaniola.

Sir Francis Drake of England led one of the most famous forays against the port of Santo Domingo in 1586, just two years before he played a key role in the English navy's defeat of the Spanish Armada. Drake failed to secure the island, but his raid, along with the arrival of corsairs and freebooters in scattered settlements, was part of a pattern of encroachment that gradually diluted Spanish dominance.

French Settlement and Sovereignty

Reportedly expelled by the Spanish from Saint Christopher (Saint Kitts), the original French residents of Tortuga Island (Île de la Tortue), off the northwest coast of Hispaniola, sustained themselves mostly through two means: curing the meat and tanning the hides of wild game, and pirating Spanish ships. The former activity lent these hardy souls the colorful designation of buccaneers, derived from the Arawak word for the smoking of meat. It took decades for the buccaneers and the more staid settlers that followed them to establish themselves on Tortuga. Skirmishes with Spanish and English forces were common. As the maintenance of the empire tried the wit, and drained the energies, of a declining Spain, however, foreign intervention became more forceful.

The freewheeling society of Tortuga that was often described in romantic literature had faded into legend by the end of the seventeenth century. The first permanent settlement on Tortuga was established in 1659 under the commission of King Louis XIV. French Huguenots had already begun to settle the north coast of Hispaniola by that time. The establishment in 1664 of the French

West India Company for the purpose of directing the expected commerce between the colony and France underscored the seriousness of the enterprise. Settlers steadily encroached upon the northwest shoulder of the island, and they took advantage of the area's relative remoteness from the Spanish capital city of Santo Domingo. In 1670 they established their first major community, Cap François (later Cap Français, now Cap-Haïtien). During this period, the western part of the island was commonly referred to as Saint-Domingue, the name it bore officially after Spain relinquished sovereignty over the area to France in the Treaty of Ryswick in 1697.

Colonial Society: The Conflicts of Color and Class

By the mid-eighteenth century, a territory largely neglected under Spanish rule had become the richest and most coveted colony in the Western Hemisphere. By the eve of the French Revolution, Saint-Domingue produced about 60 percent of the world's coffee and about 40 percent of the sugar imported by France and Britain. Saint-Domingue played a pivotal role in the French economy, accounting for almost two-thirds of French commercial interests abroad and about 40 percent of foreign trade. The system that provided such largess to the mother country, such luxury to planters, and so many jobs in France had a fatal flaw, however. That flaw was slavery.

The origins of modern Haitian society lie within the slaveholding system. The mixture of races that eventually divided Haiti into a small, mainly mulatto elite and an impoverished black majority began with the slavemasters' concubinage of African women. Today Haiti's culture and its predominant religion (voodoo) stem from the fact that the majority of slaves in Saint-Domingue were brought from Africa. (The slave population totalled at least 500,000, and perhaps as many as 700,000, by 1791.) Only a few of the slaves had been born and raised on the island. The slaveholding system in Saint-Domingue was particularly cruel and abusive, and few slaves (especially males) lived long enough to reproduce. The racially tinged conflicts that have marked Haitian history can be traced similarly to slavery.

While the masses of black slaves formed the foundation of colonial society, the upper strata evolved along lines of color and class. Most commentators have classified the population of the time into three groups: white colonists, or *blancs;* free blacks (usually mulattoes, or *gens de couleur*—people of color), or *affranchis;* and the slaves (see Social Structure, ch. 7).

Conflict and resentment permeated the society of Saint-Domingue. Beginning in 1758, the white landowners, or *grands blancs,* discriminated against the *affranchis* through legislation. Statutes forbade *gens de couleur* from taking up certain professions, marrying whites, wearing European clothing, carrying swords or firearms in public, or attending social functions where whites were present. The restrictions eventually became so detailed that they essentially defined a caste system. However, regulations did not restrict the *affranchis'* purchase of land, and some eventually accumulated substantial holdings. Others accumulated wealth through another activity permitted to *affranchis* by the *grands blancs*—in the words of historian C.L.R. James, "the privilege of lending money to white men." The mounting debt of the white planters to the *gens de couleur* provided further motivation for racial discrimination.

The Haitian Revolution

The Slave Rebellion of 1791

Violent conflicts between white colonists and black slaves were common in Saint-Domingue. Bands of runaway slaves, known as maroons (*marrons*), entrenched themselves in bastions in the colony's mountains and forests, from which they harried white-owned plantations both to secure provisions and weaponry and to avenge themselves against the inhabitants. As their numbers grew, these bands, sometimes consisting of thousands of people, began to carry out hit-and-run attacks throughout the colony. This guerrilla warfare, however, lacked centralized organization and leadership. The most famous maroon leader was François Macandal, whose six-year rebellion (1751–57) left an estimated 6,000 dead. Reportedly a *boko,* or voodoo sorcerer, Macandal drew from African traditions and religions to motivate his followers. The French burned him at the stake in Cap Français in 1758. Popular accounts of his execution that say the stake snapped during his execution have enhanced his legendary stature.

Many Haitians point to the maroons' attacks as the first manifestation of a revolt against French rule and the slaveholding system. The attacks certainly presaged the 1791 slave rebellion, which evolved into the Haitian Revolution. They also marked the beginning of a martial tradition for blacks, just as service in the colonial militia had done for the *gens de couleur.* The maroons, however, seemed incapable of staging a broad-based insurrection on their own. Although challenged and vexed by the maroons' actions, colonial authorities effectively repelled the attacks, especially with help from the *gens de couleur,* who were probably forced into cooperating.

The arrangement that enabled the whites and the landed *gens de couleur* to preserve the stability of the slaveholding system was unstable. In an economic sense, the system worked for both groups. The *gens de couleur,* however, had aspirations beyond the accumulation of goods. They desired equality with white colonists, and many of them desired power. The events set in motion in 1789 by the French Revolution shook up, and eventually shattered, the arrangement.

The National Assembly in Paris required the white Colonial Assembly to grant suffrage to the landed and tax-paying *gens de couleur.* (The white colonists had had a history of ignoring French efforts to improve the lot of the black and the mulatto populations.) The Assembly refused, leading to the first mulatto rebellion in Saint-Domingue. The rebellion, led by Vincent Ogé in 1790, failed when the white militia reinforced itself with a corps of black volunteers. (The white elite was constantly prepared to use racial tension between blacks and mulattoes to advantage.) Ogé's rebellion was a sign of broader unrest in Saint-Domingue.

A slave rebellion of 1791 finally toppled the colony. Launched in August of that year, the revolt represented the culmination of a protracted conspiracy among black leaders. According to accounts of the rebellion that have been told through the years, François-Dominique Toussaint Louverture helped plot the uprising, although this claim has never been substantiated. Among the rebellion's leaders were Boukman, a maroon and voodoo *houngan* (priest); Georges Biassou, who later made Toussaint his aide; Jean-François, who subsequently commanded forces, along with Biassou and Toussaint, under the Spanish flag; and Jeannot, the bloodthirstiest of them all. These leaders sealed their compact with a voodoo ceremony conducted by Boukman in the Bois Cayman (Alligator Woods) in early August 1791. On August 22, a little more than a week after the ceremony, the uprising of their black followers began.

The carnage that the slaves wreaked in northern settlements, such as Acul, Limbé, Flaville, and Le Normand, revealed the simmering fury of an oppressed people. The bands of slaves slaughtered every white person they encountered. As their standard, they carried a pike with the carcass of an impaled white baby. Accounts of the rebellion describe widespread torching of property, fields, factories, and anything else that belonged to, or served, slaveholders. The inferno is said to have burned almost continuously for months.

News of the slaves' uprising quickly reached Cap Français. Reprisals against nonwhites were swift and every bit as brutal as the atrocities committed by the slaves. Although outnumbered, the inhabitants of Le Cap (the local diminutive for Cap Français) were well-armed and prepared to defend themselves against the tens of thousands of blacks who descended upon the port city. Despite their voodoo-inspired heroism, the ex-slaves fell in large numbers to the colonists' firepower and were forced to withdraw. The rebellion left an estimated 10,000 blacks and 2,000 whites dead and more than 1,000 plantations sacked and razed.

Even though it failed, the slave rebellion at Cap Français set in motion events that culminated in the Haitian Revolution. Mulatto forces under the capable leadership of André Rigaud, Alexandre Pétion, and others clashed with white militiamen in the west and the south (where, once again, whites recruited black slaves to their cause). Sympathy with the Republican cause in France inspired the mulattoes. Sentiment in the National Assembly vacillated, but it finally favored the enfranchisement of *gens de couleur* and the enforcement of equal rights. Whites, who had had little respect for royal governance in the past, now rallied behind the Bourbons and rejected the radical egalitarian notions of the French revolutionaries. Commissioners from the French Republic, dispatched in 1792 to Saint-Domingue, pledged their limited support to the *gens de couleur* in the midst of an increasingly anarchic situation. In various regions of the colony, black slaves rebelled against white colonists, mulattoes battled white levies, and black royalists opposed both whites and mulattoes. Foreign interventionists found these unstable conditions irresistible; Spanish and British involvement in the unrest in Saint-Domingue opened yet another chapter in the revolution.

Toussaint Louverture

Social historian James G. Leyburn has said of Toussaint Louverture that "what he did is more easily told than what he was." Although some of Toussaint's correspondence and papers remain, they reveal little of his deepest motivations in the struggle for Haitian autonomy. Born sometime between 1743 and 1746 in Saint-Domingue, Toussaint belonged to the small, fortunate class of slaves employed by humane masters as personal servants. While serving as a house servant and coachman, Toussaint received the tutelage that helped him become one of the few literate black revolutionary leaders.

Upon hearing of the slave uprising, Toussaint took pains to secure safe expatriation of his master's family. It was only then that he joined Biassou's forces, where his intelligence, skill in strategic and tactical planning (based partly on his reading of works by Julius Caesar and others), and innate leadership ability brought him quickly to prominence.

Le Cap fell to French forces, who were reinforced by thousands of blacks in April 1793. Black forces had joined the French against the royalists on the promise of freedom. Indeed, in August Commissioner Léger-Félicité Sonthonax abolished slavery in the colony.

Two black leaders who warily refused to commit their forces to France, however, were Jean-François and Biassou. Believing allegiance to a king would be more secure than allegiance to a republic, these leaders accepted commissions from Spain. The Spanish deployed forces in coordination with these indigenous blacks to take the north of Saint-Domingue. Toussaint, who had taken up the Spanish banner in February 1793, came to command his own forces independently of Biassou's army. By the year's end, Toussaint had cut a swath through the north, had swung south to Gonaïves, and effectively controlled north-central Saint-Domingue.

Some historians believe that Spain and Britain had reached an informal arrangement to divide the French colony between them— Britain to take the south and Spain, the north. British forces landed at Jérémie and Môle Saint-Nicolas (the Môle). They besieged Port-au-Prince (or Port Républicain, as it was known under the Republic) and took it in June 1794. The Spanish had launched a two-pronged offensive from the east. French forces checked Spanish progress toward Port-au-Prince in the south, but the Spanish pushed rapidly through the north, most of which they occupied by 1794. Spain and Britain were poised to seize Saint-Domingue, but several factors foiled their grand design. One factor was illness. The British in particular fell victim to tropical disease, which thinned their ranks far more quickly than combat against the French. Southern forces led by Rigaud and northern forces led by another mulatto commander, Villatte, also forestalled a complete victory by the foreign forces. These uncertain conditions positioned Toussaint's centrally located forces as the key to victory or defeat. On May 6, 1794, Toussaint made a decision that sealed the fate of a nation.

After arranging for his family to flee from the city of Santo Domingo, Toussaint pledged his support to France. Confirmation of the National Assembly's decision on February 4, 1794, to abolish slavery appears to have been the strongest influence over Toussaint's actions. Although the Spanish had promised emancipation, they showed no signs of keeping their word in the territories that they controlled, and the British had reinstated slavery in the areas they occupied. If emancipation was Toussaint's goal, he had no choice but to cast his lot with the French.

In several raids against his former allies, Toussaint took the Artibonite region and retired briefly to Mirebalais. As Rigaud's forces achieved more limited success in the south, the tide clearly swung in favor of the French Republicans. Perhaps the key event at this point was the July 22, 1794, peace agreement between France and Spain. The agreement was not finalized until the signing of the Treaty of Basel the following year. The accord directed Spain to cede its holdings on Hispaniola to France. The move effectively denied supplies, funding, and avenues of retreat to combatants under the Spanish aegis. The armies of Jean-François and Biassou disbanded, and many flocked to the standard of Toussaint, the remaining black commander of stature.

In March 1796, Toussaint rescued the French commander, General Etienne-Maynard Laveaux, from a mulatto-led effort to depose him as the primary colonial authority. To express his gratitude, Laveaux appointed Toussaint lieutenant governor of Saint-Domingue. With this much power over the affairs of his homeland, Toussaint was in a position to gain more. Toussaint distrusted the intentions of all foreign parties—as well as those of the mulattoes—regarding the future of slavery; he believed that only black leadership could assure the continuation of an autonomous Saint-Domingue. He set out to consolidate his political and military positions, and he undercut the positions of the French and the resentful *gens de couleur*.

A new group of French commissioners appointed Toussaint commander in chief of all French forces on the island. From this position of strength, he resolved to move quickly and decisively to establish an autonomous state under black rule. He expelled Sonthonax, the leading French commissioner, who had proclaimed the abolition of slavery, and concluded an agreement to end hostilities with Britain. He sought to secure Rigaud's allegiance and thus to incorporate the majority of mulattoes into his national project, but his plan was thwarted by the French, who saw in Rigaud their last opportunity to retain dominion over the colony.

Once again, racial animosity drove events in Saint-Domingue, as Toussaint's predominantly black forces clashed with Rigaud's mulatto army. Foreign intrigue and manipulation prevailed on both sides of the conflict. Toussaint, in correspondence with United States president John Adams, pledged that in exchange for support he would deny the French the use of Saint-Domingue as a base for operations in North America. Adams, the leader of an independent, but still insecure, nation, found the arrangement desirable and dispatched arms and ships that greatly aided black forces in what is sometimes referred to as the War of the Castes. Rigaud, with his forces and ambitions crushed, fled the colony in late 1800.

After securing the port of Santo Domingo in May 1800, Toussaint held sway over the whole of Hispaniola. This position gave him an opportunity to concentrate on restoring domestic order and productivity. Like Jean-Jacques Dessalines and Henri (Henry) Christophe, Toussaint saw that the survival of his homeland depended on an export-oriented economy. He therefore reimposed the plantation system and utilized nonslaves, but he still essentially relied on forced labor to produce the sugar, coffee, and other commodities needed to support economic progress. He directed this process through his military dictatorship, the form of government that he judged most efficacious under the circumstances. A constitution, approved in 1801 by the then still-extant Colonial Assembly, granted Toussaint, as governor general for life, all effective power as well as the privilege of choosing his successor.

Toussaint's interval of freedom from foreign confrontation was unfortunately brief. Toussaint never severed the formal bond with France, but his de facto independence and autonomy rankled the leaders of the mother country and concerned the governments of slave-holding nations, such as Britain and the United States. French first consul Napoléon Bonaparte resented the temerity of the former slaves who planned to govern a nation on their own. Moreover, Bonaparte regarded Saint-Domingue as essential to potential French exploitation of the Louisiana Territory. Taking advantage of a temporary halt in the wars in Europe, Bonaparte dispatched to Saint-Domingue forces led by his brother-in-law, General Charles Victor Emmanuel Leclerc. These forces, numbering between 16,000 and 20,000—about the same size as Toussaint's army—landed at several points on the north coast in January 1802. With the help of white colonists and mulatto forces commanded by Pétion and others, the French outmatched, outmaneuvered, and wore down the black army. Two of Toussaint's chief lieutenants, Dessalines and Christophe, recognized their untenable situation, held separate parleys with the invaders, and agreed to transfer their allegiance. Recognizing his weak position, Toussaint surrendered to Leclerc on May 5, 1802. The French assured Toussaint that he would be allowed to retire quietly, but a month later, they seized him and transported him to France, where he died of neglect in the frigid dungeon of Fort de Joux in the Jura Mountains on April 7, 1803.

The betrayal of Toussaint and Bonaparte's restoration of slavery in Martinique undermined the collaboration of leaders such as Dessalines, Christophe, and Pétion. Convinced that the same fate lay in store for Saint-Domingue, these commanders and others once again battled Leclerc and his disease-riddled army. Leclerc himself died of yellow fever in November 1802, about two months after he had requested reinforcements to quash the renewed resistance. Leclerc's replacement, General Donatien Rochambeau, waged a bloody campaign against the insurgents, but events beyond the shores of Saint-Domingue doomed the campaign to failure.

By 1803 war had resumed between France and Britain, and Bonaparte once again concentrated his energies on the struggle in Europe. In April of that year, Bonaparte signed a treaty that allowed the purchase of Louisiana by the United States and ended French ambitions in the Western Hemisphere. Rochambeau's reinforcements and supplies never arrived in sufficient numbers. The general fled to Jamaica in November 1803, where he surrendered to British authorities rather than face the retribution of the rebel leadership. The era of French colonial rule in Haiti had ended.

Independent Haiti

On January 1, 1804, Haiti proclaimed its independence. Through this action, it became the second independent state in the Western Hemisphere and the first free black republic in the world. Haiti's uniqueness attracted much attention and symbolized the aspirations of enslaved and exploited peoples around the globe. Nonetheless, Haitians made no overt effort to inspire, to support, or to aid slave rebellions similar to their own because they feared that the great powers would take renewed action against them. For the sake of national survival, nonintervention became a Haitian credo.

Dessalines, who had commanded the black and the mulatto forces during the final phase of the revolution, became the new country's leader; he ruled under the dictatorial 1801 constitution. The land he governed had been devastated by years of warfare. The agricultural base was all but destroyed, and the population was uneducated and largely unskilled. Commerce was virtually nonexistent. Contemplating this bleak situation, Dessalines determined, as Toussaint had done, that a firm hand was needed.

White residents felt the sting most sharply. While Toussaint, a former privileged slave of a tolerant white master, had felt a certain magnanimity toward whites, Dessalines, a former field slave, despised them with a maniacal intensity. He reportedly agreed wholeheartedly with his aide, Boisrond-Tonnerre, who stated, "For our declaration of independence, we should have the skin of a white man for parchment, his skull for an inkwell, his blood for ink, and a bayonet for a pen!'' Accordingly, whites were slaughtered whole-sale under the rule of Dessalines.

Although blacks were not massacred under Dessalines, they wit-nessed little improvement in the quality of their lives. To restore some measure of agricultural productivity, Dessalines reestablished the plantation system. Harsh measures bound laborers to their as-signed work places, and penalties were imposed on runaways and on those who harbored them. Because Dessalines drew his only organizational experience from war, it was natural for him to use the military as a tool for governing the new nation. The rule of Dessalines set a pattern for direct involvement of the army in pol-itics that continued unchallenged for more than 150 years.

In 1805 Dessalines crowned himself Emperor of Haiti. By this point, his autocratic rule had disenchanted important sectors of Haitian society, particularly mulattoes such as Pétion. The mulat-toes resented Dessalines mostly for racial reasons, but the more educated and cultured *gens de couleur* also derided the emperor (and most of his aides and officers) for his ignorance and illiteracy. Ef-forts by Dessalines to bring mulatto families into the ruling group through marriage met with resistance. Pétion himself declined the offer of the hand of the emperor's daughter. Many mulattoes were appalled by the rampant corruption and licentiousness of the em-peror's court. Dessalines's absorption of a considerable amount of land into the hands of the state through the exploitation of ir-regularities in titling procedures also aroused the ire of landowners.

The disaffection that sealed the emperor's fate arose within the ranks of the army, where Dessalines had lost support at all levels. The voracious appetites of his ruling clique apparently left little or nothing in the treasury for military salaries and provisions. Although reportedly aware of discontent among the ranks, Dessa-lines made no effort to redress these shortcomings. Instead, he re-lied on the same iron-fisted control with which he kept rural laborers in line. That his judgement in this matter had been in error be-came apparent on the road to Port-au-Prince as he rode with a column of troops on its way to crush a mulatto-led rebellion. A group of people, probably hired by Pétion or Etienne-Elie Gérin (another mulatto officer), shot the emperor and hacked his body to pieces.

Under Dessalines the Haitian economy had made little progress despite the restoration of forced labor. Conflict between blacks and mulattoes ended the cooperation that the revolution had produced, and the brutality toward whites shocked foreign governments and isolated Haiti internationally. A lasting enmity against Haiti arose among Dominicans as a result of the emperor's unsuccessful invasion

Artist's rendering of Henri (Henry) Christophe's palace,
Sans Souci, at Cap-Haïtien
Courtesy Library of Congress Prints and Photographs Division

of Santo Domingo in 1805. Dessalines's failure to consolidate Haiti
and to unite Haitians had ramifications in the years that followed,
as the nation split into two rival enclaves.

Christophe's Kingdom and Pétion's Republic

Many candidates succeeded Dessalines, but only three approached his stature. Most Haitians saw Henry Christophe as the
most logical choice. He had served as a commander under Toussaint and could therefore claim the former leader's mantle and some
of his mystique. Christophe was black like Dessalines, but he lacked
Dessalines's consuming racial hatred, and he was much more prag-
matic in this regard. His popularity, especially in the north, however, was not strong enough to offset the mulatto elite's growing
desire to exert control over Haiti through a leader drawn from its
own ranks. The mulattoes had two other candidates in mind: Gérin and Pétion, the presumed authors of Dessalines's assassination.

In November 1806, army officers and established *anciens libres*
(pre-independence freedmen) landowners—an electorate dominated
by the mulatto elite—elected a constituent assembly that was given
the task of establishing a new government. Members of the assembly
drafted a constitution that established a weak presidency and a

215

comparatively strong legislature. They selected Christophe as president and Pétion as head of the legislature, the earliest attempt in Haiti to establish what would later be known as the *politique de doublure* (politics by understudies). Under this system, a black leader served as figurehead for mulatto elitist rule.

The only defect in the mulattoes' scheme was Christophe himself, who refused to be content with his figurehead role. He mustered his forces and marched on Port-au-Prince. His assault on the city failed, however, mainly because Pétion had artillery and Christophe did not. Indignant, but not defeated, Christophe retreated to north of the Artibonite River and established his own dominion, which he ruled from Cap-Haïtien (which he would later rechristen Cap Henry). Periodic and ineffectual clashes went on for years between this northern territory and Pétion's republic, which encompassed most of the southern half of the country and boasted Port-au-Prince as its capital.

The northern dominion became a kingdom in 1811, when Christophe crowned himself King Henry I of Haiti. Unlike Dessalines, who as emperor declared, "Only I am royal," Christophe installed a nobility of mainly black supporters and associates who assumed the titles of earls, counts, and barons.

Below this aristocratic level, life in the northern kingdom was harsh, but not nearly so cruel as the conditions that had prevailed under Dessalines. Laborers remained bound to their plantations, but working hours were liberalized, and remuneration was increased to one-fourth of the harvested crop.

Christophe was a great believer in discipline. He brought African warriors from Dahomey (present-day Benin), whom he dubbed Royal Dahomets. They served as the primary agents of his authority. Incorruptible and intensely loyal to Christophe, the Dahomets brought order to the countryside.

Many people were dissatisfied with the strictness of Christophe's regime. As productivity and export levels rose, however, the quality of their lives improved in comparison with revolutionary and immediately post-revolutionary days.

In the more permissive southern republic, where Pétion ruled as president for life, people's lives were not improving. The crucial difference between the northern kingdom and the southern republic was the way each treated landownership. Christophe gave ownership of the bulk of the land to the state and leased large tracts to estate managers. Pétion took the opposite approach and distributed state-owned land to individuals in small parcels. Pétion began distributing land in 1809, when he granted land to his soldiers. Later on, Pétion extended the land-grant plan to other beneficiaries and lowered the selling price of state land to a level where almost anyone could afford to own land.

Pétion's decision proved detrimental in the shaping of modern Haiti (see Growth and Structure of the Economy, ch. 8). Smallholders had little incentive to produce export crops instead of subsistence crops. Coffee, because of its relative ease of cultivation, came to dominate agriculture in the south. The level of coffee production, however, did not permit any substantial exports. Sugar, which had been produced in large quantities in Saint-Domingue, was no longer exported from Haiti after 1822. When the cultivation of cane ceased, sugar mills closed, and people lost their jobs. In the south, the average Haitian was an isolated, poor, free, and relatively content yeoman. In the north, the average Haitian was a resentful but comparatively prosperous laborer. The desire for personal autonomy motivated most Haitians more than the vaguer concept of contributing to a strong national economy, however, and defections to the south were frequent, much to the consternation of Christophe.

Pétion, who died in 1818, left a lasting imprint upon his homeland. He ruled under two constitutions, which were promulgated in 1806 and 1816. The 1806 document resembled in many ways the Constitution of the United States. The 1816 charter, however, replaced the elected presidency with the office of president for life.

Pétion's largely laissez-faire rule did not directly discriminate against blacks, but it did promote an entrenched mulatto elite that benefited from such policies as the restoration of land confiscated by Dessalines and cash reimbursement for crops lost during the last year of the emperor's rule. Despite the egalitarianism of land distribution, government and politics in the republic remained the province of the elite, especially because the control of commerce came to replace the production of commodities as the focus of economic power in Haiti. Pétion was a beneficent ruler, and he was beloved by the people, who referred to him as "Papa Bon Coeur" (Father Good Heart). But Pétion was neither a true statesman nor a visionary. Some have said that his impact on the nations of South America, through his support for rebels such as Simón Bolívar Palacios and Francisco de Miranda, was stronger and more positive than his impact on his own impoverished country.

Although Christophe sought a reconciliation after Pétion's death, the southern elite rejected the notion of submission to a black leader. Because the president for life had died without naming a successor, the republican senate selected Pétion's mulatto secretary and commander of the Presidential Guard (Garde Présidentielle), General Jean-Pierre Boyer, to fill the post. In the north, King Henry committed suicide in October 1820, after having suffered a severe stroke that caused him to lose control of the army, his main source of power. The kingdom, which had been ruled by an even narrower clique than the republic, was left ripe for the taking. Boyer claimed it on October 26 at Cap-Haïtien at the head of 20,000 troops. Haiti was once again a single nation.

Boyer: Expansion and Decline

Boyer shared Pétion's conciliatory approach to governance, but he lacked his stature as a leader. The length of Boyer's rule (1818–43) reflected his political acumen, but he accomplished little. Boyer took advantage of internecine conflict in Santo Domingo by invading and securing the Spanish part of Hispaniola in 1822. He succeeded where Toussaint and Dessalines had failed. Occupation of the territory, however, proved unproductive for the Haitians, and ultimately it sparked a Dominican rebellion (see Haiti and Santo Domingo, ch. 1).

Boyer faced drastically diminished productivity as a result of Pétion's economic policies. Most Haitians had fallen into comfortable isolation on their small plots of land, content to eke out a quiet living after years of turmoil and duress. Boyer enacted a Rural Code (Code Rural), designed to force yeomen into large-scale production of export crops. The nation, however, lacked the wherewithal, the enthusiasm, and the discipline to enforce the code.

Boyer perceived that France's continued refusal to settle claims remaining from the revolution and to recognize its former colony's independence constituted the gravest threat to Haitian integrity. His solution to the problem—payment in return for recognition—secured Haiti from French aggression, but it emptied the treasury and mortgaged the country's future to French banks, which eagerly provided the balance of the hefty first installment. The indemnity was later reduced in 1838 from 150 million francs to 60 million francs. By that time, however, the damage to Haiti had been done.

As the Haitian economy stagnated under Boyer, Haitian society ossified. The lines separating mulattoes and blacks sharpened, despite Boyer's efforts to appoint blacks to responsible positions in government. The overwhelming rate of illiteracy among even well-to-do blacks foiled Boyer's intentions. Still, his government effected no substantial improvements in the limited educational system that Pétion had established. The exclusivity of the social structure thus perpetuated itself. Many blacks found no avenues in the bureaucracy for social mobility, and they turned to careers in the military, where literacy was not a requirement (see The Military in Haitian History, ch. 10).

As Pétion's successor, Boyer held the title of president for life. The length and relative placidity of his rule represented a period of respite for most Haitians after the violence and disorder that had characterized the emergence of their nation. Pressures gradually built up, however, as various groups, especially young mulattoes, began to chafe at the seemingly deliberate maintenance of the political and social status quo.

In the late 1830s, legislative opposition to Boyer clustered around Hérard Dumesle, a mulatto poet and liberal political thinker. Dumesle and his followers decried the anemic state of the nation's economy and its concomitant dependence on imported goods. They also disdained the continued elite adherence to French culture and urged Haitians to forge their own national identity. Their grievances against Boyer's government included corruption, nepotism, suppression of free expression, and rule by executive fiat. Banding together in a fraternity, they christened their organization the Society for the Rights of Man and of the Citizen. The group of young mulattoes called for an end to Boyer's rule and for the establishment of a provisional government.

The government expelled Dumesle and his followers from the legislature and made no effort to address their grievances. The perceived intransigence of the Boyer government triggered violent clashes in the south near Les Cayes. Forces under the command of Charles Rivière-Hérard, a cousin of Dumesle, swept through the southern peninsula toward the capital. Boyer received word on February 11, 1843, that most of his army units had joined the rebels. A victim of what was later known as the Revolution of 1843, Boyer sailed to Jamaica. Rivière-Hérard replaced him in the established tradition of military rule.

Decades of Instability, 1843-1915

Leyburn summarizes this chaotic era in Haitian history: "Of the twenty-two heads of state between 1843 and 1915, only one served out his prescribed term of office, three died while serving, one was blown up with his palace, one presumably poisoned, one hacked to pieces by a mob, one resigned. The other fourteen were deposed by revolution after incumbencies ranging in length from three months to twelve years." During this wide gulf between the 1843 revolution and occupation by the United States in 1915, Haiti's leadership became the most valuable prize in an unprincipled competition among strongmen. The overthrow of a government usually degenerated into a business venture, with foreign merchants—frequently Germans—initially funding a rebellion in the expectation of a substantial return after its success. The weakness of Haitian governments of the period and the potential profits to be gained from supporting a corrupt leader made such investments attractive.

Rivière-Hérard enjoyed only a brief tenure as president. It was restive and rebellious Dominicans, rather than Haitians, who struck one of the more telling blows against this leader. Nationalist forces led by Juan Pablo Duarte seized control of Santo Domingo on February 27, 1844 (see The Infant Republic, ch. 1). Unprofessional and undisciplined Haitian forces in the east, unprepared for a significant uprising, capitulated to the rebels. In March Rivière-Hérard attempted to reimpose his authority, but the Dominicans put up stiff opposition. Soon after Rivière-Hérard crossed the border, domestic turmoil exploded again.

Discontent among black rural cultivators, which had flared up periodically under Boyer, re-emerged in 1844 and led to greater change. Bands of ragged *piquets* (a term derived from the word for the pikes they brandished), under the leadership of a black, former army officer named Louis Jean-Jacques Acaau, rampaged through the south. The *piquets* who were capable of articulating a political position demanded an end to mulatto rule and the election of a black president. Their demands were eventually met but not by the defeated Rivière-Hérard, who returned home to a country where he enjoyed little support and wielded no effective power. In May 1844, his ouster by several rebel groups brought to power Philippe Guerrier, an aged black officer who had been a member of the peerage under Christophe's kingdom.

Guerrier's installation by a mulatto-dominated establishment represented the formal beginning of *politique de doublure;* a succession of short-lived black leaders was chosen after Guerrier in an effort to appease the *piquets* and to avoid renewed unrest in the countryside. During this period, two exceptions to the pattern of abbreviated rule were Faustin Soulouque (1847–59) and Fabre Nicolas Geffrard (1859–67). Soulouque, a black general of no particular distinction, was considered just another understudy when he was tapped by the legislature as a compromise between competing factions. Once in office, however, he displayed a Machiavellian taste for power. He purged the military high command, established a secret police force—known as the *zinglins*—to keep dissenters in line, and eliminated mulatto opponents. In August 1849, he grandiosely proclaimed himself as Haiti's second emperor, Faustin I.

Soulouque, like Boyer, enjoyed a comparatively long period of power that yielded little of value to his country. Whereas Boyer's rule had been marked by torpor and neglect, Soulouque's was distinguished by violence, repression, and rampant corruption. Soulouque's expansive ambitions led him to mount several invasions of the Dominican Republic. The Dominicans turned back his first foray in 1849 before he reached Santo Domingo. Another invasion in 1850 proved even less successful. Failed campaigns in 1855 and in 1856 fueled mounting discontent among the military; a revolt led by Geffrard, who had led a contingent in the Dominican campaign, forced the emperor out of power in 1859.

Geffrard, a dark-skinned mulatto, restored the old order of elite rule. After the turmoil of Soulouque's regime, Geffrard's rule seemed comparatively tranquil and even somewhat progressive. Geffrard produced a new constitution based largely on Pétion's 1816 document, improved transportation, and expanded education (although the system still favored the upper classes). Geffrard also signed a concordat with the Vatican in 1860 that expanded the presence of the Roman Catholic Church and its preponderantly foreign-born clergy in Haiti, particularly through the establishment of parochial schools (see Religion, ch. 7). The move ended a period of ill will between Haiti and the church that had begun during the revolutionary period.

Intrigue and discontent among the elite and the *piquets* beset Geffrard throughout his rule. In 1867 General Sylvain Salnave— a light-skinned mulatto who received considerable support from blacks in the north and in the capital—forced Geffrard from office. The overthrow profoundly unsettled the country, and Salnave's end came quickly. Rural rebellion among anti-Salnavist peasants who called themselves *cacos* (a term of unknown derivation) triggered renewed unrest among the *piquets* in the south. After several military successes, Salnave's forces weakened, and the leader fled Port-au-Prince. *Caco* forces captured him, however, near the Dominican border, where they tried and executed him on January 15, 1870. Successive leaders claimed control of most of the country and then regularly confirmed their rule ex post facto through a vote by the legislature, but none succeeded in establishing effective authority over the entire country.

Rebellion, intrigue, and conspiracy continued to be commonplace even under the rule of Louis Lysius Félicité Salomon (1879– 88), of the National Party (Parti National—PN), the most notable and effective president of the late nineteenth century. During one seven-year term and the beginning of a second, Salomon revived agriculture to a limited degree, attracted some foreign capital, established a national bank, linked Haiti to the outside world through the telegraph, and made minor improvements in the education system. Salomon, the scion of a prominent black family, had spent many years in France after being expelled by Rivière-Hérard. Salomon's support among the rural masses, along with his energetic efforts to contain elite-instigated plots, kept him in power longer than the strongmen who preceded and followed him. Still, Salomon yielded—after years of conflict with forces led by the Liberal Party (Parti Liberal—LP) and other disgruntled, power-hungry elite elements.

Political forces during the late nineteenth century polarized around the Liberal and the National parties. Mulattoes dominated the Liberal ranks, while blacks dominated the National Party; both parties were nonideological in nature. The parties competed on the battlefield, in the legislature, within the ranks of the military, and in the more refined but limited circles of the literati. The more populist Nationalists marched under the banner of their party slogan, "the greatest good for the greatest number," while the blatantly elitist Liberals proclaimed their preference for "government by the most competent."

Haitian politics remained unstable. From the fall of Salomon until occupation by the United States in 1915, eleven men held the title of president. Their tenures in office ranged from six and one-half years in the case of Florvil Hyppolite (1889–96) to only months—especially between 1912 and 1915, the turbulent period that preceded the United States occupation—in the case of seven others.

Although domestic unrest helped pave the way for intervention by the United States, geostrategic concerns also influenced events. The United States had periodically entertained the notion of annexing Hispaniola, but the divisive issue of slavery deterred the nation from acting. Until 1862 the United States refused to recognize Haiti's independence because the free, black, island nation symbolized opposition to slavery. President Ulysses S. Grant proposed annexation of the Dominican Republic in 1870, but the United States Senate rejected the idea. By the late nineteenth century, the growth of United States power and the prospect of a transoceanic canal in either Nicaragua or Panama had increased attention given to the Caribbean. Annexation faded as a policy option, but Washington persistently pursued efforts to secure naval stations throughout the region. The United States favored the Môle Saint-Nicolas as an outpost, but Haiti refused to cede territory to a foreign power.

The French and the British still claimed interests in Haiti, but it was the Germans' activity on the island that concerned the United States most. The small German community in Haiti (approximately 200 in 1910) wielded a disproportionate amount of economic power. Germans controlled about 80 percent of the country's international commerce; they also owned and operated utilities in Cap-Haïtien and Port-au-Prince, the main wharf and a tramway in the capital, and a railroad in the north. The Germans, as did the French, aiming to collect the nation's customs receipts to cover Haiti's outstanding debts to European creditors, also sought control of the nearly insolvent National Bank of Haiti. This kind of arrangement was known technically as a customs receivership.

Officials in Washington were especially concerned about Germany's aggressive employment of military might. In December 1897, a German commodore in charge of two warships demanded and received an indemnity from the Haitian government for a German national who had been deported from the island after a legal dispute. Another German warship intervened in a Haitian uprising in September 1902. It forced the captain of a rebel gunboat (that had waylaid a German merchant ship) to resort to blowing up his ship—and himself—to avoid being seized.

Reports reached Washington that Berlin was considering setting up a coaling station at the Môle Saint-Nicolas to serve the German naval fleet. This potential strategic encroachment resonated through the White House, at a time when the Monroe Doctrine (a policy that opposed European intervention in the Western Hemisphere) and the Roosevelt Corollary (whereby the United States assumed the responsibility for direct intervention in Latin American nations in order to check the influence of European powers) strongly shaped United States foreign policy, and when war on a previously unknown scale had broken out in Europe. The administration of President Woodrow Wilson accordingly began contingency planning for an occupation of Haiti.

Escalating instability in Haiti all but invited foreign intervention. The country's most productive president of the early twentieth century, Cincinnatus Leconte, had died in a freak explosion in the National Palace (Palais National) in August 1912. Five more contenders claimed the country's leadership over the next three years. General Vilbrun Guillaume Sam, who had helped to bring Leconte to power, took the oath of office in March 1915. Like every other Haitian president of the period, he faced active rebellion to his rule. His leading opponent, Rosalvo Bobo, reputedly hostile toward the United States, represented to Washington a barrier to expanded commercial and strategic ties. A pretext for intervention came on July 27, 1915, when Guillaume Sam executed 167 political prisoners. Popular outrage provoked mob violence in the streets of Port-au-Prince. A throng of incensed citizens sought out Guillaume Sam at his sanctuary in the French embassy and literally tore him to pieces. The spectacle of an exultant rabble parading through the streets of the capital bearing the dismembered corpse of their former president shocked decision makers in the United States and spurred them to swift action. The first sailors and marines landed in Port-au-Prince on July 28. Within six weeks, representatives from the United States controlled Haitian customs houses and administrative institutions. For the next nineteen years, Haiti's powerful neighbor to the north guided and governed the country.

The United States Occupation, 1915–34

Representatives from the United States wielded veto power over all governmental decisions in Haiti, and Marine Corps commanders served as administrators in the provinces. Local institutions, however, continued to be run by Haitians, as was required under policies put in place during the presidency of Woodrow Wilson. In line with these policies, Admiral William Caperton, the initial commander of United States forces, instructed Bobo to refrain from offering himself to the legislature as a presidential candidate. Philippe Sudre Dartiguenave, the mulatto president of the Senate, agreed to accept the presidency of Haiti after several other candidates had refused on principle.

With a figurehead installed in the National Palace and other institutions maintained in form if not in function, Caperton declared martial law, a condition that persisted until 1929. A treaty passed by the Haitian legislature in November 1915 granted further authority to the United States. The treaty allowed Washington to assume complete control of Haiti's finances, and it gave the United States sole authority over the appointment of advisers and receivers. The treaty also gave the United States responsibility for establishing and running public-health and public-works programs and for supervising routine governmental affairs. The treaty also established the Gendarmerie d'Haïti (Haitian Constabulary), a step later replicated in the Dominican Republic and Nicaragua. The Gendarmerie was Haiti's first professional military force, and it was eventually to play an important political role in the country. In 1917 President Dartiguenave dissolved the legislature after its members refused to approve a constitution purportedly authored by United States assistant secretary of the navy Franklin D. Roosevelt. A referendum subsequently approved the new constitution (by a vote of 98,225 to 768), however, in 1918. Generally a liberal document, the constitution allowed foreigners to purchase land. Dessalines had forbidden land ownership by foreigners, and since 1804 most Haitians had viewed foreign ownership as anathema.

The occupation by the United States had several effects on Haiti. An early period of unrest culminated in a 1918 rebellion by up to

President Philippe Sudre Dartiguenave (seated at center)
with ministers and bodyguards
Courtesy National Archives

40,000 former *cacos* and other disgruntled people. The scale of the uprising overwhelmed the Gendarmerie, but marine reinforcements helped put down the revolt at the estimated cost of 2,000 Haitian lives. Thereafter, order prevailed to a degree that most Haitians had never witnessed. The order, however, was imposed largely by white foreigners with deep-seated racial prejudices and a disdain for the notion of self-determination by inhabitants of less-developed nations. These attitudes particularly dismayed the mulatto elite, who had heretofore believed in their innate superiority over the black masses. The whites from North America, however, did not distinguish among Haitians, regardless of their skin tone, level of education, or sophistication. This intolerance caused indignation, resentment, and eventually a racial pride that was reflected in the work of a new generation of Haitian historians, ethnologists, writers, artists, and others, many of whom later became active in politics and government. Still, as Haitians united in their reaction to the racism of the occupying forces, the mulatto elite managed to dominate the country's bureaucracy and to strengthen its role in national affairs.

The occupation had several positive aspects. It greatly improved Haiti's infrastructure. Roads were improved and expanded. Almost all roads, however, led to Port-au-Prince, resulting in a gradual concentration of economic activity in the capital. Bridges went up throughout the country; a telephone system began to function; several towns gained access to clean water; and a construction boom (in some cases employing forced labor) helped restore wharves, lighthouses, schools, and hospitals. Public health improved, partially because of United States-directed campaigns against malaria and yaws (a crippling disease caused by a spirochete). Sound fiscal management kept Haiti current on its foreign-debt payments at a time when default among Latin American nations was common. By that time, United States banks were Haiti's main creditors, an important incentive for Haiti to make timely payments.

In 1922 Louis Borno replaced Dartiguenave, who was forced out of office for temporizing over the approval of a debt-consolidation loan. Borno ruled without the benefit of a legislature (dissolved in 1917 under Dartiguenave) until elections were again permitted in 1930. The legislature, after several ballots, elected mulatto Sténio Vincent to the presidency.

The occupation of Haiti continued after World War I, despite the embarrassment that it caused Woodrow Wilson at the Paris peace conference in 1919 and the scrutiny of a congressional inquiry in 1922. By 1930 President Herbert Hoover had become concerned about the effects of the occupation, particularly after a December 1929 incident in Les Cayes in which marines killed at least ten Haitian peasants during a march to protest local economic conditions. Hoover appointed two commissions to study the situation. A former governor general of the Philippines, W. Cameron Forbes, headed the more prominent of the two. The Forbes Commission praised the material improvements that the United States administration had wrought, but it criticized the exclusion of Haitians from positions of real authority in the government and the constabulary, which had come to be known as the Garde d'Haïti. In more general terms, the commission further asserted that "the social forces that created [instability] still remain—poverty, ignorance, and the lack of a tradition or desire for orderly free government."

The Hoover administration did not implement fully the recommendations of the Forbes Commission, but United States withdrawal was well under way by 1932, when Hoover lost the presidency to Roosevelt, the presumed author of the most recent Haitian constitution. On a visit to Cap-Haïtien in July 1934, Roosevelt reaffirmed an August 1933 disengagement agreement. The last contingent of marines departed in mid-August, after a formal transfer of authority to the Garde. As in other countries occupied by the

United States in the early twentieth century, the local military was often the only cohesive and effective institution left in the wake of withdrawal.

Politics and the Military, 1934–57

The Garde was a new kind of military institution in Haiti (see Army Politics in the Twentieth Century, ch. 10). It was a force manned overwhelmingly by blacks, with a United States-trained black commander, Colonel Démosthènes Pétrus Calixte. Most of the Garde's officers, however, were mulattoes. The Garde was a national organization; it departed from the regionalism that had characterized most of Haiti's previous armies. In theory, its charge was apolitical—to maintain internal order, while supporting a popularly elected government. The Garde initially adhered to this role.

President Vincent took advantage of the comparative national stability, which was being maintained by a professionalized military, to gain absolute power. A plebiscite permitted the transfer of all authority in economic matters from the legislature to the executive, but Vincent was not content with this expansion of his power. In 1935 he forced through the legislature a new constitution, which was also approved by plebiscite. The constitution praised Vincent, and it granted the executive sweeping powers to dissolve the legislature at will, to reorganize the judiciary, to appoint ten of twenty-one senators (and to recommend the remaining eleven to the lower house), and to rule by decree when the legislature was not in session. Although Vincent implemented some improvements in infrastructure and services, he brutally repressed his opposition, censored the press, and governed largely to benefit himself and a clique of merchants and corrupt military officers.

Under Calixte the majority of Garde personnel had adhered to the doctrine of political nonintervention that their Marine Corps trainers had stressed. Over time, however, Vincent and Dominican dictator Rafael Leónidas Trujillo Molina sought to buy adherents among the ranks. Trujillo, determined to expand his influence over all of Hispaniola, in October 1937 ordered the indiscriminate butchery by the Dominican army of an estimated 15,000 to 20,000 Haitians on the Dominican side of the Massacre River (see The Era of Trujillo, ch. 1). Some observers claim that Trujillo supported an abortive coup attempt by young Garde officers in December 1937. Vincent dismissed Calixte as commander and sent him abroad, where he eventually accepted a commission in the Dominican military as a reward for his efforts while on Trujillo's payroll. The attempted coup led Vincent to purge the officer corps of all members suspected of disloyalty, marking the end of the apolitical military.

In 1941 Vincent showed every intention of standing for a third term as president, but after almost a decade of disengagement, the United States made it known that it would oppose such an extension. Vincent accommodated the Roosevelt administration and handed power over to Elie Lescot.

Lescot was a mulatto who had served in numerous government posts. He was competent and forceful, and many considered him a sterling candidate for the presidency, despite his elitist background. Like the majority of previous Haitian presidents, however, he failed to live up to his potential. His tenure paralleled that of Vincent in many ways. Lescot declared himself commander in chief of the military, and power resided in a clique that ruled with the tacit support of the Garde. He repressed his opponents, censored the press, and compelled the legislature to grant him extensive powers. He handled all budget matters without legislative sanction and filled legislative vacancies without calling elections. Lescot commonly said that Haiti's declared state of war against the Axis powers during World War II justified his repressive actions. Haiti, however, played no role in the war except for supplying the United States with raw materials and serving as a base for a United States Coast Guard detachment.

Aside from his authoritarian tendencies, Lescot had another flaw: his relationship with Trujillo. While serving as Haitian ambassador to the Dominican Republic, Lescot fell under the sway of Trujillo's influence and wealth. In fact, it was Trujillo's money that reportedly bought most of the legislative votes that brought Lescot to power. Their clandestine association persisted until 1943, when the two leaders parted ways for unknown reasons. Trujillo later made public all his correspondence with the Haitian leader. The move undermined Lescot's already dubious popular support.

In January 1946, events came to a head when Lescot jailed the Marxist editors of a journal called *La Ruche* (The Beehive). This action precipitated student strikes and protests by government workers, teachers, and shopkeepers in the capital and provincial cities. In addition, Lescot's mulatto-dominated rule had alienated the predominantly black Garde. His position became untenable, and he resigned on January 11. Radio announcements declared that the Garde had assumed power, which it would administer through a three-member junta.

The Revolution of 1946 was a novel development in Haiti's history, insofar as the Garde assumed power as an institution, not as the instrument of a particular commander. The members of the

*Residents of Port-au-Prince celebrate the fall of President
Elie Lescot, January 1946.
Courtesy National Archives*

junta, known as the Military Executive Committee (Comité Exécutif Militaire), were Garde commander Colonel Franck Lavaud, Major Antoine Levelt, and Major Paul E. Magloire, commander of the Presidential Guard. All three understood Haiti's traditional way of exercising power, but they lacked a thorough understanding of what would be required to make the transition to an elected civilian government. Upon taking power, the junta pledged to hold free elections. The junta also explored other options, but public clamor, which included public demonstrations in support of potential candidates, eventually forced the officers to make good on their promise.

Haiti elected its National Assembly in May 1946. The Assembly set August 16, 1946, as the date on which it would select a president. The leading candidates for the office—all of whom were black—were Dumarsais Estimé, a former school teacher, assembly member, and cabinet minister under Vincent; Félix d'Orléans Juste Constant, leader of the Haitian Communist Party (Parti Communiste d'Haïti—PCH); and former Garde commander Calixte, who stood as the candidate of a progressive coalition that included the Worker Peasant Movement (Mouvement Ouvrier Paysan—MOP). MOP chose to endorse Calixte, instead of a candidate from its own ranks, because the party's leader, Daniel Fignolé, was only twenty-six years old—too young to stand for the nation's highest office. Estimé, politically the most moderate of the three, drew support from the black population in the north, as well as from the emerging black middle class. The leaders of the military, who would not countenance the election of Juste Constant and who reacted warily to the populist Fignolé, also considered Estimé the safest candidate. After two rounds of polling, legislators gave Estimé the presidency.

Estimé's election represented a break with Haiti's political tradition. Although he was reputed to have received support from commanders of the Garde, Estimé was a civilian. Of humble origins, he was passionately anti-elitist and therefore generally antimulatto. He demonstrated, at least initially, a genuine concern for the welfare of the people. Operating under a new constitution that went into effect in November 1946, Estimé proposed, but never secured passage of, Haiti's first social-security legislation. He did, however, expand the school system, encourage the establishment of rural cooperatives, raise the salaries of civil servants, and increase the representation of middle-class and lower-class blacks in the public sector. He also attempted to gain the favor of the Garde—renamed the Haitian Army (Armée d'Haïti) in March 1947—by promoting Lavaud to brigadier general and by seeking United States military assistance.

Estimé eventually fell victim to two of the time-honored pitfalls of Haitian rule: elite intrigue and personal ambition. The elite had a number of grievances against Estimé. Not only had he largely excluded them from the often lucrative levers of government, but he also enacted the country's first income tax, fostered the growth of labor unions, and suggested that voodoo be considered as a religion equivalent to Roman Catholicism—a notion that the Europeanized elite abhorred. Lacking direct influence in Haitian affairs, the elite resorted to clandestine lobbying among the officer corps. Their efforts, in combination with deteriorating domestic conditions, led to a coup in May 1950.

To be sure, Estimé had hastened his own demise in several ways. His nationalization of the Standard Fruit banana concession sharply reduced the firm's revenues. He alienated workers by requiring them to invest between 10 percent and 15 percent of their salaries in national-defense bonds. The president sealed his fate by attempting to manipulate the constitution in order to extend his term in office. Seizing on this action and the popular unrest it engendered, the army forced the president to resign on May 10, 1950. The same junta that had assumed power after the fall of Lescot reinstalled itself. An army escort conducted Estimé from the National Palace and into exile in Jamaica. The events of May 1946 made an impression upon the deposed minister of labor, François Duvalier. The lesson that Duvalier drew from Estimé's ouster was that the military could not be trusted. It was a lesson that he would act upon when he gained power.

The power balance within the junta shifted between 1946 and 1950. Lavaud was the preeminent member at the time of the first coup, but Magloire, now a colonel, dominated after Estimé's overthrow. When Haiti announced that its first direct elections (all men twenty-one or over were allowed to vote) would be held on October 8, 1950, Magloire resigned from the junta and declared himself a candidate for president. In contrast to the chaotic political climate of 1946, the campaign of 1950 proceeded under the implicit understanding that only a strong candidate backed by both the army and the elite would be able to take power. Facing only token opposition, Magloire won the election and assumed office on December 6.

Magloire restored the elite to prominence. The business community and the government benefited from favorable economic conditions until Hurricane Hazel hit the island in 1954. Haiti made some improvements in its infrastructure, but most of these were financed largely by foreign loans. By Haitian standards, Magloire's rule was firm, but not harsh: he jailed political opponents, including Fignolé, and shut down their presses when their protests grew too strident, but he allowed labor unions to function, although they were not permitted to strike. It was in the arena of corruption, however, that Magloire overstepped traditional bounds. The president controlled the sisal, cement, and soap monopolies. He and other officials built imposing mansions. The injection of international hurricane relief funds into an already corrupt system boosted graft to levels that disillusioned all Haitians. To make matters worse, Magloire followed in the footsteps of many previous presidents by disputing the termination date of his stay in office. Politicians, labor leaders, and their followers flocked to the streets in May 1956 to protest Magloire's failure to step down. Although Magloire declared martial law, a general strike essentially shut down Port-au-Prince. Again like many before him, Magloire fled to Jamaica, leaving the army with the task of restoring order.

The period between the fall of Magloire and the election of Duvalier in September 1957 was a chaotic one, even by Haitian standards. Three provisional presidents held office during this interval; one resigned and the army deposed the other two, François Sylvain and Fignolé. Duvalier is said to have engaged actively in the behind-the-scenes intrigue that helped him to emerge as the presidential candidate that the military favored. The military went on to guide the campaign and the elections in a way that gave Duvalier every possible advantage. Most political actors perceived Duvalier—a medical doctor who had served as a rural administrator of a United States-funded anti-yaws campaign before entering the cabinet under Estimé—as an honest and fairly unassuming leader without a strong ideological motivation or program. When elections were finally organized, this time under terms of universal suffrage (both men and women now had the vote), Duvalier, a black, painted himself as the legitimate heir to Estimé. This approach was enhanced by the fact that Duvalier's only viable opponent, Louis Déjoie, was a mulatto and the scion of a prominent family. Duvalier scored a decisive victory at the polls. His followers took two-thirds of the legislature's lower house and all of the seats in the Senate.

François Duvalier, 1957–71

Like many Haitian leaders, Duvalier produced a constitution to solidify his power. In 1961 he proceeded to violate the provisions of that constitution, which had gone into effect in 1957. He replaced the bicameral legislature with a unicameral body and decreed presidential and legislative elections. Despite a 1957 prohibition against presidential reelection, Duvalier ran for office and won with an official tally of 1,320,748 votes to zero. Not content with this sham display of democracy, he went on in 1964 to declare himself president for life. For Duvalier, the move was a matter of political tradition; seven heads of state before him had claimed the same title.

An ill-conceived coup attempt in July 1958 spurred Duvalier to act on his conviction that Haiti's independent military threatened the security of his presidency. In December the president sacked the armed forces chief of staff and replaced him with a more reliable officer. This action helped him to expand a Presidential Palace army unit into the Presidential Guard. The Guard became the elite corps of the Haitian army, and its sole purpose was to maintain Duvalier's power. After having established his own power base within the military, Duvalier dismissed the entire general staff and replaced aging marine-trained officers with younger men who owed their positions, and presumably their loyalty, to Duvalier.

Duvalier also blunted the power of the army through a rural militia formally named the Volunteers for National Security (Volontaires de la Sécurité Nationale—VSN), but more commonly referred to as the *tonton makouts* (derived from the Creole term for a mythological bogeyman). In 1961, only two years after Duvalier had established the group, the *tonton makouts* had more than twice the power of the army. Over time, the group gained even more power. While the Presidential Guard secured Duvalier against his enemies in the capital, the *tonton makouts* expanded his authority into rural areas. The *tonton makouts* never became a true militia, but they were more than a mere secret police force. The group's pervasive influence throughout the countryside bolstered recruitment, mobilization, and patronage for the regime.

After Duvalier had displaced the established military with his own security force, he employed corruption and intimidation to create his own elite. Corruption—in the form of government rakeoffs of industries, bribery, extortion of domestic businesses, and stolen government funds—enriched the dictator's closest supporters. Most of these supporters held sufficient power to enable them to intimidate the members of the old elite who were gradually coopted or eliminated (the luckier ones were allowed to emigrate).

Duvalier was an astute observer of Haitian life and a student of his country's history. Although he had been reared in Port-au-Prince, his medical experiences in the provinces had acquainted him with the everyday concerns of the people, their predisposition toward paternalistic authority (his patients referred to him as "Papa Doc," a sobriquet that he relished and often applied to himself), the ease with which their allegiance could be bought, and the central role of voodoo in their lives. Duvalier exploited all of these points, especially voodoo. He studied voodoo practices and beliefs and was rumored to be a *houngan.* He related effectively to *houngan* and *bokò* (voodoo sorcerers) throughout the country and incorporated many of them into his intelligence network and the ranks of the *tonton makouts.* His public recognition of voodoo and its practitioners and his private adherence to voodoo ritual, combined with his reputed practice of magic and sorcery, enhanced his popular persona among the common people (who hesitated to trifle with a leader who had such dark forces at his command) and served as a peculiar form of legitimization of his rapacious and ignoble rule.

Duvalier weathered a series of foreign-policy crises early in his tenure that ultimately enhanced his power and contributed to his megalomaniacal conviction that he was, in his words, the "personification of the Haitian fatherland." Duvalier's repressive and authoritarian rule seriously disturbed United States president John F. Kennedy. The Kennedy administration registered particular concern over allegations that Duvalier had blatantly misappropriated aid money and that he intended to employ a Marine Corps mission to Haiti not to train the regular army but to strengthen the *tonton makouts.* Washington acted on these charges and suspended aid in mid-1962. Duvalier refused to accept United States demands for strict accounting procedures as a precondition of aid renewal. Duvalier, claiming to be motivated by nationalism, renounced all aid from Washington. At that time, aid from the United States constituted a substantial portion of the Haitian national budget. The move had little direct impact on the Haitian people because most of the aid had been siphoned off by Duvalierist cronies any-way. Renouncing the aid, however, allowed the incipient dictator to portray himself as a principled and lonely opponent of domina-tion by a great power. Duvalier continued to receive multilateral contributions. After Kennedy's death in November 1963, pressure on Duvalier eased, and the United States adopted a policy of grudg-ing acceptance of the Haitian regime because of the country's stra-tegic location near communist Cuba (see Foreign Relations, ch. 9).

A more tense and confrontational situation developed in April 1963 between Duvalier and Dominican Republic president Juan Bosch Gaviño. Duvalier and Bosch were confirmed adversaries; the Dominican president provided asylum and direct support to Haitian exiles who plotted against the Duvalier regime. Duvalier ordered the Presidential Guard to occupy the Dominican chancery in Pétionville in an effort to apprehend an army officer believed to have been involved in an unsuccessful attempt to kidnap the dictator's son, Jean-Claude Duvalier, and daughter, Simone Du-valier. The Dominican Republic reacted with outrage and indig-nation. Bosch publicly threatened to invade Haiti, and he ordered army units to the frontier. Although observers throughout the world anticipated military action that would lead to Duvalier's downfall, they saw events turn in the Haitian tyrant's favor. Dominican mili-tary commanders, who found Bosch's political leanings too far to the left, expressed little support for an invasion of Haiti. Bosch, because he could not count on his military, decided to let go of his dream to overthrow the neighboring dictatorship. Instead, he allowed the matter to be settled by emissaries of the Organization of American States (OAS).

Resistant to both domestic and foreign challenges, Duvalier en-trenched his rule through terror (an estimated 30,000 Haitians were killed for political reasons during his tenure), emigration (which removed the more activist elements of the population along with thousands of purely economic migrants), and limited patronage. At the time of his death in 1971, François Duvalier designated his son, Jean-Claude Duvalier, as Haiti's new leader. To the Haitian elite, who still dominated the economy, the continuation of Duvalierism without "Papa Doc" offered financial gain and a possibility for recapturing some of the political influence lost under the dictatorship.

Jean-Claude Duvalier, 1971–86

The first few years after Jean-Claude Duvalier's installation as Haiti's ninth president for life were a largely uneventful extension of his father's rule. Jean-Claude was a feckless, dissolute nineteen-year-old, who had been raised in an extremely isolated environment and who had never expressed any interest in politics or Haitian affairs. He initially resented the dynastic arrangement that had made him Haiti's leader, and he was content to leave substantive and administrative matters in the hands of his mother, Simone Ovide Duvalier, while he attended ceremonial functions and lived as a playboy.

By neglecting his role in government, Jean-Claude squandered a considerable amount of domestic and foreign goodwill and facilitated the dominance of Haitian affairs by a clique of hard-line Duvalierist cronies who later became known as the dinosaurs. The public displayed more affection toward Jean-Claude than they had displayed for his more formidable father. Foreign officials and observers also seemed more tolerant toward "Baby Doc," in areas such as human-rights monitoring, and foreign countries were more generous to him with economic assistance. The United States restored its aid program for Haiti in 1971.

Jean-Claude limited his interest in government to various fraudulent schemes and to outright misappropriations of funds. Much of the Duvaliers' wealth, which amounted to hundreds of millions of dollars over the years, came from the Régie du Tabac (Tobacco Administration). Duvalier used this "nonfiscal account," established decades earlier under Estimé, as a tobacco monopoly, but he later expanded it to include the proceeds from other government enterprises and used it as a slush fund for which no balance sheets were ever kept.

Jean-Claude's kleptocracy, along with his failure to back with actions his rhetoric endorsing economic and public-health reform, left the regime vulnerable to unanticipated crises that were exacerbated by endemic poverty, including the African Swine Fever (ASF) epidemic and the widely publicized outbreak of acquired immune deficiency syndrome (AIDS) in the 1980s. A highly contagious and fatal disease, ASF plagued pigs in the Dominican Republic in mid-1978. The United States feared that the disease would spread to North America and pressured Jean-Claude to slaughter the entire population of Haitian pigs and to replace them with animals supplied by the United States and international agencies. The Haitian government complied with this demand, but it failed to take note of the rancor that this policy produced among the peasantry. Black Haitian pigs were not only a form of "savings account" for peasants because they could be sold for cash when necessary, but they were also a breed of livestock well-suited to the rural environment because they required neither special care nor special feed. The replacement pigs required both. Peasants deeply resented this intrusion into their lives (see Livestock and Fishing, ch. 8).

Initial reporting on the AIDS outbreak in Haiti implied that the country might have been a source for the human immune deficiency virus (see Acquired Immune Deficiency Syndrome, ch. 7). This rumor, which turned out to be false, hurt the nation's tourism industry, which had grown during Jean-Claude Duvalier's tenure. Already minimal, public services deteriorated as Jean-Claude and his ruling clique continued to misappropriate funds from the national treasury.

Jean-Claude miscalculated the ramifications of his May 1980 wedding to Michèle Bennett, a mulatto divorcée with a disreputable background. (François Duvalier had jailed her father, Ernest Bennett, for bad debts and other shady financial dealings.) Although Jean-Claude himself was light-skinned, his father's legacy of support for the black middle class and antipathy toward the established mulatto elite had enhanced the appeal of Duvalierism among the black majority of the population. By marrying a mulatto, Jean-Claude appeared to be abandoning the informal bond that his father had labored to establish. The marriage also estranged the old-line Duvalierists in the government from the younger technocrats whom Jean-Claude had appointed. The Duvalierists' spiritual leader, Jean-Claude's mother, Simone, was eventually expelled from Haiti, reportedly at the request of Michèle, Jean-Claude's wife.

The extravagance of the couple's wedding, which cost an estimated US$3 million, further alienated the people. Popular discontent intensified in response to increased corruption among the Duvaliers and the Bennetts, as well as the repulsive nature of the Bennetts' dealings, which included selling Haitian cadavers to foreign medical schools and trafficking in narcotics. Increased political repression added to the volatility of the situation. By the mid-1980s, most Haitians felt hopeless, as economic conditions worsened and hunger and malnutrition spread.

Widespread discontent began in March 1983, when Pope John Paul II visited Haiti. The pontiff declared that "something must change here." He went on to call for a more equitable distribution of income, a more egalitarian social structure, more concern among the elite for the well-being of the masses, and increased popular participation in public life. This message revitalized both laymen and clergy, and it contributed to increased popular mobilization and to expanded political and social activism.

A revolt began in the provinces two years later. The city of Gonaïves was the first to have street demonstrations and raids on food-distribution warehouses. From October 1985 to January 1986, the protests spread to six other cities, including Cap-Haïtien. By the end of that month, Haitians in the south had revolted. The most significant rioting there broke out in Les Cayes.

Jean-Claude responded with a 10 percent cut in staple food prices, the closing of independent radio stations, a cabinet reshuffle, and a crackdown by police and army units, but these moves failed to dampen the momentum of the popular uprising against the dynastic dictatorship. Jean-Claude's wife and advisers, intent on maintaining their profitable grip on power, urged him to put down the rebellion and to remain in office.

A plot to remove him had been well under way, however, long before the demonstrations began. The conspirators' efforts were not connected to the popular revolt, but violence in the streets prompted Jean-Claude's opponents to act. The leaders of the plot were Lieutenant General Henri Namphy and Colonel Williams Regala. Both had privately expressed misgivings about the excesses of the regime. They and other officers saw the armed forces as the single remaining cohesive institution in the country. They viewed the army as the only vehicle for an orderly transition from Duvalierism to another form of government.

In January 1986, the unrest in Haiti alarmed United States president Ronald Reagan. The Reagan administration began to pressure Duvalier to renounce his rule and to leave Haiti. Representatives appointed by Jamaican prime minister Edward Seaga served as intermediaries who carried out the negotiations. The United States rejected a request to provide asylum for Duvalier, but offered to assist with the dictator's departure. Duvalier had initially accepted on January 30, 1986. The White House actually announced his departure prematurely. At the last minute, however, Jean-Claude decided to remain in Haiti. His decision provoked increased violence in the streets.

The United States Department of State announced a cutback in aid to Haiti on January 31. This action had both symbolic and real effect: it distanced Washington from the Duvalier regime, and it denied the regime a significant source of income. By this time, the rioting had spread to Port-au-Prince.

At this point, the military conspirators took direct action. Namphy, Regala, and others confronted the Duvaliers and demanded their departure. Left with no bases of support, Jean-Claude consented. After hastily naming a National Council of Government (Conseil National de Gouvernement—CNG) made up of Namphy, Regala, and three civilians, Jean-Claude and Michèle Duvalier departed from Haiti on February 7, 1986. They left behind them a country economically ravaged by their avarice, a country bereft of functional political institutions and devoid of any tradition of peaceful self-rule. Although the end of the Duvalier era provoked much popular rejoicing, the transitional period initiated under the CNG did not lead to any significant improvement in the lives of most Haitians (see Background: From Duvalier to Avril, 1957-89, ch. 9; The Post-Duvalier Period, ch. 10). Although most citizens expressed a desire for democracy, they had no firm grasp of what the word meant or of how it might be achieved.

* * *

The English-language historiography for Haiti is fairly rich and diverse. The two leading comprehensive works are David Nicholls's *From Dessalines to Duvalier: Race, Colour, and National Independence in Haiti* and *Written in Blood: The Story of the Haitian People, 1492-1971* by Robert Debs Heinl and Nancy Gordon Heinl. Nicholls's book goes into greater depth with regard to Haiti's sociocultural history, whereas the Heinls' volume is a more straightforward account, full of fascinating and useful detail. Another worthwhile general work is Robert Rotberg's *Haiti: The Politics of Squalor*. Rayford Logan's *Haiti and the Dominican Republic* examines Haiti's history in the larger context of European and United States competition in the Western Hemisphere. The period of the United States occupation is chronicled effectively in Hans Schmidt's *The United States Occupation of Haiti, 1915-1934*. Bernard Diederich and Al Burt's *Papa Doc: The Truth about Haiti Today* provides a riveting, although somewhat anecdotal, chronicle of François Duvalier's rule. In a similar vein, Elizabeth Abbott's *Haiti: The Duvaliers and Their Legacy* gives the reader a feel for the behind-the-scenes workings of the dynastic dictatorship. (For further information and complete citations, see Bibliography.)

Chapter 7. Haiti:
The Society and Its Environment

Figure from a painting by Prosper Pierrelouis

HAITI IS A DRAMATIC COUNTRY in its terrain, history, and culture. In comparison with other countries in the Caribbean, Haiti is country of extremes: it is the most rural in its settlement pattern, the poorest, and the most densely populated. It is also the only country in the region that was born of a successful slave rebellion, and it is the first modern black republic.

Many observers have described Haitian society as stagnant, but in recent years, changes have begun. By the 1980s, the population of Haiti surpassed 5 million. Although the country continued to be overwhelmingly rural, urbanization was accelerating as the impact of soil erosion and land fragmentation on agricultural productivity forced increasing numbers of peasants to migrate to Port-au-Prince and even overseas. The population of Port-au-Prince was expected to reach 1 million by the end of the 1980s. Haiti's peasants had traditionally relied on the extended family and cooperative labor as a means for taking care of each other, but by the late 1980s, this aspect of the culture had disintegrated. Deteriorating economic conditions were forcing the poor to find new ways to eke out a living from the land, or to survive in urban slums. An unstable, but politically significant, black middle class had emerged between the traditional, mainly mulatto, elite and the peasantry. Migration and the penetration of foreign missions and nongovernmental organizations to the more remote parts of Haiti created new kinds of relationships with the outside world. The transportation and the communications systems had been greatly improved, and Creole-language radio brought news of domestic and international affairs to the country's isolated villages (see Transportation and Communications, ch. 8).

The weight of the past bore heavily on the daily lives of all Haitians in the 1980s. The country's legacy of slavery and French colonization had left a lasting imprint on the culture. In the past, members of the upper class cherished Franco-Haitian culture because the French language and manners separated them from the masses whom they wished to rule. At the same time, former slaves created a peasant culture, but always in the shadow of their urban superiors. Haiti's dual cultural heritage resulted in negative attitudes toward Haitian peasant life, particularly toward the Creole language, traditional marriages, and voodoo, the folk religion. The recent emergence of a middle class has only exacerbated the debate over what should be considered ''true'' Haiti.

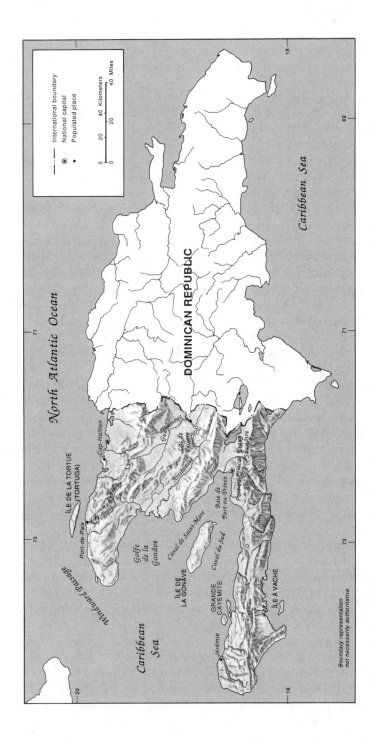

Figure 11. Haiti: Topography and Drainage

Geography

Haiti is a country of only about 28,000 square kilometers, about the size of the state of Maryland. It occupies the western third of the Caribbean island of Hispaniola (La Isla Española); the Dominican Republic takes up the eastern two-thirds. Shaped like a horseshoe on its side, Haiti has two main peninsulas, one in the north and one in the south. Between the peninsulas is the Île de la Gonâve (see fig. 11).

Northwest of the northern peninsula is the Windward Passage, a strip of water that separates Haiti from Cuba, which is about ninety kilometers away. The eastern edge of the country borders the Dominican Republic. A series of treaties and protocols—the most recent of which was the Protocol of Revision of 1936—set the 388-kilometer eastern border, which is formed partly by the Pedernales River in the south and the Massacre River in the north.

The mainland of Haiti has three regions: the northern region, which includes the northern peninsula; the central region; and the southern region, which includes the southern peninsula. In addition, Haiti controls several nearby islands.

The northern region consists of the Massif du Nord (Northern Massif) and the Plaine du Nord (Northern Plain). The Massif du Nord, an extension of the central mountain range in the Dominican Republic, begins at Haiti's eastern border, north of the Guayamouc River, and extends to the northwest through the northern peninsula. The Massif du Nord ranges in elevation from 600 to 1,100 meters. The Plaine du Nord lies along the northern border with the Dominican Republic, between the Massif du Nord and the North Atlantic Ocean. This lowland area of 2,000 square kilometers is about 150 kilometers long and 30 kilometers wide.

The central region consists of two plains and two sets of mountain ranges. The Plateau Central (Central Plateau) extends along both sides of the Guayamouc River, south of the Massif du Nord. It runs eighty-five kilometers from southeast to northwest and is thirty kilometers wide. To the southwest of the Plateau Central are the Montagnes Noires, with elevations of up to approximately 600 meters. The most northwestern part of this mountain range merges with the Massif du Nord. Southwest of the Montagnes Noires and oriented around the Artibonite River is the Plaine de l'Artibonite, measuring about 800 square kilometers. South of this plain lie the Chaîne des Matheux and the Montagnes du Trou d'Eau, which are an extension of the Sierra de Neiba range of the Dominican Republic.

The southern region consists of the Plaine du Cul-de-Sac and the mountainous southern peninsula. The Plaine du Cul-de-Sac is a natural depression, twelve kilometers wide, that extends thirty-two kilometers from the border with the Dominican Republic to the coast of the Baie de Port-au-Prince. The mountains of the southern peninsula, an extension of the southern mountain chain of the Dominican Republic (the Sierra de Baoruco), extend from the Massif de la Selle in the east to the Massif de la Hotte in the west. The range's highest peak, the Morne de la Selle, is the highest point in Haiti, rising to an altitude of 2,715 meters. The Massif de la Hotte varies in elevation from 1,270 to 2,255 meters.

The four islands of notable size in Haitian territory are Île de la Gonâve, Île de la Tortue (Tortuga Island), Grande Cayemite, and Île à Vache. Île de la Gonâve is sixty kilometers long and fifteen kilometers wide. The hills that cross the island rise to heights of up to 760 meters. Île de la Tortue is located north of the northern peninsula, separated from the city of Port-de-Paix by a twelve-kilometer channel. Île à Vache is located south of the southern peninsula; Grande Cayemite lies north of the southern peninsula.

Numerous rivers and streams, which slow to a trickle during the dry season and which carry torrential flows during the wet season, cross Haiti's plains and mountainous areas. The largest drainage system in the country is that of the Artibonite River. Rising as the Libón River in the foothills of the Massif du Nord, the river crosses the border into the Dominican Republic and then forms part of the border before reentering Haiti as the Artibonite River. At the border, the river expands to form the Lac de Péligre in the southern part of the Plateau Central. The 400-kilometer Artibonite River is only one meter deep during the dry season, and it may even dry up completely in certain spots. During the wet season, it is more than three meters deep and subject to flooding.

The ninety-five-kilometer Guayamouc River is one of the principal tributaries of the Artibonite River. The most important river in the northern region is Les Trois Rivières, or The Three Rivers. It is 150 kilometers long, has an average width of sixty meters, and is three to four meters deep.

The most prominent body of water in the southern region is the salt-water Etang Saumâtre, located at the eastern end of the Plaine du Cul-de-Sac. At an elevation of sixteen meters above sea level, the lake is twenty kilometers long and six to fourteen kilometers wide; it has a circumference of eighty-eight kilometers.

Haiti has a generally hot and humid tropical climate. The north wind brings fog and drizzle, which interrupt Haiti's dry season from December to February. But during March to November, the weather is very wet. Northeast trade winds bring rains during the wet season.

The average annual rainfall is 140 to 200 centimeters, but it is unevenly distributed. Heavier rainfall occurs in the southern peninsula and in the northern plains and mountains. Rainfall decreases from east to west across the northern peninsula. The eastern central region receives a moderate amount of precipitation, while the western coast from the northern peninsula to Port-au-Prince, the capital, is relatively dry. Temperatures are almost always high in the lowland areas, ranging from 15°C to 25°C in the winter and from 25°C to 35°C during the summer.

Population

Demographic Profile

The estimated population of Haiti in 1989 was 6.1 million, with an average population density of 182 people per square kilometer. Some 75 percent of the population lived in rural areas, while only 25 percent remained in urban areas; this was one of the lowest urban-to-rural population ratios in Latin America and the Caribbean. The estimated annual population growth rate between 1971 and 1982 was 1.4 percent. The crude mortality rate in 1982 was estimated to be 16.5 percent, with a crude birth rate of 36 percent (see table 11, Appendix A). A profile of the population reveals that the majority of Haitians are young (see fig. 12).

Haiti has conducted only a few censuses throughout its history. A survey taken during 1918 and 1919 indicated that there were about 1.9 million people in the country. The first formal census, taken in 1950, showed that the population had reached 3.1 million. The second census, in 1971, indicated a population of 4.2 million. Critics have argued that these censuses, along with one taken in 1982 (the final results of which were still unavailable as of 1989), were deficient and that they seriously undercounted the population.

Urban areas, particularly Port-au-Prince, grew significantly in the 1970s and the 1980s. The annual population growth rate of metropolitan Port-au-Prince was estimated to be 3.5 percent between 1971 and 1982, substantially above the 1.4 percent national rate for that period. The growth rate for other urban areas was estimated at 2.4 percent. Metropolitan Port-au-Prince, which includes the capital and the suburbs of Delmas and Carrefour, was by far the largest urban area in 1982, with a population of 763,188, or about 61 percent of the total urban population. The population of the second largest city, Cap-Haïtien, was estimated to be 64,400

245

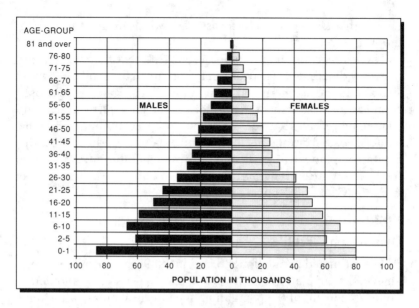

Source: Based on information from Haiti, Institut Haïtien de Statistique et d'Informatique, *Santé et Population en Haïti*, Port-au-Prince, 1986, 8.

Figure 12. Haiti: Population Distribution by Age and Sex, 1982

The next two largest towns, Gonaïves and Les Cayes, had estimated populations of slightly more than 34,000. Six other towns had populations greater than 10,000.

The rural population, which grew about 1 percent a year between 1971 and 1982, was estimated to be 3.8 million in 1982, 3.4 million in 1971, and 2.7 million in 1950. In 1982 there were about 464 people per square kilometer in rural areas, one of the highest population densities in the Western Hemisphere.

Migration

The population growth rate in Haiti's rural areas has been lower than the rate for urban areas, even though fertility rates are higher in rural areas. The main reason for this disparity is outmigration. People in rural areas have moved to cities, or they have emigrated to other countries, mostly the United States and the Dominican Republic. An estimated 1 million people left Haiti between 1957 and 1982.

Many of the emigrants in the 1950s and the 1960s were urban middle-class and upper-class opponents of the government of François Duvalier (1957–71). Throughout the 1970s, however, an increasing number of rural and lower-class urban Haitians emigrated, too.

246

In the 1980s, as many as 500,000 Haitians were living in the United States; there were large communities in New York, Miami, Boston, Chicago, and Philadelphia. Thousands of Haitians also illegally emigrated to the United States through nonimmigrant visas, while others entered the United States without any documentation at all.

The first reports of Haitians' arriving in the United States, by boat and without documentation, occurred in 1972. Between 1972 and 1981, the United States Immigration and Naturalization Service (INS) reported that more than 55,000 Haitian ''boat people'' had arrived in Florida. The INS estimated that because as many as half of the arrivals escaped detection, the actual number of boat people may have exceeded 100,000. An unknown number of Haitians are reported to have died during their attempts to reach the United States by sea. Though poorer than earlier immigrants, the boat people were often literate and skilled, and all had families who could afford the price of a passage to Florida. About 85 percent of these boat people settled in Miami.

In September 1981, the United States entered an agreement with Haiti to interdict Haitian boats and return prospective immigrants to Haiti. Under the agreement, 3,107 Haitians had been returned by 1984. Nevertheless, clandestine departures by boat continued throughout the 1980s. The Bahamas was another destination of Haitian emigrants; an estimated 50,000 arrived there by boat during the 1980s. The Bahamas had welcomed Haitian immigrants during the 1960s, but in the late 1970s, it reversed its position, leading to increased emigration to Florida.

Since the early twentieth century, the Dominican Republic has received both temporary and permanent Haitian migrants. The International Labour Office estimated that between 200,000 and 500,000 Haitians resided in the Dominican Republic in 1983. About 85,000 of them lived on cane plantations. In the early 1980s, about 80 to 90 percent of the cane cutters in the Dominican Republic were reported to be Haitians. Through an accord with the Haitian government, the Dominican Republic imported Haitian workers to cut cane. In 1983 the Dominican Republic hired an estimated 19,000 workers. Evidence presented to the United Nations (UN) Working Group on Slavery revealed that the Dominican Republic paid wages that were miserably low and that working and living conditions failed to meet standards set by the two governments. According to some reports, Haitian cane cutters were unable to leave their workplaces, and they were prevented from learning about the terms of the contracts under which they had been hired.

Emigration helped moderate Haiti's population growth. Furthermore, annual remittances from abroad, estimated to be as high as US$100 million, supported thousands of poor families and provided an important infusion of capital into the Haitian economy (see Balance of Payments, ch. 8). At the same time, emigration resulted in a heavy loss of professional and skilled personnel from urban and rural areas.

Fertility and Family Planning

A number of studies show that Haiti's fertility rate declined significantly from the early 1960s to the early 1980s. As was true in other countries, there appeared to be a correlation among declining fertility rates, urban residence, and literacy. The 1977 Haitian Fertility Survey found that between 1962 and 1977, the fertility rate of literate urban women declined by 33 percent. In contrast, the rate for illiterate rural women declined by only 7 percent during the same period. Moreover, the fertility rate of literate rural women declined by 27 percent, while that of illiterate urban women declined by 15 percent.

Haitian women interviewed in the 1977 survey indicated that they desired between three and four children, but at that time, the average woman had more than five children.

Expressed desire for family planning services exceeded available programs, and many women lacked access to modern contraceptives and birth-control information. The survey found that, despite the widespread desire for fewer children, only 7 percent of women of childbearing age were using modern contraceptives. Haitian men traditionally shunned the use of condoms. The fertility survey reported a condom-use rate of only 1 percent. The absence of more recent surveys made it impossible to determine whether or not condom use had risen in response to the high incidence of acquired immune deficiency syndrome (AIDS) in Haiti.

Social Structure

As a result of the extinction of the indigenous population by the beginning of the seventeenth century, the population of preindependence Saint-Domingue (present-day Haiti) was entirely the product of the French colonists' slaveholding policies and practices. The major planters and government officials who constituted the ruling class carefully controlled every segment of the population, especially the majority of African slaves and their descendants. Society was structured for the rapid production of wealth for the planters and their investors in France (see Colonial Society: The Conflicts of Color and Class, ch. 6).

In the colonial period, the French imposed a three-tiered social structure. At the top of the social and political ladder was the white elite (*grands blancs*). At the bottom of the social structure were the black slaves (*noirs*), most of whom had been transported from Africa. Between the white elite and the slaves arose a third group, the freedmen (*affranchis*), most of whom were descended from unions of slaveowners and slaves. Some mulatto freedmen inherited land, became relatively wealthy, and owned slaves (perhaps as many as one-fourth of all slaves in Saint-Domingue belonged to *affranchis*). Nevertheless, racial codes kept the *affranchis* socially and politically inferior to the whites. Also between the white elite and the slaves were the poor whites (*petits blancs*), who considered themselves socially superior to the mulattoes, even if they sometimes found themselves economically inferior to them. Of a population of 519,000 in 1791, 87 percent were slaves, 8 percent were whites, and 5 percent were freedmen. Because of harsh living and working conditions, many slaves died, and new slaves were imported. Thus, at the time of the slave rebellion of 1791, most slaves had been born in Africa rather than in Saint-Domingue.

The Haitian Revolution changed the country's social structure. The colonial ruling class, and most of the white population, was eliminated, and the plantation system was largely destroyed. The earliest black and mulatto leaders attempted to restore a plantation system that relied on an essentially free labor force, through strict military control, but the system collapsed during the tenure of Alexandre Pétion (1806–18) (see Independent Haiti, ch. 6). The Haitian Revolution broke up plantations and distributed land among the former slaves. Through this process, the new Haitian upper class lost control over agricultural land and labor, which had been the economic basis of colonial control. To maintain their superior economic and social position, the new Haitian upper class turned away from agricultural pursuits in favor of more urban-based activities, particularly government.

The nineteenth-century Haitian ruling class consisted of two groups, the urban elite and the military leadership. The urban elite were primarily a closed group of educated, comparatively wealthy, and French-speaking mulattoes. Birth determined an individual's social position, and shared values and intermarriage reinforced class solidarity. The military, however, was a means of advancement for disadvantaged black Haitians. In a shifting, and often uneasy, alliance with the military, the urban elite ruled the country and kept the peasantry isolated from national affairs. The urban elite promoted French norms and models as a means of separating themselves from the peasantry. Thus, French language and manners, orthodox Roman Catholicism, and light skin were important criteria of high social position. The elite disdained manual labor, industry, and commerce in favor of the more genteel professions, such as law and medicine.

A small, but politically important, middle class emerged during the twentieth century. Although social mobility increased slightly, the traditional elite retained their economic preeminence, despite countervailing efforts by François Duvalier. For the most part, the peasantry continued to be excluded from national affairs, but by the 1980s, this isolation had decreased significantly. Still, economic hardship in rural areas caused many cultivators to migrate to the cities in search of a higher standard of living, thereby increasing the size of the urban lower class.

The Upper Class

In the 1980s, Haiti's upper class constituted as little as 2 percent of the total population, but it controlled about 44 percent of the national income. The upper class included not only the traditional elite, which had not controlled the government for more than thirty years, but also individuals who had become wealthy and powerful through their connections with the governments of François Duvalier and his son, Jean-Claude Duvalier. Increased access to education helped carry some individuals into the ranks of the upper class. Others were able to move upward because of wealth they accrued in industry or export-import businesses.

The traditional elite held key positions in trade, industry, real estate, and the professions, and they were identified by membership in "good families," which claimed several generations of recognized legal status and name. Being a member of the elite also required a thorough knowledge of cultural refinements, particularly the customs of the French. Light skin and straight hair continued to be important characteristics of this group. French surnames were common among the mulatto elite, but increased immigration from Europe and the Middle East in the late nineteenth and the early twentieth centuries had introduced German, English, Danish, and Arabic names to the roster.

The only group described as an ethnic minority in Haiti was the "Arabs," people descended from Syrian, Lebanese, and Palestinian traders who began to arrive in Haiti and elsewhere in the Caribbean in the late nineteenth century. From their beginnings, as itinerant peddlers of fabrics and other dry goods, the Arabs moved into the export-import sector, engendering the hostility of Haitians and foreign rivals. Nevertheless, the Arabs remained. Many adopted French and Creole as their preferred languages, took

Jacmel, a town on the southern peninsula

Haitian citizenship, and integrated themselves into the upper and the middle classes. Formerly spurned by elite mulatto families and excluded from the best clubs, the Arabs had begun to intermarry with elite Haitians and to take part in all aspects of upper-class life, including entry into the professions and industry.

The Middle Class

The middle class was essentially nonexistent during the nineteenth century. But at about the time of the United States occupation (1915–34), it became more defined (see The United States Occupation, 1915–34, ch. 6). The creation of a professional military and the expansion of government services fostered the development of Haiti's middle class. Educational reform in the 1920s, an upsurge in black consciousness, and the wave of economic prosperity after World War II also contributed to the strengthening of the class. In the late 1980s, the middle class probably made up less than 5 percent of the total population, but it was growing, and it was becoming more politically powerful.

The mulatto elite dominated governments in the 1930s and the early 1940s and thwarted the political aspirations of the black middle class. President Dumarsais Estimé (1946–50) came to power with the aim of strengthening the middle class. The Duvalier government

251

also claimed the allegiance of the black middle class, at least through the 1970s. During the Duvalier period, many in the middle class owed their economic security to the government. A number of individuals from this class, however, benefited from institutionalized corruption.

Some members of the middle class had acquired political power by the 1980s, but most continued to be culturally ambivalent and insecure. Class solidarity, identity, and traditions were all weak. The criteria for membership in the middle class included a non-manual occupation, a moderate income, literacy, and a mastery of French. Middle-class Haitians sought upward mobility for themselves and their children, and they perceived education and urban residence as two essential keys to achieving higher status. Although they attempted to emulate the lifestyle of the upper class, middle-class Haitians resented the social preeminence and the color prejudice of the elite. Conflicts between the Franco-Haitian and the Afro-Haitian cultural traditions were most common among the middle class.

Peasants

Haiti's peasantry constituted approximately 75 percent of the total population. Unlike peasants in much of Latin America, most of Haiti's peasants had owned land since the early nineteenth century. Land was the most valuable rural commodity, and peasant families went to great lengths to retain it and to increase their holdings.

Peasants in general had control over their landholdings, but many lacked clear title to their plots. Haiti has never conducted a cadastral survey, but it is likely that many families have passed on land over generations without updating land titles. Division of land equally among male and female heirs resulted in farm plots that became too small to warrant the high costs of a surveyor. Heirs occasionally surveyed land before taking possession of it, but more frequently, heirs divided plots among themselves in the presence of community witnesses and often a notary. Some inherited land was not divided, but was used in common, for example, for pasture, or it was worked by heirs in rotation. Families commonly sold land to raise cash for such contingencies as funerals or to pay the expenses of emigration. Purchasers often held land with a notarized paper, rather than a formal deed (see Land Tenure and Land Policy, ch. 8).

There were strata within the peasantry based on the amount of property owned. Many peasants worked land as sharecroppers or tenants, and some hoped eventually to inherit the plots they worked.

Some tenant farmers owned and cultivated plots in addition to the land they worked for others. The number of entirely landless peasants who relied solely on wage labor was probably quite small. Agricultural wages were so low that peasants deprived of land were likely to migrate to urban areas in search of higher incomes. Wealthier peasants maintained their economic positions through the control of capital and influence in local politics.

Peasants maintained a strong, positive identity as Haitians and as cultivators of the land, but they exhibited a weak sense of class consciousness. Rivalries among peasants were more common than unified resentment toward the upper class.

Cooperation among peasants diminished during the twentieth century. Farms run by nuclear families and exchanges among extended families had formed the basis of the agrarian system. Until the middle of the twentieth century, collective labor teams, called *kounbit*, and larger labor-exchange groups were quite common. These groups were formed to carry out specific tasks on an individual's land; the owner provided music and a festive meal. After the 1940s, smaller groups, called *eskouad*, began to replace the *kounbit*. The *eskouad* carried out tasks on a strictly reciprocal basis or sold their collective labor to other peasants.

Although Haitian peasant villages generally lacked a sense of community and civic-mindedness, some civic-action groups had emerged over the years. After the 1960s, wealthy peasants led rural community councils, which were supervised by the government. These councils often served more to control the flow of development resources into an area than to represent the local population. In the 1980s, a countervailing movement of small peasant groups (*groupman*) emerged with support from the Roman Catholic Church, principally in the Plateau Central. The *groupman* discussed common interests and undertook some cooperative activities. Both the Duvalier governments and the succeeding National Council of Government (Conseil National de Gouvernement—CNG), headed by Lieutenant General Henri Namphy, took steps to curb the activities of these peasant groups.

The first generation of Haitian peasants pursued self-sufficiency, freedom, and peace. The necessity of devoting at least some share of their limited hectarage to the production of cash crops, however, hindered the peasants' ability to achieve self-sufficiency in the cultivation of domestic staples. Although they acquired a degree of freedom, they also found themselves isolated from the rest of the nation and the world. In the second half of the twentieth century, the Haitian peasantry gradually became much less isolated. Several factors accelerated the peasants' involvement with the outside world in the 1970s and the 1980s. Road projects improved the transportation system, and foreign religious missions and private development agencies penetrated the rural areas. These organizations brought new resources and provided an institutional link to the outside world. Many people from almost every community had migrated to Port-au-Prince or overseas, and they sent money home to rural areas. Cassette tapes enabled illiterate people who had traveled far from home to communicate with their families. Creole, which became widely used on radio, brought news of Haiti and the world to remote villages. And in 1986, media coverage of the fall of the Duvalier regime put rural Haitians in touch with the political affairs of the nation.

Urban Lower Class

The urban lower class, which made up about 15 percent of the total population in the early 1980s, was concentrated in Port-au-Prince and the major coastal towns. Increased migration from rural areas contributed greatly to the growth of this class. Industrial growth was insufficient, however, to absorb the labor surplus produced by the burgeoning urbanization; unemployment and underemployment were severe in urban areas. The urban lower class was socially heterogeneous, and it had little class consciousness. One outstanding characteristic of this group was its commitment to education. Despite economic hardships, urban lower-class parents made a real effort to keep their children in school throughout the primary curriculum. Through education and political participation, some members of the lower class achieved mobility into the middle class.

The poorest strata of the urban lower class lived under Haiti's worst sanitary and health conditions. According to the World Bank (see Glossary), one-third of the population of Port-au-Prince lived in densities of more than 1,000 people per hectare in 1976. The poorest families consumed as few as seven liters of water per person, per day, for cooking, drinking, and cleaning, and they spent about one-fifth of their income to obtain it. For many of these families, income and living conditions worsened in the 1980s.

Gender Roles and Family Life

In rural areas, men and women played complementary roles. Men were primarily responsible for farming and, especially, for heavy work, such as tilling. Women, however, often assisted with tasks such as weeding and harvesting. Women were responsible for selling agricultural produce. In general, Haitian women participated in the labor force to a much greater extent than did women

Residential street, Port-au-Prince
Children, Port-au-Prince
Courtesy United States Agency for International Development

in other Latin American countries. Haiti's culture valued women's economic contribution to the farm in that all income generated through agricultural production belonged to both husband and wife. Many women also acquired sufficient capital to become full-time market traders, and they were thus economically independent. The income that they earned from nonfarm business activities was recognized as their own; they were not required to share it with their husbands.

The most common marital relationship among peasants and the urban lower class was known as *plasaj*. The government did not recognize *plasaj* as legitimate marriage, but in lower-class communities, these relationships were considered normal and proper. The husband and wife often made an explicit agreement about their economic relationship at the beginning of a marriage. These agreements usually required the husband to cultivate at least one plot of land for the wife and to provide her with a house. Women performed most household tasks, though men often did heavy chores, such as gathering firewood.

For the most part, lower-class men and women had civil and religious marriages for reasons of prestige rather than to legitimize marital relations. Because weddings were expensive, many couples waited several years before having them. In the 1960s, this pattern began to change among Protestant families who belonged to churches that strongly encouraged legal marriage and provided affordable weddings (see Protestantism, this ch.). It was not unusual for peasants to have more than one marital relationship. Some entered into polygamous marriages, which only a few men could afford.

Legal marriages were neither more stable nor more productive than *plasaj* relationships. Also, legal marriages were not necessarily monogamous. In fact, legally married men were often more economically stable than men in *plasaj* relationships, so it was easier for them to separate from their wives or to enter into extramarital relationships.

Men and women both valued children and both contributed to child care, but women generally bore most of the burden. Parents were proud of their children, regardless of whether they were born in a marital relationship or as "outside children." Parents took pains to ensure that all of their children received equal inheritances.

Family structure in rural Haiti has changed since the nineteenth century. Until the early part of the twentieth century, the *lakou*, an extended family, usually defined along male lines, was the principal family form. The term *lakou* referred not only to the family members, but to the cluster of houses in which they lived. Members of a *lakou* worked cooperatively, and they provided each other with financial and other kinds of support. Land ownership was not cooperative, however, and successive generations of heirs inherited individual plots. Under the pressure of population growth and the increasing fragmentation of landholdings, the *lakou* system disintegrated. By the mid-twentieth century, the nuclear family had become the norm among peasants. The *lakou* survived as a typical place of residence, but the cooperative labor and the social security provided by these extended families disappeared. Haitian peasants still relied on their kin for support, but the extended family sometimes became an arena for land disputes as much as a mechanism for cooperation.

Family life among the traditional elite was substantially different from that of the lower class. Civil and religious marriages were the norm, and the "best" families could trace legally married ancestors to the nineteenth century. Because of the importance of intermarriage, mulatto elite families were often interrelated. Marital relationships have changed somewhat since the mid-twentieth century. Divorce, once rare, has become acceptable. Elite wives, once exclusively homemakers surrounded by servants, entered the labor force in increasing numbers in the 1970s and the 1980s. The legal rights of married women, including rights to property, were expanded through legislation in the 1980s. In addition, the elite had a broader choice of partners as economic change and immigration changed the composition of that group.

The Language Question
French and Creole

Two languages were spoken in Haiti: Creole and French. The social relationship between these languages was complex. Nine of every ten Haitians spoke only Creole, which was the everyday language for the entire population. About one in twenty spoke Creole and some French. And only about one in twenty was fluent in both Creole and French. Thus, Haiti was neither a francophone country nor a bilingual one. Rather, two separate speech communities existed: the monolingual majority and the bilingual elite.

All classes valued verbal facility. Public speaking played an important role in political life; the style of the speech was often more important than the content. Repartee enlivened the daily parlance of both the monolingual peasant and the sophisticated bilingual urbanite. Small groups gathered regularly in Port-au-Prince to listen to storytellers. Attitudes toward French and Creole helped to define the Haitians' cultural dilemma.

Language usually complicated interactions between members of the elite and the masses. Haitians of all classes took pride in Creole as a means of expression and as the national tongue. Nevertheless, many monolingual and bilingual Haitians regarded Creole as a nonlanguage, claiming that "it has no rules." Thus, the majority of the population did not value their native language and built a mystique around French. At the same time, almost every bilingual Haitian had ambivalent feelings about using French and did so uncomfortably. In Creole the phrase "to speak French" means "to be a hypocrite."

Fluency in French served as an even more important criterion than skin color for membership in the Haitian elite. The use of French in public life excluded the Creole-speaking majority from politics, government, and intellectual life. Bilingual families used French primarily for formal occasions. Because Creole was the language of informal gatherings, it was filled with slang and was used for telling jokes. Haitian French lacked these informal qualities. Monolingual Creole speakers avoided formal situations where their inability to communicate in French would be a disadvantage or an embarrassment. In an attempt to be accepted in formal or governmental circles, some monolingual Creole speakers used French-sounding phrases in their Creole speech, but these imitations were ultimately of little or no use. Middle-class bilinguals in Port-au-Prince suffered the greatest disadvantage because they frequently encountered situations in which the use of French would be appropriate, but their imperfect mastery of the language tended to betray their lower-class origins. It was in the middle class that the language issue was most pressing. The use of French as a class marker made middle-class Haitians more rigid in their use of French on formal occasions than Haitians who were solidly upper class.

The origins of Creole are still debated. Some scholars believe that it arose from a pidgin that developed between French colonists and African slaves in the colonies. Others believe that Creole came to the colony of Saint-Domingue as a full-fledged language, having arisen from the French maritime-trade dialect. Whatever its origins, Creole is linguistically a separate language and not just a corrupted French dialect. Although the majority of Creole words have French origins, Creole's grammar is not similar to that of French, and the two languages are not mutually comprehensible.

There are regional and class variations in Creole. Regional variations include lexical items and sound shifts, but the grammatical structure is consistent throughout the country. Bilingual speakers tend to use French phonemes in their Creole speech. The tendency

A house-raising
Courtesy Inter-American Foundation
Haitian peasants
Courtesy Pan-American Development Foundation

259

to use French sounds became common in the Port-au-Prince variant of Creole. By the 1980s, the Port-au-Prince variant was becoming perceived as the standard form of the language. The use of French and Creole during the colonial and the independence periods set speech patterns for the next century. During the colonial period, it was mostly whites and educated mulatto freedmen who spoke French. When the slaves gained their freedom and the plantation system disintegrated, the greatest barriers among the various classes of people of color collapsed. French language became a vital distinction between those who had been emancipated before the revolution (the *anciens libres*) and those who achieved freedom through the revolution, and it ensured the superior status of the *anciens libres*. French became the language not only of government and commerce, but also of culture and refinement. Even the most nationalist Haitians of the nineteenth century placed little value on Creole.

Attitudes toward Creole began to change during the twentieth century, however, especially during the United States occupation. The occupation forced Haitian intellectuals to confront their non-European heritage. A growing black consciousness and intensifying nationalism led many Haitians to consider Creole as the "authentic" language of the country. The first attempt at a Creole text appeared in 1925, and the first Creole newspaper was published in 1943.

Beginning in the 1950s, a movement to give Creole official status evolved slowly. The constitution of 1957 reaffirmed French as the official language, but it permitted the use of Creole in certain public functions. In 1969 a law was passed giving Creole limited legal status; the language could be used in the legislature, the courts, and clubs, but not in accredited educational institutions. In 1979, however, a decree permitted Creole as the language of instruction in the classroom. The constitution of 1983 declared that both Creole and French were the national languages but specified that French would be the official language. The suppressed 1987 Constitution (which was partially reinstated in 1989) gave official status to Creole (see The Constitutional Framework, ch. 4).

Changes in Language Use

The use of Creole, even in formal settings, increased throughout the 1970s and the 1980s. Conversations at elite dinner tables, once held rigidly in French, switched fluidly between French and Creole, even within the same sentence. Radio and television stations increased broadcasts in Creole as advertisers learned the utility of reaching the vast majority of their market. Radio provided widespread access to news, which helped to break down the isolation of the peasantry and to galvanize the population during the crisis that led to the fall of the Duvalier regime. In 1986 it became obvious that important changes had taken place in Haiti, as people who had been in exile for years began to return home to run for the presidency. Many arrived at the Port-au-Prince airport with French speeches in hand but found themselves confronted by journalists who insisted on speaking Creole.

The emergence of English as an important language of business affected attitudes toward French. Growing trade with the United States and the development of assembly industries funded by investors from the United States led to greater use of English in commercial settings. English also became more important as Haitians migrated to the United States and as many members of the elite sent their children to North American educational institutions.

English cut across class lines. Hundreds of French-speaking elite families spent years of exile in the United States during the Duvalier period, and they returned to Haiti fluent in English. Many Creole speakers who went to the United States also returned to Haiti as fluent English speakers. Haitian migration to the United States and trade with North America also resulted in the introduction of English words into the Creole lexicon. For many monolinguals, learning English appeared more practical than learning French, and English posed fewer psychological and social obstacles. The availability and the popularity of English-language television programs on Haiti's private cable service helped familiarize Haitians with the language. Spanish also had become fairly widespread in Haiti, largely because of migration to the Dominican Republic.

Creole, Literacy, and Education

Conflicting political interests have caused Haiti's national language policy to be inconsistent. Even governments that claimed to represent the masses hesitated to give Creole and French equal legal status. It was only in the late 1970s that the government approved the use of Creole in education. In the early 1980s, there was still some doubt about whether Creole would be used in primary education.

For almost fifty years, Haitian linguists had debated the spelling rules for Creole. But in the late 1970s, the National Pedagogic Institute (Institut Pédagogique National—IPN) developed an orthography that included elements of the two systems previously in use. The government gave semiofficial status to the new orthography as part of the education reform of 1978.

The most controversial aspect of the education reform was the introduction of Creole as the medium of instruction in primary

Boats arriving for market day in Restel, southern Haiti

schools. In many rural and urban schools, textbooks were in French, but classroom discussion of these books was in Creole. Nevertheless, French remained the official language of instruction, and a major goal of most students was to master written and spoken French.

The education reform program was intended to boost students' performance through instruction in their native language, but several groups opposed the use of Creole as the language of instruction. Bilingual families believed that the use of Creole in the schools was eroding their linguistic advantage in society by reducing the importance of French. In general, the upper class believed that by offering instruction in Creole, the schools would increase poor people's access to education; however, many poor people also opposed the reform. The poor tended to view education more as a means of escaping poverty than as a means for learning, so many parents were most concerned about having their children learn French. Private schools often ignored the curriculum changes called for under the reform. Under pressure from the public, the government declared that students would begin using French when they entered the fifth grade. Students entering fifth grade found themselves unprepared for classroom use of French, however, because their textbooks in earlier grades had been entirely in Creole. The problem remained unresolved in the late 1980s.

In the 1960s, the government had established adult literacy programs in Creole, and the Roman Catholic Church had sponsored similar nationwide programs in the mid-1980s. According to Haiti's 1982 census, 37 percent of the population over ten years of age was literate; in rural areas, only 28 percent was literate. In rural areas, the literacy rate for women was almost as high as it was for men. The census failed to note, however, the degree of literacy, or the language in which people were literate.

Monolingual speakers had little access to literature in Creole (see The Mass Media, ch. 9). The major Creole publication, the monthly *Bon Nouvel,* published by a Roman Catholic group, had a circulation of 20,000 in 1980. A Protestant group published the New Testament in Creole in 1972. Numerous booklets about hygiene and agricultural practices appeared in increasing quantities in the 1970s and the 1980s. Nevertheless, Creole literature continued to be scarce in the late 1980s. In particular, information in Creole about politics and current events was in short supply. By the late 1980s, monolingual speakers regularly used Creole in letters and personal notes. Community leaders and development workers also used the language in recording the minutes of their meetings and in project reports.

Religious Life

Roman Catholicism is the official religion of Haiti, but voodoo may be considered the country's national religion. The majority of Haitians believe in and practice at least some aspects of voodoo. Most voodooists believe that their religion can coexist with Catholicism. Most Protestants, however, strongly oppose voodoo.

Voodoo

Misconceptions about voodoo have given Haiti a reputation for sorcery and zombies. Popular images of voodoo have ignored the religion's basis as a domestic cult of family spirits. Adherents of voodoo do not perceive themselves as members of a separate religion; they consider themselves Roman Catholics. In fact, the word for voodoo does not even exist in rural Haiti. The Creole word *vodoun* refers to a kind of dance and in some areas to a category of spirits. Roman Catholics who are active voodooists say that they "serve the spirits," but they do not consider that practice as something outside of Roman Catholicism. Haitians also distinguish between the service of family spirits and the practice of magic and sorcery.

The belief system of voodoo revolves around family spirits (often called *loua* or *mistè*) who are inherited through maternal and paternal lines. *Loua* protect their "children" from misfortune. In return, families must "feed" the *loua* through periodic rituals in which food, drink, and other gifts are offered to the spirits. There are two kinds of services for the *loua*. The first is held once a year; the second is conducted much less frequently, usually only once a generation. Many poor families, however, wait until they feel a need to restore their relationship with their spirits before they conduct a service. Services are usually held at a sanctuary on family land.

In voodoo, there are many *loua*. Although there is considerable variation among families and regions, there are generally two groups of *loua*, the *rada* and the *petro*. The *rada* spirits are mostly seen as "sweet" *loua*, while the *petro* are seen as "bitter" because they are more demanding of their "children." *Rada* spirits appear to be of African origin while *petro* spirits appear to be of Haitian origin.

Loua are usually anthropomorphic and have distinct identities. They can be good, evil, capricious, or demanding. *Loua* most commonly show their displeasure by making people sick, and so voodoo is used to diagnose and treat illnesses. *Loua* are not nature spirits, and they do not make crops grow or bring rain. The *loua* of one family have no claim over members of other families, and they cannot protect or harm them. Voodooists are therefore not interested in the *loua* of other families.

Loua appear to family members in dreams and, more dramatically, through trances. Many Haitians believe that *loua* are capable of temporarily taking over the bodies of their "children." Men and women enter trances during which they assume the traits of particular *loua*. People in a trance feel giddy and usually remember nothing after they return to a normal state of consciousness. Voodooists say that the spirit temporarily replaces the human personality. Possession trances usually occur during rituals such as services for *loua* or a *vodoun* dance in honor of the *loua*. When *loua* appear to entranced people, they may bring warnings or explanations for the causes of illnesses or misfortune. *Loua* often engage the crowd around them through flirtation, jokes, or accusations.

Ancestors (*le mò*) rank with the family *loua* as the most important spiritual entities in voodoo. Elaborate funeral and mourning rites reflect the important role of the dead. Ornate tombs throughout the countryside reveal how much attention Haiti gives to its dead. Voodooists believe the dead are capable of forcing their survivors to construct tombs and sell land. In these cases, the dead act like family *loua*, which "hold" family members to make them ill or bring other misfortune. The dead also appear in dreams to provide their survivors with advice or warnings.

Voodooists also believe there are *loua* that can be paid to bring good fortune or protection from evil. And, they believe that souls can be paid to attack enemies by making them ill.

Folk belief includes zombies and witchcraft. Zombies are either spirits or people whose souls have been partially withdrawn from their bodies. Some Haitians resort to *bokò*, who are specialists in sorcery and magic. Haiti has several secret societies whose members practice sorcery.

Voodoo specialists, male *houngan* and female *manbo*, mediate between humans and spirits through divination and trance. They diagnose illnesses and reveal the origins of other misfortunes. They can also perform rituals to appease spirits or ancestors or to repel magic. Many voodoo specialists are accomplished herbalists who treat a variety of illnesses.

Voodoo lacks a fixed theology and an organized hierarchy, unlike Roman Catholicism and Protestantism. Each specialist develops his or her own reputation for helping people.

François Duvalier recruited voodoo specialists to serve as *tonton makouts* to help him control all aspects of Haitian life (see François Duvalier, 1957-71, ch. 6). Duvalier indicated that he retained power through sorcery, but because voodoo is essentially a family-based cult, Duvalier failed to politicize the religion to any great extent.

Roman Catholicism

Before the Haitian Revolution, Roman Catholicism in particular and the church in general played minor roles in colonial life. Plantation owners feared that religious education for slaves could undermine their basis for control, and they expelled the education-oriented Jesuits in 1764. Roman Catholicism gained official status in several postindependence Haitian constitutions, but there was no official Roman Catholic presence in the country until the signing of a Concordat with the Vatican in 1860. (The Vatican had previously refused to recognize the Haitian government.) The Concordat provided for the appointment of an archbishop in Port-au-Prince, designated dioceses, and established an annual government subsidy for the church. An amendment to the Concordat in 1862 assigned the Roman Catholic Church an important role in secular education.

The small number of priests and members of religious orders initially ministered mainly to the urban elite. Until the mid-twentieth century, the majority of priests were francophone Europeans, particularly Bretons, who were culturally distant from their rural parishioners. Roman Catholic clergy were generally hostile toward voodoo, and they led two major campaigns against the religion in 1896 and 1941. During these campaigns, the government outlawed voodoo services, and Catholics destroyed voodoo religious objects and persecuted practitioners. Roman Catholic clergy, however, have not been persistently militant in their opposition to voodoo, and they have had relatively little impact on the religious practices of the rural and the urban poor. The clergy have generally directed their energies more toward educating the urban population than toward eradicating voodoo. In the 1970s and the 1980s, the use of Creole and drum music became common in Roman Catholic services. Incorporating folk elements into the liturgy, however, did not mean that the Roman Catholic Church's attitude toward voodoo had changed.

Nationalists and others came to resent the Roman Catholic Church because of its European orientation and its alliance with the mulatto elite. François Duvalier opposed the church more than any other Haitian president. He expelled the archbishop of Port-au-Prince, the Jesuit order, and numerous priests between 1959 and 1961. In response to these moves, the Vatican excommunicated Duvalier. When relations with the church were restored in 1966, Duvalier prevailed. A Haitian archbishop was named for the first time, and the president gained the right to nominate bishops.

The mid-1980s marked a profound change in the church's stance on issues related to peasants and the urban poor. Reflecting this change was the statement by Pope John Paul II, during a visit to Haiti in 1983, that "things must change here" (see Jean-Claude Duvalier, 1971–86, ch. 6). Galvanized by the Vatican's concern, Roman Catholic clergy and lay workers called for improved human rights. Lay workers helped develop a peasant-community movement, especially at a center in the Plateau Central. The Roman Catholic radio station, Radio Soleil, played a key role in disseminating news about government actions during the 1985–86 crisis and encouraging opponents of the Duvalier government. The bishops, particularly in Jérémie and Cap-Haïtien, actively denounced Duvalierist repression and human-rights violations.

In the aftermath of Jean-Claude Duvalier's departure, the church took a less active role in Haiti's politics. The church hierarchy strongly supported the suppressed 1987 Constitution, which granted official status to Creole and guaranteed basic human rights, including the right to practice voodoo. The alliance with the lower classes left the Catholic Church with two unresolved problems in the late 1980s: its uneasy relationship with voodoo and its relationship to the more radical elements of the political movement that it had supported (see Interest Groups, ch. 9).

Protestantism

Protestantism has existed in Haiti since the earliest days of the republic. By the mid-nineteenth century, there were small numbers of Protestant missions, principally Baptist, Methodist, and Episcopalian. Protestant churches, mostly from North America, have sent many foreign missions to Haiti. Almost half of Haiti's Protestants were Baptists; Pentecostals were the second largest group. Many other denominations also were present, including Seventh Day Adventists, Mormons, and Presbyterians. Widespread Protestant proselytization began in the 1950s. Since the late 1950s, about 20 percent of the population has identified itself as Protestant. Protestantism has appealed mainly to the middle and the upper classes, and it played an important role in educational life.

Protestant churches focused their appeal on the lower classes long before the Roman Catholics did. Churches and clergy were found even in the smaller villages. Protestant clergy used Creole rather than French. Schools and clinics provided much-needed services. Protestant congregations encouraged baptisms and marriages and performed them free. For many Haitians, Protestantism represented an opposition to voodoo. When people converted to Protestantism, they usually did not reject voodoo, but they often came to view the folk religion as diabolical. Most Protestant denominations considered all *loua,* including family spirits, as demons. Some Haitians converted to Protestantism when they wanted to reject family spirits that they felt had failed to protect them. Others chose to become Protestants merely as a way to gain an alternative form of protection from misfortune.

François Duvalier, in his struggle with the Roman Catholic Church, welcomed Protestant missionaries, especially from the United States. Dependent on the government for their presence in Haiti, and competing with each other as well as with the Roman Catholics, Protestant missions generally accepted the policies of the Duvalier regimes. Numerous Protestant leaders did, however, join with Roman Catholics in their public opposition to the government during the waning days of Jean-Claude Duvalier's power.

Education

Haiti's postcolonial leaders promoted education, at least in principle. The 1805 constitution called for free and compulsory primary education. The early rulers, Henri (Henry) Christophe (1807–20) and Alexandre Pétion (1806–18), constructed schools; by 1820 there were nineteen primary schools and three secondary lycées. The Education Act of 1848 created rural primary schools with a more limited curriculum and established colleges of medicine and law. A comprehensive system was never developed, however, and the emerging elite who could afford the cost preferred to send their children to school in France. The signing of the Concordat with the Vatican in 1860 resulted in the arrival of clerical teachers, further emphasizing the influence of the Roman Catholic Church among the educated class. Roman Catholic schools essentially became nonsecular public schools, jointly funded by the Haitian government and the Vatican. The new teachers, mainly French clergy, promoted an attachment to France in their classrooms.

Clerical teachers concentrated on developing the urban elite, especially in the excellent new secondary schools. To their students, they emphasized the greatness of France, while they expounded on Haiti's backwardness and its lack of capacity for self-rule. Throughout the nineteenth century, only a few priests ventured to the rural areas to educate peasants. In both urban and rural settings, they followed a classical curriculum, which emphasized literature and rote learning. This curriculum remained unaltered until the 1980s, except during the United States occupation, when efforts were made to establish vocational schools. The elite resisted these efforts, and the government restored the old system in 1934.

Education in Haiti changed during the 1970s and the 1980s. Primary enrollments increased greatly, especially in urban areas. The Jean-Claude Duvalier regime initiated administrative and curriculum reforms. Nevertheless, as of 1982 about 65 percent of the population over ten years of age had received no education and only 8 percent was educated beyond the primary level.

Primary Schools

Primary education was compulsory in the late 1980s, but scarce government funds and a limited number of schools resulted in low enrollments in many rural areas. The school year began in October and ended in July, with two-week vacations at Christmas and Easter. Regular primary education consisted of six grades, preceded by two years of kindergarten (*enfantin*), which was heavily attended and which counted statistically in primary enrollments. Primary education consisted of preparatory, elementary, and intermediate cycles, each of which lasted two years. Promotion between grades depended on final examinations and on class marks recorded in trimesters. At the end of the sixth year, students who had passed their final examinations received a graduation certificate (*certificat d'études primaires*). After receiving the certificate, students could take examinations for entry into either secondary school or higher-primary school that led to an elementary certificate (*brevet élémentaire*) after three years. It was therefore possible for a student to take two years of kindergarten, six years of primary school, and three years of higher-primary studies for a total of eleven primary-school years. This primary-education system, however, was expected to change in the 1980s because of measures included in the 1978 Education Reform.

Primary-school enrollment was estimated at 642,000 in 1981, more than twice the official figure for 1970. According to the 1982 census, 40 percent of children in the six-year-old to eleven-year-old bracket were enrolled in school, compared with only 25 percent in 1971. Primary-school enrollment was 74 percent in metropolitan Port-au-Prince, but it was only 32 percent in rural areas. Most primary-school students were enrolled in private establishments in 1981, a reversal from the previous decade. An increase in the number of private primary schools accounted for the switch.

School nutrition programs, which increased about 12 percent annually between 1976 and 1984, contributed to increased primary-school enrollments. By 1986 about three out of four students received meals at school. The United States and Europe supported the meal programs through surplus commodities. Private development agencies also provided support. At the same time, a

Classroom, University of Haiti, Faculty of Medicine and Pharmacy, Port-au-Prince
Partially completed addition to an elementary school
Courtesy Inter-American Development Bank

number of private agencies, mostly from the United States, sponsored students in primary schools, helping to pay for tuition, books, and uniforms. By 1985 at least 75,000 primary students received such support. One-third of these students, however, were in Port-au-Prince. Enrollments of rural children continued to be low.

Dropout rates for primary students were high. According to some estimates for the mid-1980s, more than half of Haiti's urban primary-school students dropped out before completing the six-year primary cycle. In rural areas, the dropout rate was 80 percent. In addition, dropout and repetition rates in rural areas were so high that three of every five primary-school students were in either first or second grade.

There were more than 14,000 primary-school teachers in Haiti in the early 1980s; however, only about 40 percent of the public primary-school teachers and about 30 percent of those in private schools had a secondary-level or teacher training certificate. In 1979 public school teachers were earning US$100 a month—the same salary paid to teachers in 1905, when the profession was considered prestigious. Private school salaries were about 50 percent lower than those of public school teachers. The National Council of Government (Conseil National de Gouvernement—CNG), reacting to demonstrations by teachers, agreed to raise salaries in 1986. Private school teachers' salaries, however, remained low. Because of the low salaries, many teachers left the profession.

In the 1970s, the Haitian government, with support from the World Bank and the United Nations Educational, Scientific, and Cultural Organization (UNESCO), began to reform its educational system, mostly at the primary level. In 1978 the government unified educational administration for the first time by putting rural schools under the authority of the Department of National Education. Before 1978 rural schools had been administered by the Ministry of Agriculture and Natural Resources. The education reform also introduced a new structure for primary classes, established Creole as the language of instruction, and introduced new curricula and procedures for teacher certification. The new structure consisted of ten years of primary education in one four-year and two three-year cycles, followed by three years of secondary education. Promotion from first to second grade and from third to fourth grade was to be automatic in order to prevent large numbers of students from repeating grades and overloading the system at the lower grades. The new curriculum for first through fourth grades included three months of study skills and classes in reading, writing, mathematics, and environmental sciences.

Secondary Education

General secondary education consisted of a three-year basic cycle and a four-year upper cycle that led to a baccalaureate (*baccalauréat*) and possible university matriculation. The curriculum emphasized the classics and the arts to the detriment of the sciences. Despite these limitations, general secondary education was often of high quality. Secondary-school graduates usually qualified for admission to the University of Haiti or to institutions of higher learning abroad.

In 1981 there were 248 secondary-level schools in Haiti; 205 of them were private. Between 1974 and 1981, the number of private secondary schools almost tripled, while only two new public lycées were built. About 100,000 students attended these secondary schools, which employed 4,400 teachers. In addition to general secondary schools, several vocational and business schools existed, most of them in metropolitan Port-au-Prince.

Higher Education

Haiti's most important institution of higher education in the 1980s was the University of Haiti. Its origins date to the 1820s, when colleges of medicine and law were established. In 1942 the various faculties merged into the University of Haiti. After a student strike in 1960, the Duvalier government brought the university under firm government control and renamed it the State University. The government restored the original name in 1986.

In 1981 there were 4,099 students at the University of Haiti, of whom 26 percent were enrolled in the Faculty of Law and Economics; 25 percent, in the Faculty of Medicine and Pharmacy; 17 percent, in the Faculty of Administration and Management; and 11 percent, in the Faculty of Science and Topography. Despite the important role played by agriculture in the Haitian economy, only 5 percent of the university's students were enrolled in the Faculty of Agronomy and Veterinary Medicine. In 1981 the University of Haiti had 559 professors, compared with 207 in 1967. Most professors worked part time, were paid on an hourly basis, and had little time for contact with students. The University of Haiti also suffered severe shortages of books and other materials.

Two private post-secondary institutions were established in the 1980s—the Institut Universitaire Roi Christophe in Cap-Haïtien and the Institut International d'Etudes Universitaires in Port-au-Prince. Other private institutions of higher learning included a school of theology and law schools in Cap-Haïtien, Gonaïves, Les Cayes, Jérémie, and Fort Liberté. A business school, the Institut de Hautes Etudes Economiques et Commerciales, was established in Port-au-Prince in 1961. An engineering school, the Institut Supérieur Technique d'Haïti, was founded in Port-au-Prince in 1962. The Institut de Technique Electronique d'Haïti, also in Port-au-Prince, provided instruction in electrical engineering.

Health

Nutrition and Disease

In the mid-1980s, the Haitian government estimated that the average daily nutritional consumption level in the country was 1,901 calories per person, including 41.1 grams of protein. These figures represented 86 percent and 69 percent, respectively, of the World Health Organization's recommendations for adequate nutrition. In rural areas, the average person consumed about 1,300 calories, including 30 grams of protein per day. A national survey in 1978 showed that 77 percent of children in Haiti were malnourished. Anemia was also a common problem among children and women.

Infant and child health were poor. The infant mortality rate was 124 per 1,000 live births in 1983. A quarter of all registered deaths occurred among infants who were younger than one year old; half of all deaths occurred among children under five. Most of these deaths resulted from infectious diseases, especially diarrheal illnesses. Malnutrition and acute respiratory illness also presented serious problems for infants and children. For adults, malaria was among the more serious problems; some 85 percent of the population lived in malarial areas. Tuberculosis and parasitic infections continued to be serious health hazards, and typhoid fever was endemic. Poor sanitation contributed to poor health indicators. In 1984 less than 20 percent of the population had toilets or latrines. Only one-fourth of the rural population had access to potable water. Life expectancy at birth was forty-eight years in 1983, and the general mortality rate was 17 per 1,000 population.

Acquired Immune Deficiency Syndrome

In 1987 there were an estimated 1,500 people suffering from acquired immune deficiency syndrome (AIDS) in Haiti. Most of the cases were reported in Port-au-Prince. The earliest reported case of human immunodeficiency virus (HIV) infection was in 1978, and the earliest case of AIDS-related Karposi's sarcoma was in 1979. About two of every five AIDS patients in Haiti in 1987 were women. The exact number of people infected with HIV was unknown, but one sample of pregnant women in a poor neighborhood

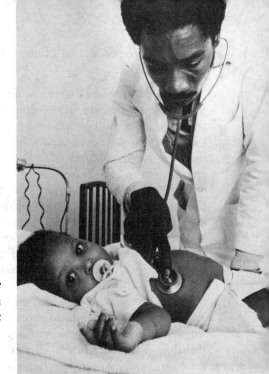

*Doctor examining infant,
Miragoâne
Courtesy Inter-American
Development Bank*

of the capital revealed that 8 percent tested positive for the virus. Most people infected with HIV appear to have contracted the virus through heterosexual intercourse. Transfusions of infected blood also were responsible for transmitting the virus to large numbers of people, especially women, who routinely received blood after childbirth. The Haitian Red Cross did not begin screening the blood supply in Port-au-Prince for HIV until 1986. Blood supplies outside the capital continued to be unscreened in the late 1980s. The use of contaminated needles accounted for 5 percent of the country's AIDS cases.

Homosexual activity has contributed to the spread of AIDS in Haiti. AIDS transmission was also related to female and male prostitution. At least 50 percent of the female prostitutes in the capital city's main prostitution center were believed to be infected with HIV.

Because of the prevalence of AIDS in the Haitian immigrant population, the United States Centers for Disease Control classified Haitians as a high-risk group for the disease in 1982. It rescinded the classification in 1985, however. Early studies suggested that Haiti might have been the origin of the disease. By the late 1980s, most AIDS researchers in Haiti claimed that male homosexual tourists brought the disease to the country in the late 1970s.

Health Services

Modern health services were inadequate in the late 1980s. In

275

1982 the country had 810 physicians, 83 dentists, 758 nurses, 1,564 auxiliary nurses, and 403 health agents. Haiti had about one doctor for every 6,600 people and one nurse for every 8,000 people. Health services were concentrated in the capital area. Thus, in the most poorly served area of the country, there was only one physician for every 21,000 people. In the mid-1980s, there were thirty-eight hospitals in the country, more than half of which were in the Port-au-Prince area. Nongovernmental organizations provided almost half of the health services in the country in the late 1980s.

Most Haitians continued to meet their health-care needs through traditional remedies. Herbal medicine was widely used, especially in rural areas, although environmental deterioration made some herbs more difficult to obtain. In addition to home remedies, herbal specialists (*doktè fey*) provided massage and herbal remedies. Many voodoo specialists were also experts in herbal remedies. Traditional midwives assisted at most rural births. Many midwives received training in modern methods from the government. Traditional religion, used by many to diagnose and treat illnesses, has served well in some cases when modern medicine was not available.

Welfare

In the 1980s, public assistance continued to be limited. The government provided pensions to some retired public officials and military officers, but it did not guarantee them to civil servants. A social-insurance system for employees of industrial, commercial, and agricultural firms provided pensions at age fifty-five, after twenty years of service, and compensation for total incapacity, after fifteen years of service. A system of work-injury benefits also covered private and public employees, providing partial or total disability compensation. These programs were administered by the Ministry of Social Affairs. In general, however, the dearth of social programs offered by the government forced most Haitians to rely mainly on their families and on the services provided by nongovernmental organizations. As has been true in so many other areas of life, Haitians have cultivated self-reliance in the face of hardship, scarcity, and the inadequacy of existing institutions.

* * *

Among works on Haitian society in English, James G. Leyburn's *The Haitian People* continues to be a useful overview. The introduction, by Sidney Mintz, to the second edition is one of the most lucid analyses of the Duvalier regimes. Another classic is Melville J. Herskovits's ethnography, *Life in a Haitian Valley*, detailing the life of peasants and townspeople in the 1930s. More recent analyses of Haitian society and economics include Mats Lundahl's *Peasants and Poverty: A Study of Haiti,* which views Haitian economic decline in terms of overpopulation, environmental degradation, and governmental passivity over the course of Haiti's history. A contrasting analysis can be found in Alex Dupuy's *Haiti in the World Economy: Class, Race, and Underdevelopment since 1970,* which examines the country's social and economic problems primarily in terms of Haiti's relations with foreign powers.

The volume of essays edited by Charles R. Foster and Albert Valdman, *Haiti—Today and Tomorrow: An Interdisciplinary Study,* provides a useful discussion of many aspects of Haitian society in the 1980s, including issues of language, education, religion, cultural orientation, male-female relationships, migration, and the economy. Simon Fass's *Political Economy in Haiti: The Drama of Survival* is the first detailed examination of the urban lower class. The work of David Nicholls, especially his *From Dessalines to Duvalier: Race, Colour, and National Independence in Haiti,* provides an analysis of political and social ideologies through the course of Haitian history. For an overview of Haitian immigrants in the United States, the chapter on Haitians in David W. Haines's *Refugees in the United States: A Reference Handbook* is helpful. (For further information and complete citations, see Bibliography.)

Chapter 8. Haiti: The Economy

Figure from a painting by Prosper Pierrelouis

HAITI'S LOW-INCOME, PEASANT-BASED economy faced serious economic and ecological obstacles to development in the late 1980s. The country's gross domestic product (GDP—see Glossary) in 1987 was approximately US$1.95 billion, or about US$330 per capita, ranking Haiti as the poorest country in the Western Hemisphere and as the twenty-seventh most impoverished nation in the world. The only low-income country—defined by the World Bank (see Glossary) as a country with a per capita GDP in 1988 below US$425—in the Americas, Haiti fell even farther behind other low-income countries in Africa and Asia during the 1980s.

Haiti's economy continued to be fundamentally agricultural in the 1980s, although agriculture's role in the economy—as measured by its share of GDP, the labor force, and exports—had fallen sharply after 1950. Highly inefficient exploitation of the scarce natural resources of the countryside caused severe deforestation and soil erosion and constituted the primary cause of the decline in agricultural productivity. Manufacturing became the most dynamic sector in Haiti during the 1970s, as the country's abundant supply of low-cost labor stimulated the growth of assembly operations. Services such as banking, tourism, and transportation played comparatively minor roles in the economy. Tourism, a potential source of foreign-exchange earnings, expanded rapidly in the 1970s, but it contracted during the 1980s as a consequence of political upheaval and news coverage that erroneously identified Haiti as the origin of acquired immune deficiency syndrome (AIDS—see Fertility and Family Planning, ch. 7).

Haiti's agricultural wealth, coveted by many in colonial times, had waned by the mid-nineteenth century as land reform divided the island's plantations into small plots farmed by emancipated slaves. Changes in land tenure contributed significantly to falling agricultural output, but the failure of Haiti's leaders to manage the economy also contributed to the country's long-term impoverishment. Haiti's economy reflected the cleavages (i.e., rural-urban, black-mulatto, poor-rich, Creole-French, traditional-modern) that defined Haitian society (see Social Structure, ch. 7). The mulatto elite dominated the capital, showed little interest in the countryside, and had outright disdain for the black peasantry. Disparities between rural and urban dwellers worsened during the twentieth century under the dynastic rule of François Duvalier (1957–71) and his son, Jean-Claude Duvalier (1971–86); Haiti's tradition of corruption reached new heights as government funds that could have aided economic and social development enriched the Duvaliers and their associates. By the 1980s, an estimated 1 percent of the population received 45 percent of the national income, and an estimated 200 millionaires in Haiti enjoyed a life of unparalleled extravagance. In stark contrast, as many as three of every four Haitians lived in abject poverty, with incomes well below US$150, according to the World Bank. Similarly, virtually every social indicator pointed to ubiquitous destitution.

As a result of the traditional passivity of the government and the country's dire poverty, Haiti has depended extensively, since the mid-1970s, on foreign development aid for budget support. The United States has been the largest donor, but it has frequently interrupted the flow of aid because of alleged human rights abuses, corruption, and election fraud. Most other development agencies have followed the United States lead, thus extending United States influence over events in Haiti (see Foreign Relations, ch. 9). Although the major multilateral and bilateral development agencies have provided the bulk of foreign funding, hundreds of nongovernmental organizations have also played a prominent role in development assistance. These nongovernmental organizations, afiliated for the most part with religious groups, have sustained hundreds of thousands of Haitians through countrywide feeding stations. They also contributed to the country's political upheaval in 1986 by underscoring the Duvalier regime's neglect of social programs. The accomplishments of the nongovernmental organizations have proved that concerted efforts at economic development could achieve results in Haiti.

The prospects for development improved temporarily following Jean-Claude Duvalier's February 1986 departure; some important economic reforms took place, and the economy began to grow. Subsequently, however, renewed political instability forestalled continued reform. Economic progress was feasible, but entrenched political and social obstacles prevented Haiti from reaching that goal.

Growth and Structure of the Economy

After Christopher Columbus's discovery of Hispaniola (La Isla Española) in 1492, Spanish mercantilists generally neglected the island and instead focused their endeavors on the more richly endowed areas of Mexico and Peru (see Spanish Discovery and Colonization, ch. 6). In 1664 France successfully converted the western third of Hispaniola into an unofficial territory; over the next 140 years, French colonialists transformed the colony of Saint-Domingue into a slave-based plantation economy known as the "pearl of the Antilles." By the late eighteenth century, Saint-Domingue boasted thousands of profitable plantations: 800 produced sugar; 3,000, coffee; 800, cotton; and nearly 3,000, indigo. Haiti became France's most lucrative overseas possession. In his classic 1776 publication, *The Wealth of Nations,* economist Adam Smith declared Saint-Domingue "the most important of the sugar colonies of the West Indies."

The Haitian Revolution (1791–1803) devastated agricultural output. The leadership of the new nation faced the daunting task of reviving economic activity without relying on slavery. After the 1806 assassination of Haiti's first national leader, Jean-Jacques Dessalines, Haiti operated under a dual economy, with forced labor on large plantations in the north and small-scale farming in partitioned land in the south. The 1820 unification of the nation entailed the abandonment of plantation agriculture and the establishment of a peasant-based agricultural economy (see Boyer: Expansion and Decline, ch. 6). Although policies of land redistribution and limited social and economic reform improved the lives of the former slaves, the policies also produced a severe and ultimately irreversible decline in agricultural production.

Successive Haitian presidents gave priority to self-enrichment and to the payment of a controversial debt with France, which left little capital for improving the standard of living. The rigid social stratification and the political disparity between mulattoes and blacks further widened the gap between the rich elite and the poor.

The nineteen-year United States occupation of Haiti (1915–34) brought unquestionable economic benefits. United States administrators controlled fiscal and monetary policy largely to the country's benefit. The United States military built major roads, introduced automatic telephones in Port-au-Prince, constructed bridges, dredged harbors, erected schools, established clinics, and undertook other previously neglected public works. The troops departed in 1934, but economic advisers remained in Haiti to manage the national treasury until 1941. The Haitian economy enjoyed some growth in the 1940s and the early 1950s, partly because of improvements in the country's infrastructure, but mostly because of improved prices for its exports.

François Duvalier fashioned the modern Haitian economy into a system dominated by personal patronage, institutionalized corruption, and internal security concerns. Bent on retaining power at all costs, Duvalier heavily taxed the citizenry to finance the military, the paramilitary security forces known as the *tonton makouts,* and his family's vast expenses. His subordinates, from cabinet ministers to rural section chiefs (*chefs de section*), followed Duvalier's example, essentially plundering the peasantry at every level of the economy. The most notorious example of Duvalier's overt corruption was his administration of a tax agency, the Régie du Tabac (Tobacco Administration), for which no accounting records were kept. Although he proclaimed himself a champion of black nationalism, Duvalier almost completely ignored the impoverished rural black population in his government expenditures. As a result, many Haitians—rich, poor, educated, and uneducated—left the countryside or fled the country altogether. "Brain drain" became a serious problem. In 1969, for example, some observers believed that there were more Haitian health professionals in Montreal than in all of Haiti.

Overall, Duvalier's policies had no positive effect in Haiti. According to the United Nations (UN), Haiti was the only country in the world that did not experience real economic growth for most of the 1950s and the 1960s, a period when the world economy expanded at its most rapid rate in history.

During the 1970s, Haiti enjoyed a 5 percent annual economic growth rate as foreign aid, overseas investment, and higher commodity prices buoyed the economy. A key factor in this growth was the 1973 renewal of foreign aid from the United States and other donors after a ten-year suspension. The rapid development of assembly manufacturing that began in the late 1960s also stimulated economic expansion. Higher prices for coffee, sugar, cocoa, and essential oils boosted previously depressed cash-crop production. Infrastructure development proceeded, construction boomed, banking prospered, and tourist arrivals more than doubled. Haiti modernized considerably, especially in Port-au-Prince and the major provincial cities. Agriculture stagnated, however, and per capita food production in real terms continued to decline. Jean-Claude Duvalier showed some interest in developing the nonagricultural sectors of the economy during his regime, and the state slowly expanded its role.

Haiti's fortunes soured in the 1980s, as real economic growth declined by 2.5 percent a year from 1980 to 1985. Inflation rose over the same period from 6 to 8 percent, and official unemployment jumped from 22 percent to more than 30 percent. After an interval of positive growth in 1986 and 1987, the negative growth trend continued in 1988, when the economy contracted by 5 percent. Although the country's poor performance in the 1980s to some extent reflected hemispheric trends, Haiti faced its own peculiar obstacles, many of which stemmed from decades of government indifference to economic development. Uneven foreign aid flows, resulting from disputes over human rights violations and a lack of progress toward democracy, hampered government spending. Worsening ecological problems hindered agricultural development, and tourist arrivals plummeted because of negative media coverage of the island's political situation and the high incidence of AIDS among Haitians.

The most fundamental problems of the Haitian economy, however, were economic mismanagement and corruption. More avaricious than his father, Jean-Claude Duvalier overstepped even the traditionally accepted boundaries of Haitian corruption. Duvalierists under Jean-Claude engaged in, among other activities, drug trafficking, pilferage of development and food aid, illegal resale and export of subsidized oil, fraudulent lotteries, export of cadavers and blood plasma, manipulation of government contracts, tampering with pension funds, and skimming of budgeted funds. As a result, the president for life and his wife lived luxuriously, in stark contrast to the absolute poverty of most Haitians. Allegations of official corruption surfaced when Duvalier appointed a former World Bank official, Marc Bazin, to the post of finance minister in 1982. Bazin sought to investigate corruption and to reform fiscal accounting practices in connection with a 1981 International Monetary Fund (IMF—see Glossary) economic stabilization agreement. More zealous than Duvalier had anticipated, Bazin documented case after case of corruption, determined that at least 36 percent of government revenue was embezzled, and declared the country the "most mismanaged in the region." Although quickly replaced, Bazin gave credence to foreign complaints of corruption, such as that contained in a 1982 report by the Canadian government that deemed Duvalier's Haiti a kleptocracy.

After the fall of Duvalier, the provisional National Council of Governmentz (Conseil National de Gouvernement—CNG) enacted numerous policy reforms mandated by structural adjustment lending programs from the IMF and the World Bank. These reforms included the privatization of unprofitable state-owned enterprises, trade liberalization, and export promotion. The CNG, however, never fully implemented the economic reforms because of nagging political instability (see Background: From Duvalier to Avril, 1957–89, ch. 9). At the close of the decade, the economic direction of the military government, led by Lieutenant General Prosper Avril, remained unclear.

Economic Policy

Fiscal Policy

Despite irregularities in the allocation of funds under the François Duvalier regime, government revenues traditionally equaled, or surpassed, budget outlays, technically yielding balanced budgets. Jean-Claude Duvalier's unprecedented intervention in the economy in the 1980s, however, broke this tradition. The public sector under Duvalier established, or expanded, its ownership of an international fishing fleet, a flour mill, a cement company, a vegetable-oil processing plant, and two sugar factories. Duvalierist officials based these investment decisions primarily on the amount of personal profit that would accrue to themselves, to Duvalier, and to the rest of his coterie. They ignored the potential negative impact on the economy. Poorly managed, the state's newly acquired enterprises drained fiscal accounts, causing the overall public-sector deficit to reach 10.6 percent of GDP in fiscal year (FY—see Glossary) 1985, despite sharp reductions in spending on already meager social programs in accordance with an IMF stabilization program. In July 1986, the Ministry of Finance, under the CNG, revamped fiscal policies through tax reform, privatization, and revisions of the tariff code. Although the CNG greatly increased spending on health and education, the reform measures served to lower the government's deficit to 7 percent of GDP by FY 1987. General Avril's FY 1989 budget attempted further to curtail deficit spending, but that prospect remained unlikely without stable flows of economic assistance.

Expenditures

The misallocation of public revenues for private use and the low government allocations for economic and social development have contributed directly to Haiti's extreme poverty. After 1986, national budgets included a significantly larger portion for development efforts, but they continued to allocate the largest share—17 percent in FY 1987-88—to the armed forces and internal security forces (see Military Spending and Foreign Assistance, ch. 10). About 57 percent of FY 1988 expenditures were for wages and salaries; 26 percent, for goods and services; 10 percent, for interest payments; 4 percent, for extrabudgetary spending; and 3 percent, for transfers and subsidies. Compared with previous budgets in the 1980s, this budget included increased spending on wages and interest payments and decreased spending on goods and services, as well as an allocation for unspecified expenses. The FY 1989 budget continued these fiscal trends. The leading expenditure items in the FY 1989 budget were defense (16.4 percent), debt payments (15.8 percent), education (14.5 percent), health and social services (13.7 percent), and finance, public service, and commerce (12.4 percent). According to some reports, however, discrepancies existed between budget allocations and actual disbursements.

Revenues

The structure of government revenues changed distinctly as a consequence of the tax and tariff revisions of 1986. Haiti's taxes and tariffs historically exacted revenues from directly productive activities—mainly agriculture—and from international trade. This revenue structure eventually created disincentives for the production of cash crops and other export products, while it stimulated the development of uncompetitive industries. Over time, Haiti's authorities created a public-finance pattern that, when combined with a highly regressive income tax, raised approximately 85 percent of its revenue from the rural population, but spent only about 20 percent on those same taxpayers.

A 10 percent value-added tax was introduced in 1983, but it was not until 1986 that tax and tariff reforms began to shift the source of revenues. New tax laws simplified the income-tax process, altered tax brackets, and strengthened tax-collection efforts. In the area of trade regulations, the new government phased out export taxes and replaced quantitative restrictions on all but five goods with ad valorem tariffs of a maximum of 40 percent, thus essentially lowering import protection and liberalizing trade. As a result of these policies, revenues derived from international trade dropped from 35 percent in FY 1984 to an estimated 22 percent in FY 1989; the revenue balance in both years was derived from internal taxes.

Monetary and Exchange-Rate Policies

The Bank of the Republic of Haiti (Banque de la République d'Haïti—BRH) represented one of the few well-established, public-sector institutions dedicated to economic management. Founded in 1880 as the National Bank of Haiti, the BRH—a commercial bank—did not begin to act as a central bank until 1934, when it became known as the National Republic Bank of Haiti. Since the 1930s, the bank has performed the functions of a central bank, a commercial bank, and a development-finance institution; it also has been involved in other matters, such as the management of the Port-au-Prince wharf. As a central bank, the BRH also issued Haiti's national currency, the gourde (G; for value of gourde— see Glossary).

On August 17, 1979, new banking laws gave the BRH its present name and empowered it with the monetary-management responsibilities associated with most central banks. The BRH subsequently became actively involved in controlling credit, setting interest rates, assessing reserve ratios, and restraining inflation. In the late 1980s, the BRH pursued generally conservative monetary policies, and it employed high cash-reserve ratios in commercial banks as the key policy tool to regulate the money supply. In an effort to increase the dynamism of the economy, the BRH sought to inject more credit into the private sector, particularly for long-term uses.

Since 1919 the Haitian currency has been pegged to the United States currency at the rate of five gourdes to the dollar. Since that same date, the United States dollar has served as legal tender on the island and has circulated freely. Remarkably, the value of Haiti's fixed exchange rate remained strong for decades; it fluctuated only with the movements of the currency of the United States, its main trading partner. Until the 1980s, no black market existed for gourdes, but unusually high inflation and large budget deficits eroded their value and brought premiums of up to 25 percent for black-market transactions in the early 1980s. The black market subsided considerably in the late 1980s, but the gourde's real rate of exchange remained above the 1980 level.

Labor

Haiti's 1989 labor force was estimated at 2.8 million people. The economically active population (those over age ten), however, represented more than half of the country's total 6.1 million population. Forty-two percent of the official work force was female, ranking the country's female participation as one of the highest among developing countries. In rural areas, however, the role of women in production and commerce was apparently much greater than these statistics indicated (see Gender Roles and Family Life, ch. 7).

The distribution of the labor force by economic sector from 1950 to 1987 reflected a shift from agriculture to services, with some growth in industry. Despite these changes, agriculture continued to dominate economic activity in the 1980s, employing 66 percent of the labor force; it was followed by services, 24 percent, and industry, 10 percent. Based on these figures, Haiti continued to be the most agrarian, and the least industrial, society in the Western Hemisphere. The country's employment of only 50,000 salaried workers in 1988 was further evidence of the traditional character of the work force (see fig. 13).

Statistics on employment and the methodologies used to gather such data varied widely; most unemployment figures were only estimates. In 1987 the United States Department of Labor estimated that Haiti's unemployment rate was 49 percent. Other estimates ranged from 30 to 70 percent. Official unemployment was severe in Port-au-Prince, but comparatively low in rural areas, reflecting urban migration trends, rapid population growth, and the low number of skilled and semi-skilled workers.

Haiti established a labor code in 1961, but revised it in March 1984 to bring legislation more in line with standards set by the International Labour Office (ILO). Conformity with ILO guidelines was a prerequisite for certification under the Caribbean Basin Initiative (CBI—see Appendix B) enacted by the United States Congress in 1983.

Haiti's most fundamental labor law, the minimum wage, was also the most controversial. Low wage rates attracted foreign assembly operations. In 1989 the average minimum wage stood at the equivalent of US$3 a day, with some small variations for different types of assembly work. The minimum wage in the late 1980s was below the 1970 level in real terms, but assembly manufacturers and government officials refused to increase wages because they needed to remain competitive with other Caribbean countries. Labor laws included an array of provisions protecting workers in the areas of overtime, holidays, night-shift work, and sick leave. The government, however, did not universally enforce many of these provisions. The greatest number of workers' complaints came from assembly plants where seasonal layoffs were common.

The organized-labor movement, generally suppressed under the Duvaliers, grew rapidly in the wake of the dynasty's collapse. Three major trade unions dominated organized-labor activity in the 1980s. The newest of these three was the Federation of Union Workers (Fédération des Ouvriers Syndiqués—FOS). Established in 1983 after negotiations over the CBI opened the way for public labor organization, the FOS by 1987 represented forty-four member unions, nineteen of which were registered with the government. Its combined membership in Port-au-Prince and Les Cayes totaled approximately 15,000. Politically moderate, the FOS was affiliated with the American Federation of Labor-Congress of Industrial Organizations (AFL-CIO) and with the International Confederation of Free Trade Unions in Brussels. The oldest union of influence, the Autonomous Federation of Haitian Workers/Federation of Latin American Workers (Centrale Autonome des Travailleurs Haïtiens/Centrale Latino-Américaine des Travailleurs—CATH/CLAT), was affiliated with the Latin American trade-union movement and shared its history of political activism. CATH/CLAT consisted of 150 unions, including 63 that were registered with the

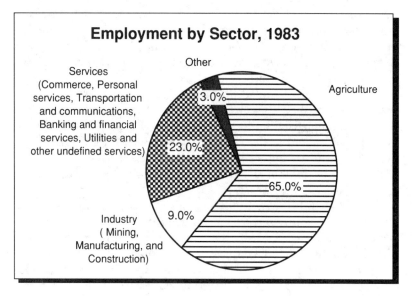

Source: Based on information from International Labour Office, *Yearbook of Labor Statistics, 1987*, Geneva, section 3B.

Figure 13. Haiti: Employment by Sector, 1983

government. It professed a membership of 7,000. Haiti's third principal union, the CATH, had splintered from CATH/CLAT in 1980; it had managed to take with it forty-four member unions, all recognized by the state. CATH claimed a membership of 5,000. CATH and CATH/CLAT primarily represented assembly workers. The Ministry of Social Affairs registered only unions and not individual members; this practice allowed unions to exaggerate their membership, which probably amounted to fewer than 5,000 by 1987. By the end of the decade, trade unions had made only small organizational inroads among assembly workers; the role of union activity in that sector was the central point of debate in the organized-labor movement.

Agriculture

Agriculture continued to be the mainstay of the economy in the late 1980s; it employed approximately 66 percent of the labor force and accounted for about 35 percent of GDP and for 24 percent of exports in 1987 (see fig. 14). The role of agriculture in the economy has declined severely since the 1950s, when the sector employed 80 percent of the labor force, represented 50 percent of GDP, and contributed 90 percent of exports. Many factors have contributed to this decline. Some of the major ones included the continuing fragmentation of landholdings, low levels of agricultural technology, migration out of rural areas, insecure land tenure, a lack of capital investment, high commodity taxes, the low productivity of undernourished farmers, animal and plant diseases, and inadequate infrastructure. Neither the government nor the private sector invested much in rural ventures; in FY 1989 only 5 percent of the national budget went to the Ministry of Agriculture, Natural Resources, and Rural Development (Ministère de l'Agriculture, des Resources Naturelles et du Développement Rural—MARNDR). As Haiti entered the 1990s, however, the main challenge to agriculture was not economic, but ecological. Extreme deforestation, soil erosion, droughts, flooding, and the ravages of other natural disasters had all led to a critical environmental situation.

Land Tenure and Land Policy

After independence from France, Alexandre Pétion (and later Jean-Pierre Boyer) undertook Latin America's first, and perhaps most radical, land reform by subdividing plantations for the use of emancipated slaves (see Christophe's Kingdom and Pétion's Republic, ch. 6). The reform measures were so extensive that by 1842 no plantation was its original size. By the mid-nineteenth century, therefore, Haiti's present-day land structure was largely in place. The basic structures of land tenure remained remarkably stable during the twentieth century, despite steadily increasing pressure for land, the fragmentation of land parcels, and a slight increase in the concentration of ownership.

For historical reasons, Haiti's patterns of land tenure were quite different from those of other countries in Latin America and the Caribbean. Most Haitians owned at least some of their land. Complex forms of tenancy also distinguished Haitian land tenure. Moreover, land owned by peasants often varied in the size and number of plots, the location and topography of the parcels, and other factors.

Scholars have debated issues related to land tenure and agriculture in Haiti because they considered census data unreliable. Other primary data available to them were geographically limited and frequently out of date. The three national censuses of 1950, 1971, and 1982 provided core information on land tenure, but other studies financed by the United States Agency for International Development (AID) supplemented and updated census data. The final tabulations of the 1982 census were still unavailable in late 1989.

The 1971 census revealed that there were 616,700 farms in Haiti, and that an average holding of 1.4 hectares consisted of several

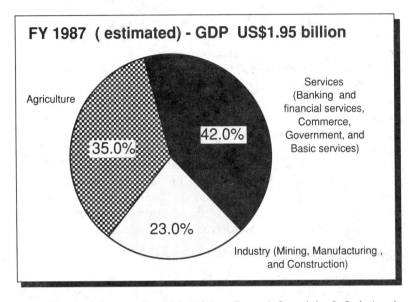

FY 1987 (estimated) - GDP US$1.95 billion

Agriculture

35.0%

42.0%

23.0%

Services (Banking and financial services, Commerce, Government, and Basic services)

Industry (Mining, Manufacturing , and Construction)

Source: Based on information from United Nations, Economic Commission for Latin America and the Caribbean, *Estudio Económico de América Latina y el Caribe, 1987: Haiti*,
Santiago, Chile, 1988; and Economist Intelligence Unit, *Country Report: Cuba, Dominican Republic, Haiti, Puerto Rico*, No. 2, London, 1989, 4.

*Figure 14. Haiti: Estimated Gross Domestic Product (GDP) by Sector,
Fiscal Year (FY) 1987*

and that an average holding of 1.4 hectares consisted of several
plots of less than 1 hectare. Haitians, however, most commonly
measured their land by the common standard, a *carreau*, equal to
about 3.3 hectares. The survey concluded that the largest farms
made up only 3 percent of the total number of farms and that they
comprised less than 20 percent of the total land. It also documented that 60 percent of farmers owned their land, although some
lacked official title to it. Twenty-eight percent of all farmers rented and sharecropped land. Only a small percentage of farms belonged to cooperatives. The 1950 census, by contrast, had found
that 85 percent of farmers owned their land.

Studies in the 1980s indicated a trend toward increased fragmentation of peasant lands, an expanding role for sharecropping and
renting, and a growing concentration of higher-quality land, particularly in the irrigated plains. As a consequence of high rural
population density and deteriorating soils, competition over land
appeared to be intensifying. Haiti's land density, that is, the number
of people per square kilometer of arable land, jumped from 296

in 1965 to 408 by the mid-1980s—a density greater than that in India (see Demographic Profile, ch. 7).

The three major forms of land tenancy in Haiti were ownership, renting (or subleasing), and sharecropping. Smallholders typically acquired their land through purchase, inheritance, or a claim of long-term use. Many farmers also rented land temporarily from the state, absentee landlords, local owners, or relatives. In turn, renters frequently subleased some of these lands, particularly parcels owned by the state. Renters generally enjoyed more rights to the land they worked than did sharecroppers. Unlike sharecroppers, however, renters had to pay for land in advance, typically for a period of one year. The prevalence of renting made the land market exceedingly dynamic; even small farmers rented land, depending on the amount of extra income they derived from raising cash crops. Sharecropping, also very common, was usually a shorter-term agreement, perhaps lasting only one growing season. Sharecropper and landowner partnerships were less exploitive than those in many other Latin American countries; in most agreements, farmers gave landowners half the goods they produced on the land.

Other land arrangements included managing land for absentee landlords, squatting, and wage labor. The practice of having an on-site overseer (*jéran*) manage land for another owner, usually another peasant residing far away, was a variation of sharecropping. *Jérans* were generally paid in-kind for their custodial services. Overgrazing, or unregulated gardening, was the most common form of squatting, which took place on most kinds of lands, especially state-owned land. A small minority of peasants were landless; they worked as day laborers or leased subsistence plots. In addition, thousands of Haitians migrated seasonally to the Dominican Republic as braceros (temporary laborers) to cut sugarcane under wretched conditions.

Land Use and Farming Technology

It is difficult to understand the complex variations in land tenancy without an appreciation of land use and peasant attitudes toward land. More mountainous than Switzerland, Haiti has a limited amount of cultivable land. According to soil surveys by the United States Department of Agriculture in the early 1980s, 11.3 percent of the land was highly suitable for crops, while 31.7 percent was suitable with some restrictions related to erosion, topography, or conservation. The surveys revealed that 2.3 percent was mediocre because of poor drainage, but was acceptable for rice cultivation, and 54.7 percent was appropriate only for tree crops or pastures because of severe erosion or steep slopes. According to

293

estimates of land use in 1978, 42.2 percent of land was under constant or shifting cultivation, 19.2 percent was pasture land, and 38.6 percent was not cultivated.

The use of purchased inputs, such as fertilizers, pesticides, machinery, and irrigation, was rare; farmers in Haiti employed traditional agricultural practices more than did farmers in any other part of the Western Hemisphere. Although Haitian farmers used increased amounts of chemical fertilizers in the 1970s and the 1980s, their use of an average of only seven kilograms per hectare ranked Haiti ahead only of Bolivia among Western Hemisphere countries. Peasants applied mostly natural fertilizers, such as manure, mulch, and bat guano. Large landowners consumed most of the country's small amounts of chemical fertilizers, and they benefited from subsidized fertilizers imported from the Dominican Republic and mixed in Port-au-Prince. Five importers controlled the 400,000 kilograms of pesticides that entered the country each year; malaria-carrying mosquitoes and rodents in the rice fields were the main targets of pesticide application. Most rural cultivators used small hand tools, such as hoes, machetes, digging sticks, and a local machete-like tool called the *serpette.* There was an average of one tractor per 1,700 hectares; most farmers considered such machinery inappropriate for use on tiny plots scattered along deeply graded hillsides. The insecurity of land tenure further discouraged the use of capital inputs.

The amount of irrigated crop land in the 1980s, estimated at between 70,000 and 110,00 hectares, was substantially less than the 140,000 hectares of colonial times. Of the nearly 130 irrigation systems in place, many lacked adequate maintenance, were clogged with silt, or provided irregular supplies to their 80,000 users. By the 1980s, the irrigation network had been extended as far as was possible.

The minimal amount of research on agriculture and the limited number of extension officers that MARNDR provided gave little assistance to already low levels of farming technology. Foreign organizations, such as the Inter-American Institute for Cooperation in Agriculture, carried out the most research. Foreign organizations also provided more technical assistance in agriculture than the government.

Peasant attitudes and limited access to credit also helped to explain the traditional nature of farming. Most observers blamed agricultural underdevelopment on peasants' individualistic nature, their proclivity toward superstition, and their unwillingness to innovate (see Social Structure, ch. 7). Small farmers also lacked access to credit. Informal credit markets flourished, but credit was not always available at planting time. When credit was available, it was usually provided at usurious rates. The country's major public financial institutions provided loans to the agricultural sector, but this lending benefited less than 10 percent of all farmers. Major credit sources included the Agricultural Credit Bureau, agriculture credit societies, credit unions, cooperatives, and institutions created by nongovernmental organizations.

Crops

Cash Crops

Despite its relative decline, coffee endured as the leading agricultural export during the 1980s. The French had introduced coffee to Haiti from Martinique in 1726, and soon coffee became an important colonial commodity. Coffee production peaked in 1790, and it declined steadily after independence. Production dropped precipitously during the 1960s. After a boom in prices and in the production of coffee in the late 1970s, output declined again from 42,900 tons in 1980 to 30,088 tons by 1987. Coffee trees covered an estimated 133,000 hectares in the 1980s, with an average annual yield of 35,900 tons. Haiti was a member of the International Coffee Organization (ICO), but found itself increasingly unable to fulfill its ICO export quota, which stood at 300,000 bags, of 60 kilograms each, in 1988. Most analysts believed that excessive taxation and the low prices afforded to peasant farmers had contributed to the decline in coffee production.

Coffee provides one of the best examples of the market orientation of Haiti's peasant economy. Most peasants grew coffee, usually alongside other crops. More than 1 million Haitians participated in the coffee industry as growers, marketers (known as Madame Sarahs), middlemen (*spéculateurs*), or exporters. The peasants' widespread participation throughout the coffee industry demonstrated that they were not merely subsistence farmers, but that they were also actively engaged in the market economy. After harvest by peasants, female Madame Sarahs transported coffee to local and urban markets and sold the beans. Middlemen, in turn, sold coffee to members of the Coffee Exporters Association (Association des Exportateurs de Café—Asdec), which set prices and thereby passed on the traditionally high coffee-export taxes directly to producers. Because of its prominent role in agriculture and the inequitable nature of the trade, the coffee industry was the subject of numerous studies. The majority of these studies highlighted imperfect competition and the systematic enrichment of a small group of Port-au-Prince exporters.

Sugar was another cash crop with a long history in Haiti. Columbus brought sugarcane to present-day Haiti on his second voyage to Hispaniola, and sugar rapidly became the colony's most important cash crop. After 1804, production never returned to preindependence levels, but sugar production and low-level exports continued. Unlike the system in other Caribbean countries, sugar in Haiti was a cash crop raised by peasants rather than by large-scale plantations. The sugar harvest dipped to under 4 million tons by the early 1970s, but it rebounded to nearly 6 million tons of cane by the middle of the decade with a sharp increase in the world price of the commodity. Lower world prices and structural problems combined to cause a drop in sugar output in the 1980s; by the end of the decade, sugarcane covered fewer than 114,000 hectares of the coastal plains, and it yielded fewer than 4.5 million tons annually.

Further expansion of the sugar industry faced serious deep-rooted obstacles. For example, the production cost of Haitian sugar was three times more than the world price in the 1980s. Shifts in the world sugar market, caused mainly by the international substitution of corn-based fructose for sugarcane, exerted further pressure on Haitian producers. One result of this situation was the practice of importing sugar, which was then re-exported to the United States under the Haitian sugar quota. Reductions in Haiti's quota during the 1980s, however, limited exchanges of this sort.

Total sugar exports dropped from 19,200 tons in 1980 to 6,500 tons in 1987. In 1981, 1982, and 1988, Haiti exported no sugar. Haiti's four sugar mills closed temporarily on several occasions during the decade (see Manufacturing, this ch.). The oldest mill, the Haitian American Sugar Company (HASCO), was the only plant that maintained a large cane plantation. Realizing the dim future for sugar, outside development agencies proposed alternatives to sugar, such as soybeans, for Haiti's plains.

Cocoa, sisal, essential oils, and cotton were other significant cash crops. Cacao trees covered an estimated 10,400 hectares in 1987, and they yielded 4,000 tons of cocoa a year. Mennonite missionaries played a growing role in the cocoa industry, mostly around southern departments, especially Grande'Anse (see fig. 10). Sisal, exported as a twine since 1927, peaked in the 1950s, as the Korean War demanded much of the nation's 40,000-ton output. By the 1980s, however, Haiti exported an average of only 6,500 tons a year, mainly to the Dominican Republic and Puerto Rico. The substitution of synthetic fibers for sisal reduced most large-scale growing of the plant, but many peasants continued to harvest the natural fiber for its use in hats, shoes, carpets, and handbags.

Workers at a cotton gin, Gonaïves
Courtesy Inter-American Development Bank
Squeezing sugarcane, Petit Goâve
Courtesy Inter-American Foundation

The export of essential oils, derived from vetiver, lime, amyris, and bitter orange, peaked in 1976 at 395 tons. Exports leveled off at a little more than 200 tons during the 1980s, generating an average of US$5 million in foreign exchange. Cotton cultivation peaked in the 1930s, before Mexican boll weevil beetles ravaged the crop. Growers introduced a higher quality of cotton, in the 1960s, which was processed in local cotton gins and then exported to Europe. Cotton prices fell in the 1980s, however, and cotton plantings shrank from 12,400 hectares in 1979 to under 8,000 hectares by 1986. Exports ceased. Government policies in the 1980s emphasized diversification into nontraditional export crops that would benefit under the terms of the CBI; the poor performance of traditional cash crops enhanced the importance of these efforts for the Haitian economy.

Food Crops

Food crops fared somewhat better than cash crops in the 1980s, as prices for cash crops dropped, and economic uncertainty increased. Nonetheless, real per capita food production declined, and the country continued to import millions of tons of grains. The trend toward increased production of food crops had negative ecological consequences as the planting and the harvesting of tuber staples accelerated soil erosion. Haiti's peasants were already underfed. It was therefore unlikely that farmers would grow tree crops in place of staples without appropriate incentives (see Forestry, this ch.).

Peasants cultivated a variety of cereals for food and animal feeds, notably corn, sorghum, and rice. Corn, also referred to as maize, was the leading food crop; it was sown on more hectares—220,000 in 1987—than any other crop. Farmers in southern departments grew corn separately, but elsewhere they mixed it with other crops, mostly legumes. Total production averaged approximately 185,000 tons during the 1980s; yields increased in some areas. Drought-resistant sorghum often replaced corn during the second growing season as the leading crop, but total hectares planted and total production averaged only 156,250 and 125,000 tons, respectively. Rice became an increasingly common cereal, beginning in the 1960s, when increased irrigation of the Artibonite Valley aided larger-scale farming (see fig. 11). Rice production, however, fluctuated considerably, and it remained dependent on government subsidies. An estimated 60,000 hectares of rice yielded an average of 123,000 tons, from 1980 to 1987.

Tubers were also cultivated as food. Sweet potatoes, one of the nation's largest crops, grew on an estimated 100,000 hectares, and they yielded 260,000 tons of produce a year in the 1980s. Manioc,

Harvesting rice in the Artibonite Valley
Courtesy Inter-American Development Bank
Family sowing black beans in the Cul-de-Sac region
Courtesy Inter-American Development Bank

or cassava, another major tuber, was mix-cropped on upwards of 60,000 hectares to produce between 150,000 and 260,000 tons a year, much of which was for direct consumption. The cultivation of yams, limited by the lack of deep moist soils, took up only 26,000 hectares. The tropical Pacific tuber taro, called *malangá* in Haiti, grew with other tubers on more than 27,000 hectares.

Haitians also cultivated dozens of other food crops. Red, black, and other kinds of beans were very popular; they provided the main source of protein in the diet of millions. As many as 129,000 hectares provided 67,000 tons of beans in 1987. Banana and plantain trees were also common and provided as much as 500,000 tons of produce, almost entirely for domestic consumption. Although the flimsy trees were vulnerable to hurricanes and to droughts, rapid replanting helped sustain the crop. Mangoes, another tree crop, were a daily source of food, and they provided some exports. Other food crops included citrus fruit, avocados, pineapples, watermelons, almonds, coconut, okra, peanuts, tomatoes, breadfruit, and *mamey* (tropical apricot). In addition, Haitians grew a wide variety of spices for food, medicine, and other purposes, including thyme, anise, marjoram, absinthe, oregano, black pepper, cinnamon, cloves, nutmeg, garlic, and horseradish.

Forestry

Nothing better symbolized the vicious cycle of poverty in Haiti than the process of deforestation. Haiti was once a lush tropical island, replete with pines and broad leaf trees; however, by 1988 only about 2 percent of the country had tree cover.

The most direct effect of deforestation was soil erosion. In turn, soil erosion lowered the productivity of the land, worsened droughts, and eventually led to desertification, all of which increased the pressure on the remaining land and trees. The United Nations Food and Agriculture Organization estimated that this cycle destroyed 6,000 hectares of arable land a year in the 1980s. Analysts calculated that, at the rate of deforestation prevailing in the late 1980s, the country's tree cover would be completely depleted by 2008.

Deforestation accelerated after Hurricane Hazel downed trees throughout the island in 1954. Beginning in about 1954, concessionaires stepped up their logging operations, in response to Port-au-Prince's intensified demand for charcoal, thus accelerating deforestation, which had already become a problem because of environmentally unsound agricultural practices, rapid population growth, and increased competition over scarce land.

Most of Haiti's governments paid only lip service to the imperative of reforestation. As was the case in other areas of Haitian life, the main impetus to act came from abroad. AID's Agroforestry Outreach Program, Projè Pyebwa, was the country's major reforestation program in the 1980s. Peasants planted more than 25 million trees under Projè Pyebwa, but as many as seven trees were cut for each new tree planted. Later efforts to save Haiti's trees—and thus its ecosystem—focused on intensifying reforestation programs, reducing waste in charcoal production, introducing more wood-efficient stoves, and importing wood under AID's Food for Peace program.

Livestock and Fishing

Most peasants possessed a few farm animals, usually goats, pigs, chickens, and cattle. Few holdings, however, were large, and few peasants raised only livestock. Many farm animals, serving as a kind of savings account, were sold or were slaughtered to pay for marriages, medical emergencies, schooling, seeds for crops, or a voodoo ceremony.

From the perspective of rural peasants, perhaps the most important event to occur in Haiti during the 1980s was the slaughter of the nation's pig stock, which had become infected with the highly contagious African Swine Fever (ASF) in the late 1970s. Having spread from Spain to the Dominican Republic and then to Haiti via the Artibonite River, ASF infected approximately one-third of the nation's pigs from 1978 to 1982. Farmers slaughtered their infected animals. Fear of further infection persuaded peasants to slaughter another one-third in panic sales. A government eradication program virtually wiped out what remained of the 1.2-million pig population by 1982.

At the grassroots level, the government's eradication and repopulation programs became highly controversial. Farmers complained that they were not fairly compensated for—or not paid at all for—their slaughtered livestock and that the sentinel breed of pigs imported from the United States to replace the hardy creole pigs was inappropriate for the Haitian environment and economy. Nonetheless, repopulation of the nation's pigs with both sentinel and Jamaican creole pigs augmented the national stock from an official figure of zero in 1982 to about 500,000 by 1989. Many analysts noted, however, that ASF and the pig slaughter had further impoverished already struggling peasants. The disaster forced many children to quit school. Small farmers mortgaged their land; others cut down trees for cash income from charcoal. The loss of the creole pigs to ASF undoubtedly increased the hardships of the rural population, and it may well have fueled to some degree the popular revolt that forced Jean-Claude Duvalier from power.

Goats were one of the most plentiful farm animals in Haiti. Like the creole pigs, they were well adapted to the rugged terrain and sparse vegetation. Approximately 54 percent of all farmers owned goats; the total had climbed from 400,000 in 1981 to more than 1 million by the late 1980s. Peasants owned the majority of the country's estimated 1 million head of cattle in 1987; about 48 percent of the farmers owned at least one head of cattle. Until 1985 the primary export market for beef cattle was the American baby food industry. Farmers raised sheep in some areas, but these animals were not particularly well adapted to the country's climate. Chickens, ducks, turkeys, and guinea hens were raised throughout Haiti under little supervision, although one medium-sized hatchery raised chickens for domestic consumption. After the swine-fever epidemic and the subsequent slaughter of pigs, chicken replaced pork as the most widely consumed meat in the Haitian diet.

About 11,000 Haitians fished the nation's 1,500-kilometer coastline on a full-time or part-time basis, netting an average annual catch of 5,000 tons. The country imported an additional 12,000 tons a year of fish products to satisfy domestic demand. The island's coastal waters suffered from low productivity, and few fishermen ventured far from shore. Nevertheless, Haiti managed to export about US$4 million worth of lobster, conch, and other shellfish in the 1980s. Some minor aquaculture also existed.

Industry

Manufacturing

Manufacturing was the most dynamic sector of the economy in the 1980s. Growth in this sector had averaged more than 10 percent a year during the 1970s; manufactures replaced agricultural commodities as the country's leading export goods during this decade. In 1988 manufacturing accounted for 17 percent of GDP and for 53 percent of exports; it employed about 6 percent of the labor force. In addition to the dynamic assembly subsector, which experienced 22 percent real annual growth in the 1970s, manufacturing included small-scale local enterprises and large-scale, state-owned organizations.

The manufacturing sector in the late 1980s comprised 500 enterprises, most of which were small or medium in size and family-owned. Their major products included processed foods, electrical equipment, textiles, and clothing. Small enterprises, employing up to 50 workers, represented 57 percent of all manufacturing firms, but they employed only 10 percent of the industrial labor force. Medium enterprises, with 51 to 300 workers, accounted for 35

*Cleaning drinkers at a
chicken farm
Courtesy Inter-American
Development Bank*

percent of the sector's firms and employed 44 percent of the industrial labor force. Large enterprises, those with more than 300 employees, constituted only 8 percent of the companies, but they employed 43 percent of all manufacturing workers, mostly in large assembly factories in the industrial parks of Port-au-Prince.

Assembly Manufacturing

The development of assembly manufacturing in Haiti was an outgrowth of the island's cheap labor, its proximity to the United States market, the increasing multinational nature of modern firms, and changes in the United States Tariff Code, which in 1962 began to exact duties only on the value-added of products assembled overseas. Assembly operations—typical examples included the sewing of garments, the stuffing of toys, or the stringing of baseballs—grew modestly in the depressed economic climate of the 1960s, but they accelerated rapidly in the early 1970s in response to new fiscal incentives enacted by the government. The warming of Haitian-United States relations after 1973 encouraged foreign investment. The number of assembly enterprises swelled from only 13 companies in 1966 to 67 by 1973 and then to 127 by 1978. When the subsector peaked in 1980, an estimated 200 assembly firms employed early 60,000 workers. Political instability, increased regional competition under the CBI, nascent union activity, and the failure of government institutions to attract further investment all contributed to a decline in assembly investment and employment after 1986. In 1989 approximately 150 assembly companies employed only 41,000 workers, more than three-quarters of them women. Assembly exports continued to expand, however, as a result of increased productivity on the part of assembly exporters.

Despite the low wages paid to workers, future growth in the assembly subsector was uncertain. Numerous constraints to growth included the highest utility costs in the Caribbean, excessive shipping and warehousing costs, underdeveloped infrastructure, a largely illiterate work force, scarce managerial personnel, foreign-exchange shortages, expensive or inferior-quality local inputs, political instability, and the personalized nature of business activity. Some United States officials predicted in the 1980s that Haiti would progress to become the "Taiwan of the Caribbean." The implementation of the CBI, however, appeared to hurt Haiti's position in assembly production, as other countries, such as the Dominican Republic, Jamaica, and Costa Rica, began to capitalize more effectively on the advantages of the initiative. In the mid-1980s, more than 40 percent of all assembly operations were owned by Haitians. The other operations were either owned by firms based in the United States or jointly owned by Haitian and United States interests. Asian investment in the country continued to grow.

Four industrial parks catered to the assembly industry; two were run by the government's National Industrial Park Company (Société Nationale des Parcs Industriels—Sonapi) and two by a private company. Most firms operated with short-term subcontracting arrangements under which Haitian factories filled requests of American companies that provided partial products, inputs, and machinery. Workers earned piece-work wages, with a guaranteed minimum wage of US$3 a day in 1989, and most made slightly more than that amount. These workers were among the best paid in Haiti, but most of them supported an average of four people on their wages.

The major products assembled in Haiti were garments, electronics, baseballs, games, sporting goods, toys, footwear, and leather products. The largest assembly activity in the late 1980s produced garments. The fastest-growing activity produced electronics; it included subcontracting work for the United States Department of Defense. One of the island's major baseball producers, MacGregor Sporting Goods, decided in 1988 to move its baseball-sewing operations to Mexico, however; and, as a result of the deteriorating political situation in Haiti, other assembly companies decided to fill their orders at the Free Zone of San Isidro, Dominican Republic.

Craftsman with a woven soleil *(sunburst)*
Courtesy Inter-American Foundation
Apparel assembly operation, Port-au-Prince Industrial Park
Courtesy Inter-American Development Bank

Many Haitians were eager to find jobs in the assembly sector, but some criticized the effects of the industry on workers and on the economy. For example, unions complained that new employees earned only 60 percent of the minimum wage for their first few months and that short-term contracts and seasonal demand led to job instability and the annual dismissal of as many as 5,000 workers with no compensation. Some economists noted that, although assembly operations provided badly needed urban jobs, these industries forged few linkages with the rest of the economy. A few local plants utilized domestically produced glue, thread, sisal, and textiles, but the overwhelming share of producers opted for imported inputs, which were generally cheaper, of better quality, and more plentiful. Finally, others disapproved of the generous tax holidays and the duty-free imports that both domestic and foreign manufacturers enjoyed.

Domestic Manufacturing

Attempts at import-substitution (see Glossary) manufacturing gave most local factories generous import protection from the 1970s to the mid-1980s, thereby insulating them from foreign competition. Industries of this kind produced paper, matches, cardboard, footwear, leather, food products, beverages, rubber, plastics, metals, building materials, textiles, cigarettes, soap, beer, and other basic goods. Most local factories were small or medium in size. Some very small producers demonstrated incredible ingenuity in transforming virtual junk into usable goods, but the limited domestic market and the weak purchasing power of most Haitians severely limited economies of scale, forcing most enterprises to function inefficiently and below capacity. A handful of local manufacturers, who produced rum, paints, essential oils, leather, and handicrafts, were able to expand their businesses through exports. Haitian rum was of exceptional quality, as were the country's handicrafts. Nongovernmental organizations were particularly active in marketing handicrafts in the United States and Europe.

In 1986 the CNG enacted broad import-liberalization policies and abolished long-standing import protection, forcing local producers to compete internationally. As a consequence, domestic manufacturing, already hampered by competition with lower-priced goods smuggled into Haiti from the Dominican Republic, experienced a painful transition in the late 1980s. Many manufacturers closed their doors.

The other major manufacturing subsector was large-scale production by state-owned enterprises of items such as vegetable oils, sugar, flour, and cement. From 1980 to 1985, the government either built, or bought, a majority share in five of the country's largest manufacturing companies. As the losses of these inefficient parastatals mounted, reaching more than 4 percent of GDP from 1982 to 1985, international lenders increasingly pressured the government to divest its interests in these ventures, a process that began after 1986.

Construction

After a meager annual growth rate of 1.8 percent a year in the 1960s, construction boomed in the 1970s, expanding nearly 14 percent a year, faster than any other sector except assembly manufacturing. From the 1970s onward, the construction industry had concentrated on infrastructure developments, industrial structures related to the assembly subsector, and extravagant residential housing in Port-au-Prince and its exclusive suburb, Pétionville. The growing demand for construction caused cement output to increase from 150,000 tons a year in 1975 to 220,000 tons a year by 1985. Growth was positive, but uneven, in the 1980s, mainly as a result of political and economic turmoil. The construction industry generally failed to benefit Haiti's poor, who continued to build their own dwellings with a mixture of raw materials, mostly wood and palm thatch in rural areas and corrugated metal, cardboard, or wood in urban shantytowns.

Mining

Endowed with few commercially valuable natural resources, Haiti maintained only a small mining sector in the late 1980s; mining accounted for less than 1 percent of GDP, and it employed less than 1 percent of the labor force. The country's only bauxite mine, the Miragoâne mine in the southern peninsula, produced an average of 500,000 tons of bauxite a year in the early 1980s; however, in 1982 the declining metal content of the ore, high production costs, and the oversupplied international bauxite market forced the mine to close. Bauxite had at one time been the country's second leading export. Copper also was mined, beginning in the 1960s, but production of the ore was sporadic.

Haiti contained relatively small amounts of gold, silver, antimony, tin, lignite, sulphur, coal, nickel, gypsum, limestone, manganese, marble, iron, tungsten, salt, clay, and various building stones. Mining activity in the late 1980s focused on raw materials for the construction industry. The government announced the discovery of new gold deposits in the northern peninsula in 1985, but long-standing plans for gold production proceeded slowly. With funding from the Inter-American Development Bank (IDB), the government planned to perform its first comprehensive geological survey in the late 1980s.

Energy

Haiti had limited energy resources in the late 1980s. The country had no petroleum resources, little hydroelectricity potential, and rapidly diminishing supplies of wood fuels. Wood accounted for 75 percent of the nation's energy consumption. Petroleum accounted for 15 percent; bagasse (sugarcane residue), for 5 percent; and hydroelectric power, for 5 percent. Energy consumption was paltry, even for a low-income country. Haiti's per capita energy use in 1985 was equivalent to that in Bangladesh and about seventeen times less than that of neighboring Jamaica. Having virtually no access to electricity, Haiti's poor depended on the felling of trees for the production of charcoal. Similarly, many rural and provincial small businesses used wood as a fuel in powering their operations.

Beginning in the late 1940s, various international oil companies had unsuccessfully explored for oil in Haiti's Artibonite Basin and Cul-de-Sac Basin. The prospects for drilling deeper wells or attempting even higher-risk offshore exploration were not promising. Oil imports, mainly from the Netherlands Antilles and Trinidad and Tobago, amounted to about 15 percent of total imports.

Electricity consumption increased sixfold between 1970 and 1987, but only 10 percent of the population had access to electricity by 1986. About 45 percent of the residents of Port-au-Prince had access to electricity—a reflection of the concentration of national economic efforts and resources in the capital—while a mere 3 percent of those outside the capital enjoyed similar access.

Installed electricity capacity in the late 1980s was estimated at about 150 megawatts (MW), and it was expected to increase to 190 MW by the late 1990s. The National Electricity Company (Electricité d'Haïti—EdH), created in 1971 to control the newly built Péligre hydroelectric plant, operated the nation's power system in the late 1980s. As was true of other enterprises throughout the economy, the president was the nominal head of EdH. The company administered the 47–MW Péligre hydroelectric plant, the 22–MW Guayamouc hydroelectric plant, a series of smaller hydroelectric plants, two large thermoelectric operations (42–MW Varreux and 38–MW Carrefour), small generators, and the distribution system. The national system, however, was highly disjointed; no power links extended from the capital to provincial cities. Supplies of imported petroleum used in thermal plants fluctuated because of

Charcoal depot
Courtesy Pan-American Development Foundation

foreign-exchange shortages, and dry-season water shortfalls hampered production at hydroelectric dams. EdH's generation was unreliable. Under these conditions, rationing of electricity was common in the 1980s, and most larger businesses maintained back-up generators. EdH, which had suffered financial problems in the 1970s, charged the highest electricity rates in the Caribbean in the 1980s. Many people illegally tapped into power lines, and by the late 1980s, as many as one in four urban residents reportedly engaged in this practice. International development agencies had explored alternative sources of energy, such as wind power, solar power, methanol production from sorghum, and power generation from organic waste, but none appeared to be immediately feasible.

Services

Banking and Financial Services

Banking and financial services expanded by almost 10 percent a year during the 1970s, in the wake of the growth of assembly manufacturing, construction, and tourism. By the 1980s, however, the country's financial institutions suffered from negative growth as a result of political instability and the consequently insecure investment climate. In the late 1980s, banking and related services accounted for 10 percent of GDP, and they employed about 4 percent of the labor force.

Nine commercial banks—five Haitian and four foreign—constituted the heart of the financial system. In 1989 the five local banks were the Haitian Popular Bank (Banque Populaire Haïtienne), Union Bank of Haiti (Banque de l'Union d'Haïti), Industrial and Commercial Bank of Haiti (Banque Industrielle et Commerciale d'Haïti), Commercial Bank of Haiti (Banque Commerciale d'Haïti), and the Haitian General Banking Society (Société Générale Haïtienne de Banque—Sogebank). Sogebank expanded its holdings in 1986 to encompass the two branches of the Royal Bank of Canada, previously the oldest and largest foreign-owned bank in Haiti. Of the four foreign-owned banks, two were based in the United States (Citibank and the Bank of Boston), one in Canada (the Bank of Nova Scotia), and one in France (Banque Nationale de Paris). Haiti considered the United States dollar legal tender, but the government prohibited foreign banks from maintaining foreign-currency accounts. Seventy-five percent of all commercial credit went to manufacturing and commerce; only 3 percent went to agriculture. Excessive collateral requirements, high interest rates, and a proclivity toward short-term financing diminished the role of commercial banks in stimulating output, especially among small producers.

Five development-finance institutions—both public and private—helped to offset deficiencies in commercial-bank financing. The main lenders for agriculture were the Agricultural Credit Bank (Bureau de Crédit Agricole—BCA) and the National Agricultural and Industrial Development Bank (Banque Nationale de Développement Agricole et Industriel—BNDAI). BCA provided short-term credit to nearly 20,000 small-scale farmers for the purchase of inputs and tools. Established in 1951, BNDAI lent to all categories of farmers, but it provided mostly short-term financing to larger, more capital-intensive producers, particularly those cultivating irrigated rice. BNDAI also lent to industrial enterprises, generally on a long-term basis. Private and public funds helped to set up the Industrial Development Fund (Fonds de Développement Industriel—FDI) and the Haitian Financial Development Society (Société Financière Haïtienne de Développement—Sofihdes) in the 1980s. FDI, founded in 1981 to aid firms with ownership that was at least 51 percent Haitian, offered no direct lending to industry, but it assisted existing companies or new ventures in acquiring credit, supplied guarantees on new loans, and provided technical assistance. Sofihdes, established in 1983 with funds from the CBI, AID, and the Haitian private sector, supplied credit with extended repayment schedules to manufacturing firms and agribusinesses ineligible for commercial bank loans. A fifth development-finance institution was the Mortgage Bank (Banque de Crédit Immobilier—BCI). Established in 1986 with 98 percent private capital, the BCI provided loans of up to US$100,000 for the housing industry, and it offered technical assistance and special loans for some low-income workers.

Other financial institutions included insurance companies, credit unions, finance institutions for the informal sector, and an extensive underground credit system. Several dozen companies wrote insurance policies in Haiti in the 1980s, but only a few were locally owned. Credit unions, established in the 1940s, mobilized savings primarily for agricultural cooperatives. The Haitian Development Foundation and the Haitian Fund for Assistance to Women were instrumental in the late 1980s in lending to small businesses that could not obtain commercial bank credit. There was no Haitian stock exchange.

Transportation and Communications

Haiti's transportation system was still inadequate in the 1980s, in spite of the major infrastructural improvements that had accompanied the growth period of the 1970s. Poor transportation hindered economic growth, particularly in the agricultural sector. Like other services in the economy, transportation—when it was available—was prohibitively expensive for most citizens. One study in the 1980s revealed that some assembly workers spent as much as one-quarter of their daily wages and two hours of their time on transportation.

The country's road system was the most important part of the transportation system. In 1989 there were more than 3,700 kilometers of roads: 17 percent were paved; 27 percent were gravel or were otherwise improved; and 56 percent were unimproved and were generally impassible following heavy rains. Besides the paved streets in the capital, there were only two paved highways, which linked the northern and the southern regions of the country. National Highway One extended north from Port-au-Prince to Cap-Haïtien via the coastal towns of Montrouis and Gonaïves. National Highway Two proceeded south from the capital to Les Cayes by way of Miragoâne with a spur to Jacmel (see fig. 15). Both were paved in 1973 with funding from AID. Despite international funding and some government improvement efforts by the National Road Maintenance Service (Service Entretien Permanent du

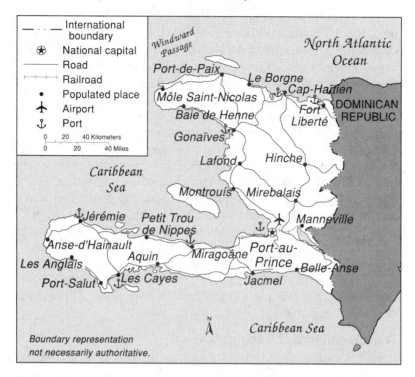

Figure 15. Haiti: Transportation System, 1989

Réseau Routier National—Serrin), inadequate road maintenance persisted.

Haiti imported all its vehicles, about 4,000 a year in the late 1980s. According to government sources, more than 36,600 vehicles were in use in 1981, three times the number in 1960. Travel outside the capital generally required four-wheel-drive vehicles, which were equipped to ride on poorly maintained and washed-out roads. The government offered limited and unreliable public transportation. The majority of Haitians who traveled by vehicle used tap-taps, brightly colored and overcrowded jitneys that serviced most of the island.

Haiti's fourteen ports constituted another major component of the transportation sector. Port-au-Prince was the central shipping site, accounting for as much as 90 percent of registered imports and most exports. Upgraded in 1978, Port-au-Prince was the only modern port in Haiti in the late 1980s; it offered mechanical handling equipment, two transit warehouses, and container capability. The capital's port, however, was expensive and therefore underutilized; wharfage costs were four times higher than those of ports in the Dominican Republic. Cap-Haïtien, the second major port, handled most cruise-ship traffic as well as domestic and international merchant ships. Cap-Haïtien, like some other small ports, underwent renovations during the 1980s. Lesser-used ports included Miragoâne, Les Cayes, Fort Liberté, Gonaïves, Jacmel, Montrouis, and Jérémie.

As a result of the poor road system, cabotage via provincial ports played an important role in internal commerce. Smaller ports also dealt extensively in the pervasive contraband trade out of the Dominican Republic and Miami. Smuggling stimulated economic activity at depressed provincial ports, but it also resulted in the loss of millions of dollars in import duties.

Port-au-Prince had the country's only international airport. Located about ten kilometers outside the capital, this airport, opened in 1965, was fully equipped for all international flights, and it handled the majority of domestic flights. More than a dozen airlines from North America, South America, the Caribbean, and Europe serviced the airport. The government-owned airline, Air Haiti, operating under the control of the National Civil Aviation Office (Office Nationale de l'Aviation Civile—ONAC), flew domestic flights to many provincial airports. Eleven other airfields of varying quality were also operational. The National Airport Authority (Autorité Aéroportuaire Nationale—AAN) regulated the country's airports.

There was no passenger rail service in Haiti. The 80-kilometer railroad that operated southwest and east of Port-au-Prince for the Haitian American Sugar Company (Hasco) was the country's only railroad system.

Haitians were the most isolated citizens of the Western Hemisphere in terms of their low per capita use of telephones, radios, and televisions. There were only six telephones for every 1,000 people in Haiti, compared with the average of eight telephones for every 1,000 people in Africa.

The Haitian Telecommunications Company (Telecommunications d'Haïti—Teleco), under the Ministry of Public Works, Transport, and Communications, was responsible for the nation's telephone service and other telecommunications. The government owned 96 percent of Teleco, which modernized the national telephone industry in the late 1980s, with French financing, by introducing digital dialing to the Port-au-Prince area. The capital also enjoyed direct dialing to the United States and Europe, via a satellite station at Sabourin, although at very high rates. Telephones, however, continued to be a luxury item. In the mid-1980s, more than 80 percent of the country's 39,000 telephones were in Port-au-Prince, where only about 20 percent of Haiti's population lived. Telephone service to provincial cities was so unreliable that many rural areas relied on two-way radios. Rapid expansion of the telephone system was expected by the early 1990s, when the number of telephones in Port-au-Prince was slated nearly to double from 39,000 to 69,000 and the number outside the capital, more than to triple from 7,000 to 23,000. About 400 telex lines and an elementary mail service functioned in the late 1980s.

Tourism

A new international airport in 1965 and improved relations with the United States helped Haiti's tourism industry to flourish in the 1970s. Tourist arrivals (139,000 by air and 163,000 by sea) peaked in 1980, and net expenditures on tourism (US$44 million) reached their highest level in 1981 before a series of events made Haiti unpopular among tourists. One of these events was publicity surrounding Haiti as a possible origin of acquired immune deficiency syndrome (AIDS) and the high number of AIDS cases among Haitians. The former allegation proved false, but the portrait lingered, along with television images of political violence, dire poverty, "boat people," and general instability.

For the tourists who ventured to the "land of mountains," Haiti held a number of attractions: exotic culture, exquisite French cuisine, distinctive and colorful art and handicrafts, castles, hotels, and a resort setting virtually free of street crime. Its warm climate, friendly people, and low prices were further attractions. In the late 1980s, North Americans, especially people from the United States, continued to account for more than three-quarters of all visitors. Large numbers of Haitian émigrés also visited the country after the fall of Jean-Claude Duvalier. The declining number of tourists in general forced many hotels to close, however, and the total number of rooms registered in the industry dropped from 3,000 in 1981 to 1,500 in 1987. In contrast, the number of hotel rooms in the neighboring Dominican Republic quadrupled over the same time period. Haiti's tourist industry tended to be an enclave economic activity, distinguished by all-inclusive, self-contained beach resorts and brief cruise ship dockings in Cap-Haïtien or Port-au-Prince. Prospects for reviving tourism dimmed in the late 1980s, when the Haitian government closed its tourist-promotion office in New York City.

Foreign Economic Relations
Foreign Trade

Throughout Haiti's history, foreign trade has played a major

314

*Riders on a "tap-tap" (jitney)
near Gonaïves
Courtesy Inter-American
Development Bank*

*Colorful "tap-taps" on Avenue
Dessalines, Port-au-Prince
Courtesy Inter-American
Development Bank*

economic role. Trade provided crucial foreign exchange for Haiti, but the structure of trade and government policies resulted in falling incomes and poorly distributed wealth. In the mid-1980s, about twenty families dominated the importation of basic consumer items. Traditionally, government import-licensing schemes and tariff policies supported import monopolies, a major cause of prevailing high consumer prices. This same structure also permitted the plentiful importation of luxury items at relatively low tariffs. A small group of businessmen also controlled exports, particularly coffee, and its members generally favored commerce over more productive investment. The effects of major trade reforms enacted in 1986 remained to be seen in the late 1980s.

Officially, imports in 1987 reached US$307.7 million, the second lowest level of the decade (after the 1986 level of US$303.2 million). An export level of only US$198.4 million in 1987 created a trade deficit of US$110 million (see table 12, Appendix A). Not reflected in these data, however, were sizable amounts of contraband. The structure of the country's imports changed little during the 1980s. Foodstuffs continued to account for the greatest share (19 percent) of imports in 1987, followed by machinery and transport equipment (17 percent), manufacturing (16 percent), petroleum (13 percent), chemicals (10 percent), edible oils (10 percent), and other categories (15 percent). The United States was the leading exporter to Haiti, supplying 64 percent of all goods and services in 1987.

In July 1986, the National Council of Government (Conseil National de Gouvernement—CNG) swiftly introduced import-liberalization policies that eliminated all quantitative restrictions on import items, with the exception of seven (later amended to five) basic consumer goods. Ad valorem tariffs replaced import quotas; this reform also lowered other tariffs significantly. At the same time, authorities began a complete revision of the Tariff Code that resulted in markedly lower overall protection by the end of 1986. In addition, the government revoked the tariff subsidies enjoyed by state-owned enterprises. Additional trade reform streamlined complex import-licensing schemes, which often favored traditional merchants. The government also attempted to expedite customs procedures, something the private sector had long advocated. Import policies, however, conspicuously lacked a serious and comprehensive policy to halt widespread smuggling.

Exports generally increased during the 1980s, but political instability started to weaken export performance toward the end of the decade. The structure of exports changed dramatically as the result of the long decline in agriculture, the termination of bauxite mining, and the implementation of the CBI. In 1987 manufacturing contributed 53 percent of total exports, followed by coffee (18 percent), handicrafts (14 percent), essential oils (2 percent), cocoa (2 percent), and other goods (11 percent). Agriculture, which accounted for 52 percent of exports in 1980, contributed only 24 percent by 1987; exports of traditional commodities, such as sugar, sisal, and meat, either declined to insignificant levels or ceased altogether. Haiti exported goods mostly to the United States, the destination of 84 percent of the country's overseas sales in 1987. France and Italy, the main purchasers of Haiti's coffee, accounted for 3 percent and 4 percent, respectively, of 1987 exports. The balance of exports went to the Dominican Republic (2 percent) and other West European and Latin American countries (7 percent).

Trade policy in the late 1980s strongly favored export promotion within the framework of the CBI, the expansion of assembly manufacturing, and the maintenance of the country's export competitiveness. In an effort to generate more exports, the Duvalier government solicited increased foreign investment through revisions in the foreign investment code during 1985. With funding from AID, the private sector in February 1987 established an export-promotion office to spearhead new investment and to recoup the momentum of exports that had been lost to political upheaval. Other economic reforms, such as budget cuts that helped to maintain the value of the gourde, maintenance of low minimum wages, and trade liberalization, were intended to stimulate investment and exports. The duty-free entry of additional Haitian goods into the United States under the CBI favored the overall growth in exports. In a bid to revitalize traditional exports, the government in 1986 also eliminated long-standing export taxes on coffee, cocoa, sisal, and other items. Haiti had applied for membership in the free-trade association, the Caribbean Community and Common Market (Caricom), in the early 1970s, but it had not been accepted as of 1989.

Balance of Payments

Chronic trade deficits, dating back to 1965, had contributed to the country's current-account deficits throughout the 1980s. Tourism receipts cushioned negative trade performance, but not enough to balance the current account. Many Haitians living in other countries sent foreign currency to their families still living in Haiti. These remittances continued to grow during the 1980s; in some of these years, they equaled more than half of the total value of exports, and they thus partially offset export shortfalls.

Haiti had a negative balance of payments in the 1980s, although surpluses in the capital account, mainly the result of official aid flows, helped to cover current-account deficits for FY 1987 and FY 1988. Electoral violence in November 1987, however, moved some donor nations to reduce or cut off aid flows in 1988. Along with accelerated capital flight, this move turned overall accounts negative, draining foreign-exchange reserves to a level equal to only four weeks of imports.

Foreign Debt

The nation's foreign debt was modest and manageable, in contrast to the foreign debts of neighboring countries. Total external debt was estimated at US$800 million in 1989; furthermore, the terms of Haiti's foreign debt—interest rates, maturity of loans, and grace periods—were extremely favorable. Nevertheless, the country's foreign debt doubled during the 1980s, and its debt-service payments, as a percentage of exports, increased from 6 percent to more than 15 percent. New International Monetary Fund (IMF— see Glossary) and World Bank lending during the decade boosted the share of national debt owed to multilateral organizations from 67 percent in 1983 to 74 percent by 1987. Bilateral agencies held 18 percent of the foreign debt, and private banks were responsible for the remaining 8 percent. The government of the Federal Republic of Germany (West Germany) had canceled a small bilateral debt owed by Haiti in 1985, and the Haitian government generally kept up payments to its other creditors. As of 1989, Haiti had not rescheduled its foreign debt.

Foreign Assistance

Foreign assistance played a critical role in the economy. As the poorest country in the Western Hemisphere, Haiti was the recipient of economic assistance from numerous multilateral and bilateral development agencies and more than 300 nongovernmental foreign organizations. Some analysts went so far as to call the development community in Haiti a shadow government because overseas funding contributed as much as 70 percent of spending on economic and social development and 40 percent of the national budget. This situation was largely a legacy of the Duvalier governments, which conserved spending on development projects by soliciting generous foreign-aid commitments. Nevertheless, per capita foreign economic assistance to Haiti continued to be well below the level of assistance in most other Caribbean and Central American nations, as a consequence of the government's weak commitment, minimal counterpart funding, ineffectual public institutions, and history of corruption.

Unloading containers, Port-au-Prince harbor
Courtesy Inter-American Development Bank
Section of National Highway Two near Miragoâne
Courtesy Inter-American Development Bank

The United States was the most important source of bilateral economic assistance, and it was the only country that maintained a resident aid mission. United States economic assistance to Haiti began in 1944, only three years after the last economic advisers of the occupation departed. This assistance ended when United States president John F. Kennedy terminated all but humanitarian aid to the François Duvalier government in 1963. Consequently, Haiti did not participate in the Alliance for Progress (the Latin American development program initiated under the Kennedy administration and continued under the administration of Lyndon B. Johnson). United States assistance resumed in 1973 under Jean-Claude Duvalier, and it continued until January 1986, a month before the end of the Duvalier era. The United States restored aid in unprecedented amounts three weeks after Duvalier's exile, but the administration of President Ronald Reagan again severed non-humanitarian aid flows after the electoral violence of November 1987. Development assistance was resumed in the late 1980s, but it continued to be tied to progress toward fair elections.

AID's major goals in Haiti were to improve rural conditions through soil conversion, agro-forestry, and watershed management; to augment the country's human resources through increased nutrition, family planning, and educational opportunities; and to foster economic policy reform aimed at private-sector development and export promotion. AID also pursued narcotics interdiction, migration control, and political reform. In 1982 AID began to channel an increasing percentage of its assistance through nongovernmental organizations rather than through Haitian ministries. The United States had legislated this policy shift through the 1981 Foreign Assistance Act. Canada, West Germany and other foreign donors also decided to circumvent government agencies in favor of nongovernmental organizations. This approach proved so much more efficient and effective that, by the late 1980s, AID distributed all of its humanitarian aid through a network of nongovernmental institutions.

The Inter-American Foundation and the Peace Corps also supported the United States development effort in Haiti. The Peace Corps entered the country in 1983, after more than a decade of negotiations. Political instability in 1988 and 1989, however, led to the dismissal of the Corps' volunteers. Other foreign donors included Belgium, Canada, France, Israel, Italy, Japan, the Netherlands, Switzerland, West Germany, and Taiwan.

Multilateral development agencies underwrote most major infrastructural projects, and they financed most payment shortfalls during the 1970s and the 1980s. The IMF was the most influential multilateral agency in the country. Since the early 1950s, Haiti had signed more than twenty standby agreements—more than any other member country—with the IMF. The IMF in 1988 made Haiti a test case for its Enhanced Structural Adjustment Facility, a special financing arrangement reserved for only the poorest countries. The World Bank, the supplier of one-quarter of multilateral aid in the late 1980s, lent extensively for highways, electricity, education, institution building, and policy reform. Beginning in the early 1960s, the IDB approved more than US$300 million for improved irrigation, rural water systems, public health, and road construction. Other multilaterals included several other United Nations (UN) agencies, the European Economic Community, the Organization of American States, and the Organization of Petroleum Exporting Countries.

A 1985 survey of nongovernmental organizations in Haiti revealed that one-third of these organizations had arrived in the country before 1960. Many had come in response to Hurricane Hazel in 1954. Nongovernmental organizations reportedly donated as much as US$65 million in annual assistance, food aid, other goods, and project financing.

Some Haitian officials complained about the lack of coordination among nongovernmental organizations. Partially in response to this criticism, AID in 1981 financed the creation of an umbrella nongovernmental organization, the Haitian Association of Voluntary Agencies (HAVA), to share ideas, technology, and lessons learned. By 1989 HAVA included over 100 members.

The case for supporting Haiti's economic development was indisputable. Haiti had the potential for development. The government and the urban elite had failed, however, to tap the strengths of the nation's hard-working people, except in an exploitive fashion. Development problems in Haiti were, in many ways, political rather than economic. Politics exacerbated the country's economic and ecological problems, but the resourcefulness of the people and the prospect of political change provided some hope. The many small successes of the hundreds of nongovernmental organizations that worked with rural residents to improve their status were proof that better economic management and determined efforts could make a difference.

*   *   *

Compared with research on Haiti's history, politics, and security, the volume of literature on the nation's economy is modest. Nonetheless, the small group of scholars that concentrate on Haiti are dedicated and well-informed. Many of the most important studies on the economy in recent years have been funded by AID in Port-au-Prince, notably *Agriculture Sector Assessment: Haiti,* by Marguerite Blemur, et al.; "Land Tenure Issues in Rural Haiti," by Peter Bloch, et al.; and *Haiti: Country Environmental Profile,* by Marko Ehrlich, et al. Other major works on agriculture include Mats Lundahl's *The Haitian Economy: Man, Land, and Markets,* which previously appeared in French. "Foreign Assembly in Haiti," by Joseph Grunwald, et al., and *Le Système Bancaire Haïtien: Fonctionnement et Perspectives,* by Charles A. Beaulieu, are the definitive works on their respective topics. More general publications that merit recognition are Brian Weinstein and Aaron Segal's *Haiti: Political Failures, Cultural Successes* and Simon Fass's *Political Economy in Haiti. Haiti's Future,* edited by Richard M. Morse, reveals the views of twelve Haitian leaders on the post-Duvalier era. The Bank of the Republic of Haiti publishes the most current available statistics through its annual reports and monthly bulletins. The Ministry of Economy and Finance's Haitian Institute for Statistics and Information (République d'Haïti, Ministère de l'Economic et des Finances) provides the most comprehensive data by means of *Recueil des Statistiques de Base* and other publications. The World Bank, the IMF, AID, and the IDB compile the best data on Haiti outside the island. (For further information and complete citations, see Bibliography.)

Chapter 9. Haiti:
Government and Politics

Figure from a painting by Dieuseul Paul

WHEN IT SECURED ITS INDEPENDENCE from France, Haiti moved to the forefront of political history. The Haitian Revolution took place at the same period as the American and the French revolutions, and Haiti was one of the first nations to abolish slavery. In some ways, however, Haiti's political development lagged behind that of other nations. Its government functioned like a proto-state compared with the more modern systems that evolved in other states. Authoritarianism, typical among archaic states based on monarchy and despotism, characterized Haiti's political history. Haitian governments historically had lacked well-developed institutions, elaborate bureaucracies, and an ability to do more than maintain power and extract wealth from a large peasant base. Haiti's rural areas, where the majority of the population lives, traditionally have benefited least from government expenditures, and they have suffered for the past 500 years from virtually uninterrupted military domination.

In the late 1980s, the Haitian political system was in a profound state of crisis, which became acute during the waning months of 1985 as swelling popular unrest led to the fall of the Jean-Claude Duvalier government on February 7, 1986. After Duvalier's fall, a series of short-lived governments ruled the country.

In retrospect, the post-Duvalier period may be viewed as a transition to consolidation of longer-term control over the Haitian state by one (or more) of several competing political factions. In mid-1989, however, the political situation continued to be in a state of flux; many claimants to power competed with each other, while Haiti's public institutions languished. Even Haiti's armed forces, the country's most powerful institution, suffered from factionalism, corruption, and a general breakdown in the chain of command. Pressure to overhaul the political system mounted. To a significant degree, the political crisis of the transitional period pitted regressive Duvalierist elements, who advocated complete or partial restoration of the ancien régime, against popular aspirations for change.

The spectacle of five successive governments between February 1986 and September 1988 reflected the nation's political instability. This period witnessed the election of a constituent assembly, the popular ratification of a new constitution, repeated massacres of citizens exercising their political rights—such as the right to vote in free elections—and battles between army factions. The succession of governments included the decaying, hereditary dynasty of the Duvaliers; the military-civilian National Council of Government (Conseil National de Gouvernement—CNG) led by Lieutenant General Henri Namphy, which underwent several changes in membership, leading to a reduction in the size of, and the civilian representation in, the government; a four-month civilian government headed by President Leslie F. Manigat, who rose to power because the armed forces rigged the election; another government headed by Namphy as military dictator, originating after a coup against Manigat; and the replacement of Namphy by Lieutenant General Prosper Avril in yet another military coup. Threats from army factions and opposition from the old Duvalierist right wing continued to plague the Avril government (see The Post-Duvalier Period, ch. 10).

This apparent instability, however, tended to mask underlying political continuities. Before the fall of the Duvaliers, the last crisis of succession in Haiti had taken place in 1956–57, when President Paul Magloire attempted to extend his constitutional term of office (see Politics and the Military, 1934–57, ch. 6). During the period following Magloire's overthrow, five governments rose and fell within the nine-month period prior to the accession of François Duvalier to the presidency. There were also battles between competing army factions during this period. From a longer-term perspective, the post-Duvalier period resembled the nineteenth century in Haiti, when transitory governments held power between relatively long periods of stability (see Decades of Instability, 1843–1915, ch. 6).

Background: From Duvalier to Avril, 1957–89

Although François Duvalier came to power through elections in 1957, he lost all credibility because of a fraudulent re-election in 1961, a rigged referendum in 1964 that confirmed him as Haiti's president for life, and the severe and unrelenting repression he dealt out, primarily through the Volunteers for National Security (Volontaires de la Sécurité Nationale—VSN), or *tonton makouts* (bogeymen). Duvalier ("Papa Doc") extended his illegitimate rule beyond his death by naming his son Jean-Claude ("Baby Doc") as his successor.

Jean-Claude Duvalier came to power in 1971, under the informal regency of his mother, Simone Ovide Duvalier, and a small inner circle of Duvalierists. As Jean-Claude matured and began to assert his power independently of his mother and her advisers, some minor reforms in Haitian life took place. By the late 1970s, Jean-Claude had restored some freedom of the press and had

*Jean-Claude Duvalier (third from right) with wife Michèle
Duvalier and others at a military ceremony
Courtesy United States Department of Defense*

allowed the formation of fledgling opposition political parties as
well as the organization of a human rights league. This brief period
of liberalization, however, ended with the arrest and the expul-
sion of a number of union leaders, journalists, party activists, and
human-rights advocates in November 1980. Representatives of the
Roman Catholic Church and leaders of peasant organizations also
suffered arrest and intimidation. These arrests heralded a period
of heightened government repression that lasted throughout the
balance of Duvalier's tenure.

Duvalier's 1980 marriage to Michèle Bennett resulted in Simone
Duvalier's exile and created new factional alliances within the ruling
group. The Duvalier-Bennett clique amassed wealth at an unprecedented rate during the remainder of Jean-Claude's presidency for
life. The concomitant sharp deterioration in the already dismal
quality of life of most Haitians prompted Pope John Paul II to
declare in a speech in Haiti in 1983 that "things must change here."
His call for social and political justice signaled a new era of church
activism in Haiti (see Roman Catholicism, ch. 7).

The 1983 promulgation of a new constitution—Haiti's twentieth
since 1801—and the February 1984 legislative elections, heavily
weighted in favor of Duvalierist candidates, did little or nothing

to legitimize Duvalier's rule. These efforts were met by antigovernment riots in Gonaïves in 1984 and 1985. In response, "Baby Doc" attempted to manipulate further the "liberalized" system he had established. Constitutional amendments, approved in 1985 by a fraudulent referendum (a traditional Duvalierist legalism), created the post of prime minister, confirmed the presidency for life as a permanent institution, guaranteed the president the right to name his successor, and provided for severe restrictions on the registration of political parties. Duvalierists organized into the National Progressive Party (Parti National Progressiste—PNP) in anticipation of future manipulated elections. New outbreaks of popular unrest shattered Duvalier's plans, however, and he was eventually forced into exile in February 1986 (see Jean-Claude Duvalier, 1971–86, ch. 6).

The popular revolt, known in Creole as *operation déchoukaj* (operation uprooting), sought to destroy the foundations of Duvalierism. Its strikes and mass demonstrations reflected the Duvalier regime's general loss of support. In response, the CNG annulled the Duvalierist constitution and held elections for a constituent assembly in October 1986. This assembly produced a new constitution in 1987. Haitians overwhelmingly ratified the document by popular vote on March 29, 1987. At that point, a number of observers seemed optimistic about Haiti's potential transition to democracy. This optimism proved short-lived, however.

The Constitution mandated the formation of an independent electoral council. The Provisional Electoral Council (Conseil Electoral Provisoire—CEP), established in early 1987, initially fulfilled this requirement. Relations between the CEP and the CNG, however, weakened, and by June they had degenerated into open conflict over proposed electoral guidelines. The CNG disbanded the CEP, proposed its own electoral council, and abolished an important opposition trade union. This attempt by the military-dominated CNG to control the electoral process met with strong popular opposition. Strikes and civil unrest eventually forced the CNG to reinstate the independent electoral council, which set presidential elections for November 29, 1987, but postponed local elections.

The presidential campaign was a volatile affair. Two presidential candidates were assassinated, and controversy gripped the CEP with regard to the application of Article 291 of the Constitution, which banned participation by Duvalierist candidates. The campaign officially opened in October, with thirty-five presidential candidates registered. The CEP eventually recognized twenty-three of these candidates and disbarred twelve as Duvalierists. In apparent retaliation, Duvalierist provocateurs are reported to have burned

CEP headquarters. By election day, about 2.2 million voters—73 percent of the voting-age population—had registered. Voter turnout on the morning of November 29 was reported to be heavy. Balloting was suspended, however, by midmorning because armed paramilitary groups, linked to old *tonton makout* leaders who were reportedly protected by certain army officers, massacred an estimated thirty-four voters at the polls.

After the 1987 electoral debacle, the CNG announced the formation of a new electoral council, controlled by the government, and scheduled new elections for January 17, 1988. Four leading presidential candidates withdrew from the race in protest over the military's attempts to control the electoral process. The balloting went ahead as scheduled, however, amid a low voter turnout and allegations of fraud. The CNG's electoral council declared Leslie F. Manigat, of the small Coalition of Progressive National Democrats (Rassemblement des Démocrates Nationaux Progressistes— RDNP) the winner. Manigat took office on February 7. Namphy and the army deposed Manigat, following a dispute over army appointments. Manigat made the mistake of trying to assert constitutional control over the armed forces rather than serving as a figurehead. In response, Namphy and the army deposed Manigat on June 20 of that same year, and Haiti returned to direct military government for the first time since 1956. Namphy formally rescinded the 1987 Constitution in July 1988.

Human-rights abuses increased during Namphy's tenure as the army did little to discourage the violent backlash of Duvalierist groups. These abuses climaxed on Sunday, September 11, when a group of former *tonton makouts* entered the Church of Saint John Bosco in Port-au-Prince (pastored by a prominent opposition priest), murdered a number of worshipers, and set the church on fire. On September 17, noncommissioned officers of the Presidential Guard (Garde Présidentielle) ousted Namphy and replaced him with Lieutenant General Prosper Avril. Avril proceeded to purge the army command and the government cabinet in an attempt to solidify his position. In October Avril arrested fifteen soldiers and noncommissioned officers who had helped to bring him to power.

In early 1989, instability intensified as labor unions and other groups staged demonstrations throughout the country. In an attempt to achieve some sort of stability, Avril convened a National Forum on February 7, with strong participation from centrist politicians, to explore the possibility of re-establishing an electoral calendar. In a further conciliatory move, the government excluded key Duvalerists from the forum. Avril also partially restored the 1987 Constitution on March 13. In line with the Constitution, the government announced the formation of a new independent electoral commission, the Permanent Electoral Council (Conseil Electoral Permanent—CEP). The CEP members took office in April.

From April 2 to 8, factional struggles in the military evolved into two attempted coups supported by old-line Duvalierists, former *tonton makout* leaders, and high-level army officers implicated in drug trafficking (see The Post-Duvalier Period, ch. 10). Key elements of the Presidential Palace Guard, however, remained loyal to Avril, who survived the coup attempts and emerged with a strengthened hand. In an attempt to head off future challenges, Avril abolished the rebel army units and began to disperse their troops into scattered provincial outposts. Avril managed to retain power, but the events of April 1989 had left the armed forces divided. The domestic situation continued to be extremely unstable, and the future political course of the nation was unpredictable.

The Constitutional Framework

Haitian heads of state have often drafted and abolished the nation's constitutions at will, treating the documents as their own personal charters. However, when the 1987 Constitution replaced the Duvalierist 1983 constitution, the popular referendum that ratified the Constitution was free and fair; it demonstrated widespread support for the new document. Nevertheless, the interim governments have not taken the provisions of the Constitution seriously. Through a simple presidential decree, Namphy suspended the document in 1988, and Avril only partially reinstated it in 1989.

The 1987 Constitution is a modern, progressive, democratic document. It guarantees a series of basic rights to the citizenry. It declares the intent to establish democracy in Haiti, and it includes ideological pluralism, electoral competition, and the separation of powers. Several provisions seek to reshape the system and the political tradition bequeathed to the nation by the Duvaliers. In particular, the Constitution reduces the president's constitutional powers, decentralizes governmental authority, and establishes elected councils for local government. Police and army functions are disaggregated. The Constitution also establishes an independent judiciary and subordinates military personnel to civilian courts in all cases that involve civilians. Under the Constitution, individuals are barred from public office for ten years if they have served as ''architects'' of the Duvalierist dictatorship, enriched themselves from public funds, inflicted torture on political prisoners, or committed political assassinations. The Constitution abolishes the death penalty and focuses on the protection of civil rights through detailed restrictions on the arrest and the detainment of citizens. It calls for the establishment of a career civil service based on merit and for job security, and it recognizes both Creole and French as official languages.

The Constitution establishes three major branches of government—legislative, executive, and judicial—and notes that these branches are essential to a civil state and that they must be independent of each other. Legislative powers are vested in two chambers, the House of Deputies and the Senate. Deputies and senators are elected by direct suffrage. Deputies represent municipalities (or communes), and senators represent geographic departments (see fig. 16).

In the executive branch, the president of the republic serves as head of state. A prime minister, chosen by the president from the majority party in the legislature, heads the government. Other components of the executive branch include cabinet ministers and secretaries of state.

The judiciary consists of the Court of Cassation (supreme court), courts of appeal, and other smaller courts. The president appoints judges on the basis of lists submitted by various elected bodies, including the Senate and departmental and municipal assemblies.

The Constitution also provides for several special institutions and autonomous governmental offices that include the CEP, the Superior Court of Auditors and Administrative Disputes, the Conciliation Commission (a body responsible for settling disputes between executive and legislative branches and between the two houses of the legislature), the Office of Citizen Protection (an ombudsman organization established to protect citizens against abuse by the government), the State University of Haiti, the Haitian Academy (responsible for standardizing the Creole language), and the National Institute of Agrarian Reform.

The Constitution contains a number of provisions intended to guide the country during transitions between elected governments. These provisions include the creation of an electoral council with sufficient autonomy to hold local and national elections, free of outside interference. The Constitution calls for the replacement of the provisional council by a permanent electoral council following a transition to civilian government.

When General Avril reinstated the Constitution in March 1989, he created an electoral council according to the constitutional formula, but he also temporarily suspended thirty-eight articles. Under the partially restored Constitution, the president of the military government could exercise power until a presidential election was organized. Legislative powers were similarly suspended pending elections. The suspended constitutional elements included

331

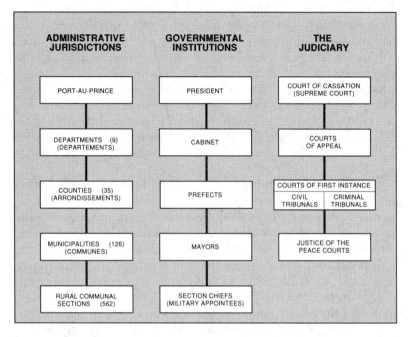

Figure 16. Haiti: Civil Jurisdictions and Governmental Institutions, 1989

Article 42-1, Article 42-2, and Article 42-3, which require the trial of military personnel in civilian courts for charges of high treason or of conflicts and abuses involving civilians. Other suspended articles refer to the constitutional separation of powers among the executive, the legislative, and the judicial branches of government and the military. These suspensions immunized military personnel against legal charges stemming from the constitutional protection of citizen rights. They also allowed the military to carry out activities that the Constitution reserved for the executive or the legislative branches.

The Governmental System

The formally reinstated 1987 Constitution did not accurately reflect the government of Haiti in 1989, however. The only constitutional reform that the Avril government had actually implemented was the new CEP. The reinstatement of the Constitution was essentially a mere gesture and not a restoration of the political process initiated by the 1986–87 constituent assembly. Under the partially restored Constitution, the Haitian president, drawn from the military, actually controlled all executive, legislative, and military functions. In the absence of a legislature, the president ruled by decree. This form of transitional military government also usurped judicial functions.

Governmental Institutions

Avril's military government administered the country through a cabinet that included thirteen ministerial portfolios as of mid-1989. The most powerful of these posts was the Ministry of Interior and National Defense, which combined administrative responsibilities over the nation's armed forces and the police. As of the end of 1989, no legislative body existed in Haiti.

A number of military and civil jurisdictions existed throughout Haiti. The jurisdictional system resulted in preferential treatment for the government of Port-au-Prince over the rest of the country. Most institutions were concentrated in the capital city. Moreover, the military either ran or dominated the most elaborate institutions. At the level of departments (*départements*) and rural communal sections, a military office served as the sole government representative. Thus, both the largest and the smallest subdivisions were exclusively military jurisdictions.

Furthermore, the structure of jurisdictions and the distribution of government institutions were generally asymmetrical. The military subdivisions of departments (i.e., districts, subdistricts, and guard posts) did not correspond to civil jurisdictions such as counties (*arrondissements*) or municipalities. Units identified as police functioned only in Port-au-Prince. The technical ministries, such as agriculture or public health, generally did not maintain offices at the level of municipalities or rural communal sections. At the municipality level, the most widely diffused national civil institution was the tax office. In any case, most people in Haiti lived in rural sections, where the civil functions of government were virtually nonexistent.

Under transitional military government, the judiciary did not function as the Constitution directed. Moreover, the formal structure of the judiciary was in a state of flux. The Haitian judiciary had usually had a marginal relationship to society, and it had generally failed to protect the rights of citizens. The masses of the citizenry were largely excluded from the duly constituted system of courts and due process. Under the dictatorial rule of François Duvalier, the court system was virtually suspended.

Haiti derived the formal aspects of its legal system from Roman law, the Napoleonic Code, and the French system of civil law. The highest court, the Court of Cassation, consisted of a president, a vice president, and ten judges. It functioned in two chambers, with five judges in each, but it would function as a whole when it heard appeals and pleas of the unconstitutionality of laws and decrees. Judges of the Court of Cassation had to be at least thirty years old, had to have practiced law for at least ten years, and had to have held the position of judge or public attorney for at least seven years.

Below the Court of Cassation were four courts of appeal, located in Port-au-Prince, Les Cayes, Gonaïves, and Cap-Haïtien. The court at Port-au-Prince had a president and five judges, whereas the others had a president and four judges. These courts heard both civil and criminal cases, including all appeals from courts of first instance and criminal appeals from justice of the peace courts when a serious matter was involved. To be appointed to these courts, judges had to have been either judges of courts of first instance for three years or military advocates for at least ten years.

Courts of first instance were either civil tribunals or criminal tribunals. Both were located in major cities. Each court had one judge and various other officers. These courts heard many first-instance civil cases and all criminal cases other than police matters. Judges in these courts were required to have practiced law for at least two years.

The justice of the peace courts were located in each of the country's 126 municipalities and in other places. Each court had at least one judge and other officials. According to the law, a justice of the peace was required to have a law degree, to be at least twenty-five years old, to be in full enjoyment of civil and political rights, and to have completed a probationary period of at least one year. These courts heard all cases involving limited amounts of money, including first-instance cases. They also handled landlord and tenant cases. Their jurisdiction in criminal matters extended only to cases where the penalty did not exceed six months in jail (see The Legal Framework, ch. 10).

In addition, there were special courts that dealt with administrative contracts, property rights, juveniles, and labor conflicts.

The president of Haiti appointed all judges. Those in the Court of Cassation and the courts of appeal served ten years; the others served seven years.

The Functions of the State

Most Haitians viewed government functionaries as beneficiaries of patronage and the spoils system rather than as public servants. The state traditionally supported and maintained the established political order and extracted wealth from the population. Citizens therefore expected little or nothing from government. Rather, they saw the state as an entity that confiscated, taxed, prohibited, or imprisoned.

The Haitian government also traditionally served as a source of jobs. Political favoritism and bribery characterized the system. One common Creole expression holds that *"Jijman se kob"* (court rulings are money). Political scientists have used terms such as *kleptocracy, predatory state, government-by-franchise,* and *autocolonization* in their descriptions of the Haitian system of taxation, patronage, corruption, public monopolies, and private monopolies protected by the state.

The state had developed a relatively elaborate apparatus for taxation, but it provided only limited public services. Most Haitians relied on foreign-assistance agencies and on nongovernmental institutions for services provided by most other governments. For example, education was the most elaborate public-service sector, but the majority of children still attended nongovernmental schools (see Education, ch. 7). The state's abdication of its role as service provider created a situation in which foreign-assistance agencies served as a kind of shadow government.

Government institutions in Port-au-Prince provided at least the facade of public services through the Ministry of Public Health and Population; the Ministry of Agriculture, Natural Resources, and Rural Development; the Ministry of National Education, Youth, and Sports; and other ministries. These ministries had no representatives in most rural areas, however, and they provided relatively few services even in Port-au-Prince. Government budgets for public services generally accounted for salaries, but they provided little or no budget support for program implementation.

Aside from the army, Haiti's key state institution had traditionally been the customs house, the primary source of tax revenues. The state also extracted wealth through its control over certain essential services and through public and private monopoly ownership of key commodity-based enterprises (see Economic Policy, ch. 8). This system contributed to the country's political instability because it politicized important sectors of the country's economy.

Urban Dominance, Rural Stagnation

A sharp administrative division existed between rural and urban jurisdictions. The capital city dominated the urban sector. National political institutions and decisions focused on Port-au-Prince, and they were far removed from the lives of most Haitians. References to the "Republic of Port-au-Prince" reflected this reality. The political system affected all Haitians, but changes in government generally had little direct impact on the lives of rural Haitians.

Data from 1984 suggested that the government spent about 65 percent of its revenues in Port-au-Prince, a city with roughly

20 percent of the nation's population. In effect, taxes levied in rural areas paid the salaries of a privileged group of city dwellers.

Foreign assistance also tended to exacerbate rural-urban differences. About 40 percent of all public foreign aid benefited Port-au-Prince.

In rural Haiti, the army was the government. The official role of the armed forces was national defense, but most members of the military carried out police functions (see The Role of the Armed Forces, ch. 10). Perhaps the most influential presence was that of the denim-uniformed corps of 562 rural section chiefs (*chefs de section*) and their assistants. People commonly referred to the section chief and his corps of assistants as *leta* (the state), although the section chiefs constituted more an auxiliary corps and were not members of the regular army.

The rural section chiefs were usually recruited from a small class of landed peasant families known as *gro neg* (big man) or *gran abitan* (large peasant). These families generally had other economic interests in addition to farming, including grain speculation, money-lending, and various forms of commerce. Appointments of section chiefs were usually based on political ties, factional alliances, and bribes. In many cases the positions were inherited.

The role of section chief involved much more than conventional police functions. As the sole government representative in rural areas, the section chief levied taxes and fines, mediated disputes, and served as a civil registry. These responsibilities placed the section chief in a powerful political and economic position. He was well situated to collect bribes; rural police refused to provide services to citizens who did not make special payments to them. The virtual absence of competing power brokers buttressed the section chiefs' positions. The 1987 Constitution set up rural government councils in an attempt to curb abuses by section chiefs and to mediate the interests of rural citizens in the political process. These councils, however, were also subject to graft and corruption.

Centralized authority in the presidency contrasted with the decentralized exercise of authority by local government officials. Port-au-Prince provided no policy direction for local governments, and it did little to monitor them. Few funds were made available to local governments for expenses other than salaries. Certain local officials, such as section chiefs, exercised absolute power within their local jurisdictions. They did not depend on salaries for their income; in a sense, they purchased from the state the privilege of collecting revenues by virtue of their authority and their power to grant favors.

Political Dynamics

The Haitian political system has historically displayed certain enduring features. The post-Duvalier transition, for example, was similar in some ways to previous crises of succession.

Power Maintenance

According to the Duvaliers, Haiti was a republic, wherein power passed smoothly from father to son in 1971. In reality, however, the country resembled a monarchy. This "dynastic republicanism" was merely a new variant of the traditional Haitian system of competition among personalist factions. The dynastic republicanism began when François Duvalier simply extended his term in office beyond its prescribed six years. As Duvalier was well aware, there was ample precedent in Haitian history for this move. Duvalier's immediate predecessors all tried to extend their prescribed terms in office (see Politics and the Military, 1934–57, ch. 6). After extending his term, Duvalier declared himself president. Nine of Duvalier's predecessors had designated themselves chiefs of state for life. Duvalier then established the hereditary presidency. Haitian monarchs Henri (Henry) Christophe (1807–20) and Faustin Soulouque (1847–59) had attempted to establish hereditary succession more than a century earlier (see Christophe's Kingdom and Pétion's Republic; Decades of Instability, 1843–1915, ch. 6). In short, the primary goal of most Haitian leaders has been to maintain themselves in power for as long as possible.

Army Politics: Force and Counterforce

The Haitian army has traditionally played the role of political arbiter. The precedent for this role can be traced to eighteenth-century colonial Saint-Domingue. The early leaders of Haiti established strong military rule during the revolutionary period (1791–1804). The leading general of the revolution, François-Dominique Toussaint Louverture, declared himself the French governor for life in the preindependence constitution of 1801 (see Toussaint Louverture, ch. 6; The Military in Haitian History, ch. 10). The French Revolution also affected events in Haiti. At the time that Haiti achieved independence, France was ruled by Napoléon Bonaparte, a preeminent military figure who eventually declared himself emperor. Jean-Jacques Dessalines, the first Haitian head of state, was also a victorious general who declared himself emperor. From 1804 to 1913, almost all Haitian heads of state were military officers. Military occupation by the United States (1915–34) served to reinforce the central role of military power in society (see The United States Occupation, 1915–34, ch. 6).

The army clearly exercised its power, as the supreme arbiter of political destinies, during the political succession of François Duvalier in 1957. At that point, however, history took a different turn. By 1962 Duvalier had effectively undermined the authority of the regular army by legitimizing the *tonton makouts* as a paramilitary counterforce, the VSN. The VSN, devoted to maintaining power and repressing political opposition, was considerably larger than the army; it consisted primarily of rural dwellers.

Duvalier's ability to maintain power can be attributed largely to his neutralization of the military as an independent political force. The idea of a paramilitary counterforce also had historical precedent. Soulouque made effective use of the *zinglins,* precursors to the *tonton makouts.* During his presidential campaign, François Duvalier organized a private paramilitary group known as *cagoulards* (hooded men).

For years the VSN has had a strong base of support in rural Haiti, from the same segments of the population that filled the ranks of the irregular military forces known as *cacos* and *piquets* during the pre-occupation era (see Decades of Instability, 1843–1915, ch. 6). Duvalier's decision to legitimize the VSN was clever, partly because it co-opted disenfranchised groups into the established political system at relatively little cost to the regime. Militia members were volunteers who were even willing to pay fees to local VSN commanders for permission to join the force. Volunteers were familiar with the VSN's opportunities for personal gain through corruption. To raise money, local VSN commanders periodically disbanded their units and recruited new members who would pay to join the force.

Forces that countered military power were set up within the military itself at certain points in Haiti's history. President Sténio Vincent (1930–41) first created a presidential guard in the 1930s, and he had heavy weapons brought into the presidential palace. This guard helped Vincent maintain power for eleven years; it played a key role in the political fates of all of Vincent's successors. The Leopards Corps, created by Jean-Claude Duvalier in the 1970s, represented yet another variant of a specialized army corps assigned the responsibilities of maintaining presidential power and discouraging coups d'état.

More recently, Avril's core of support also lay clearly within the Presidential Guard. As of mid-1989, Avril had not fully consolidated his power base, and contenders vied for his position as military chief of state. Avril was also forced to contend with army and nonmilitary groups linked to the *tonton makouts.* The *tonton makouts,* although abolished in 1986, were never effectively disbanded. They

Presidential Palace with statue of the Unknown Maroon
in foreground, Port-au-Prince
Courtesy United States Agency
for International Development (John Metelsky)

continued to play a leading role in the politics of the army, and they, together with the Duvalierists, appeared to represent the central obstacle to Avril's consolidation of power. Ironically, these were the same people to whom he owed personal and political debts.

The President as Strongman

The focus of Haitian politics has always been the presidency. The weakly developed separation of powers has reflected this situation. Legislative bodies and elections, which have existed for centuries, have generally only assisted the chief of state in obtaining whatever he wished.

Haitian writers have often described the country's obsession with the presidency in pathological terms. As a young writer, long before he became president, François Duvalier identified the historical "mania for the presidency" as the disease of "presidentitis." Earlier generations of Haitian intellectuals had also bemoaned the destructive social effects of the presidency for life. This obsession continued to be an important political issue throughout the twentieth century.

As a result of the life-and-death power he wielded over the citizenry, the president has historically acquired a godlike quality.

Presidents rarely represented a coalition of interest groups that joined forces through Western-style debate, compromise over party platforms, and competition at the polls. Rather, the president usually headed a faction that seized control of the state by any means possible, with the support of the army. In the process, the president became the personal embodiment of the state. François Duvalier wrote it in lights on the public square, proclaiming "I am the Haitian flag. He who is my enemy is the enemy of the fatherland." State and nation merged in the person of the president. In Haitian politics, there was no real distinction between state and government. Presidents could therefore claim with some justification that they were the state.

Political parties and candidates also focused on the presidency. A plethora of individuals competed for the presidency; no true political parties existed. The emphasis on the presidency has hampered constitutional reforms designed to establish a sharing of power, free elections, and local representation. The emphasis also conflicted with the wave of popular expectations unleashed by the fall of Duvalier in 1986. Heightened expectations for change clashed with the regressive politics of old-line Duvalierists and *tonton makouts*. This clash contributed to the protracted post-Duvalier crisis of succession.

Perceptions of Democracy

The presidency depended on the nonparticipation of average citizens in the political process, except when they had personal ties to a power holder. Presidential contenders often rhetorically invoked the masses in their transitions to power; still, the common citizen played an insignificant role in the day-to-day politics of the country. This situation fueled popular cynicism regarding elections.

Participation in the political arena, however, has traditionally involved great personal risk. The threat of arrest, injury, and death was very real for those who challenged the prevailing government. The fact that political detainees were not entitled to due process of law further magnified this risk.

After the fall of Jean-Claude Duvalier, everyone spoke of democracy. Some Creole observers have described the post-Duvalier period as *diyari demokratik* (democratic diarrhea) or *bambosh demokrasi* (revelry of democracy). Average Haitians expected that life would somehow dramatically improve with the departure of the Duvaliers and that there would be democracy; however, for most Haitians, democracy was only an abstract concept. Haitians had never experienced true democracy, and communities had never had a voice in the political process.

The political role models for most Haitians emerged during the Duvalier era. For many people, post-Duvalier notions of democracy meant only a change in the factions and the personalities of the people in power. For others, democracy meant their finally being able to take their turn at the spoils system. Some people believed that democracy meant an opportunity to do what one pleased—liberty without responsibility (an attitude noted and reproved in Toussaint Louverture's remark, "I have never considered that liberty is synonymous with license"). Many people felt that a democracy should provide everyone with jobs, food, and material goods. In any case, the constitutional referendum in March 1987 and the November 29 elections of that same year clearly demonstrated overwhelming support for genuine change that would lead to a better quality of life.

The Mass Media

The mass media in Haiti expanded remarkably between 1957 and 1989; radio led the way. The transistor radio brought news and information to previously isolated rural areas. Since the 1950s, Protestant missionaries have proselytized through their own radio stations (see Protestantism, ch. 7). Radio Soleil, a Roman Catholic station, and other radio stations contributed to the fall of Duvalier in 1986.

Approximately two dozen radio stations were broadcasting in Haiti in the late 1980s; slightly more than half of them were in the Port-au-Prince area. There were a similar number of newspapers and other periodicals, including four daily papers with an estimated combined circulation of 25,000, four monthlies, and a dozen or so weeklies. The number of publications varied over time. Some publications were produced irregularly. During the post-Duvalier period, a relatively large number of publications appeared, but many of them published only a few issues before folding.

Two television stations, one private and one public, were broadcasting in the late 1980s. There was also a cable television network. Many wealthy families owned satellite dishes that picked up television signals from abroad. Television played a growing role among the Haitian media, but its influence continued to be greatest among higher-income residents of Port-au-Prince. In general, increased freedom of expression and an absence of formal government censorship or control characterized the post-Duvalier period.

Spoken and written Creole became commonplace in radio, television, and publications, as well as in community organizations and development projects (see Changes in Language Use, ch. 7). The production of materials written in Creole expanded exponentially in the late 1980s and increased the participation of the majority of the population in Haitian politics. Creole also became increasingly important in advertising.

Interest Groups

During the post-Duvalier period, other developments in the media, party organization, labor unions, and professional associations took place. Understanding these changes is essential to understanding Haiti's political environment.

The *Tonton Makout* Network

The Duvalier dynasty held power longer than any other regime in Haitian history. The duration of the dynasty enabled the thorough entrenchment of Duvalierist institutions and the development of a patronage system. One of the more important of these institutions was the VSN. After the VSN's dissolution, former *tonton makout* leaders remained at large, and some were politically active throughout the post-Duvalier period. The old *tonton makout* networks also continued to function within the army. As of 1989, they were the main obstacle to free, fair, and popular elections in Haiti, and they were the most significant threat to domestic security (see Public Order, ch. 10).

Through the VSN, the Duvalier regime had politicized rural Haiti. The VSN had expanded the president's influence to remote areas, and it had incorporated rural Haiti into a political system once limited almost exclusively to Port-au-Prince. The VSN had assured political control of the hinterlands, but it had given peasants no new voice in the political process. It had, however, created a rural awareness of Port-au-Prince and events there, a consciousness of the national political system, and new political aspirations. The VSN had engendered a generalized disrespect for political institutions, and it had heightened expectations of profit from the political system.

Political Parties

During presidential campaigns, political parties organized under the banner of specific personalities. Political parties have existed in name for a long time, but they have not exerted any independent influence on the political system. Rather, parties have served as campaign vehicles for individual politicians.

In the 1870s and the 1880s, the emergence of the Liberal Party (Parti Liberal—PL) and the National Party (Parti National—PN) reflected the polarization between black and mulatto elites (see Decades of Instability, 1843–1915, ch. 6). In the wake of the United

States occupation (1915–34), nationalist parties organized around the issue of resistance to foreign occupation. These parties included the Patriotic Union (L'Union Patriotique) and the Nationalist Union (L'Union Nationaliste). During the presidential campaign of 1946, there were many candidates and parties, including the Popular Socialist Party (Parti Socialiste Populaire—PSP), the Unified Democrat Party (Parti Démocrate Unifié—PDU), the Worker Peasant Movement (Mouvement Ouvrier Paysan—MOP), the Popular Democratic Party of Haitian Youth (Parti Démocratique Populaire de la Jeunesse Haïtienne—PDPJH), the Communist Party of Haiti (Parti Communiste d'Haïti—PCH), and a federation of groups known as the Haitian Revolutionary Front (Front Révolutionnaire Haïtien—FRH).

The presidential campaign of 1956–57 included candidates who ran under the banners of the National Agricultural Industrial Party (Parti Agricole et Industriel National—PAIN); led by Louis Déjoie; the MOP, led by Daniel Fignolé, the PN, led by Clément Jumelle; and the National Unity Party (Parti Unité Nationale—PUN), led by François Duvalier. During the Duvalier years, the three non-Duvalierist parties continued to function in exile on the United States mainland and in Puerto Rico.

Both Duvalier governments banned, or severely restricted, opposition political parties. Consequently, about a dozen opposition parties operated in exile, including Leslie Manigat's RDNP based in Caracas; the Unified Haitian Communist Party (Parti Unifié Communiste Haïtien—PUCH) based in France; the National Progressive Revolutionary Haitian Party (Parti National Progressiste Révolutionnaire Haïtien—Panpra) headed by Serge Gilles and based in France; and the Democratic Revolutionary Party of Haiti (Parti Révolutionnaire Démocratique d'Haïti) based in the Dominican Republic and subsequently known in Haiti as the Democratic Movement for the Liberation of Haiti (Mouvement Démocratique pour la Libération d'Haïti—Modelh), headed by François Latortue.

During the presidential campaign of 1987, more than 100 candidates announced their candidacy. As of August 1987, twenty-one political parties had registered. None of these parties, however, developed a nationwide organization. At the time of the sabotaged elections of November 19, 1987, the race was expected to be won by one of four candidates: Sylvio C. Claude, standard bearer of the Christian Democrat Party of Haiti (Parti Démocrate Chrétien d'Haïti—PDCH); Marc Bazin of the Movement for the Installation of Democracy in Haiti (Mouvement pour l'Instauration de la Démocratie en Haïti—MIDH); Louis Dejoie II, son of the 1957 presidential candidate, representing PAIN; and Gérard Gourgue of the National Cooperation Front (Front National de Concertation—FNC). The Gourgue candidacy under the FNC appeared to have considerable support in urban and rural areas. The FNC was a loose federation of parties, community groups, and trade unions based on an organization called the Group of 57. The party included the National Committee of the Congress of Democratic Movements (Comité National du Congrès des Mouvements Démocratiques—Conacom), the Patriotic Unity Bloc (Bloc Unité Patriotique—BUP), and Panpra, which had re-established itself in Haiti with the return of Serge Gilles. Bazin and Dejoie also returned from exile to organize their presidential campaigns. Claude's PDCH and the Social Christian Party of Haiti (Parti Social Chrétien d'Haïti—PSCH) led by Grégoire Eugène were the only two political parties organized in Haiti that sought to operate openly during the Jean-Claude Duvalier years. The remaining parties had either formed during the post-Duvalier period or had returned from exile to join the campaign.

The Upper and the Middle Classes

The system of public and private monopolies, including parastatals and import-substitution industries, developed under the Duvaliers (see Growth and Structure of the Economy, ch. 3). These industries generated great wealth for a handful of powerful families in Port-au-Prince, which resulted in politicized economic decision making. This elite sector saw itself threatened by the fall of the Duvalier regime. Under interim rule, volatile competition arose among certain business interests and military factions. Key members of the business community backed Duvalierist presidential candidates who were likely to protect the lucrative business privileges established under the old regime.

Intermediary classes (those between the wealthy elite and the impoverished masses) grew significantly during the Duvalier era. François Duvalier's political strategy of appealing to the black middle class created a new constituency for political patronage, government employment, and the rapid accumulation of wealth through the political system. The growth of the black middle class was closely linked to the Duvalier era, and it contributed to the tremendous growth of Port-au-Prince after the 1950s (see Demographic Profile, ch. 7).

The long-standing tendencies toward the centralization of wealth and of power in Port-au-Prince greatly increased during the Duvalier era. The income gap between upper and lower income groups widened, and rural areas suffered accordingly. Growing rural-to-urban migration, primarily to Port-au-Prince, and emigration, especially to the United States, also had an impact on the political environment and on aspirations for change (see Migration, ch. 7). The Duvalier era saw an unprecedented level of emigration to North America along with smaller waves of emigration to other Caribbean countries, Latin America, Europe, and Africa. Emigration had an important impact on Haitian politics. Emigrés maintained numerous fragmented political parties in exile. Emigration also caused huge sums of foreign currency to enter into the economy through remittances. It raised Haitians' consciousness of the outside world, and it led to easier upward social mobility for members of the new intermediary classes by alleviating competition for scarce jobs.

Other Groups

The Duvaliers suppressed labor unions. A number of loosely organized unions and federations emerged after the fall of Jean-Claude, but labor generally lacked institutional development (see Labor, ch. 3). Unions exercised little clout in industry. Their importance as pressure groups, however, grew during the post-Duvalier period. Professional and trade associations played an active political role in the fall of Jean-Claude Duvalier and during the period that followed. The most active associations represented teachers, students, agronomists, physicians, journalists, lawyers, and engineers. The Association of Industries of Haiti (Association des Industries d'Haïti), representing businesspeople involved in the assembly industry, exercised a great deal of influence over government economic policy. The two Port-au-Prince chambers of commerce—the Chamber of Commerce and Industry of Haiti (Chambre de Commerce et de l'Industrie d'Haïti) and the Haitian-American Chamber of Commerce and Industry (Chambre de Commerce et de l'Industrie Haïtiano-Américaine—Hamcham)—were less active after 1986 than they had been under Jean-Claude Duvalier. The Association of Coffee Exporters (Association des Exportateurs de Café—Asdec) had long exerted influence in politics and the economy.

Approximately ten human rights organizations functioned in Haiti in 1989. Although most formed after the fall of Jean-Claude Duvalier, one had been in existence since the late 1970s. Most of these organizations maintained their headquarters in Port-au-Prince. A number of them had links to Haitians who lived abroad or who had been exiled during the Duvalier era. Some individuals working in human rights harbored broader political ambitions, and they sought to influence presidential politics.

Foreign Relations

Throughout its history, Haiti's relative isolation has constrained its foreign relations. Haiti achieved some prominence as a result of its successful revolution, but the governments of slaveholding countries either ignored or decried the country during the first half of the nineteenth century. In the United States, the question of recognizing Haiti provoked sharp debate between abolitionists, who favored recognition, and slaveholders, who vehemently opposed such an action. The advent of the Civil War, however, allowed President Abraham Lincoln to recognize Haiti without controversy. Haiti became a focus of interest for the great powers in the early twentieth century mainly because of the country's strategic location. Competition among the United States, Germany, France, and Britain resulted in the breaching of Haiti's sovereignty and the nineteen-year occupation by United States forces (see The United States Occupation, 1915–34, ch. 6). Subsequent isolation stemmed from Haiti's cultural and linguistic uniqueness, its economic underdevelopment, and from international condemnation of the repressive Duvalier regimes.

Haiti has maintained a long-standing relationship with the United States. Haitians have perceived economic ties to the United States as vital. The United States was Haiti's primary trading partner for both exports and imports, its most important source of foreign assistance, and the primary target of Haitian emigration. A large number of private voluntary agencies from the United States functioned in Haiti. The assembly industry of Port-au-Prince was closely tied to the United States economy. In short, the economic and the political influence of the United States in Haiti was more powerful than the influence of any other country.

Still, contemporary American diplomatic interest in Haiti has been minimal. Washington's interest in Haiti arose chiefly because of the country's proximity to the Panama Canal and Central America. Haiti also controls the Windward Passage, a narrow body of water that could be easily closed, disrupting maritime traffic. In the nineteenth century, the United States considered establishing a naval base in Haiti (see Decades of Instability, 1843–1915, ch. 6). At about the time of World War I, the United States occupied Haiti along with a number of other countries in the Caribbean and Central America. Since the 1960s, Washington has viewed Haiti as an anticommunist bulwark, partly because of the country's proximity to Cuba. François Duvalier, exploiting United States' hostility toward the Cuban regime of Fidel Castro Ruz and United States fears of communist expansion in the Caribbean, deterred the United

States government from exerting excessive pressure against his own dictatorship.

In the 1980s, the United States expressed a special interest in curbing illegal Haitian immigration (see Migration, ch. 7).·Washington also attempted to curtail shipments of illegal drugs to and from Haiti.

From the 1970s until 1987, United States assistance to Haiti grew. After the violently disrupted elections of November 1987, however, United States president Ronald Reagan suspended all aid to Haiti. In August 1989, President George Bush restored US$10 million in food aid because the Avril government had made progress toward holding free elections and had agreed to cooperate in efforts to control international drug trafficking.

The Dominican Republic was the second most important country to Haiti because the two nations shared a border, but the two countries were ambivalent toward each other. Haiti supplied cheap labor to the Dominican Republic, mostly to help harvest sugarcane. Under the Duvaliers, this arrangement involved an annual intergovernmental exchange of funds for the supply of cane cutters.

For generations Haitians had informally crossed the Dominican Republic's border in search of work. An estimated 250,000 people of Haitian parentage lived in the Dominican Republic. This perceived "blackening" of the Dominican population motivated dictator Rafael Leónidas Trujillo Molina to carry out a notorious massacre of Haitians in 1937 (see Politics and the Military, 1934–57, ch. 6; The Era of Trujillo, ch. 1). The border has been an issue of contention in other respects as well. The Haitian economy has proved to be a desirable market for Dominican products, effectively undercutting Haitian production of certain commodities and reducing the domestic market for some Haitian goods. Also, exiled Haitian politicians have readily sought refuge in the Dominican Republic and have gained allies there in efforts to bring down Haitian governments.

Ties with other Caribbean nations were limited. Historically, Britain and France strove to limit contacts between their dependencies and Haiti, in order to discourage independence movements. Haiti's cultural and linguistic distinctiveness also prevented close relations in the Caribbean. As of mid-1989, Haiti did not belong to the Caribbean Community and Common Market (Caricom), and it had not been included in the Lomé Convention (see Glossary), although there had been some discussion with Caricom officials on both points. Haiti also maintained few productive relationships in Latin America.

Other countries important to Haiti included the primary donor countries for foreign assistance, especially France, Canada, and the Federal Republic of Germany. Haiti maintained special cultural ties to France, even though the two countries were not major trading partners. Haiti also enjoyed a supportive relationship with the Canadian province of Quebec, one of the few linguistically compatible entities in the Western Hemisphere; most Haitian émigrés in Canada lived in Quebec, and the majority of administrators of Canadian aid projects came from Quebec. Haiti's memberships in international and multilateral organizations included the United Nations and its associated organizations, the Organization of American States, the Inter-American Development Bank, the International Monetary Fund (see Glossary), and the General Agreement on Tariffs and Trade.

In many ways, Haitians were proud of their history, particularly the accomplishments of such revolutionary figures as Dessalines and Toussaint. However, the nation has suffered both from its uniqueness and from its similarity to other less developed nations. Largely isolated in the Western Hemisphere, Haiti nonetheless has experienced political instability, repression, and impoverishment equal to, or exceeding that of, other Latin American states. As the 1990s approached, Haiti still could not count itself among the democratic nations of the hemisphere, despite the sincere desire of its people for some form of representative government.

* * *

James Leyburn's general social history, *The Haitian People,* originally published in 1941, continues to be the classic introduction to Haitian political issues. The 1956 edition has a useful introduction by Sidney Mintz, a historically oriented anthropologist. The classic work on Haitian-United States relations is Ludwell Lee Montague's *Haiti and the United States, 1714-1938.* Hans Schmidt's *The United States Occupation of Haiti, 1915-1934* reveals certain features of Haitian politics and relations with the United States. Other important political studies include Robert Rotberg and Christopher Clague's *Haiti: The Politics of Squalor* as well as Robert Debs Heinl and Nancy Gordon Heinl's *Written in Blood: The Story of the Haitian People, 1492-1971.* (Robert Debs Heinl was head of the United States Marine Mission to Haiti under François Duvalier.) The Heinls cover Haitian history from 1492 to 1971, but the treatment of the François Duvalier years is the most useful portion of this work.

David Nicholls's *From Dessalines to Duvalier: Race, Colour, and National Independence in Haiti* provides careful treatment of the role of race, color, and class in Haitian political history since independence in 1804. This work provides good insights into the factionalism and the rotating political elites that characterize Haitian political history. *Haiti: Political Failures, Cultural Successes,* by Brian Weinstein and Aaron Segal, gives good coverage of the Jean-Claude Duvalier years. Recent works include James Ferguson's *Papa Doc, Baby Doc: Haiti and the Duvaliers,* a journalistic account focused on the fall of Jean-Claude Duvalier and events of the following year, and Elizabeth Abbott's *Haiti: The Duvaliers and Their Legacy,* a detailed and rather personal journalistic account of the Duvaliers, especially the Jean-Claude Duvalier regime in the 1980s and the Namphy regime that followed. Simon M. Fass's *Political Economy in Haiti: The Drama of Survival* gives an interesting politico-economic analysis of how the system works to extract wealth and how the urban poor maneuver the economics of survival. (For further information and complete citations, see Bibliography.)

Figure from a painting by Prosper Pierrelouis

CONSOLIDATION OF POLITICAL POWER in the hands of strongmen has made the armed forces the institutional pillar of Haitian society. Born of revolutionary violence and plagued by socioeconomic deterioration, Haiti never succeeded in building civilian institutions capable of rivaling military rule.

Part of Haiti's history is the story of competing mercenary bands (*cacos*) and peasant groups (*piquets*), who fought a ramshackle military. The United States occupation, after 1915, reversed the collapse of national institutions that had marked this part of Haiti's history. But the most visible product of the occupation, ironically, turned out to be the Garde d'Haïti, which has evolved into today's armed forces, the Haitian Armed Forces (Forces Armées d'Haïti— FAd'H). The military has continued to be Haiti's only truly national organization with any degree of institutional cohesion.

A shrewd autocrat, François Duvalier (1957–71) ruthlessly suppressed all opposition groups. Duvalier purged the army of individuals suspected of disloyalty and brought the remaining soldiers under his absolute control. A powerful paramilitary counterbalancing organization—the Volunteers for National Security (Volontaires de la Sécurité Nationale—VSN), or *tonton makouts* (bogeymen)— was created to protect the regime and to enforce its directives. François Duvalier's son, Jean-Claude Duvalier, assumed power in 1971 and demonstrated initial political endurance. During Jean-Claude's tenure, a reconstituted officer corps emerged, partly to counterbalance the overwhelming power of the paramilitary forces organized by his father. A vague strategy to modernize Haiti's economic and political structure in the 1970s also led to a brief upgrading of the armed forces. Jean-Claude's regime added a tactical unit (the Leopards Corps), purchased new equipment for the Air Corps (Corps d'Aviation), reopened the Military Academy, and secured a small amount of military assistance from the United States. Yet the authoritarian, and often aimless, governance isolated the regime from national realities, leading to a tide of popular discontent between 1983 and 1985 and to the fall of the regime in February 1986.

Under pressure from the international community, Duvalier fled Haiti. A hastily constructed interim junta replaced him. The junta was put together mostly by the armed forces, the only institution in a position of authority. The junta fared badly in its political mission, however, and the failed and flawed elections of 1987 and 1988 reflected the military's institutional unraveling and its inability to control the nation. A succession of coups in 1988 and a serious intramilitary revolt in early 1989 underscored the gravity of the problem.

The character of Haiti's domestic security situation has attracted considerable international attention. Reports of brutal violence and human-rights infractions have outraged many countries and international agencies. The government's inability—or unwillingness— to control paramilitary violence and a rise in crime since 1986 have undermined the military's credibility. A growing narcotics network, involving Haitian military personnel, has also reduced the credibility of the armed forces.

Behind domestic security problems is an antiquated and unresponsive legal system. The 1987 Constitution separates the functions of the police and the conventional military, but the FAd'H continued to be the government's primary law-enforcement agency. Haiti had no national police force in the late 1980s. The armed forces handled rural security duties, and in Port-au-Prince police duties were carried out by a part of the army. Several national political crises and budgetary constraints have led to a recent streamlining of FAd'H's operations and to improvement in its administration.

The Military in Haitian History

The origins of Haiti's military lie in the country's revolution (see The Haitian Revolution, ch. 6). A decade of warfare produced a military cadre from which Haiti's early leaders emerged. Defeat of the French demonstrated Haiti's considerable strategic stamina and tactical capabilities, but Haiti's victory did not translate into a successful national government or a strong economy. Lacking a strong constitution, Haiti was usually ruled by force. The armed forces, who had been united against the French, fragmented into warring regional factions. The military very soon took control of almost every aspect of Haitian life. Officers assumed responsibility for the administration of justice and for municipal management. According to a Haitian diplomat, the country was in its earlier days "an immense military camp." Without viable civilian institutions, Haiti was vulnerable to military personalities, who permanently shaped the nation's authoritarian, personalist, and coercive style of governance.

During the latter half of the nineteenth century, the army either failed to protect the central government or directly caused the government's collapse. Rural insurgent movements led by *piquets* and *cacos* limited the central government's authority in outlying areas. These groups carried on war into the twentieth century; they were finally put down by the United States Marines in 1919.

Prolonged instability weakened the military. By the end of the nineteenth century, Haiti's military had become little more than an undisciplined, ill-fed, and poorly paid militia that shifted its allegiances as battles were won or lost and as new leaders came to power. Between 1806 and 1879, an estimated sixty-nine revolts against existing governments took place; another twenty uprisings, or attempted insurrections, broke out between 1908 and 1915. At the beginning of the twentieth century, Haiti's political problems attracted increasing foreign involvement. France, Germany, and the United States were the major actors; the latter occupied the country in 1915 (see The United States Occupation, 1915–34, ch. 6). During the occupation, the United States made an unsuccessful attempt to modernize Haiti's armed forces.

The United States Marines disbanded Haiti's army, which consisted of an estimated 9,000 men, including 308 generals. In February 1916, the Haitian Constabulary (Gendarmerie d'Haïti) was formed. United States Marine and United States Navy officers and noncommissioned officers (NCOs) commanded the group. The Gendarmerie attempted to secure public safety, initially by subduing the *cacos*; to promote development, particularly road construction; and to modernize the military through the introduction of a training structure, a health service, and other improvements.

The United States administration of Haiti (1915–34) brought order and resulted in some economic and social development. At the same time, the United States overhauled Haiti's disintegrated military infrastructure. The Gendarmerie became the Garde d'Haïti in 1928; the Garde formed the core of Haiti's armed forces after the United States administration ended. The United States sought to establish a modern, apolitical military force in Haiti. On the surface, it succeeded; the organization, the training, and the equipment of the Garde all represented improvements over the military conditions existing before the occupation. What the United States did not (and probably could not) reform was the basic authoritarian inclination of Haitian society, an inclination antithetical to the goal of military depoliticization.

Army Politics in the Twentieth Century

Some professionalization of the army continued for a few years after the United States occupation, but Haiti's political structure deteriorated rapidly after 1934, weakening civil-military relations and ultimately affecting the character of the armed forces. After the coup of 1946 and after Colonel Paul E. Magloire's election to the presidency in 1950, the army again assumed a political role. This development divided the army internally, and it set the stage for François Duvalier's ascent to power in late 1957 (see Politics and the Military, 1934–57, ch. 6).

During the three decades of despotic Duvalier rule, a parallel security force, the VSN, emerged. The Duvaliers maintained control of the country through this brutal force, which was independent of the armed forces. Both Duvaliers lacked military experience; still, they managed to neutralize the army's influence through intimidation, bribery, and political maneuvering. The Duvaliers also managed to stave off a number of low-level opposition plots and invasion attempts, mostly during the 1960s.

François Duvalier, 1957–71

When François Duvalier came to power in 1957, the armed forces were at their lowest point, professionally, since 1915. Internal tension stemmed from political, generational, and racial divisions within the army command. The leadership of the former Garde d'Haïti, trained by the United States Marines, was aging and was slowly giving way to a younger cadre of Military Academy graduates from the 1940s. Duvalier hastened this process by retiring a group of senior officers and promoting a number of junior officers.

Duvalier's establishment of a parallel security apparatus posed the most serious challenge to the crumbling integrity of the armed forces. In late 1958, Duvalier reinstated, and took direct control of, the Presidential Guard (Garde Présidentielle), and he eliminated the Maison Militaire (military household), which had served as the presidential security unit before the Duvalier era. In 1959 the regime began recruiting a civilian militia (Milice Civile), ostensibly as an adjunct to the Presidential Guard. Drawn initially from the capital city's slums and equipped with antiquated small arms found in the basement of the Presidential Palace, the civilian militia became the VSN after 1962. The VSN's control extended into the countryside, through a system of information, intelligence, and command tied directly to the Presidential Palace.

The armed forces yielded political power to the new regime and lost many of their institutionalized features, developed during the previous thirty years. Duvalier closed down the Military Academy in 1961. A professional and elitist institution, the academy represented a potential source of opposition to the regime. Officers who attempted to resist Duvalier forfeited their careers. In 1963 Duvalier expelled the United States military mission, which he had invited to Haiti in 1959, because he believed that military-modernization values imparted by United States instructors could lead to resistance to the government's restructuring of the armed forces.

Duvalier succeeded in overpowering the mainstream military establishment, but the process was painful; it required several abrupt attacks. For example, Duvalier eliminated, or exiled, anyone who opposed him. Duvalier's ruthlessness and suspicion caused members of his own security apparatus to turn against him—most notably Clément Barbot, one of the original VSN chiefs.

By the mid-1960s, the VSN and the army routinely cooperated on internal security matters, even though the two groups were suspicious of each other. There were occasional lapses in the security apparatus, however. In 1967 several bombs exploded near the palace, and the regime subsequently executed nineteen officers of the Presidential Guard. In 1970 the entire membership of Haiti's small Coast Guard staged an abortive mutiny.

The regime referred to the VSN as a militia. This designation masked the organization's role as the Duvaliers' front-line security force. The VSN acted as political cadres, secret police, and instruments of terror. In addition, they played a crucial political role for the regime: they countered the influence of the armed forces, historically the nation's foremost institutional power. François Duvalier went farther than any of his predecessors in his efforts to reduce the ability of the military to influence selection of the country's leaders. The VSN's success in keeping the army and the rest of Haitian society in check created what has been described as a VSN-led ''parabureaucracy.''

The VSN gained its deadly reputation partially because its members received no salary, even though they worked for the National Palace (Palais National). They made their livings, instead, through extortion and petty crime. Rural members of the VSN, who wore blue denim uniforms, had received some training from the army, while the plainclothed members, with their dark glasses, served as Haiti's criminal-investigation force (see Public Order, this ch.).

Jean-Claude Duvalier, 1971–86

When Jean-Claude Duvalier (''Baby Doc'') came to power in 1971, the country's security forces became less abusive, but they still used some brutality. During Jean-Claude's regime, the balance between the VSN and the armed forces changed. The new regime sought to realign these competing power bases, if only to ensure control over the nation's security apparatus. Furthermore, Jean-Claude's half-hearted attempt to open Haiti to the outside world and to secure renewed foreign assistance from the United States suggested a need to restrain the abuses of the VSN, which included more than 9,000 members and an informal circle of thousands in early 1986.

The creation of the Leopards counterinsurgency unit, with United States support, provided the regime with a relatively modern tool for responding to internal threats. The Leopards also provided Baby Doc with a new force, the capability and the allegiance of which bridged the gap between the armed forces and the VSN. A reorganization integrated some senior VSN members into the army, effecting a partial merger of Haiti's two security institutions. In 1972 the Military Academy reopened, and a politically well-connected class—the first since 1961—graduated in 1973. The reopening of the academy represented a small step toward reprofessionalizing the military. Some modernization of army equipment was also undertaken during this period.

The armed forces entered the 1980s as a mere shadow of the powerful, disciplined, trained institution that had existed forty years earlier. Although the army successfully repelled a number of attempts against the regime, it ultimately failed to prevent Duvalier's fall under pressure from his own populace. With last-minute assistance from the United States, the army's senior leadership provided the political transition required to ease Duvalier out of power in February 1986. A number of senior officers pushed for Duvalier's abdication, despite strong resistance from Jean-Claude and the senior leadership of the VSN. The army was interested in protecting itself from the explosive sociopolitical situation in Haiti in late 1985 and early 1986. Nationalism and concern for the best interests of Haiti exerted only a secondary influence on the officers' actions.

The armed forces largely escaped the immediate wrath of a population clearly bent on putting an end to Duvalier rule. Popular violence had erupted in 1984, and it continued into early 1986 in an expanding sequence of local revolts. In its waning days, the regime relied heavily on the VSN and on limited local police capabilities to curb violence. Many Haitians detected the fissures growing in the nation's security apparatus, and some rumors held that the army would move against Duvalier. These rumors, however, proved incorrect; still, Duvalier's inability to contain the widespread rioting through political measures and the VSN's failure to control the unrest placed the military in a pivotal position. Conscious of his precarious hold on power, Duvalier reshuffled the cabinet and the military leadership in the last days of 1985, but to no avail. Reports of brutal excesses by the increasingly desperate VSN further weakened Duvalier's position.

Troops of the Leopards Corps in camouflage uniforms
Courtesy United States Department of Defense

The army became discontent with the crumbling regime. In several instances, troops refused to fire on demonstrators, and in a few cases, army personnel turned against the VSN. According to one account, several senior military figures threatened Duvalier and his wife, Michèle Duvalier, at gunpoint.

The Post-Duvalier Period

Jean-Claude Duvalier left behind a hastily constructed interim junta, controlled by the armed forces. Lieutenant General Henri Namphy, army chief of staff, became head of the interim National Council of Government (Conseil National de Gouvernement—CNG). Colonel Williams Regala, the head of the Military Academy; Lieutenant General Prosper Avril of the Presidential Guard; and Colonel Jean-Claude Paul of the regular army were also key figures in the interim government. The CNG officially disbanded the VSN a few days after Duvalier's departure, but it avoided the politically difficult measure of effectively halting the VSN's activities. This nonfeasance prompted angry mobs to murder known members of the VSN and set in motion a cycle of instability from which Haiti had yet to recover in the late 1980s. Despite the popular backlash, some members of the VSN managed to survive by integrating themselves into military circles.

The consequences of the army's failure to dismantle the VSN became obvious in the bloody events leading up to the aborted elections of November 1987 (see Background: From Duvalier to Avril, 1957–89, ch. 9). The CNG's attempt to balance demands for, and resistance to, reforms gave way to chaos. By 1987 the armed forces had lost the favorable reputation they had enjoyed a year earlier. Worse, the senior military command appeared to be doing little to stop attacks against the electoral process. The disastrous elections of 1987 and 1988 isolated the Haitian military from the international community, which had grown skeptical about the role of the armed forces.

The situation unraveled further in 1988, under the short-lived civilian government of Leslie Manigat (February–June 1988), who was overthrown when he retired the Port-au-Prince police chief and attempted to reshuffle the army command. CNG leader Namphy returned as head of government, with the support of other commanders. In September 1988, another coup brought Prosper Avril to power. Avril was an experienced officer with a career dating back to the Duvalier era.

The armed forces continued to face problems, however, even after Avril came to power. From September 1988 through March 1989, 140 officers reportedly were retired or were fired, some because they were suspected of drug smuggling. Allegations that government officials were involved in drug trafficking became widely known after a United States court indicted Colonel Paul, then commander of the Dessalines Battalion, on charges of cocaine distribution. Paul's wife had previously been arrested in Miami on cocaine charges. Paul's mysterious death in the fall of 1988 only partially resolved the issue of military involvement in drug trafficking. At about the same time, United States authorities arrested and convicted a former CNG associate of Namphy, Colonel Gary Léon, on drug-trafficking charges.

Avril's attempts to purge the government of Duvalierist forces included ousting individuals who had graduated from the Military Academy in 1973. The move reflected additional political rifts within the senior command. Sensing the low stature of the Avril government, segments of the senior command split into warring factions in April 1989. Reports alleged that pro-Duvalierist elements had helped to provoke dissension within the officer corps. The loyalty of the Presidential Guard and support from many NCOs helped Avril prevail in a week of internecine conflict with the officer corps. The conflict, however, left the military in a state of crisis. Duvalier's collapse initially had enhanced the national standing of the FAd'H. But the group's senior commanders, when thrust by events to the forefront of governance, had reverted to the traditional use of force to carry out a vaguely defined political program. Other actors, such as the Roman Catholic Church or political parties, remained divided in the post-1986 period, and they were therefore generally ineffectual politically (see Interest Groups, ch. 9). The failure of Haiti's civilian leadership to negotiate an alternative political course further reinforced the FAd'H's self-characterization as the decisive agent of Haitian affairs.

The Role of the Armed Forces

Haiti's defense traditionally has fallen victim to political vagaries. A readiness for battle and the initiation of defense-related engineering projects in the first two decades of the nineteenth century turned out to be costly preparation for conflict against phantom armies. The engineering projects included construction of the citadel of La Ferrière in northern Haiti. Soon afterward, Haiti turned its attention toward the rest of the island of Hispaniola (La Isla Española), which Haiti controlled between 1822 and 1844. Controlling the whole island, however, drained the national treasury and induced torpor in the battle-hardened veterans of the wars of independence.

The gap between Haiti's fears and its military capabilities widened. The army lost institutional coherence and its ability to pursue missions of national defense. The only thing that assured the nation's safety until the twentieth century was the jealousy among the great powers—France, Germany, and, by the turn of the century, the United States. Washington's increasing interest in Haiti prompted the United States Navy to deploy to the country's ports fifteen times between 1876 and 1913 in order to protect American lives and property.

The United States Marines occupied the country in 1915. They formulated a policy designed to ensure domestic law and order that the Garde d'Haïti was given the responsibility of implementing. This concern with internal law and order, rather than with external security, endured throughout the twentieth century.

Haiti is a party to a number of international agreements, including the Inter-American Treaty of Reciprocal Assistance (the Rio Treaty), the Charter of the Organization of American States, and the earlier Act of Chapultepec (1945). The nation's security concerns regarding neighboring Cuba and the Dominican Republic have been viewed since World War II within the broader framework of United States strategic interests in the Caribbean. The fact that the FAd'H deployed relatively few of its units along the Dominican border, despite a history of conflicts with its neighbor, reflects Haiti's limited national security concerns.

Cuban and other external threats have had little impact on Haiti's security. The Duvaliers' tight control eliminated all Marxist influences in the country. It was not until 1986 that a communist party, the Unified Haitian Communist Party (Parti Unifié Communiste Haïtien—PUCH), openly operated in the country. Cuba helped some Haitian refugees travel to Florida in the 1980s, but its overall interest in Haitian affairs has been unclear. The severity of Haiti's political and economic crises, along with the high profile of the United States in the region, has limited involvement by other countries in Haitian affairs.

Threats to Haiti's internal security, however, have been numerous during the past four decades. Between 1968 and 1970, the government repulsed three invasions supported by exiled Haitians. In 1970 the Coast Guard mutinied. The Coast Guard's five ships, low on fuel and ammunition, went into exile at the United States military base at Guantánamo, Cuba. In the early 1980s, Haitian military forces and members of the VSN defeated a small exile force on the Île de la Tortue (Tortuga Island). An airplane dropped a bomb on the National Palace in 1982, and a car bomb exploded nearby in 1983. Exile groups, however, never posed a significant military challenge to the army and the VSN. The real challenge to these forces came in the popular domestic disturbances that developed after 1984.

After the collapse of the Duvalier regime in 1986, the FAd'H developed an agenda to exert national political leadership, to restore public order, and to gain control over the VSN and other paramilitary groups, but carrying out this program proved difficult, given Haiti's political, economic, and foreign policy situations.

The main mission of Haiti's armed forces in the late 1980s continued to be internal security. After 1986, however, this mission regularly conflicted with the national leadership role of the FAd'H. Generational and political differences among officers and a scarcity of resources for the military led to chronic instability that culminated in military coups. These coups caused the government to change hands four times in 1988. A fifth coup in early 1989, however, failed to topple the government. The two most important problems that the FAd'H had to face were, first, a divided senior military command and, second, suspicious junior officers and NCO personnel. These problems became apparent in 1988 when Avril ousted Namphy and subsequently dismissed a number of senior officers. The degree to which NCOs may have been manipulated in this process and the extent to which lower army echelons had begun to shape their own political attitudes caused some observers to doubt the military's future as an institution.

The challenges facing the FAd'H in the late 1980s were more political than military. The largest and most immediate questions revolved around the institution's ability to govern Haiti during a period of political transition and modernization. It remained unclear, in mid-1989, how and when the military planned to transfer power to a legitimate civilian government. Another important problem concerned the personal political ambitions of some army commanders. It was also unclear how the FAd'H would respond to these challenges because the institution had not demonstrated viable national political capabilities. The FAd'H was ill-prepared for this broad new role in national life because François Duvalier had severely limited its role in government affairs.

Other security-related problems included narcotics trafficking. United States officials have expressed concern over Haiti's role as a major transshipment area for narcotics, mainly Colombian cocaine bound for the United States. This role apparently expanded after Jean-Claude's fall. The United States Drug Enforcement Administration opened an office in Port-au-Prince in October 1987 to help Haitian authorities control drug trafficking; however, the lack of a professional police force in Haiti hindered these efforts. The FAd'H appeared ambivalent toward the narcotics issue because drug-related corruption reportedly involved hundreds of members of the officer corps and because some officers resented pressure from Washington. Avril, however, attempted to placate United States concerns by dismissing some officers linked to drug trafficking. The most prominent among the dismissed officers was Paul, a former commander of the Dessalines Battalion, who was indicted in March 1988 by a Florida grand jury on charges of cocaine distribution. Haiti had signed an extradition treaty with the United States, but the agreement did not cover narcotics-related offenses, so Paul never faced trial on the charges.

Paul's continued service in the army posed a political problem, and Avril asked him to retire. In November 1988, however, Paul died mysteriously, possibly a victim of poisoning. Paul's death removed a major narcotics figure and a potential threat to Avril's political power.

Unstable and unstructured civilian politics and institutions also undermined Haiti's stability. Some Duvalierists sought to use the armed forces completely or partially to restore the ancien régime. At the same time, more democracy-oriented civilian groups, all of which lacked strong institutional bases, continued to be suspicious of the army's political leadership. The weak economy and the international media's criticism of Haitian affairs resulted in financial and public-relations problems for the army; and, because

Haiti's political environment remained volatile and because the army did not always appear to be in control of the country, Haiti faced more unrest and the possible development of insurgency movements. On the one hand, Haiti's armed forces was still one of the few institutions of national magnitude, but, on the other hand, the armed forces suffered from serious institutional deterioration and diminished cohesion. In 1989 the military was struggling to provide political leadership at a time when it faced its own disintegration.

Military Spending and Foreign Assistance

Budgetary irregularities have impeded assessments of Haiti's expenditures on national defense and the police forces. Throughout much of the Duvalier era, significant portions of the nation's security budget either went unrecorded or disappeared in a maze of interdepartmental transfers directed by officials in the Presidential Palace. Therefore, it was difficult to judge how these payments affected Haiti's economy. Defense expenditures that were recorded were generally modest. Moreover, because of Haiti's convoluted politics, it is impossible to determine whether the money allocated for defense ever benefited the nation's army or police force. Undetermined amounts were undoubtedly siphoned off by corrupt individuals.

Haiti's defense expenditures grew slowly in the 1970s and the 1980s. Some efforts in the late 1970s to modernize the military, especially the air corps, coupled with the Duvalier regime's growing sense of insecurity, led to increased expenditures. After that period, however, military spending remained constant at about US$30 million a year. Between 1975 and 1985, military spending averaged about 8 percent of government expenditures, or between 1.2 percent and 1.9 percent of the gross national product (GNP—see Glossary; table 13, Appendix A).

In the twentieth century, the United States has been the primary source of foreign military support in terms of matériel and financing. Moderate levels of military expenditure and a marginal amount of foreign influence on Haiti's national security reflected the deinstitutionalization of the Haitian armed forces that took place after the 1950s.

The United States occupation resulted in a technically competent and logistically well-equipped Haitian military that was really a national constabulary. United States military missions to Haiti during World War II, the 1950s, and the early 1960s helped to maintain links between the two countries; and, despite François Duvalier's displeasure with United States efforts to modernize the

Haitian armed forces, he agreed to several purchases of military equipment and services from Washington. Between 1964 and 1970, these purchases included a number of aging aircraft, the overhaul of all five Haitian F–51s, a mix of small arms, and a number of patrol boats. By the early 1970s, the newly created Leopards Corps had become the focus of procurement efforts, and Washington openly approved private arms sales and training programs. Overall, between 1950 and 1977 the United States provided an estimated US$3.4 million in military aid and training for 610 Haitian students in the United States.

During the late 1970s, Haiti acquired small arms from other countries. The aircraft were never put to use because of chronic training deficiencies and maintenance problems; still, when the regime encountered difficulties in the early to mid-1980s, it grounded much of the Air Corps and removed its ordnance to prevent bombing runs on the Presidential Palace.

In the 1980s, the United States intermittently provided aid and assistance in support of Haitian security needs through credits or commercial military sales, a Military Assistance Program (MAP), and an International Military Education and Training (IMET) program. Commercial sales of military goods, primarily crowd-control equipment, increased substantially in the last two years of Jean-Claude Duvalier's regime; they amounted to US$3.2 million in 1985. Earlier in the 1980s, the United States had sustained a Foreign Military Sales (FMS) financing program for Haiti that amounted to about US$300,000 a year. Expenditures on the IMET program ranged from US$150,000 to US$250,000 a year. About 200 Haitian students benefited from the IMET from 1980 to 1985.

Military assistance from the United States came to a halt when the elections of 1987 failed. The United States also cut off resources to upgrade the nation's justice and police system, although some funding for narcotics-control efforts continued. In 1989 only an IMET training program was likely to receive funding from the United States. Washington was also considering, however, some support for efforts to disarm Duvalierist forces.

Armed Forces Organization and Structure

A 1987 decree prescribed the structure and the administration of Haiti's armed forces, but the terms of the decree had not been fully implemented by 1989. The FAd'H served as the military arm of the Ministry of Interior and National Defense. This arrangement blurred police and national-defense functions. The minister who holds the portfolio of interior and national defense has historically been viewed as the senior administrator of the cabinet and the government. The 1987 Constitution modified this structure by creating the post of prime minister during the brief presidency of Leslie Manigat (see Constitutional Framework, ch. 9). (In most countries, the president and his prime minister are responsible for matters of national defense.) Constitutional reforms also called for a national police structure, tied to a strengthened Ministry of Justice. As of 1989, few of these reforms had been implemented.

The 1987 Constitution and FAd'H regulations defined the missions, the command structure, and the general organization of the armed forces. On paper, these details differed only slightly from the way the military had been structured prior to the collapse of the Duvalier regime in 1986. In practice, however, the military was quite different from that outlined in the Constitution. First, Haiti's political upheavals had caused the armed forces to assume the role of the decisive national institution, although the upheavals also had overburdened the political organization and the operations of the FAd'H. Second, the unofficial remnants of the VSN continued to challenge Haiti's domestic security, requiring increased attention to internal security concerns over external defense considerations.

The commander of the FAd'H was appointed by the president for a renewable three-year term. An assistant commander acted as deputy (see fig. 17). The FAd'H had a central planning and coordinating unit—as part of the office of the commander in chief—the head of which oversaw personnel, intelligence, operations and training, and logistics. The organization of the FAd'H also provided for an inspector general of the armed forces and an adjutant general. A military attaché's office, reporting to the commander of the FAd'H, acted as liaison for military personnel at Haitian embassies and for attachés stationed at foreign missions. The FAd'H had undergone some restructuring, but some changes called for in 1987 had not been implemented by late 1989.

Only the Metropolitan Military Region maintained a significant tactical capability. The forces in this region had a direct impact on the viability of the government. The strongest of the region's units was the 1,300-member Presidential Guard, which was generally regarded as well-trained and disciplined. The Guard was essentially the president's security force. Many members of the guard were stationed on the grounds of the Presidential Palace. The second largest force was the 750-member Dessalines Battalion, a conventional light-infantry unit stationed at the Dessalines barracks located behind the Presidential Palace (the battalion was disbanded after battles within the army in April 1989). Finally, there was the 700-member Leopards Corps, a tactical unit created in the early 1970s and based at the outskirts of the capital in Pétion-ville. In the 1980s, the Leopards Corps' police functions often superseded its counterinsurgency functions. The Leopards were disbanded within a month of the attempted coup of 1989.

The FAd'H controlled the Port-au-Prince police and the prison system, an arrangement that further blurred the boundaries between law-enforcement and military institutions. The Port-au-Prince police force consisted of about 1,000 ill-trained members. This force was actually a low-level constabulary under military command. Portions of this force belonged to the armed forces' security-services command. Other parts were organizationally under the command of the Metropolitan Military Region. The armed forces administered the capital city's (and for all practical purposes, the nation's) fire fighters and the country's immigration and narcotics-control programs.

About 8,000 personnel from military and police units served in Haiti's security services. In 1989 the services included about 6,200 personnel in the FAd'H, about 1,000 in the police, and several hundred in specialized units.

Despite efforts by the United States Marine Corps to modernize Haiti's military during the occupation (1915–34), World War II, and the 1960s, Haitian military training programs continued to be flawed. The Military Academy at Frères (near Pétionville) was the senior school of instruction. The academy's student body averaged about sixty students during the 1980s. François Duvalier had closed the academy in 1961, but his son, Jean-Claude, reopened it in 1972. Cadets had to be nominated to the academy. After a three-year course, academy graduates became career officers and many later held senior FAd'H posts. An NCO school and training camp at Lamentin (near Carrefour) outside Port-au-Prince was not operational as of 1989. Graduates of this school were directed toward mainstream army units, or even rural police duty. Training was normally accomplished at the unit level. Enlistment was theoretically voluntary. Article 268 of the 1987 Constitution requires all men to serve in the military when they reach their eighteenth birthday. Women in the military were limited to participating in the medical corps.

The Haitian armed forces had eight officer ranks in the army; six, in the air corps; and six, in the navy. For enlisted personnel, there were eight grades in the army; seven, in the air corps; and five, in the navy. The three categories of uniform for the Haitian armed forces were dress, duty (or garrison), and field. The army and the air corps dress uniform consisted of a blue shirt, a dark blue blouse and trousers, a blue belt, black shoes, and a dark blue

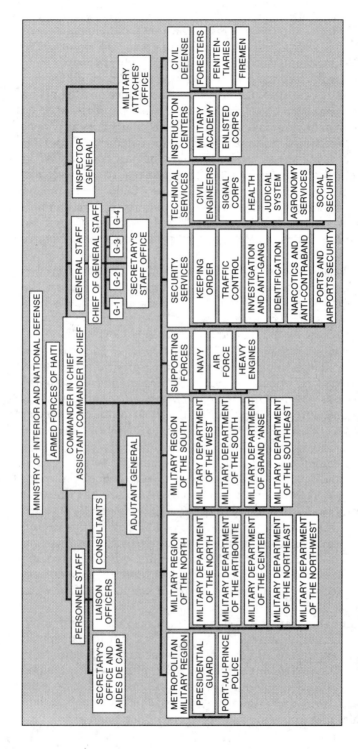

Source: Based on information from Règlements Généraux des Forces Armées d'Haïti, Port-au-Prince, 1987.

Figure 17. Haiti: Organization of the Armed Forces, 1989

cap with black visor. Their duty uniform included khaki shirt and trousers, tan belt, and brown or black shoes. Navy officers and enlisted personnel wore uniforms identical to those of the United States Navy. The field uniform for the army, the navy, and the air corps was similar in design, color, and material to the United States Army fatigue uniform.

Army and air corps officers wore their rank insignia on shoulder boards. One to three gold chevrons indicated company-grade officers; field-grade officers displayed one to three gold stars; and general officers wore one to three silver stars. Navy insignia consisted of gold bands worn on shoulder boards or on the lower sleeve of the dress uniform. Enlisted personnel wore gold chevrons for the army, black chevrons for the navy, and blue chevrons for the air corps (see fig. 18; fig. 19).

Of the three services that composed the FAd'H, the army (with 6,200 members) was the largest and, for all practical purposes, the only relevant one. The marginal capabilities of the navy and the air corps were reflected in their limited weapons systems, low technical sophistication, and poor readiness. Although the army had the largest number of personnel, it also generally suffered from antiquated equipment and inefficient procedures. Because of the nation's desperate economic situation and its political turmoil, modernization of the army was unlikely in the late 1980s.

The Presidential Guard was the largest of the military components based at Port-au-Prince. It consisted of four companies that were reinforced in April 1989. The nine regional military departments operated principally as district police. The Port-au-Prince police, the prison guard company, and the Port-au-Prince fire brigade rounded out the forces assigned to the capital.

The M1 Garand rifle, developed during World War II, continued to be the principal small arm of the Haitian military. Small quantities of the West German G3 and the American M16 rifles, however, had been acquired to equip the elite units. The Israeli-made Uzi submachine gun had superseded the Thompson as the principal light automatic. Infantry-support arms, used only by the Presidential Guard, included .30-caliber Browning M1919 and .50-caliber M2HB machine guns along with M18 57mm and M40 106mm recoilless launchers and M2 60mm and M1 81mm mortars (see table 14). Few of the army's light tanks remained in serviceable condition in 1989. The effective armored force therefore consisted of V-150 Commando and M2 armored personnel carriers. The Presidential Guard operated all armored vehicles and artillery pieces, some of which were totally obsolete. There were no separate armored or artillery units.

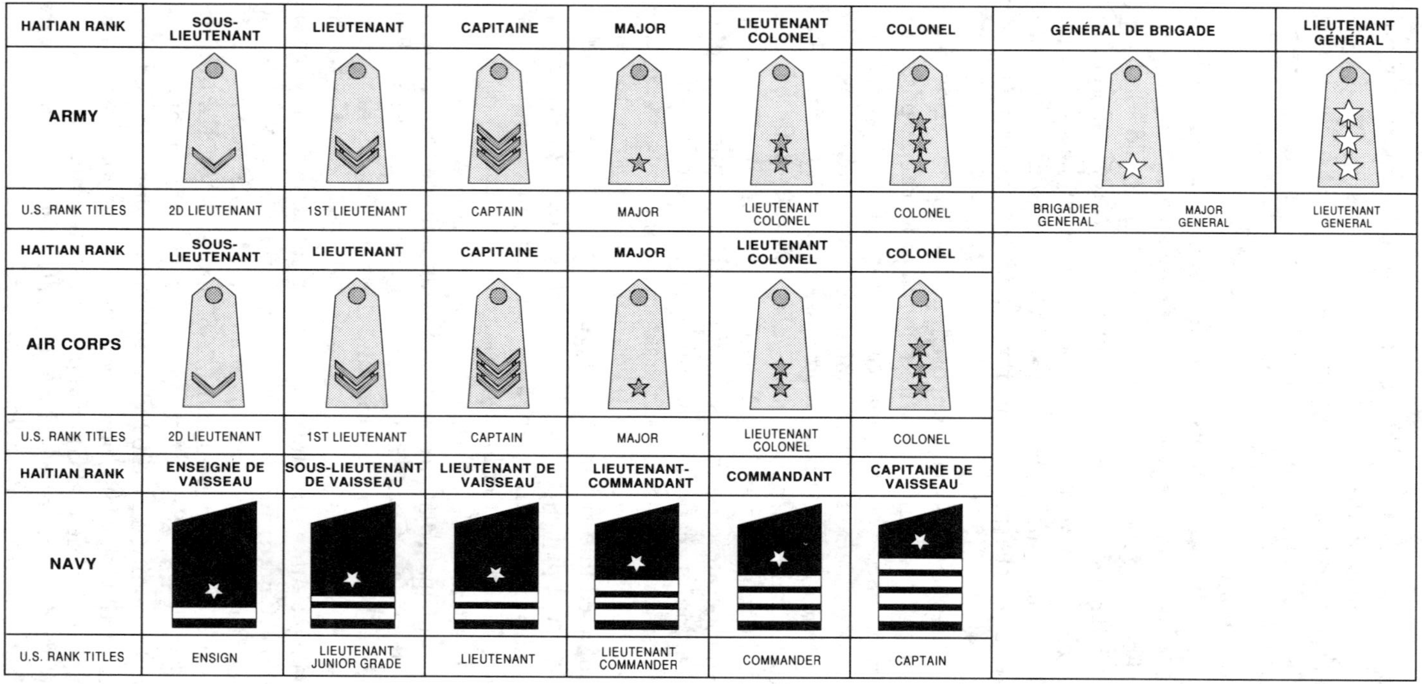

HAITIAN RANK	SOUS-LIEUTENANT	LIEUTENANT	CAPITAINE	MAJOR	LIEUTENANT COLONEL	COLONEL	GÉNÉRAL DE BRIGADE	LIEUTENANT GÉNÉRAL
ARMY								
U.S. RANK TITLES	2D LIEUTENANT	1ST LIEUTENANT	CAPTAIN	MAJOR	LIEUTENANT COLONEL	COLONEL	BRIGADIER GENERAL	LIEUTENANT GENERAL
HAITIAN RANK	SOUS-LIEUTENANT	LIEUTENANT	CAPITAINE	MAJOR	LIEUTENANT COLONEL	COLONEL	MAJOR GENERAL	
AIR CORPS								
U.S. RANK TITLES	2D LIEUTENANT	1ST LIEUTENANT	CAPTAIN	MAJOR	LIEUTENANT COLONEL	COLONEL		
HAITIAN RANK	ENSEIGNE DE VAISSEAU	SOUS-LIEUTENANT DE VAISSEAU	LIEUTENANT DE VAISSEAU	LIEUTENANT-COMMANDANT	COMMANDANT	CAPITAINE DE VAISSEAU		
NAVY								
U.S. RANK TITLES	ENSIGN	LIEUTENANT JUNIOR GRADE	LIEUTENANT	LIEUTENANT COMMANDER	COMMANDER	CAPTAIN		

Figure 18. Haiti: Officer Ranks and Insignia, 1989

370

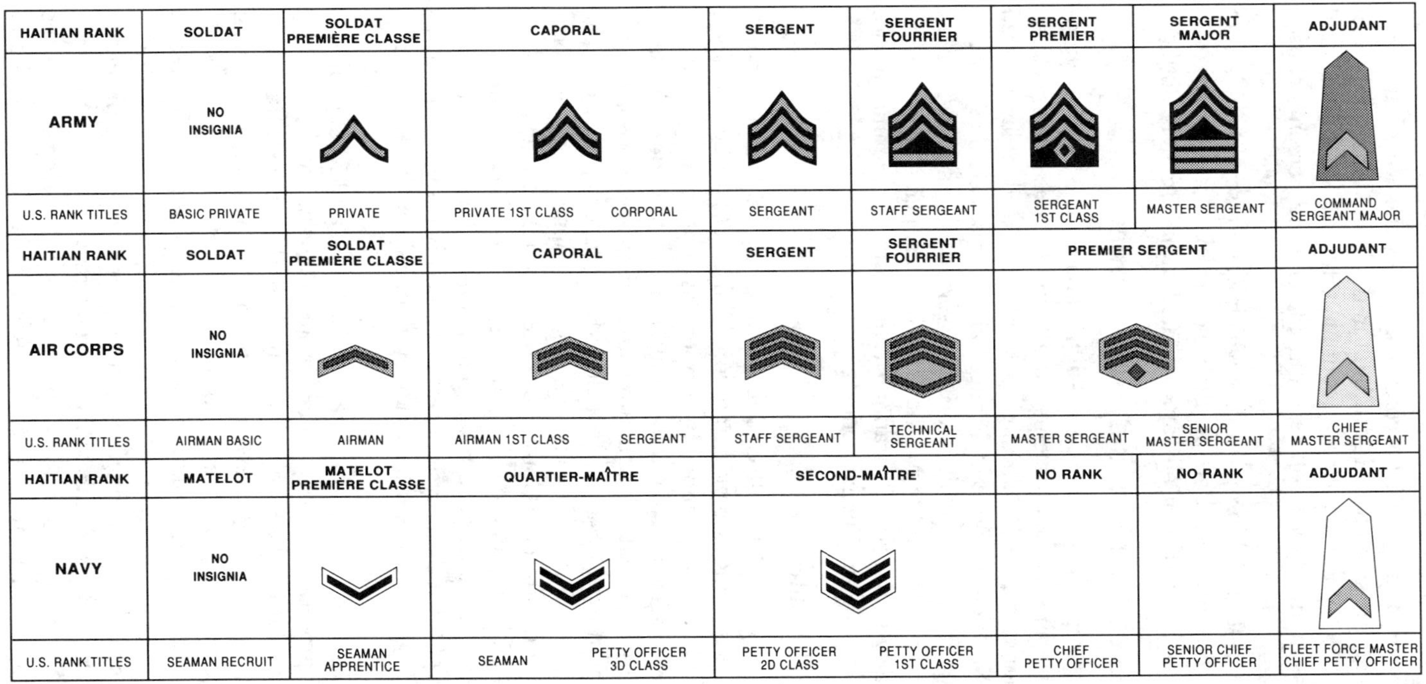

Category	1	2	3	4	5	6	7	8
ARMY — HAITIAN RANK	SOLDAT	SOLDAT PREMIÈRE CLASSE	CAPORAL	SERGENT	SERGENT FOURRIER	SERGENT PREMIER	SERGENT MAJOR	ADJUDANT
ARMY — Insignia	NO INSIGNIA							
ARMY — U.S. RANK TITLES	BASIC PRIVATE	PRIVATE	PRIVATE 1ST CLASS / CORPORAL	SERGEANT	STAFF SERGEANT	SERGEANT 1ST CLASS	MASTER SERGEANT	COMMAND SERGEANT MAJOR
AIR CORPS — HAITIAN RANK	SOLDAT	SOLDAT PREMIÈRE CLASSE	CAPORAL	SERGENT	SERGENT FOURRIER	PREMIER SERGENT		ADJUDANT
AIR CORPS — Insignia	NO INSIGNIA							
AIR CORPS — U.S. RANK TITLES	AIRMAN BASIC	AIRMAN	AIRMAN 1ST CLASS / SERGEANT	STAFF SERGEANT	TECHNICAL SERGEANT	MASTER SERGEANT	SENIOR MASTER SERGEANT	CHIEF MASTER SERGEANT
NAVY — HAITIAN RANK	MATELOT	MATELOT PREMIÈRE CLASSE	QUARTIER-MAÎTRE	SECOND-MAÎTRE	MASTER SERGEANT	NO RANK	NO RANK	ADJUDANT
NAVY — Insignia	NO INSIGNIA							
NAVY — U.S. RANK TITLES	SEAMAN RECRUIT	SEAMAN APPRENTICE	SEAMAN / PETTY OFFICER 3D CLASS	PETTY OFFICER 2D CLASS	PETTY OFFICER 1ST CLASS	CHIEF PETTY OFFICER	SENIOR CHIEF PETTY OFFICER	FLEET FORCE MASTER CHIEF PETTY OFFICER

Figure 19. Haiti: Enlisted Ranks and Insignia, 1989

371

The navy in the late 1980s consisted of only the armed tug *Henri Christophe,* nine small patrol craft built in the United States between 1976 and 1981, and the old presidential yacht *Sans Souci.* This small force was manned by 45 officers and 280 enlisted personnel based at Port-au-Prince.

All aircraft, a high proportion of which were unserviceable, were based at Bowen Field, Port-au-Prince (see table 15, Appendix A). Air Corps personnel of all ranks totaled approximately 300.

The Judicial System and Public Order

Haiti's reputation for human-rights abuses was only a symptom of deeper societal problems. As a United States Marine Corps report noted in 1934, "Although possessed of excellent laws, based on the Napoleonic Code of France, Haiti possessed no means of enforcing them. . . . Haiti's prisons were a disgrace to humanity. . . ." Some might argue that little has changed over the years, particularly in the administration of the country's criminal justice system and military penal code.

The Legal Framework

Haiti's legal system reflected its colonial origins. It had a French structure superimposed on a traditional African-Caribbean society. Although Haiti was founded by former slaves, it lacked the parallel or indigenous legal system often found in modern Africa. The legal framework followed the structures and the procedures of French and Roman legal systems. It included local courts, justice of the peace courts, courts of first instance, courts of appeal, and the Court of Cassation (Supreme Court). But the system had little relevance for most of the population. The more senior members of the court system catered to a small urbanized business clientele. The lower echelons of the judicial system employed poorly trained individuals who were likely to be influenced by political and financial pressures at the local level.

Because Haiti was a rural nation, land law and local civil and criminal procedures were of much greater relevance to the majority of the population than were decisions posted by the senior courts in Port-au-Prince and a few larger towns. French was the official language of the legal system, however, even though most people living in rural areas spoke only Creole (see French and Creole, ch. 7).

Judges in Haiti were often subject to intimidation, and the entire legal system suffered from a lack of administrative and financial capabilities. Many local courthouses were destroyed during or after the 1986 collapse of the Duvalier regime. Few facilities have been rebuilt.

The Duvalier regimes had selected most of the country's judges. Post-Duvalier governments faced the daunting task of selecting credible judges to preside over courts at all levels. This process had barely begun as of 1989.

Except for brief periods in Haiti's history, military officials controlled the country's legal system (see Army Politics: Force and Counterforce, ch. 9). As a consequence, an equitable and functioning judicial system was still largely an abstraction for most Haitians. The army or paramilitary groups, with political or personal motivations, arbitrarily fulfilled law-enforcement functions.

Problems in the country's legal system originated in Haiti's skewed experience with its constitutions. One of the first goals of Haiti's early leaders was to establish law and order while organizing a new government. The solution adopted by figures such as François-Dominique Toussaint Louverture, Jean-Jacques Dessalines, Henri (Henry) Christophe, and many of their successors emphasized executive authority along with limited civil or technical administration. A judicial system and municipal powers became extensions of central authority. This arrangement ensured military presence at all levels and branches of government. Incompetence, graft, and violence complicated this structure. One observer, writing at the turn of the century, noted that "Haiti is governed by generals in all sizes." In 1936, two years after the departure of the United States Marines, Haitian president Sténio Vincent drew up a new constitution that provided a legislature and a judiciary wholly dependent upon the whims of the executive branch (see Politics and the Military, 1934–57, ch. 6). The new constitution stated that "the government makes the constitution, the laws, the regulations and agreements."

Haitian law required that detainees appear before a judge within forty-eight hours, except when they were arrested in the act of committing a crime or when they were detained pursuant to a judicial warrant. In practice, however, prisoners frequently spent long periods in jail while they awaited trial. The absence of a bail system also led to lengthy pretrial detentions. The law further required officials formally to file charges against the accused at least two weeks before trial. The accused had the right to meet with an attorney before trial, but had to pay for it. The state provided no free counsel to the indigent.

Arraignments and trials took place in public, and defendants had the right to be present at their trials. Overall, the criminal justice system suffered from backlogs, the intimidation and influencing of jurists, and the population's widespread reluctance to serve as jurors.

Public Order

Although the armed forces continued to be the nation's ultimate law-enforcement agency, they had almost no juridical capability. Armed forces regulations provide for a judicial service, however, and the 1987 Constitution indicates the existence of a Military Court, the jurisdiction of which is limited to times of war or military discipline.

The 1987 Constitution presents a significant theoretical departure from Haiti's past. It proposes a separate police corps and a new police academy under the jurisdiction of the Ministry of Justice. Political developments in Haiti since 1987, however, have precluded implementation of these changes. Nevertheless, the mission of the police corps was almost indistinguishable from the mission spelled out for the FAd'H. The characterization of the police as a *corps armé* (armed corps) reinforced this similarity in missions.

The only identifiable police force in Haiti operated in Port-au-Prince as part of the armed forces. This 1,000-member force had few operational or technical capabilities, even though it was responsible for narcotics and immigration control and criminal investigations. In the late 1980s, the Narcotics Bureau, commanded by an army major, had acquired some visibility and resources of its own, with a reported staff of about twenty-five people.

There was no true rural police. Small garrisons, operating under military department command, with some cooperation from the lowest central government administrative head, section chief (*chef de section*), were responsible for rural security. In effect, the heads of these 562 rural communal sections (*sections rurales communales*) functioned as police chiefs, as adjuncts of the nation's military infrastructure. This fusion of civil and military administration continued to be possible because of the broad range of responsibilities assigned to the Ministry of Interior and National Defense.

After 1986 the armed forces failed to reestablish a nationwide police force and to subdue the VSN and other vigilante groups. Some observers have argued that links between the senior army command and remnants of the VSN have paralyzed reforms in Haiti's judicial system. An illustration of their point was the reported incorporation of some VSN personnel into FAd'H units and some members of the VSN, as plainclothes paramilitary agents, in the Dessalines Battalion. Other VSN members found their way into cadres of the Port-au-Prince police force, particularly in the Criminal Investigation Unit (Recherches Criminelles—renamed in 1988 the Anti-Gang Investigations Bureau), which was traditionally based at the

National Police, Port-au-Prince
Courtesy United States Agency for International Development

Dessalines barracks. The demise of the Dessalines Battalion and the Leopards, the latter of which had served as Haiti's special weapons and tactics unit, raised questions in the spring of 1989 about the future of a national police force.

The Avril government reported some success in cracking down on abuses within the security services, but violence continued to be a serious problem. Insecurity rose dramatically after 1986 with the formation of ad hoc paramilitary groups that had direct links to the VSN and indirect links to the military. Many of these paramilitary groups engaged in banditry with no political motivation. The security situation in rural regions and at the section chief level remained unclear in 1989.

The human-rights record of post-Duvalier governments was generally negative. A major problem was the inability, or the unwillingness, of the FAd'H to contain domestic political violence. Government and military personnel apparently sanctioned and participated in attacks on politicians and other activists, particularly during the second Namphy government. The Avril government boasted an improved record in this area, but as of mid-1989, it had proved incapable of restoring order.

Haitian military and police often brutally interrogated detainees. Rural section chiefs, who wielded considerable power within their

375

limited jurisdictions, arbitrarily harassed and physically abused citizens, according to some reports. In an effort to address this problem, Avril dismissed a number of section chiefs and issued a decree in December 1988 that ended appointments of section chiefs and proposed putting the posts up for election (see Urban Dominance, Rural Stagnation, ch. 9).

Harsh conditions prevailed in the prison system. Hygiene, food, and health care were inadequate, and prison staff regularly mistreated inmates. The Avril government closed two facilities closely associated with the repression of the Duvalier regimes—Fort Dimanche and the detention center of the Criminal Investigation Unit, both in Port-au-Prince—because of the abuses that had commonly taken place there.

Political turmoil between 1986 and 1989 resulted in popular justice and mob violence. The international media reported on some of this violence and featured scenes of burning or dismembered bodies. Continued human-rights violations were likely to attract international criticism during the 1990s. Lasting improvements in internal security, however, appeared unlikely without the establishment of functional civilian institutions and some resolution of the status of the former members of the *tonton makouts.*

* * *

Serious research on Haiti's military is scarce. Part of the problem lies in the nation's chaotic history, which has resulted in the destruction of primary documentation, or has simply made research in the country risky or unwelcome. Much of Haiti's archives burned down in 1883, and in 1912 the National Palace blew up. Obtaining material on Haiti has been difficult. For example, Robert Rotberg notes that the research for *Haiti, the Politics of Squalor* was ''possible only with the personally granted authorization of Dr. François Duvalier.''

Contemporary sources on Haiti's national security are practically nonexistent in either French or English. Useful information can be found in three specialized studies, one in French, *Armée et Politique en Haïti* by Kern Delince, and two from a British military analyst, Adrian J. English, *Armed Forces of Latin America* and *Regional Defense Portfolio, No. 1: Latin America.* There are also lively secondary sources that can be useful but must be read with a careful eye. These include *Papa Doc: The Truth about Haiti Today,* by Bernard Diederich and Al Burt, and *Haiti: The Duvaliers and Their Legacy,* by Elizabeth Abbott.

Alternatively, the reader is directed to more scholarly volumes that intermittently make reference to Haiti's national security. English sources include the monumental work by Robert Debs Heinl and Nancy Gordon Heinl, *Written in Blood: The Story of the Haitian People,* as well as Rotberg and Christopher Clague's *Haiti, the Politics of Squalor.* The United States military occupation is well covered by David Healy's *Gunboat Diplomacy in the Wilson Era: The U.S. Navy in Haiti, 1915–1916* and Hans Schmidt's *The United States Occupation of Haiti, 1915–1934.* See also the opinionated studies by Alex Dupuy, *Haiti in the World Economy,* and Patrick Bellegarde-Smith, *Haiti, the Breached Citadel.* Both of these works contain useful references to the military's role in politics. Specialized, and often politically motivated, coverage can be found in the occasional records from United States Congressional hearings on Haiti and the reports published by human rights organizations. (For further information and complete citations, see Bibliography.)

Appendix A

Table

1   Metric Conversion Coefficients and Factors
2   Dominican Republic: Estimated Population by Region, Sub-
    region, and Province, 1990
3   Dominican Republic: Years of School Attended, Population
    over Twenty-five Years of Age, by Subregion, 1981
4   Dominican Republic: Health Facilities and Personnel by Sub-
    region, 1981
5   Dominican Republic: Leading Causes of Death, 1982
6   Dominican Republic: Production of Selected Minerals, 1980–
    85
7   Dominican Republic: Value of Exports, 1982–87
8   Dominican Republic: Major Army Equipment, 1989
9   Dominican Republic: Major Navy Equipment, 1989
10 Dominican Republic: Major Air Force Equipment, 1989
11 Haiti: Leading Causes of Death by Age-Group and Sex, 1984
12 Haiti: Value of Trade and Current Account Balance, Fiscal
    Years, 1984–88
13 Haiti: Military Expenditures, Selected Years, 1975–85
14 Haiti: Major Army Equipment, 1989
15 Haiti: Major Air Corps Equipment, 1989

379

Table 1. Metric Conversion Coefficients and Factors

When you know	Multiply by	To find
Millimeters	0.04	inches
Centimeters	0.39	inches
Meters	3.3	feet
Kilometers	0.62	miles
Hectares (10,000 m²)	2.47	acres
Square kilometers	0.39	square miles
Cubic meters	35.3	cubic feet
Liters	0.26	gallons
Kilograms	2.2	pounds
Metric tons	0.98	long tons
	1.1	short tons
	2,204	pounds
Degrees Celsius	9	degrees Fahrenheit
(Centigrade)	divide by 5 and add 32	

Table 2. *Dominican Republic: Estimated Population by Region,*
Subregion, and Province, 1990

Region Subregion Province	Population
Cibao	
Central Cibao	
Espaillat	182,248
La Vega	303,047
Monseñor Nouel	124,794
Puerto Plata	229,738
Santiago	704,835
Total Central Cibao	1,544,662
Eastern Cibao	
Duarte	261,725
María Trinidad Sánchez	125,148
Salcedo	110,216
Samaná	73,002
Sánchez Ramírez	140,635
Total Eastern Cibao	710,726
Western Cibao	
Dajabón	64,123
Monte Cristi	92,678
Santiago Rodríguez	61,570
Valverde	111,470
Total Western Cibao	329,841
Total Cibao	2,585,229
Southeast	
Valdesia	
Monte Plata	174,799
National District	2,411,895
Peravia	186,810
San Cristóbal	320,921
Total Valdesia	3,094,425
Yuma	
El Seibo	97,590
Hato Mayor	77,823
La Altagracia	111,241
La Romana	169,223
San Pedro de Macorís	197,862
Total Yuma	653,739
Total Southeast	3,748,164

Table 2. Continued.

Region Subregion Province	Population
Southwest	
Del Valle	
Azua	195,420
Elías Piña	72,651
San Juan	266,628
Total Del Valle	534,699
Enriquillo	
Barahona	152,405
Baoruco	87,376
Independencia	43,077
Pedernales	18,896
Total Enriquillo	301,754
Total Southwest	836,453
TOTAL	7,169,846

Source: Based on information from Dominican Republic, Oficina Nacional de Estadística, *La República Dominicana en Cifras, 1987,* 14, Santo Domingo, 1987.

Table 3. Dominican Republic: Years of School Attended, Population over Twenty-five Years of Age, by Subregion, 1981 (in percentages)

	Number of Years of School Attended					
Subregion	0	1–4	5–8	9–12	13 and over	Total
Central Cibao	34	33	23	7	3	100
Del Valle	50	30	15	4	1	100
Eastern Cibao	39	35	19	5	2	100
Enriquillo	40	31	20	7	2	100
Valdesia	25	26	28	13	8	100
Western Cibao	35	37	21	5	2	100
Yuma	38	31	22	6	3	100
TOTAL: Dominican Republic	32	30	24	9	5	100

Source: Based on informtion from Nelson Ramírez, et al., *Población y Salud en la República Dominicana,* Estudio No. 5, Santo Domingo, 1986, 56.

Table 4. Dominican Republic: Health Facilities and Personnel by Subregion, 1981

Subregion	Clinics Private [1]	Rural	Hospital Beds	Physicians	Nurses
Central Cibao	46	67	1,567	379	98
Del Valle	9	44	543	109	22
Eastern Cibao	14	57	775	174	32
Enriquillo	7	34	218	67	18
Valdesia [2]	8	43	543	145	36
Western Cibao	0	38	421	79	20
Yuma	10	39	432	113	22
National District	76	15	2,987	1,452	165
TOTAL	170	337	7,486	2,518	413

[1] Facilities not run by Secretariat of State for Public Health and Social Welfare (Secretaría de Estado de Salud Pública y Asistencia Social—SESPAS).
[2] Excluding National District.

Source: Based on information from Dominican Republic, Secretaría de Estado de Salud Pública y Asistencia Social, *Política de Salud del Gobierno de Concentración Nacional, 1983-1986,* Santo Domingo, 1983, various pages.

Table 5. Dominican Republic: Leading Causes of Death, 1982

Causes of Death	Death Rate (per 100,000)
Pulmonary circulatory disease, other forms of heart disease	32.1
Intestinal infections	23.3
Perinatal diseases, unspecified	22.3
Cardiovascular diseases	21.2
Myocardial infarction	20.5
Hypoxia, asphyxia, fetal and newborn conditions and complications	14.2
Pneumonia	12.1
Cirrhosis and chronic liver disease	12.1
Other respiratory diseases	9.9

Source: Based on information from Pan American Health Organization, *Health Conditions in the Americas, 1981-84,* Washington, 1986, 102.

Table 6. *Dominican Republic: Production of Selected Minerals, 1980–85*

Mineral	1980	1981	1982	1983	1984	1985
Gold [1]	369,603	407,813	380,254	348,065	330,000	n.a.
Silver [1]	1,623	2,034	2,198	1,329	1,207	1,560 [2]
Nickel [3]	18,019 [4]	20,601	5,926	21,552	26,371 [4]	29,000 [4]
Gypsum [3]	259,000	225,000 [2]	230,000 [4]	230,000 [4]	230,000 [4]	255,000 [4]

n.a.—not available.
[1] In thousands of troy ounces.
[2] Reported figure.
[3] In short tons.
[4] Preliminary, provisional, or estimated figure.

Source: Based on information from James W. Wilkie, David E. Lorey, and Enrique Ochoa (eds.), *Statistical Abstract of Latin America*, 26, Los Angeles, 1988, 354, 357–58.

Table 7. *Dominican Republic: Value of Exports, 1982–87* (in millions of United States dollars [1])

Kind of Export	1982	1983	1984	1985	1986	1987
Traditional [2]	475	452	514	380	360	308
Free-zone	148	175	194	205	250	323
Other	294	336	358	365	363	410
TOTAL	917	963	1,066	950	973	1,041

[1] Free on board.
[2] Sugar and derivatives, green coffee, tobacco, and cocoa.

Source: Based on information from Centro Dominicano de Promoción de Exportaciones, *Boletín Estadístico, 1987*, Santo Domingo, 1988, 4, 6.

Table 8. Dominican Republic: Major Army Equipment, 1989

Description	Country of Origin	Inventory
AMX-13 light tanks	France	2
M4A1 (76mm) Sherman light tanks	United States	12
AML armored cars	France	20
V-150 Commando armored personnel carriers	United States	8
M-3A1 half-track armored personnel carriers	–do–	2
M-101 105mm howitzers, towed	–do–	22
81mm mortars	–do–	n.a.
120mm mortars	–do–	24
M40 106mm recoilless launchers	–do–	n.a.

n.a.—not available.

Source: Based on information from *The Military Balance, 1988–89*, London, 1988, 194.

Table 9. *Dominican Republic: Major Navy Equipment, 1989*

Description	Country of Origin	Inventory
Frigate		
River class, modified for use as presidential yacht and cadet training ship, 1,445 tons	Canada	1
Corvettes		
Cohoe class, 650 tons	United States	3
Admiral class, 650 tons	-do-	2
Large patrol craft		
Argo class, 337 tons	-do-	3
PGM71 class, 130 tons	-do-	1
Capitán Alsina, wood, 100 tons	Dominican Republic	1
Swiftship, 93.5 tons	United States	2
Bellatrix class, 60 tons	-do-	4
Amphibious vessel		
LCU, 150 tons	-do-	1
Tankers		
Self-propelled fuel barges	-do-	2
Tugs		
Various types	-do-	10
Floating dock	-do-	1

Source: Based on information from *Jane's Fighting Ships, 1988–89*, London, 1988, 136–39.

Table 10. *Dominican Republic: Major Air Force Equipment, 1989*

Description	Country of Origin	Inventory
Combat aircraft		
Cessna A–37B Dragonflies	United States	8
Transports		
C–47 Douglas Dakotas	-do-	6
Beech Queen Air 80	-do-	3
Aero Commander	-do-	2
Cessna 310	-do-	1
Mitsubishi MU-2J	Japan	1
Trainers		
Beech T–34B Mentors	United States	10
Beech T–41D Mescaleros	-do-	7
Helicopters		
Bell 205	-do-	8
Hughes OH–6A	-do-	2
Alouette II/III	France	2
Aérospatiale SA–360	-do-	1

Source: Based on information from *The Military Balance, 1988–89*, London, 1988, 195.

Table 11. Haiti: Leading Causes of Death by Age-Group and Sex, 1984
(in percentages)

Cause of Death	Age-Group										Sex		
	Under 1	1-4	5-14	15-24	25-34	35-44	45-54	55 and over	Unknown	Total	Male	Female	Total
Intestinal infections	55.4	11.6	7.4	6.5	6.1	3.2	2.6	6.1	1.1	100.0	32.4	67.6	100.0
Malnutrition	35.8	45.4	6.3	1.4	1.8	0.7	0.7	3.0	4.9	100.0	50.3	49.7	100.0
Tuberculosis	7.6	9.4	2.9	15.6	25.6	16.6	8.3	8.9	5.1	100.0	47.7	52.3	100.0
Pulmonary circulatory disease	2.0	5.5	3.9	3.7	7.1	8.1	6.7	56.9	6.1	100.0	57.9	42.1	100.0
Respiratory disease	42.4	16.8	3.8	4.4	5.7	3.6	3.0	15.8	4.5	100.0	54.1	45.9	100.0
Perinatal infections	92.6	n.a.	n.a.	0.2	0.2	n.a.	n.a.	n.a.	7.0	100.0	47.4	52.6	100.0
Nervous system diseases	37.8	26.6	5.2	3.9	7.9	2.5	3.1	8.2	4.8	100.0	56.2	43.8	100.0
AIDS	19.3	6.7	1.1	7.8	21.3	9.4	8.4	18.4	7.6	100.0	88.6	11.4	100.0
Cerebrovascular diseases	5.3	1.2	1.2	2.6	1.7	7.4	11.2	62.9	6.5	100.0	61.8	38.2	100.0
Hypertension	0.6	0.6	1.3	2.7	4.7	4.9	13.8	62.5	8.9	100.0	33.2	66.8	100.0

n.a.—not available.

Source: Based on information from Haiti, *Santé et Population en Haiti*, Port-au-Prince, 1986, Table 13.

Table 12. Haiti: Value of Trade and Current Account Balance,
Fiscal Years 1984-88
(in millions of United States dollars)

	1984	1985	1986	1987	1988
Trade*					
Exports	215	223	191	198	156
Imports	360	345	303	308	284
Trade balance	− 145	− 122	− 112	− 110	− 128
Current account balance	− 103	− 95	− 45	− 31	− 53

*Free on board.

Source: Based on information from Economist Intelligence Unit, *Country Report: Cuba, Domini-can Republic, Haiti, Puerto Rico,* 3, London, 1989, 4; and *Direction of Trade Statistics Yearbook, 1988,* Washington, 1988, 263-64.

Table 13. Haiti: Military Expenditures,
Selected Years, 1975-85

Year	Expenditures [1]	Expenditures as Percentages of GNP [2]	Expenditures as Percentages of National Budget
1975	21	1.5	8.2
1977	19	1.2	5.9
1979	22	1.2	6.6
1981	35	1.9	9.6
1983	28	1.6	8.9
1985	29	1.6	8.4

[1] In millions of constant 1984 United States dollars.
[2] GNP—gross national product (see Glossary).

Source: Based on information from United States, Arms Control and Disarmament Agency, *World Military Expenditures and Arms Transfers, 1987,* Washington, 1987, 61.

Table 14. *Haiti: Major Army Equipment, 1989*

Description	Country of Origin	Inventory
M2 60mm mortar	United States	36
M1 81mm mortar	--do--	n.a.
M3A1 light tank	-do-	6
M5A1 light tank	-do-	3
V-150 Commando armored personnel carrier	-do-	6
M2 armored personnel carrier	-do-	5
M116 75mm howitzer	-do-	4
M2A1 105mm howitzer	-do-	6
M3 37mm antitank gun	-do-	10
M1 57mm antitank gun	-do-	10
M1 40mm antiaircraft gun	-do-	6
RAMTA TCM-20 20mm antiaircraft gun	Israel	6

n.a.—not available.

Source: Based on information from Adrian J. English, *Regional Defense Profile, No. 1: Latin America,* London, 1988; *The Military Balance, 1988-89,* London, 1988; and *Jane's Infantry Weapons, 1988-89,* London, 1988, 769.

Table 15. *Haiti: Major Air Corps Equipment, 1989*

Description	Country of Origin	Inventory
Combat aircraft		
Cessna 337 light strike	United States	7
Transports		
Beechcraft Baron	–do–	1
Cessna 401	–do–	1
Cessna 402	–do–	1
Curtiss C–46 Commando	–do–	1
Douglas C–47	–do–	3
DHC–2	–do–	2
DHC–6	–do–	1
Trainers		
S1A1 S–211	Italy	4
S1A1–Marchetti SF.260TP	–do–	4
Cessna 152	United States	3
Cessna 172	–do–	1
Beech Bonanza	–do–	1
Helicopters		
Sikorsky S–58	–do–	4
Hughes 269C	–do–	2
Hughes 369C	–do–	2

Source: Based on information from Adrian J. English, *Regional Defense Profile No. 1: Latin America*, London, 1988; *The Military Balance, 1988–89*, London, 1988, 198; and *Journal of Defense and Diplomacy*, 6, No. 6, 1988, 30.

Appendix B

Caribbean Basin Initiative

The Caribbean Basin Initiative (CBI), enacted by the United States Congress in 1982–83, represented one of the major United States foreign economic policies toward Latin America and the Caribbean in the 1980s. Mainly a trade promotion program, the Initiative provided duty-free access to the United States market for about 3,000 products; it expanded bilateral economic assistance; and it allowed some limited tax breaks for new United States investors in the region. A number of United States agencies contributed to the formulation and implementation of the policy. As a result of the early failure of the CBI to stimulate exports from many of the countries involved, legislators attempted to amplify the program, and by 1990 Congress and the White House were expected to approve an expanded version. Whereas the CBI had improved the region's prosperity only slightly, by 1989 it had served nonetheless as a catalyst toward economic diversification in a number of Caribbean Basin countries.

The Reagan Administration's Proposal and Congressional Amendments

On February 24, 1982, in a speech before the Organization of American States, President Ronald Reagan unveiled a new proposal for the economic recovery of Central America and the Caribbean. The Reagan plan expanded duty-free entry of Caribbean Basin exports for up to twelve years, as well as increased economic assistance and tax incentives for new United States investment in the region. The administration's proposal arose in the political context of a successful revolution in Nicaragua, active insurgencies in El Salvador and Guatemala, and coups in Grenada and Suriname that had established radical leftist regimes. Dramatic political change, coupled with an international economic crisis characterized by high oil prices, unprecedented interest rates, and declining commodity prices rekindled the interest of United States policy makers in the region.

In September 1982, the 97th Congress passed the foreign aid portion of the president's plan in the form of Public Law 97–257, after scaling back some portions of the proposal, most notably the amount of aid earmarked for El Salvador. Even with congressional amendments, the overwhelming share of the US$350 million in supplemental assistance under the Caribbean Basin Economic Recovery Act, the bill's official name, went toward the most strategically important nations in the region: El Salvador, Costa Rica, Jamaica, the Dominican Republic, and Honduras. Impoverished Haiti, for example, received only US$10 million in supplementary aid. As a result of opposition from domestic labor and industrial interests, the 98th Congress did not pass the trade provisions of the Act (as Public Law 98–67) until July 1983. The bill's final version, however, excluded the following items from duty-free coverage: petroleum and petroleum products, sugar, canned tuna, luggage, handbags, certain other leather goods, flat goods, rubber and plastic gloves, footwear, textiles and apparel subject to the Multifiber Agreement, and watches or watch parts manufactured in communist countries. Critics of the Initiative argued that with or without these exclusions, it represented more a political policy than a developmental one because new duty-free provisions would provide only limited economic benefits. Congressional sentiment ran against the investment tax exemptions originally included in the bill, and these measures were never approved. Some tax breaks were extended, however, to companies holding business meetings in certain countries.

Section 212 of the Act provided the president with the authority to designate beneficiary countries. To qualify, countries had to have a noncommunist government, had to meet specific requirements concerning the expropriation of United States property, had to cooperate in regional antinarcotics efforts, had to recognize arbitral awards to United States citizens, could not provide preferential treatment to the products of developing countries in such a manner as to adversely affect United States trade, had to abstain from the illegal broadcast of United States copyrighted material, and had to maintain an extradition treaty with the United States. In addition, the Act authorized the president to consider eleven discretionary criteria to qualify potential beneficiaries. These included such considerations as the use of subsidies, acceptance of the rules of international trade, and guarantees of workers' rights. President Reagan initially announced twenty-one beneficiary nations or territories from the Caribbean, Central America, and the Northern coast of South America. Countries excluded from the list included Cuba, Nicaragua, Guyana, Suriname, Anguilla, the Cayman Islands, and the Turks and Caicos Islands, none of which applied for designation. The Bahamas became a beneficiary nation in March 1985; Aruba became one in January 1986 (its independence date); and Guyana, in November 1988. In March 1988, President Reagan suspended Panama's eligibility because of reported links between that country's government and international narcotic traffickers.

The CBI legislation also encompassed other important provisions. Section 213 stipulated the basic product eligibility rule that at least 35 percent of the value-added of the imported product had to originate in a beneficiary country for that country to qualify for duty-free treatment. This section also empowered the president to withdraw duty-free treatment in case of injury to domestic industries resulting from CBI imports. As a result of complaints from Puerto Rico and the United States Virgin Islands that the CBI extended benefits previously reserved for United States overseas territories, Section 214 set forth special benefits under the law. These included an increase in foreign content for product eligibility of up to 70 percent, as well as other more technical exemptions. Section 221 also transferred all rum taxes proceeds to the treasuries of the two United States possessions. Puerto Rico also benefited from the twin plant plan (see Glossary), which encouraged United States investors to operate complementary factories in Puerto Rico and in other beneficiary countries. This framework enabled investors to tap funds accumulated under Section 936 (see Glossary) of the United States Internal Revenue Code in order to develop complementary operations if the recipient country had signed a Tax Information Exchange Agreement (TIEA) with the United States. Finally, Section 222 permitted tax deductions for business conventions in the region if the country had signed a TIEA.

The CBI Network

The United States Department of State played a central role in designing and implementing the Initiative, but many other executive-branch agencies contributed extensively to the policy. The United States Agency for International Development (AID) administered most economic assistance flows, concentrating its efforts on the private sector. The Overseas Private Investment Corporation, the Peace Corps, the Department of Transportation, the Export-Import Bank, and the Customs Service of the Department of the Treasury all enhanced and complemented AID's endeavors. The Department of Commerce, through its Caribbean Basin Information Center and its normal regional offices, provided information packages, investment climate statements, economic trend reports, special product advice, investment missions, a monthly networking newsletter, and other information and services for potential investors. The Department of Agriculture similarly promoted the CBI through frequent agribusiness marketing workshops and technical assistance missions, and by supplying important regulatory information on United States import standards. The International Trade Commission and the Department of Labor took part by issuing in-depth annual reports on the progress of the CBI and its impact on the United States. The Office of the United States Trade Representative oversaw bilateral investment and textile agreements; and, beginning in 1987, that office hired an ombudsman to direct the CBI Operations Committee, an interagency task force dedicated to the policy's success. Finally, public and private monies helped to create a strong private business and advocacy network to further the aims of the CBI.

The United States government also generated a certain amount of multilateral and bilateral support for the Initiative. Mexico, Venezuela, Colombia, and the European Economic Community supported the CBI in a limited way, mainly through the extension of existing programs. Japan increased its aid to the region, as did Canada; on February 17, 1986, the Canadian government offered its own import preference program for the region, a package it dubbed Caribcan. Multilaterals such as the Inter-American Development Bank, the World Bank (see Glossary), and the International Monetary Fund (see Glossary) also cooperated with the Initiative through a variety of programs, particularly policy reform efforts coordinated with AID.

Expansion of CBI Benefits and Programs

Visiting the island of Grenada on February 20, 1986, President Reagan announced increased access to the United States market for apparel assembled in the Caribbean Basin in an effort to enlarge the impact of the CBI. The program, referred to either as 807-A (see 807 program, Glossary) or "Super 807" provided guaranteed access levels for CBI beneficiary countries through import quota negotiations based on previous exports and expected growth. The proposal was the direct result of regional discontent with the limited benefits of the Initiative and the expressed fears of regional leaders with regard to mounting protectionist sentiment in the United States. A group of leaders of the English-speaking Caribbean had expressed their dissatisfaction through a detailed letter to President Reagan in late 1985. Regional leaders generally welcomed the small improvement made through the 807-A announcement because of the extraordinary growth in textile production since the inauguration of the CBI.

After a series of regional and Washington-based hearings, in 1987 members of Congress introduced legislation to improve further the benefits of the Initiative. By mid-1989, a number of proposals had been combined under the Caribbean Basin Economic Recovery

Expansion Act of 1989 (H.R. 1233), most of which was expected to become law. Stating that "the existing program has not fully achieved the positive results that were intended," the House's Expansion Act, dubbed CBI II, proposed an indefinite time extension for duty-free entry of CBI covered products (previously scheduled to expire September 30, 1995) and the addition of several specific garments and fabrics to be provided reduced or exempted duties. It also guaranteed market access for textiles and footwear via bilateral agreements with all beneficiary nations; potential increases for beneficiary countries in their sugar quotas, through reallocations from other countries that did not reach their allotted share; increased duty-free allowances for United States tourists visiting the region; more flexible criteria for ethanol imports; increased postsecondary scholarships for study in the United States; greater promotion of tourist development; and the trial establishment of preinspection customs facilities to expedite exports. CBI II also sought special measures to enable the Eastern Caribbean and Belize to reap greater benefits from the program, as well as the application of new rules of origin for determining the content of duty-free imports, the employment of internationally recognized workers' rights criteria in evaluating the compliance of beneficiary countries, and a requirement that the president report to Congress every three years on the progress of the Initiative.

An Assessment of the First Five Years

One of the major aims of the plan was to increase economic assistance in order to foster sustained economic growth through stimulation of the private sector and the expansion of exports. Beneficiary nations sought increased aid to cushion the impact of the recession of the early 1980s and to provide support during the difficult economic adjustment period of the mid-1980s. The US$350 million in assistance to the region, provided under the auspices of the CBI as a supplement to annual allocations, contributed to a dramatic increase in United States assistance to Central America and the Caribbean, from US$300 million in 1981 to nearly US$1.5 billion in 1985. A large portion of this assistance, however, was motivated by United States strategic concerns rather than developmental ones. For example, El Salvador, engaged in a war against leftist insurgents, received nearly one-third of all assistance throughout this period. Similarly, some strategic countries received allocations in excess of their absorptive capacities while other countries pursued additional United States support. Increased assistance gave the United States significant leverage in encouraging recipient countries to reform their economic policies in such areas as exchange rates, the promotion of increased and diversified exports, the expansion of light manufacturing, reductions in import controls, privatization of state-owned enterprises, the balancing of fiscal accounts, promotion of small business development, and the upgrading of infrastructure. Evidence of the impact of these reforms continued to be inconclusive at the close of the decade, but several countries had begun to open and to diversify their economies, thereby setting the stage, it was hoped, for sustained future growth.

The promotion of increased foreign investment, although not part of the final CBI legislation, continued to be one of the overall goals of the Initiative. In 1988 the United States Department of Commerce surveyed Caribbean investment trends in a comprehensive manner, after a previously unsuccessful attempt to quantify CBI-related ventures in 1986. The 1988 survey revealed that significant new investment had taken place in the region during the 1984–88 period, despite the lack of tax credits for United States companies. The 642 United States companies participating in the study accounted for US$1.6 billion in new investment in CBI countries (excluding Panama) and for 116,000 new jobs. Only 150 of these firms (23 percent), however, exported CBI-eligible products; therefore, the CBI was directly related to the creation of only 15 percent of the new jobs. Furthermore, the new investment was highly concentrated; five countries accounted for 67 percent of all new investment. By 1988 the Dominican Republic had surpassed Jamaica as the prime investment location, and it received one-fifth of all the Caribbean Basin's new investment because of the vibrant growth of its industrial free zones. By contrast, Haiti suffered disinvestment because of political unrest, high nonwage costs, and increased regional competition for investment in labor-intensive industry. More than half of all foreign investment was from the United States, followed by the Republic of Korea (South Korea), Canada, and Hong Kong. Although new CBI-related and other foreign investment helped the balance-of-payments positions of several countries and provided badly needed jobs in manufacturing and tourism, foreign exchange remained scarce in the late 1980s, and unemployment continued to hover at dangerously high levels in most countries.

The centerpiece of the Initiative, however, was neither aid nor investment, but one-way duty-free trade with the United States. An assessment of CBI trade data demonstrated both negative and positive trends. On the negative side, the value of total Caribbean Basin exports generally declined throughout the 1980s because of dwindling prices for the region's traditional exports, such as petroleum, sugar, and bauxite. Except in the case of sugar, this poor performance was attributable almost solely to the vagaries of primary product prices. United States policy clearly damaged sugar exports, however, through the reimposition of sugar quotas in 1981 and through the 75 percent reduction in Caribbean and Central America quotas from 1981 to 1987, a trend that offset export growth among CBI-exempted products. Not only did the region's total exports drop by US$2.7 billion from 1983 to 1988, but its share of the United States market weakened, dropping from 6.5 percent of United States imports in 1980 to 1.6 percent by 1987. As was true of investment, only a small percentage (less than 20 percent) of the growth in nontraditional exports resulted from duty-free entry extended through the CBI. Furthermore, only ten items accounted for the great majority of products that entered the United States market duty-free. Moreover, exports, like investments, were concentrated; only a handful of countries generated the overwhelming share of CBI 806.3 (see 807 program, Glossary) and 807 exports, while some countries suffered substantial declines in exports. Overall, despite import exemptions in the United States market, the United States ran a trade surplus with the region from 1987 to 1989. After years of pursuing the goal of "trade, not aid," United States policy through the CBI in 1989 continued to provide fewer economic benefits from trade than from aid.

Despite some negative trends, Caribbean Basin countries experienced substantial growth in nontraditional exports during the 1980s. For example, although the Basin's total exports lagged behind other regions, growth in manufactures and other nontraditional exports far surpassed that of other regions. In fact, some Basin countries outperformed even the newly industrialized countries of Asia. The composition of trade shifted markedly away from agricultural commodities and raw materials in favor of nontraditional exports, textiles, and apparel. In 1983 the region's exports broke down as being 78 percent traditional commodities, 17 percent nontraditional ones, and 4 percent textiles and apparel; by 1988, however, traditional exports represented only 37 percent of total exports, compared with 44 percent for nontraditionals, and 19 percent for textiles and apparel. This shift was particularly true of United States imports covered under the 807 provisions; the value of these imports more than doubled from 1983 to 1988. Judging by these statistics, it appeared that although the CBI directly stimulated only limited export growth, its emphasis on nontraditional exports contributed to the restructuring of much of the region's external trade. Such restructuring was especially found among Caribbean countries because of the larger share of depressed primary products in their export baskets relative to those of Central America.

Bibliography

Chapter 1

Atkins, G. Pope, and Larman C. Wilson. *The United States and the Trujillo Regime.* New Brunswick: Rutgers University Press, 1972.

Black, Jan Knippers. *The Dominican Republic: Politics and Development in an Unsovereign State.* Boston: Allen and Unwin, 1986.

Calder, Bruce J. *The Impact of Intervention: The Dominican Republic During the U.S. Occupation of 1916–1924.* (The Texas Pan American Series.) Austin: University of Texas Press, 1984.

Campillo Pérez, Julio G. *Historia Electoral Dominicana, 1848–1986: El Grillo y El Ruiseñor.* Santo Domingo: Editora Corripio, 1986.

Crassweller, Robert D. *Trujillo: The Life and Times of a Caribbean Dictator.* New York: Macmillan, 1966.

Diederich, Bernard. *Trujillo: The Death of the Goat.* Boston: Little, Brown, 1978.

Fagg, John Edwin. *Cuba, Haiti, and the Dominican Republic.* (Modern Nations in Historical Perspective Series.) Englewood Cliffs, New Jersey: Prentice-Hall, 1965.

Knight, Melvin M. *The Americans in Santo Domingo.* (Studies in American Imperialism.) New York: Vanguard Press, 1928.

Logan, Rayford W. *Haiti and the Dominican Republic.* New York: Oxford University Press, 1968.

Mejía Ricart, Gustavo Adolfo. *Biografía del Caudillo Pedro Santana.* (Colección "Temas Históricos," 1.) Santo Domingo: Fundación Mejía Ricart—Guzmán Boom, 1980.

Moya Pons, Frank. *La Dominación Haitiana, 1822–1844.* (Colección 'Estudios.') Santiago, República Dominicana: Universidad Católica Madre y Maestra, 1972.

_____. *Historia Dominicana.* (2 vols.) (Colecciones Dominicanas.) Santo Domingo: Caribe Grolier, 1982.

Pérez, Carlos Federico. *El Pensamiento y la Acción en la Vida de Juan Pablo Duarte.* Santo Domingo: Organización de Estados Americanos, Universidad Nacional Pedro Henríquez Ureña, 1979.

Rodman, Selden. *Quisqueya: A History of the Dominican Republic.* Seattle: University of Washington Press, 1964.

Rotberg, Robert I., with Christopher K. Clague. *Haiti: The Politics of Squalor.* Boston: Houghton Mifflin, 1971.

Slater, Jerome. *Intervention and Negotiation: The United States and the Dominican Revolution.* New York: Harper and Row, 1970.

Welles, Sumner. *Naboth's Vineyard: The Dominican Republic, 1844–1924.* (World Affairs: National and International Viewpoints.) New York: Payson and Clarke, 1928. Reprint. New York: Arno Press, 1972.

Wiarda, Howard. J. *The Dominican Republic: Nation in Transition.* New York: Praeger, 1969.

Wiarda, Howard J., and Michael J. Kryzanek. *The Dominican Republic: A Caribbean Crucible.* (Nations of Contemporary Latin America Series.) Boulder, Colorado: Westview Press, 1982.

_____. *The Politics of External Influence in the Dominican Republic.* (Politics in Latin America: A Hoover Institution Series.) New York: Praeger/Hoover Institution Press, 1988.

Chapter 2

Alcantara, Elsa (ed.). *Guía de las Universidades de Santo Domingo.* Santo Domingo: Fundación Friedrich Ebert, 1968.

Antonini, Gustavo A. (ed.). *Public Policy and Urbanization in the Dominican Republic and Costa Rica.* (Proceedings of the 22nd Annual Latin American Conference.) Gainesville: Center for Latin American Studies, University of Florida, 1972.

Atkins, G. Pope. "The April 1986 Elections in the Dominican Republic." Pages 153–71 in Scott B. MacDonald, Harold M. Sandstrom, and Paul B. Goodwin, Jr. (eds.), *The Caribbean after Grenada: Revolution, Conflict, and Democracy.* New York: Praeger, 1988.

Balmori, Diana, Stuart F. Voss, and Miles Wortman. *Notable Family Networks in Latin America.* Chicago: University of Chicago Press, 1984.

Baud, Michiel. "The Origins of Capitalist Agriculture in the Dominican Republic," *Latin American Research Review,* 22, No. 2, 1987, 135–53.

Bell, Ian. *The Dominican Republic.* Boulder, Colorado: Westview Press, 1981.

Black, Jan Knippers. *The Dominican Republic: Politics and Development in an Unsovereign State.* Boston: Allen and Unwin, 1986.

Bray, David. "Economic Development: The Middle Class and International Migration in the Dominican Republic," *International Migration Review,* 18, No. 2, Summer 1984, 217–36.

Carvajal, M.J., and David T. Geithman. "Migration Flows and Economic Conditions in the Dominican Republic," *Land Economics,* 52, No. 2, May 1976, 207–20.

Carter, Michael R. "Risk Sharing and Incentives in the Decollectivization of Agriculture," *Oxford Economic Papers*, 39, No. 3, September 1987, 577–95.

Castillo, José del, and Martin F. Murphy. "Migration, National Identity, and Cultural Policy in the Dominican Republic," *Journal of Ethnic Studies*, 15, No. 3, Fall 1987, 49–69.

Chardon, Roland. "Sugar Plantations in the Dominican Republic," *Geographical Review*, 74, No. 4, October 1984, 441–54.

Clausner, Marlin D. *Rural Santo Domingo: Settled, Unsettled, and Resettled.* Philadelphia: Temple University Press, 1973.

Dominican Republic. Oficina Nacional de Estadística. *República Dominicana en Cifras 1987*, 14. Santo Domingo: 1987.

_____. Secretaría de Estado de Salud Pública y Asistencia Social. *Política de Salud del Gobierno de Concentración Nacional, 1983–1986.* Santo Domingo: 1983.

Fanger, Ulrich. "Urban Policy Implementation in the Dominican Republic, Jamaica, and Puerto Rico," *Ekistics*, 45, No. 266, January 1978, 20–29.

Fernandez, J.M. "Dominican Republic: System of Education." Pages 1450–53 in Torsten Husén and T. Neville Postlewaite (eds.), *The International Encyclopedia of Education.* New York: Pergamon Press, 1985.

Garrison, Vivian, and Carol I. Weiss. "Dominican Family Networks and United States Immigration Policy: Case Study," *International Migration Review*, 13, No. 2, Summer 1979, 264–83.

Grasmuck, Sherri. "Migration Within the Periphery: Haitian Labor in the Dominican Sugar and Coffee Industries," *International Migration Review*, 16, No. 2, Summer 1982, 365–77.

Haza, Luis Orlando. "Urban Growth in the Dominican Republic: A Descriptive Overview." Pages 23–54 in Gustavo A. Antonini (ed.), *Public Policy and Urbanization in the Dominican Republic and Costa Rica.* (Proceedings of the 22nd Annual Latin American Conference.) Gainesville: Center for Latin American Studies, University of Florida, 1972.

Hendricks, Glenn. *The Dominican Diaspora: From the Dominican Republic to New York City—Villagers in Transition.* New York: Teachers College Press, 1974.

Hoetink, H. *The Dominican People: Notes for a Historical Sociology.* (Trans., Stephen K. Ault.) Baltimore: Johns Hopkins University Press, 1982.

Kearney, Richard C. "Spoils in the Caribbean: The Struggle for Merit-Based Civil Service in the Dominican Republic," *Public Administration Review*, 46, No. 2, March–April, 1986, 144–51.

Lemoine, Maurice. *Bitter Sugar: Slaves Today in the Caribbean.* (Trans., Andrea Johnston.) Chicago: Banner Press, 1985.

Lernoux, Penny. *Cry of the People.* Garden City, New York: Doubleday, 1980.

Mones, Belkis, and Lydia Grant. "Agricultural Development, the Economic Crisis, and Rural Women in the Dominican Republic." Pages 35–50 in Carmen Diana Deere and Magdalena León (eds.), *Rural Women and State Policy: Feminist Perspectives on Latin American Agricultural Development.* Boulder, Colorado: Westview Press, 1987.

Morrison, Thomas K., and Richard Sinkin. "International Migration in the Dominican Republic: Implications for Development Planning," *International Migration Review,* 16, No. 4, Winter 1982, 819–36.

Pan American Health Organization. *Health Conditions in the Americas, 1981–84.* Washington: 1986.

Perusek, Glenn. "Haitian Emigration in the Early Twentieth Century," *International Migration Review,* 18, No. 1, Spring 1984, 4–18.

Pessar, Patricia R. "The Linkage Between the Household and Workplace of Dominican Women in the U.S," *International Migration Review,* 18, No. 4, Winter 1984, 1188–211.

_____. "The Role of Households in International Migration and the Case of U.S.-Bound Migration from the Dominican Republic," *International Migration Review,* 16, No. 2, Summer 1982, 342–62.

Ramírez, Nelson, Isis Duarte, and Carmen Gómez. *Población y Salud en la República Dominicana.* (Estudio No. 5.) Santo Domingo: Instituto de Estudios de Población y Desarrollo de Profamilia, 1986.

Rodríguez Sepúlveda, Bienvenida. *Evaluación de la encuesta nacional de fecundidad de la República Dominicana de 1980.* (World Fertility Survey, Scientific Reports, No. 63.) London: World Fertility Survey, October 1984.

Schneider, Curt R., Robert A. Hiatt, Emile A. Malek, and Ernesto Ruiz-Tiben. "Assessment of Schistosomiasis in the Dominican Republic," *Public Health Reports,* 100, No. 5, September–October 1985, 524–30.

Sharpe, Kenneth Evan. *Peasant Politics: Struggle in a Dominican Village.* Baltimore: Johns Hopkins University Press, 1977.

Ugalde, Antonio. "Where There Is a Doctor: Strategies to Increase Productivity at Lower Costs," *Social Science and Medicine,* 19, No. 4, 1984, 441–50.

United States. Department of Health and Human Services. Social Security Administration. Office of Policy, Office of Research,

Statistics, and International Policy. *Social Security Programs Throughout the World, 1985.* (Research Report No. 60.) Washington: 1986.
Walker, Malcolm T. *Politics and the Power Structure: A Rural Community in the Dominican Republic.* New York: Teachers College Press, 1972.
Wiarda, Howard J. *The Dominican Republic: Nation in Transition.* New York: Praeger, 1969.
Wiarda, Howard J., and Michael J. Kryzanek. *The Dominican Republic: A Caribbean Crucible.* Boulder, Colorado: Westview Press, 1982.
Wilke, James W., David E. Lorey, and Enrique Ochoa (eds.). *Statistical Abstract of Latin America,* 25. Los Angeles: University of California Press, 1987.
World Bank. *World Development Report, 1986.* New York: Oxford University Press for the World Bank, 1986.

Chapter 3

"Aging President Balaguer Blocks Much Overdue Economic Policy Changes," *Latin American Times* [London], 9, No. 2, December 1988, 10–15.
Alburquerque, Ramón. "Historia de Minería Dominicana." Pages 59–69 in Antonio Lluberes, José del Castillo, and Ramón Alburquerque (eds.), *Tabaco, Azúcar, Minería.* Santo Domingo: Editora La Palabra, 1984.
Alemán, José Luis. *27 Ensayos Sobre Economía y Sociedad Dominicanas.* Santo Domingo: Universidad Católica Madre y Maestra, 1982.
Alvarez Betancourt, Opinio. *La Reforma Financiera en la República Dominicana.* Santo Domingo: Editora La Palabra, 1986.
American Chamber of Commerce of the Dominican Republic. *Dominican Republic: Investors Handbook, 1986–87.* Santo Domingo: 1986.
Araujo, Frank, Ana María Viveros-Long, and Jim Murprey. *Agricultural Credit in the Dominican Republic.* (AID Project Impact Evaluation Report No. 58.) Washington: United States Agency for International Development, 1985.
Báez, E. Franc. *Braceros Haitianos en la República Dominicana.* Santo Domingo: Taller, 1986.
Barry, Tom, Beth Wood, and Deb Preusch. *The Other Side of Paradise: Foreign Control in the Caribbean.* New York: Grove Press, 1984.
Baud, Michiel. "The Origins of Capitalist Agriculture in the Dominican Republic," *Latin American Research Review,* 22, No. 2, 1987, 135–53.

Black, Jan Knippers. "Development and Dependency in the Dominican Republic," *Third World Quarterly* [London], 8, No. 1, January 1986, 235–57.

————. *The Dominican Republic: Politics and Development in an Unsovereign State.* Boston: Allen and Unwin, 1986.

Borgatti, Joseph J., and Edgar J. Gordon. *A Study of Debt Conversion: Dominican Republic.* (Center for Privatization, Project No. 219/1.) Washington: United States Agency for International Development, 1988.

Cassá, Roberto. *Capitalismo y Dictadura.* Santo Domingo: Editora de la Universidad Autónoma de Santo Domingo, 1982.

Ceara Hatton, Miguel, with Fernando Pellerano and Héctor Guiliani Cury. *Tendencias Estructurales y Coyuntura de la Economía Dominicana, 1963–1972.* Santo Domingo: Nuevas Rutas, 1984.

Centro Dominicano de Promoción de Exportaciones. *Boletín Estadístico* [Santo Domingo], January–December 1987.

————. *Estudio Oferta Exportable.* Santo Domingo: 1984.

Centro de Estudios Monetarios y Bancarios. *Los Bancos de Desarrollo.* Santo Domingo: Editora la Palabra, 1987.

————. *Los Bancos Hipotecarios de la Construcción.* Santo Domingo: Editora la Palabra, 1987.

————. *Las Instituciones Financieras y el Mercado de Valores en la República Dominicana.* Santo Domingo: Editora la Palabra, 1982.

Coutts, K.J., Héctor Guiliani Cury, and Fernando Pellerano. "Stabilisation Programmes and Structural Adjustment Policies in the Dominican Republic," *Labour and Society* [Geneva], 11, No. 3, August 1986.

Cuello H., José Israel. *Tres Ponencias Sobre Política Económica.* Santo Domingo: Ediciones de Taller, 1985.

Culbertson, Robert, Earl Jones, and Roberto Corpeno. *Private Sector Evaluation: The Dominican Republic.* (AID Evaluation Special Study No. 16.) Washington: United States Agency for International Development, 1983.

Dauhajre, Andrés. "La República Dominicana: 18 Años de Política Económica, 1966–1983." Pages 15–65 in Frank Moya Pons (ed.), *La Situación Cambiaria en la República Dominicana.* Santo Domingo: Forum, 1984.

Diederich, Bernard. "The Troubled Island of Hispaniola: Riots in Haiti and the Dominican Republic," *Caribbean Review,* 13, No. 3, Summer 1984, 18–21, 45.

Direction of Trade Statistics Yearbook. Washington: International Monetary Fund, 1988.

Dominican Republic. Central Bank. *Annual Economic Report, 1980.* Santo Domingo: 1980.

_____. Central Bank. *Boletín Mensual* [Santo Domingo], 41, No. 5, May 1987.

_____. Central Bank. Departamento de Estudios Económicos. *Cuentas Nacionales, 1980–1984.* Santo Domingo: n.d.

_____. Oficina Nacional de Presupuesto, Secretaría Técnico de la Presidencia. *Presupuesto de Ingresos y Ley de Gastos Públicos del Gobierno Central.* Santo Domingo: 1988.

_____. Secretariat of State for Industry and Commerce. *Directorio de Establecimientos Industriales de la República Dominicana.* Santo Domingo: 1983.

Economist Intelligence Unit. *Country Report, 1988–89: Cuba, Dominican Republic, Haiti, Puerto Rico.* London: 1988.

Evaluation Technologies. *Dominican Republic: A Country Profile.* Washington: United States Agency for International Development, 1984.

Greene, Duty D., and Terry L. Roe. *Trade, Exchange Rate, and Agricultural Pricing Policies in the Dominican Republic.* (Political Economy of Agricultural Pricing Policy Series.) Washington: World Bank, 1989.

Guiliani Cury, Héctor. *El Sistema Tributaria Dominicano.* Santo Domingo: Fundación Friedrich Ebert, 1987.

Guiliani Cury, Hugo. *Deuda Externa: Un Proceso de Renegociación.* Santo Domingo: Editora La Palabra, 1986.

Halper, Sam. "Twenty-one Years after Trujillo: The Cloud over the Dominican Republic," *New Leader,* 65, No. 12, June 14, 1982, 4–7.

Hansen, David O., Gustavo A. Antonini, and John Strasma. *The Superior Institute of Agriculture: Development of a Private Institution of Higher Agricultural Education.* (AID Project Impact Evaluation Report No. 67.) Washington: United States Agency for International Development, 1988.

Harrison, Lawrence E. *Underdevelopment Is a State of Mind: The Latin American Case.* Lanham, Maryland: University Press of America, 1985.

Hartshorn, Gary, Gustavo Antonini, Random DuBois, David Harcharik, Stanley Heckadon, Harvey Newton, Carlos Quesada, John Shores, and George Staples. *Dominican Republic: Country Environmental Profile: A Field Study.* Washington: United States Agency for International Developmental, 1981.

Hermann, Hamlet. *Recursos.* Santo Domingo: Directorio Comercial e Industrial, 1981.

Institute for Inter-American Cooperation on Agriculture. *Annual Report, 1987.* San José, Costa Rica: 1988.

Inter-American Development Bank. *Annual Report, 1987.* Washington: 1988.

―――. *El BID en la República Dominicana.* Washington: n.d.

International Monetary Fund. *International Exchange Agreements.* Washington: 1988.

Investment Promotion Council of the Dominican Republic. "Dominican Republic Industrial Free Zones: Main Figures." Santo Domingo: 1989.

―――. *Investing in the Dominican Republic.* Santo Domingo: 1988.

―――. *Investment Opportunity in the Dominican Republic: Free Zones.* Santo Domingo: 1988.

―――. *Sector Profile: Information Industries in the Dominican Republic.* Santo Domingo: 1988.

Ivey, Ronald J. *Preliminary Privatization Strategy for Corporación Dominicana de Empresas Estatales (CORDE).* (Project No. 82.) Washington: Center for Privatization, 1988.

James, Canute. "Dominican Republic." Pages 162–65 in *Latin American and Caribbean Review, 1988.* Cambridge: World of Information, 1987.

Kearney, Richard C. "Dominican Update: Can Politics Contain the Economic Crisis?," *Caribbean Review,* 14, No. 4, Fall 1985, 12–14, 38.

Kritz Ernesto, Eileen Evans, Agustin Llona, and Mauricio Perea. *Dominican Republic: Urban Migrations, Labor Markets, and Free Trade Zones.* Washington: Anita F. Allen and Associates and the International Science and Technology Institute, 1988.

Kurlansky, Mark. "The Dominican Republic: In the Land of the Blind Caudillo," *New York Times Magazine,* August 6, 1989, 24–43.

Leyba, Eddy Enrique. *El Sector Privado y la Economía Dominicana.* Santo Domingo: Centro de Estudios Monetarios y Bancarios, 1985.

López, José Manuel. "El Sistema Financiero en La República Dominicana," *Monetaria* [Mexico City], 10, No. 1, February–March 1987.

McCarthy, Desmond F. *Dominican Republic: Its Main Economic Development Problems.* Washington: World Bank, 1978.

―――. *Macroeconomic Policy Alternatives in the Dominican Republic.* Washington: World Bank, 1984.

Management Systems International. *The Impact on the Poor of USAID's Private Sector Programs in the Dominican Republic: Final Report.* Washington: United States Agency for International Development, 1989.

Mathieson, John A. "The Dominican Republic." Pages 41–63 in Eva Paus (ed.), *Struggles Against Dependence: Nontraditional Export Growth in Central America and the Caribbean.* Boulder, Colorado: Westview Press, 1988.

Merrick, Thomas W. "Population Pressures in Latin America," *Population Bulletin,* 41, No. 3, July 1986.

Moya Pons, Frank. *Régimen de Incentivos en la Economía Dominicana.* Santo Domingo: Amigo del Hogar, 1983.

Najri, José Antonio. *Crisis, Producción, y Desarrollo (Discursos y Ponencias).* Santo Domingo: Editora Corripio, 1986.

Pan American Development Foundation and the Distributive Education Clubs of America. *The Way Up from Poverty: Microenterprise in Latin America and the Caribbean.* Washington: 1988.

Pozo, Jeffrey. "Deposit Mobilization and the Political Economy of Specialized Financial Institutions: The Case of the Dominican Republic." (Economics and Sociology Occasional Paper No. 1467.) Columbus: Agricultural Finance Program, Department of Agricultural Economics and Rural Sociology, Ohio State University, May 1988.

Sabre Foundation. *Free Zones in Developing Countries: Expanding Opportunities for the Private Sector.* (AID Program Evaluation Discussion Paper No. 18.) Washington: United States Agency for International Development, 1983.

Sharpe, Kenneth Evan. *Peasant Politics: Struggle in a Dominican Village.* Baltimore: Johns Hopkins University Press, 1977.

Stanfield, J. David. "Agrarian Reform in the Dominican Republic." Pages 305–37 in William C. Thiesenhusen (ed.), *Searching for Agrarian Reform in Latin America.* Boston: Unwin Hyman, 1989.

Storrs, K. Larry, with Dianne E. Rennack. "U.S. Bilateral Economic and Military Assistance to Latin America and the Caribbean, Fiscal Years 1946–1987." (Library of Congress, Congressional Research Service, Major Issues.) Washington: July 31, 1987.

Tejera, Eduardo J. *Una Década de Desarrollo Económico Dominicano, 1963–1972.* Santo Domingo: n. pub., 1975.

Thoumi, Francisco E. "Long-Term Industrialization Trends in Two Small Caribbean Countries: The Cases of the Dominican Republic and Trinidad and Tobago." Washington: *Inter-American Development Bank,* March 1988.

United Nations. Economic and Social Council. Economic Commission on Latin America and the Caribbean. *Estudio Económico de América Latina y el Caribe, 1987: República Dominicana.* Santiago, Chile: 1988.

_____. Economic Commission on Latin America and the Caribbean. *República Dominicana: Repercusiones de Los Huracanes David y Federico Sobre La Economía y Las Condiciones Sociales.* Santiago, Chile: 1979.

United States. Agency for International Development. *Country Development Strategy Statement, Fiscal Year 1990–91, Action Plan: Dominican Republic.* Washington: 1989.

_____. Agency for International Development. *Economic Assistance Program to the Dominican Republic.* Washington: 1988.

_____. Department of Agriculture. Economic Research Service. *World Agricultural Trends and Indicators, 1970–1988.* Washington: 1989.

_____. Department of Agriculture. Foreign Agricultural Service (Santo Domingo). *Dominican Republic: 1988 Agricultural Situation Report.* (Report DR–8006.) Santo Domingo: 1988.

_____. Department of Commerce. *Guide to Telecommunication Markets in Latin America.* Washington: 1989.

_____. Department of Commerce. *Investment Climate Statement: Dominican Republic.* Washington: GPO, January 1988.

_____. Department of Commerce. Embassy in Santo Domingo. "Dominican Republic." (Foreign Economic Trends and Their Implications for the United States.) Washington: October 1988.

_____. Department of Commerce. Foreign Commercial Service. Embassy in Santo Domingo. "Summary of Investment Laws." Washington: January 1985.

_____. Department of Labor. *Foreign Labor Trends: Dominican Republic.* Washington: 1988.

_____. Department of State. Bureau of Public Affairs. *Background Notes: Dominican Republic.* Washington: GPO, August 1987.

_____. General Accounting Office. "Foreign Assistance: U.S. Use of Conditions to Achieve Economic Reforms." (GAO/NSIAD–86–157.) Washington: August 1986.

Vedovato, Claudio. *Politics, Foreign Trade, and Economic Development: A Study of the Dominican Republic.* New York: St. Martin's Press, 1986.

Vetter, Stephen. "Building the Infrastructure for Progress: Private Development Organizations in the Dominican Republic," *Grassroots Development,* 10, No. 1, 1986, 2–9.

_____. "Portrait of a Peasant Leader: Ramón Aybar," *Grassroots Development,* 8, No. 1, 1984, 2–11.

Wiarda, Howard J. *The Dominican Republic: Nation in Transition.* New York: Praeger, 1969.

Wiarda, Howard J., and Michael J. Kryzanek. *The Dominican Republic: A Caribbean Crucible.* Boulder, Colorado: Westview Press, 1982.

————. *The Politics of External Influence in the Dominican Republic.* (Politics in Latin America: A Hoover Institution Series.) New York: Praeger, 1988.

Wilkie, James W., David E. Lorey, and Enrique Ochoa. *Statistical Abstract of Latin America,* 26. (Latin American Center Publications.) Los Angeles: University of California Press, 1988.

Williams, Eric. *From Columbus to Castro: The History of the Caribbean.* New York: Viking Press, 1970.

Wines, Sarah H. "Stages of Microenterprise Growth in the Dominican Informal Sector," *Grassroots Development,* 9, No. 2, 1985, 33–41.

Winrock International Institute for Agricultural Development. *Agricultural Development Indicators.* Morrilton, Arkansas: 1987.

World Bank. *Annual Report, 1988.* Washington: 1988.

————. *World Debt Tables, 1988–89.* Washington: 1989.

————. *World Debt Tables, 1988–89: First Supplement.* Washington: 1989.

————. *World Development Report, 1989.* New York: Oxford University Press for the World Bank, 1989.

Zinser, James Edward, and Claudio Gonzalo Vega. *Los Mercados Financieros y Cambiarios Regulados y No Regulados y La Distribución del Ingreso en la República Dominicana.* Santo Domingo: Editora La Palabra, 1986.

Chapter 4

Alexander, Robert H. "Prospects for Democracy in the Dominican Republic," *Freedom at Issue,* 48, November–December 1978, 25–27.

Atkins, G. Pope. *Arms and Politics in the Dominican Republic.* Boulder, Colorado: Westview Press, 1981.

Atkins, G. Pope, and Larman Wilson. *The United States and the Trujillo Regime.* New Brunswick, New Jersey: Rutgers University Press, 1972.

Bell, Ian. *The Dominican Republic.* Boulder, Colorado: Westview Press, 1981.

Black, Jan Knippers. "Development and Dependency in the Dominican Republic," *Third World Quarterly* [London], 8, January 1986, 236–57.

————. *The Dominican Republic: Politics and Development in an Unsovereign State.* Boston: Allen and Unwin, 1986.

Bosch, Juan. *The Unfinished Experiment: Democracy in the Dominican Republic.* New York: Praeger, 1964.

Calder, Bruce. *The Impact of Intervention: The Dominican Republic During the U.S. Marine Occupation of 1916–24*. Austin: University of Texas Press, 1984.

Crassweller, Robert. *Trujillo: The Life and Times of a Caribbean Dictator*. New York: Macmillan, 1966.

Diederich, Bernard. *Trujillo: The Death of the Goat*. Boston: Little, Brown, 1978.

Draper, Theodore. *The Dominican Revolt*. New York: Commentary, 1968.

Galíndez, Jesús de. *The Era of Trujillo*. Tucson: University of Arizona Press, 1973.

Gleijeses, Piero. *The Dominican Crisis*. Baltimore: Johns Hopkins University Press, 1978.

Kryzanek, Michael J. "Diversion, Subversion, and Repression: The Strategies of Anti-Regime Politics in Balaguer's Dominican Republic," *Caribbean Studies* [Río Piedras, Puerto Rico], 19, Nos. 1 and 2, 1979, 51–74.

_____. "Political Party Decline and the Failure of Liberal Democracy: The PRD in Dominican Politics," *Journal of Latin American Studies*, 9, 1977, 115–43.

Kryzanek, Michael J., and Howard J. Wiarda. *The Politics of External Influence in the Dominican Republic*. (Politics in Latin America: A Hoover Institution Series.) New York: Praeger/Hoover Institution Press, 1988.

Kumar, U. Shiv. *Intervention in Latin America: Dominican Crisis and the OAS*. New York: Advent, 1987.

Kurzman, Dan. *Santo Domingo: Revolt of the Damned*. New York: Putnam, 1965.

Lang, James. *Inside Development in Latin America: A Report from the Dominican Republic, Colombia, and Brazil*. Chapel Hill: University of North Carolina Press, 1988.

Logan, Rayford. *Haiti and the Dominican Republic*. New York: Oxford University Press, 1968.

Lowenthal, Abraham. *The Dominican Intervention*. Cambridge: Harvard University Press, 1972.

Martin, John Bartlow. *Overtaken by Events: The Dominican Crisis from the Fall of Trujillo to the Civil War*. Garden City, New York: Doubleday, 1966.

Moreno, Jose. *Barrio in Arms: Revolution in Santo Domingo*. Pittsburgh, Pennsylvania: University of Pittsburgh Press, 1970.

Rodman, Selden. *Quisqueya: A History of the Dominican Republic*. Seattle: University of Washington Press, 1964.

Sharpe, Kenneth E. *Peasant Politics: Struggle in a Dominican Village*. Baltimore: Johns Hopkins University Press, 1977.

Slater, Jerome. *Intervention and Negotiation: The United States and the Dominican Republic.* New York: Harper and Row, 1970.

Szulc, Tad. *Dominican Diary.* New York: Delacorte Press, 1965.

Vedovato, Claudio. *Politics, Foreign Trade, and Economic Development: A Study of the Dominican Republic.* New York: St. Martin's Press, 1986.

Walker, Malcolm. *Politics and the Power Structure: A Rural Community in the Dominican Republic.* New York: Teachers College Press, 1972.

Wiarda, Howard J. *Dictatorship and Development: The Methods of Control in Trujillo's Dominican Republic.* Gainesville: University of Florida Press, 1968.

_____. *Dictatorship, Development, and Disintegration: Politics and Social Change in the Dominican Republic.* (3 vols.) Ann Arbor: Xerox University Microfilms, 1975.

_____. *The Dominican Republic: Nation in Transition.* New York: Praeger, 1969.

Wiarda, Howard J., and Michael J. Kryzanek. *The Dominican Republic: A Caribbean Crucible.* Boulder, Colorado: Westview Press, 1982.

Chapter 5

Amnesty International. *Amnesty International Report, 1988.* London: 1988.

Andrade, John. *World Police and Paramilitary Forces.* New York: Stockton Press, 1985.

Atkins, G. Pope. *Arms and Politics in the Dominican Republic.* Boulder, Colorado: Westview Press, 1981.

Becker, Harold K., and Donna Lee Becker. *Handbook of the World's Police.* Metuchen, New Jersey: Scarecrow Press, 1986.

Bell, Ian. *The Dominican Republic.* Boulder, Colorado: Westview Press, 1981.

Black, Jan Knippers. *The Dominican Republic: Politics and Development in an Unsovereign State.* Boston: Allen and Unwin, 1986.

Defense Marketing Services. *DMS Market Intelligence Reports: South America/Australasia.* Greenwich, Connecticut: Defense Marketing Services, 1985.

Dominican Republic. *Código de Procedimiento Criminal de la República Dominicana.* Santo Domingo: Editora Alfa y Omega, 1980.

_____. *Código Penal.* Santo Domingo: Empresa Elena, 1980.

_____. *Constitution.* (Constitutions of the World Series.) Dobbs Ferry, New York: Oceana, 1973.

English, Adrian J. *Armed Forces of Latin America.* London: Jane's, 1984.

Government Finance Statistics Yearbook, 12. Washington: International Monetary Fund, 1988.

Hobday, Charles. *Communist and Marxist Parties of the World.* Burnt Mill, Harlow, Essex, United Kingdom: Longman Group, 1986.

Huskey, James L. (ed.). *Lambert's Worldwide Directory of Defense Authorities with International Defense Organizations and Treaties.* Washington: Lambert, 1984.

Ingleton, Roy D. *Police of the World.* New York: Scribners, 1979.

Jane's All the World's Aircraft, 1988–89. (Ed., John W.R. Taylor.) London: Jane's, 1988.

Jane's Fighting Ships, 1988–89. (Ed., Richard Sharpe.) London: Jane's, 1988.

Keegan, John. *World Armies.* New York: Facts on File, 1984.

Labayle Couhat, Jean, and Bernard Prézelin (eds.). *Combat Fleets of the World 1988–89: Their Ships, Aircraft, and Armament.* Annapolis, Maryland: Naval Institute Press, 1987.

Levinson, Macha. *Defense Market Profiles: Latin American and the Caribbean.* Geneva: Interavia, 1982.

The Military Balance, 1988–89. London: International Institute for Strategic Studies, 1988.

Sivard, Ruth Leger. *World Military and Social Expenditures, 1987–88.* Washington: World Priorities, 1987.

South America, Central America, and the Caribbean, 1988. London: Europa, 1987.

United States. Arms Control and Disarmament Agency. *World Military Expenditures and Arms Transfers, 1987.* Washington: GPO, 1988.

_____. Department of Defense. *Congressional Presentation for Security Assistance Programs, Fiscal Year 1988.* Washington: 1987.

_____. Department of Defense. *Congressional Presentation for Security Assistance Programs, Fiscal Year 1990.* Washington: 1989.

_____. Department of Defense. Security Assistance Agency. *Foreign Military Sales, Foreign Military Construction Sales, and Military Assistance Facts as of September 30, 1988.* Washington: 1988.

_____. Department of State. *Country Reports on Human Rights Practices for 1985.* (Report submitted to United States Congress, 99th, 2d Session, Senate, Committee on Foreign Relations, and House of Representatives, Committee on Foreign Affairs.) Washington: GPO, 1986.

_____. Department of State. *Country Reports on Human Rights Practices for 1986.* (Report submitted to United States Congress, 100th, 1st Session, Senate, Committee on Foreign Relations, and House of Representatives, Committee on Foreign Affairs.) Washington: GPO, 1987.

_____. Department of State. *Country Reports on Human Rights Practices for 1987.* (Report submitted to United States Congress, 100th, 2d Session, Senate, Committee on Foreign Relations, and House of Representatives, Committee on Foreign Affairs.) Washington: GPO, 1988.

_____. Department of State. *Country Reports on Human Rights Practices for 1988.* (Report submitted to United States Congress, 101st, 1st Session, Senate, Committee on Foreign Relations, and House of Representatives, Committee on Foreign Affairs.) Washington: GPO, 1989.

_____. Department of State. Bureau of Public Affairs. *Background Notes: Dominican Republic.* Washington: GPO, 1987.

Wiarda, Howard J. *Dictatorship and Development: The Methods of Control in Trujillo's Dominican Republic.* Gainesville: University of Florida Press, 1968.

Wiarda, Howard J., and Michael J. Kryzanek. *The Dominican Republic: A Caribbean Crucible.* Boulder, Colorado: Westview Press, 1982.

Yearbook on International Communist Affairs, 1988. (Ed., Richard F. Staar.) Stanford, California: Hoover Institution Press, 1988.

"Year in Judiciary Summarized," *Listín Diario* [Santo Domingo], December 31, 1985. Joint Publications Research Service, *Latin America Report.* (JPRS-LAM-86-018.) February 19, 1986, 111-13.

(Various issues of the following publication were also used in the preparation of this chapter: Foreign Broadcast Information Service, *Daily Report: Latin America.*)

Chapter 6

Abbott, Elizabeth. *Haiti: The Duvaliers and Their Legacy.* New York: McGraw-Hill, 1988.

Bellegarde-Smith, Patrick. *In the Shadow of Powers: Dantès Bellegarde in Haitian Social Thought.* (AIMS Historical Series, No. 11.) Atlantic Highlands: Humanities Press International, 1985.

Cole, Hubert. *Christophe: King of Haiti.* New York: Viking, 1967.

Dash, J. Michael. *Haiti and the United States: National Stereotypes and the Literary Imagination.* New York: St. Martin's Press, 1988.

Davis, Wade. *The Serpent and the Rainbow.* New York: Simon and Schuster, 1985.

Diederich, Bernard. "Swine Fever Ironies: The Slaughter of the Haitian Black Pig," *Caribbean Review,* 14, No. 1, Winter 1985, 16-17, 41.

_____. "The Troubled Island of Hispaniola: Riots in Haiti and the Dominican Republic," *Caribbean Review,* 13, No. 3, Summer 1984, 18-21, 45.

Diederich, Bernard, and Al Burt. *Papa Doc: The Truth about Haiti Today.* New York: McGraw-Hill, 1969.

Fauriol, Georges. "The Duvaliers and Haiti," *Orbis: A Journal of World Affairs,* 32, No. 4, Fall 1988, 587-607.

Gingras, Jean-Pierre O. *Duvalier, Caribbean Cyclone: The History of Haiti and Its Present Government.* New York: Exposition Press, 1967.

Heinl, Robert Debs, Jr., and Nancy Gordon Heinl. *Written in Blood: The Story of the Haitian People, 1492-1971.* Boston: Houghton Mifflin, 1978.

James, C.L.R. *The Black Jacobins.* New York: Vintage, 1963.

Keegan, John E. "The Catholic Church in the Struggle Against Duvalierism," *America,* 158, April 23, 1988, 429-32.

Laguerre, Michel S. "The Haitian Political Crisis," *America,* 155, December 27, 1986, 416-20.

Leyburn, James G. *The Haitian People.* (Rev. ed., with introduction by Sidney W. Mintz.) New Haven: Yale University Press, 1966.

Logan, Rayford W. *Haiti and the Dominican Republic.* New York: Oxford University Press, 1968.

Luce, Phillip Abbott. *Haiti: Ready for Revolution.* Washington: Council for Inter-American Security, 1980.

Maingot, Anthony P. "Haiti: Problems of a Transition to Democracy in an Authoritarian Soft State," *Journal of Interamerican Studies and World Affairs,* 28, No. 4, Winter 1986-87, 75-102.

Moran, Charles. *Black Triumvirate: A Study of Louverture, Dessalines, Christophe—the Men Who Made Haiti.* New York: Exposition Press, 1957.

Morse, Richard M. "Haiti, 1492-1988." Pages 3-12 in Richard M. Morse (ed.), *Haiti's Future: Views of Twelve Haitian Leaders.* Washington: Wilson Center Press, 1988.

Nicholls, David. *From Dessalines to Duvalier: Race, Colour, and National Independence in Haiti.* London: Cambridge University Press, 1979.

_____. "Haiti: The Rise and Fall of Duvalierism," *Third World Quarterly* [London], 8, No. 4, October 1986, 1239-52.

_____. "Past and Present in Haitian Politics." Pages 253-64 in Charles R. Foster and Albert Valdman (eds.), *Haiti—Today and Tomorrow: An Interdisciplinary Study.* Lanham, Maryland: University Press of America, 1984.

Ott, Thomas O. *The Haitian Revolution, 1789–1804.* Knoxville: University of Tennessee Press, 1973.
Paley, William. "Haiti's Dynastic Despotism: From Father to Son to . . .," *Caribbean Review,* 13, No. 1, Winter 1984, 13–15, 45.
Paquin, Lyonel. *The Haitians: Class and Color Politics.* Brooklyn, New York: Multi-Type, 1983.
Parkinson, Wenda. *'This Gilded African' Toussaint L'Ouverture.* London: Quarter Books, 1978.
Price-Mars, Jean. *So Spoke the Uncle (Ainsi Parla l'Oncle).* (Trans. and introduction, Magdaline W. Shannon.) Washington: Three Continents Press, 1983.
Prince, Rod. *Haiti: Family Business.* London: Latin America Bureau, 1985.
Rotberg, Robert I. "Haiti's Past Mortgages Its Future," *Foreign Affairs,* 67, No. 1, 1988, 93–109.
Rotberg, Robert I., with Christopher K. Clague. *Haiti: The Politics of Squalor.* Boston: Houghton Mifflin, 1971.
Schmidt, Hans. *The United States Occupation of Haiti, 1915–1934.* New Brunswick, New Jersey: Rutgers University Press, 1971.
Tyson, George F., Jr. (ed.). *Toussaint L'Ouverture.* (Great Lives Observed: A Spectrum Book Series.) Englewood Cliffs, New Jersey: Prentice-Hall, 1973.
Weinstein, Brian, and Aaron Segal. *Haiti: Political Failures, Cultural Successes.* New York: Praeger, 1984.

Chapter 7

"AIDS in Haiti," *Washington Post,* September 29, 1987, Health Section.
Brinkerhoff, Derick W., and Jean Claude Garcia-Zamor (eds.). *Politics, Projects, and People: Institutional Development in Haiti.* New York: Praeger, 1986.
Conway, Frederick J. *The Decision-Making Framework for Tree Planting in the Agroforestry Outreach Project.* Port-au-Prince: University of Maine Agroforestry Outreach Research Project, 1986.
_____. "Pentecostalism in the Context of Haitian Religion and Health Practice." (Ph.D. dissertation.) Washington: American University, 1978.
Courbage, Youssef. *Méthodes d'estimation de niveau futur de la fécondité à partir du nombre d'enfants désiré et des facteurs socio-économiques en Haïti.* (World Fertility Survey Scientific Reports, No. 66.) Voorburg, Netherlands: International Statistical Institute, 1984.

DeWind, Josh, and David H. Kinley. *Aiding Migration: The Impact of International Development Assistance on Haiti.* Boulder, Colorado: Westview Press, 1988.

Dupuy, Alex. *Haiti in the World Economy: Class, Race, and Underdevelopment since 1700.* Boulder, Colorado: Westview Press, 1989.

Fass, Simon M. *Political Economy in Haiti: The Drama of Survival.* New Brunswick, New Jersey: Transaction Books, 1988.

Foster, Charles R., and Albert Valdman (eds.). *Haiti—Today and Tomorrow: An Interdisciplinary Study.* Lanham, Maryland: University Press of America, 1984.

Haines, David W. (ed.). *Refugees in the United States: A Reference Handbook.* Westport, Connecticut: Greenwood Press, 1985.

_____. *The Haitian Economy: Man, Land, and Markets.* London: Croom Helm, 1983.

Haiti. Ministère de l'Economie et des Finances. Institut Haïtien de Statistique et d'Informatique. *La Religion en Haïti (une étude basée sur un échantillon de 2.5% du recensement de 1982).* Port-au-Prince: 1986.

_____. *Santé et Population en Haïti.* Port-au-Prince: 1986.

_____. *La Scolarisation en Haïti: Analyse des résultats anticipés du recensement de 1982.* Port-au-Prince: 1984.

Herskovits, Melville J. *Life in a Haitian Valley.* Garden City, New York: Doubleday, 1971.

Hurbon, Laennec. *Comprendre Haiti: Essaie sur l'état, la nation, la culture.* Paris: Karthala, 1987.

Labelle, Micheline. *Idéologie de Couleur et Classes Sociales en Haiti.* Montreal: Les Presses Universitaires de Montréal, 1978.

Leyburn, James G. *The Haitian People.* (Rev. ed., with introduction by Sidney W. Mintz.) New Haven: Yale University Press, 1966.

Lowenthal, Ira P. *Two to Tango: Haitian Men and Family Planning.* Port-au-Prince: United States Agency for International Development, 1984.

Lundahl, Mats. *The Haitian Economy: Man, Land, and Markets.* London: Croom Helm, 1983.

_____. *Peasants and Poverty: A Study of Haiti.* New York: St. Martin's Press, 1979.

Métraux, Alfred. *Voodoo in Haiti.* New York: Schocken Books, 1972.

Nicholls, David. *From Dessalines to Duvalier: Race, Colour, and National Independence in Haiti.* London: Cambridge University Press, 1979.

Salomé, Bernard. *Education and Development: The Case of Haiti.* Paris: Organisation for Economic Co-operation and Development, 1984.

United States. Department of Health and Human Services. Social Security Administration. *Social Security Programs Throughout the World, 1985.* (Research Report No. 60.) Washington: 1985.

Zuvekas, Clarence, Jr. *Land Tenure, Income, and Employment in Rural Haiti: A Survey.* (General Document No. 2.) Washington: United States Agency for International Development, 1978.

Chapter 8

Abbott, Elizabeth. *Haiti: The Duvaliers and Their Legacy.* New York: McGraw-Hill, 1988.

Allman, T.D. "After Baby Doc," *Vanity Fair,* January 1, 1989, 75–81.

Banque de la République d'Haïti. *Bulletin,* No. 15, July 1988.

_____. *Rapport Annuel.* Port-au-Prince: 1988.

Barry, Tom, Beth Wood, and Deb Preusch. *The Other Side of Paradise: Foreign Control in the Caribbean.* New York: Grove Press, 1984.

Beaulieu, Charles A. *Le Système Bancaire Haïtien: Fonctionnement et Perspectives,* 1. Port-au-Prince: Banque de la République d'Haïti, 1987.

Blemur, Marguerite, et al. *Agriculture Sector Assessment: Haiti.* Washington: RONCO Consulting, 1987.

Bloch, Peter, Virginia Lambert, and Norman Singer. "Land Tenure in Rural Haiti." Madison, Wisconsin: Land Tenure Center, May 1987.

Brand, W. *Impressions of Haiti,* 8. (Publications of the Institute of Social Studies.) The Hague: Mouton, 1965.

Brisson, Jean. "A Look at the Poor Majority." (Research paper.) Port-au-Prince: United States Agency for International Development, March 21, 1977.

_____. *C/CAA's 1989 Caribbean and Central American Databook.* Washington: 1988.

Carty, Winthrop P. "The Regreening of Haiti: Is Tree Cropping the Answer?," *Américas,* 35, No. 5, September 10, 1983, 5–7, 36–38.

Chamberlain, Greg. "Haiti." Pages 168–70 in World of Information, *The Latin America and Caribbean Review.* Saffron Walden, Essex, United Kingdom: World of Information, 1987.

Dewind, Josh, and David H. Kinley, III. *Aiding Migration: The Impact of International Development Assistance on Haiti.* Boulder, Colorado: Westview Press, 1988.

Diederich, Bernard. "The Troubled Island of Hispaniola: Riots in Haiti and the Dominican Republic," *Caribbean Review,* 13, No. 3, 1984, 18–21, 45.

Direction of Trade Statistics Yearbook, 1988. Washington: International Monetary Fund, 1988.

Dufumier, Marc. "Quelles Options pour l'Agriculture en Haïti?," *Conjonction* [Port-au-Prince], 172, No. 1, 1987, 23–47.

Depuy, Alex. *Haiti in the World Economy: Class, Race, and Under-Development since 1700.* Boulder, Colorado: Westview Press, 1989.

Economist Intelligence Unit. *Country Profile, 1988–89: Cuba, Dominican Republic, Haiti, Puerto Rico.* London: 1988.

Ehrlich, Marko, et al. *Haiti: Country Environmental Profile (A Field Study).* Washington: Institute for International Environmental Development, 1985.

Evaluation Technologies. *Haiti: A Country Profile.* (Office of Foreign Disaster Assistance Profiles Series.) Washington: United States Agency for International Development, 1984.

Fass, Simon. *Political Economy in Haiti: The Drama of Survival.* New Brunswick, New Jersey: Transaction Books, 1988.

Fauriol, Georges A. "U.S. Aid and Haitian Democratization." (Testimony Before the United States House of Representatives, Committee on Foreign Affairs, Subcommittee on Western Hemisphere Affairs.) Washington: GPO, March 14, 1989.

Garcia Zamor, Jean-Claude. "Obstacles to Institutional Development in Haiti." Pages 63–92 in Derick W. Brinkerhoff and Jean-Claude Garcia Zamor (eds.), *Politics, Projects, and People: Institutional Development in Haiti.* New York: Praeger, 1986.

Garrity, Monique P. "The Assembly Industries in Haiti: Causes and Effects," *Review of Black Political Economy,* 11, No. 2, Winter 1981, 203–15.

Girault, Christian A. *El Comercio Del Café en Haití.* Santo Domingo: Ediciones de Taller, 1985.

———. "Commerce in the Haitian Economy." Pages 173–80 in Charles R. Foster and Albert Valdman (eds.), *Haiti—Today and Tomorrow: An Interdisciplinary Study.* Lanham, Maryland: University Press of America, 1984.

Grunwald, Joseph, Leslie Delatour, and Karl Voltaire. "Foreign Assembly in Haiti." Pages 180–205 in Joseph Grunwald and Kenneth Flamm (eds.), *The Global Factory: Foreign Assembly in International Trade.* Washington: Brookings Institution, 1985.

Haiti. Ministère de l'Economie et des Finances. Institut Haïtien de Statistique et d'Informatique. *Indicateurs de la Conjoncture* [Port-au-Prince], No. 3, 1986.

———. Ministère de l'Economie et des Finances. Institut Haïtien de Statistique et d'Informatique. *Recueil des Statistiques de Base.* Port-au-Prince: 1986.

————. Ministère de l'Industrie et du Commerce. *Haiti: A Guide for Investors.* Port-au-Prince: n.d.

————. Ministère du Plan. *Plan Biennal, 1984–86: Partie Globale et Regionale.* Port-au-Prince: 1984.

————. Office Nationale pour la Promotion des Investissements (ONAPI). *Invest in Haiti.* Port-au-Prince: 1982.

"Haiti: Land of Poverty and Fear," *Los Angeles Times,* December 15, 1985, 1, 6–7.

Haitian Development Foundation. *Annual Report, 1986–87.* Port-au-Prince: 1987.

Harrison, Lawrence E. *Underdevelopment Is a State of Mind: The Latin American Case.* Lanham, Maryland: University Press of America and the Center for International Affairs, Harvard University, 1985.

Institute for Inter-American Cooperation in Agriculture. *Annual Report, 1988.* San José, Costa Rica: 1988.

Inter-American Development Bank. *Annual Report, 1987.* Washington: 1988.

International Monetary Fund. *Annual Report of Exchange Arrangements and Exchange Restrictions, 1988.* Washington: 1988.

————. *Balance of Payments Statistics,* 39, Pt 1. Washington: 1988, 186–89.

————. *International Financial Statistics.* Washington: 1988.

Joseph, Raymond. "Statement of Raymond Joseph." (Testimony Before the United States House of Representatives, Committee on Foreign Affairs, Subcommittee on Western Hemisphere Affairs.) Washington: March 14, 1989.

Lappé, Frances Moore, Joseph Collins, and David Kinley. *Aid as Obstacle: Twenty Questions about Our Foreign Aid and the Hungry.* San Francisco: Institute for Food and Development Policy, 1981.

Lundahl, Mats. *The Haitian Economy: Man, Land, and Markets.* New York: St. Martin's Press, 1983.

————. "Haitian Underdevelopment in a Historical Perspective," *Journal of Latin American Studies,* 14, No. 2, November 1982, 465–75.

McLain, Rebecca J., and Douglas M. Steinbarger. "Land Tenure and Land Use in Southern Haiti. Case Studies of Les Anglais and Grand Ravine du Sud Watersheds." (Research Paper Series, No. 95.) Madison, Wisconsin: Land Tenure Center, April 1988.

Maguire, Robert. *Bottom-Up Development in Haiti.* (2d ed.) Rosslyn, Virginia: Inter-American Foundation, April 1981.

Maingot, Anthony P. "Haiti: Problems of a Transition to Democracy in an Authoritarian Soft State," *Journal of Interamerican Studies and World Affairs,* 28, No. 4, Winter 1986–87, 75–102.

_____. "Leslie Manigat on Haitian Modernization and the Pursuit of Happiness," *Hemisphere*, 1, No. 1, Fall 1988, 19–23.

Martino, Orland D. *Mineral Industries of Latin America*. Washington: GPO, 1988.

Merrick, Thomas W. "Population Pressures in Latin America," *Population Bulletin*, 41, No. 3, July 1986.

Morse, Richard M. (ed.). *Haiti's Future: Views of Twelve Haitian Leaders*. (Wilson Center Perspectives Series.) Washington: Wilson Center Press, 1988.

Murray, Gerald F. "Seeing the Forests While Planting the Trees: An Anthropological Approach to Agroforestry in Rural Haiti." Pages 193–226 in Derick W. Brinkerhoff and Jean-Claude Garcia Zamor (eds.), *Politics, Projects, and People: Institutional Development in Haiti*. New York: Praeger, 1986.

_____. "The Wood Tree as a Cash Crop: An Anthropological Strategy for the Domestication of Energy." Pages 141–60 in Charles R. Foster and Albert Valdman (eds.), *Haiti—Today and Tomorrow: An Interdisciplinary Study*. Lanham, Maryland: University Press of America, 1984.

Nicholls, David. *Haiti in Caribbean Context: Ethnicity, Economy, and Revolt*. New York: St. Martin's Press, 1985.

_____. "Haiti: The Rise and Fall of Duvalierism," *Third World Quarterly* [London], 8, No. 4, October 1986, 1239–52.

Organization of American States. *Haïti: Mission d'Assistance Technique Intégrée*. Washington: 1972.

_____. *Statistical Bulletin of the OAS*, 8, No. 3–4, July 12, 1986.

Pan American Development Foundation. *Annual Report, 1988*. Washington: 1989.

Paquin, Lyonel. *The Haitians: Class and Color Politics*. New York: Multi-Type, 1983.

Pfefferman, Guy P. *Public Expenditure in Latin America: Effects on Poverty*. (World Bank Discussion Papers.) Washington: World Bank, 1987.

Preeg, Ernest H. "Migration and Development in Hispaniola." Pages 140–56 in Robert A. Pastor (ed.), *Migration and Development in the Caribbean: The Unexplored Connection*. (Westview Special Studies on Latin America and the Caribbean Series.) Boulder, Colorado: Westview Press, 1985.

Prince, Rod. *Haiti: Family Business*. London: Latin America Bureau, 1985.

Prominex Haiti. "Business Line," 1, No. 1, September–October 1988.

Rotberg, Robert I. "Haiti's Past Mortgages Its Future," *Foreign Affairs*, 67, No. 1, Fall 1988, 93–109.

Rotberg, Robert I., with Christopher K. Clague. *Haiti: The Politics of Squalor*. Boston: Houghton Mifflin, 1971.

Smucker, Glenn R. "Some Reflections on the Relation of the Peasant Farmer to the Environment: A Sociocultural Assessment." (Internal memorandum.) Pan American Development Foundation: May 12, 1985.

Taft-Morales, Maureen. "Haiti: Political Developments and U.S. Policy Concerns." (Library of Congress, Congressional Research Service, Foreign Affairs and National Defense Division, Issue Brief.) Washington: January 6, 1989.

Tata, Robert J. *Haiti: Land of Poverty*. Lanham, Maryland: University Press of America, 1982.

Thoumi, Francisco E. "Social and Political Obstacles to Economic Development in Haiti." (Inter-American Development Bank Reprint Series, No. 137.) Washington: Inter-American Development Bank, 1983.

United Nations. Economic Commission for Latin America and the Caribbean. *Estudio Económico de América Latina y el Caribe 1987: Haiti*. Santiago, Chile: 1988.

United States. Agency for International Development. *Congressional Presentation, FY 1990: Latin America and Caribbean Region*. (Annex III.) Washington: GPO, 1989.

––––––. Agency for International Development. *Haiti: Development Assistance Program, FY 1979*. Washington: June 1977.

––––––. Agency for International Development. "Haiti: Fact Sheet." Washington: March 1989.

––––––. Department of Commerce. International Trade Commission. *Annual Report on the Impact of the Caribbean Basin Economic Recovery Act on U.S. Industries and Consumers*. (2d Report.) Washington: GPO, 1987.

––––––. Department of Commerce. International Trade Commission. *Caribbean Basin Investment Survey*. Washington: November 1988.

––––––. Department of Commerce. International Trade Commission. "Doing Business with Haiti." (Overseas Business Reports Series, No. OBR 85-11.) Washington: GPO, June 1985.

––––––. Department of Commerce. International Trade Commission. "Foreign Economic Trends and Their Implications for the United States: Haiti." (International Marketing Information Series.) Washington: GPO, July 1988.

––––––. Department of Commerce. International Trade Commission. *A Guide to Telecommunications Markets in Latin America*. Washington: 1989.

_____. Department of Commerce. "Investment Climate Statement: Haiti." Washington: April 1988.

_____. Department of Commerce. "1988 Commercial Activities Report: Haiti." Washington: 1988.

_____. Department of Labor. Bureau of International Labor Affairs. "Foreign Labor Trends: Haiti." Washington: GPO, 1987.

_____. Department of State. Bureau of Public Affairs. *Background Notes: Haiti.* Washington: GPO, April 1987.

_____. Department of State. Office of Foreign Disaster Assistance (OFDA). "History Report: Haiti." Washington: December 1988.

_____. General Accounting Office. "Assistance to Haiti: Barriers, Recent Program Changes, and Future Options." Washington: GPO, February 22, 1982.

_____. General Accounting Office. *Caribbean Basin Initiative: Impact on Selected Countries.* (GAO/NSIAD-88-177.) Washington: GPO, July 1988.

_____. General Accounting Office. "United States Assistance to Haiti: Progress Made, Challenges Remain." Washington: GPO, June 12, 1985.

Weinstein, Brian, and Aaron Segal. *Haiti: Political Failures, Cultural Successes.* (Politics in Latin America Series.) New York: Praeger, 1984.

Williams, Eric. *From Columbus to Castro: The History of the Caribbean, 1492-1969.* New York: Vintage, 1970.

Winrock International Institute for Agricultural Development. *Agricultural Development Indicators.* Morrilton, Arkansas: 1987.

The World Bank. *Annual Report, 1987.* Washington: 1987.

_____. *Annual Report, 1988.* Washington: 1988.

_____. *Haiti: Public Expenditures Review.* Washington: 1987.

_____. *1987-1988 World Bank Debt Tables, Second Supplement: External Debt of Developing Countries.* Washington: 1988.

_____. *World Development Report, 1988.* Washington: 1988.

Zuvekas, Clarence Jr. *Agricultural Development in Haiti: An Assessment of Sector Problems, Policies, and Prospects under Conditions of Severe Soil Erosion.* Washington: 1978.

_____. "An Annotated Bibliography of Agricultural Development in Haiti." (United States Department of Agriculture Economic Research Service, General Working Document No. 1.) Washington: GPO, August 1977.

(Various issues of the following publications were also used in the preparation of this chapter: *Business Haiti* [Port-au-Prince]; and *Grassroots Development.*)

Chapter 9

Abbott, Elizabeth. *Haiti: The Duvaliers and Their Legacy.* New York: McGraw-Hill, 1988.

Americas Watch, National Coalition for Haitian Refugees, Caribbean Rights. *The More Things Change . . . Human Rights in Haiti.* New York: 1989.

Anglade, Georges. *Atlas Critique d'Haïti.* Montreal: Centre De Recherches Caraïbes, University of Montreal, 1982.

_____. *Espace et Liberté en Haïti.* Montreal: Centre De Recherches Caraïbes, University of Montreal, 1982.

Bazin, Marc. "Democratic Transition in Haiti: An Unfinished Agenda," *Yale Journal of International Law,* 13, Summer 1988.

Blaustein, Albert P., and Grisbert H. Flanz (eds.). *Constitutions of the Countries of the World.* Dobbs Ferry, New York: Oceana, 1989.

Castor, Suzy. *Le Massacre de 1937 et les Relations Haitiano-Dominicaines.* Port-au-Prince: Le Natal, 1988.

Dalvius, Gerald. *Une Armée pour la Démocratie en Haïti.* Port-au-Prince: Le Natal, 1987.

Daudet, Yves, and François Blanc. "The Training of Managerial Administrative Personnel in Haiti." Pages 303–13 in Charles Foster and Albert Valdman (eds.), *Haiti—Today and Tomorrow: An Interdisciplinary Study.* Lanham, Maryland: University Press of America, 1984.

Diederich, Bernard. "Haiti." Pages 547–69 in Jack W. Hopkins (ed.), *Latin America and Caribbean Contemporary Record,* 5. New York: Holmes and Meier, 1986.

Doubout, Jean-Jacques, and Joly Ulrick. *Notes sur le Développement Syndical en Haïti.* Port-au-Prince: Imprimerie Abece, 1974.

Economist Intelligence Unit. *Country Report, 1988–89: Cuba, Dominican Republic, Haiti, Puerto Rico.* London: 1988.

Fass, Simon. *Political Economy in Haiti: The Drama of Survival.* New Brunswick, New Jersey: Transaction Books, 1988.

Ferguson, James. *Papa Doc, Baby Doc: Haiti and the Duvaliers.* Oxford: Blackwell, 1987.

Garcia Zamor, Jean-Claude. "Haiti." Pages 577–86 in Jack W. Hopkins (ed.), *Latin America and Caribbean Contemporary Record,* 1. New York: Holmes and Meier, 1982.

Haïti Information Libre. "Neuf Mois Après: Quoi de Neuf pour la Presse Haïtienne," *Haïti Information Libre* [Paris], No. 14, November 1986, 1–12.

Heinl, Robert Debs, Jr., and Nancy Gordon Heinl. *Written in Blood: The Story of the Haitian People, 1492–1971.* Boston: Houghton-Mifflin, 1978.

Hooper, Michael. *Duvalierism since Duvalier.* New York: Americas Watch, National Coalition for Haitian Refugees, 1986.
_____. "Haiti." Pages 808–31 in Jack W. Hopkins (ed.), *Latin America and Caribbean Contemporary Record,* 3. New York: Holmes and Meier, 1984.
_____. "Haiti." Pages 727–41 in Jack W. Hopkins (ed.), *Latin America and Caribbean Contemporary Record,* 4. New York: Holmes and Meier, 1985.
_____. "The Politicization of Human Rights in Haiti." Pages 283–302 in Charles Foster and Albert Valdman (eds.), *Haiti— Today and Tomorrow: An Interdisciplinary Study.* Lanham, Maryland: University Press of America, 1984.
Latortue, Gérard. "Contemporary Political Development in Haiti." Pages 51–72 in T. G. Mathews and F. M. Andic (eds.), *Politics and Economics in the Caribbean.* San Juan, Puerto Rico: Institute of Caribbean Studies, 1971.
Leyburn, James G. *The Haitian People.* New Haven: Yale University Press, 1941.
Maingot, Anthony P. "Haiti: Problems of a Transition to Democracy in an Authoritarian Soft State," *Journal of Interamerican Studies and World Affairs,* 28, No. 4, Winter 1986–87, 75–102.
Manigat, Leslie F. *Haiti of the Sixties, Object of International Concern.* Baltimore: School of Advanced International Studies, Johns Hopkins University Press, 1964.
Montague, Ludwell Lee. *Haiti and the United States, 1714–1938.* Durham, North Carolina: Duke University Press, 1940.
Nicholls, David. *From Dessalines to Duvalier: Race, Colour, and National Independence in Haiti.* London: Cambridge University Press, 1979.
_____. *Haiti in Caribbean Context: Ethnicity, Economy, and Revolt.* London: Macmillan, 1985.
Paquin, Lyonel. *The Haitians: Class and Color Politics.* Brooklyn, New York: Multi-Type, 1983.
Rotberg, Robert I., with Christopher K. Clague. *Haiti: The Politics of Squalor.* Boston: Houghton Mifflin, 1971.
Schmidt, Hans. *The United States Occupation of Haiti, 1915–1934.* New Brunswick, New Jersey: Rutgers University Press, 1971.
Smucker, Glenn R. "Peasant Councils and the Politics of Community." Pages 93–113 in Derick W. Brinkerhoff and Jean-Claude Garcia Zamor (eds.), *Politics, Projects, and People: Institutional Development in Haiti.* New York: Praeger, 1986.
_____. "Peasants and Development Politics: A Study in Haitian Class and Culture." (Ph.D. dissertation, New School for Social Research, New York, 1984.) Ann Arbor: Xerox University Microfilms.

_____. "Politics and Class Differentiation in Rural Haiti." (Paper presented at the American Anthropological Association, November 20, 1983, Chicago, 1983.)

_____. "The Social Character of Religion in Rural Haiti." Pages 35–56 in Charles Foster and Albert Valdman (eds.), *Haiti— Today and Tomorrow: An Interdisciplinary Study.* Lanham, Maryland: University Press of America, 1984.

Smucker, Glenn R., and Marilyn Rak. "Haiti Democratic Needs Assessment." Washington: United States Agency for International Development, May 1989.

Trouillot, Michel-Rolph. *Les Racines Historiques de L'Etat Duvalierien.* Port-au-Prince: Henri Deschamps, 1986.

United States. Agency for International Development. *Haiti Project Paper, Legal Assistance to the Poor.* Washington: 1979.

_____. Department of State. Bureau of Inter-American Affairs. Office of Public Diplomacy for Latin America and the Caribbean. "The Elections in Haiti 1987." (Department of State Publication No. 9623.) Washington: 1987.

Vieux, Serge. "Research Problems and Perspectives of the Haitian Civil Service." Pages 240–72 in Vera Rubin and Richard Schaedel (eds.), *The Haitian Potential.* New York: Teachers College Press, 1975.

Weinstein, Brian, and Aaron Segal. *Haiti: Political Failures, Cultural Successes.* (Politics in Latin America Series.) New York: Praeger, 1984.

Chapter 10

Abbott, Elizabeth. *Haiti: The Duvaliers and Their Legacy.* New York: McGraw-Hill, 1988.

Americas Watch, National Coalition for Haitian Refugees, Caribbean Rights. *The More Things Change . . . Human Rights in Haiti.* New York: 1989.

Constitution de la République d'Haïti: Commentaries et Prises de Position. Port-au-Prince: Editions SCOLHA, 1987.

Delince, Kern. *Armée et Politique en Haïti.* Paris: Editions L'Harmattan, 1979.

Diederich, Bernard, and Al Burt. *Papa Doc: The Truth about Haiti Today.* New York: McGraw-Hill, 1969.

English, Adrian J. *Armed Forces of Latin America.* London: Jane's, 1984.

_____. *Regional Defense Profile, No. 1: Latin America.* London: Jane's, 1988.

Healy, David. *Gunboat Diplomacy in the Wilson Era: The U.S. Navy in Haiti, 1915-1916.* Madison: University of Wisconsin Press, 1976.

Heine, Jorge. "Transition to Nowhere," *Caribbean Review*, 16, No. 2, Winter 1988, 4-6, 26.

Heinl, Robert Debs, Jr., and Nancy Gordon Heinl. *Written in Blood: The Story of the Haitian People, 1492-1971.* Boston: Houghton Mifflin, 1978.

Hooper, Michael S. "The Politicization of Human Rights in Haiti." Pages 283-302 in Charles R. Foster and Albert Valdman (eds.), *Haiti—Today and Tomorrow: An Interdisciplinary Study.* Lanham, Maryland: University Press of America, 1984.

Jane's Infantry Weapons, 1988-89. (Ed., Ian V. Hogg.) London: Jane's, 1988.

Levine, Barry B. "After the Fall," *Caribbean Review*, 16, No. 2, Winter 1988, 8-9, 32-34.

Logan, Rayford W. *The Diplomatic Relations of the United States with Haiti, 1776-1891.* Chapel Hill: University of North Carolina Press, 1941.

The Military Balance, 1988-89. London: International Institute for Strategic Studies, 1988.

Preeg, Ernest H., and Anthony Maingot. *The Haitian Crisis: Two Perspectives.* Miami: Institute of Interamerican Studies, University of Miami, 1988.

Rotberg, Robert I., with Christopher K. Clague. *Haiti: The Politics of Squalor.* Boston: Houghton Mifflin, 1971.

Schmidt, Hans. *The United States Occupation of Haiti, 1915-1934.* New Brunswick, New Jersey: Rutgers University Press, 1971.

Weinstein, Brian, and Aaron Segal. *Haiti: Political Failures, Cultural Successes.* New York: Praeger, 1984.

Appendix B

American Chamber of Commerce of Mexico. *Business Opportunities under the Caribbean Basin Initiative, 1987.* Mexico City: 1986.

Canada. Ministry of External Affairs. *Caribcan.* (Communique Series.) Ottawa: February 17, 1986.

Caribbean and Central American Action. *1988 Caribbean and Central American Databook.* Washington: 1987.

The Development Group for Alternative Policies. "Supporting Central American and Caribbean Development: A Critique of the Caribbean Basin Initiative and an Alternative Regional Assistance Plan." Washington: 1983.

Feinberg, Richard E., Richard Newfarmer, and Bernadette Orr. "Caribbean Basin Initiative: Pros and Cons." Pages 113–28 in Mark Falcoff and Robert Royal (eds.), *The Continuing Crisis: U.S. Policy in Central America and the Caribbean.* Washington: Ethics and Public Policy Center, 1987.

Fox, James W. "Is the Caribbean Basin Initiative Working?" Washington: United States Agency for International Development, March 7, 1989.

Gordon, Richard A., and John Venuti. "Exchange of Information under Tax Treaties—An Update," *Tax Management International Journal,* 15, August 8, 1986, 292–98.

Martin, Atherton, Steve Hellinger, and Daniel Soloman. *Prospects and Reality: The CBI Revisited.* Washington: The Development Group for Alternative Policies, 1985.

Mye, L. Randolph. *Caribbean and Central American Export Performance, 1980 to 1987.* Washington: United States Department of Commerce, 1988.

Pregelj, Vladimir N. "CBI II: Expanding the Caribbean Basin Economic Recovery Act." (Library of Congress, Congressional Research Service, Economics Division, IB89096.) Washington: June 7, 1989.

Sanford, Jonathan. "Caribbean Basin Initiative." (Library of Congress, Congressional Research Service, Foreign Affairs and National Defense Division, IB82074.) Washington: May 27, 1983.

Seyler, Daniel J. "The Politics of Development: The Case of Jamaica and the Caribbean Basin Initiative." (Research paper.) Washington: School of International Service, American University, 1986.

Sixth Meeting of the Conference of Caricom Heads of Government. Review of the Caribbean Basin Initiative. (Agenda item No. 11.) Caricom: July 1–4, 1985.

United States. Congress. 97th, 2d Session. House of Representatives. Committee on Foreign Affairs. *Hearings and Markup Before the Committee on Foreign Affairs and the Subcommittee on International Economic Policy and Trade and on Inter-American Affairs: The Caribbean Basin Initiative.* Washington: GPO, 1982.

_____. Congress. 97th, 2d Session. House of Representatives. Subcommittee on Trade. *Hearings Before the Subcommittee: The Caribbean Basin Initiative.* Washington: GPO, 1982.

_____. Congress. 97th, 2d Session. Senate. Committee on Foreign Relations. *Hearings Before the Committee on Foreign Relations: Caribbean Basin Initiative.* Washington: GPO, 1982.

_____. Congress. 100th, 1st Session. House of Representatives. Committee on Ways and Means. Subcommitte on Oversight. *Report on the Committee Delegation Mission to the Caribbean Basin and the Recommendations to Improve the Effectiveness of the Caribbean Basin Initiative.* Washington: GPO, 1987.

_____. Congress. 101st, 1st Session. House of Representatives. Committee on Ways and Means. *Caribbean Basin Economic Recovery Expansion Act of 1989.* (Report Nos. 101–36.) Washington: GPO, 1989.

_____. Department of Commerce. *Caribbean Basin Initiative: 1986 Guidebook.* Washington: 1985.

_____. Department of Commerce. *Caribbean Basin Initiative: 1987 Guidebook.* Washington: 1986.

_____. Department of Commerce, in cooperation with the United States Agency for International Development. *Caribbean Basin Initiative (CBI): 1988 Guidebook for Caribbean Basin Exporters.* Washington: 1988.

_____. Department of Commerce. International Trade Commission. *Annual Report on the Impact of the Caribbean Basin Economic Recovery Act on U.S. Industries and Consumers.* (2d Annual Report, 1986.) Washington: 1987.

_____. Department of Commerce. International Trade Commission. *Annual Report on the Impact of the Caribbean Basin Economic Recovery Act on U.S. Industries and Consumers.* (3d Annual Report, 1987.) Washington: 1988.

_____. Department of Commerce. International Trade Commission. *Caribbean Basin Investment Survey.* Washington: 1988. Washington: July 12, 1989.

_____. Department of Labor. *Trade and Employment Effects of the Caribbean Basin Economic Recovery Act.* (3d Annual Report.) Washington: GPO, 1987.

_____. Department of Labor. *Trade and Employment Effects of the Caribbean Basin Economic Recovery Act.* (4th Annual Report.) Washington: GPO, 1988.

_____. Department of State. Bureau of Inter-American Affairs. Office of Regional Economic Policy. *Report by the United States Department of State on the Caribbean Basin Initiative (CBI).* Washington: GPO, May 1989.

_____. General Accounting Office. *Caribbean Basin Initiative: Impact on Selected Countries.* (No. GAO/NSIAD–88–177.) Washington: GPO, July 1988.

_____. General Accounting Office. *Caribbean Basin Initiative: Legislative and Agency Actions Relating to the CBI. Fact Sheet for the Chairman, Subcommittee on Oversight.* (Report to the United States House of Representatives, Committee on Ways and Means.) Washington: GPO, 1986.

_____. General Accounting Office. *Caribbean Basin Initiative: Need for More Reliable Data on Business Activity Resulting from the Initiative.* (No. GAO/NSIAD-86-201BR.) Washington: GPO, 1986.

Van Grasstek, Craig. "The Caribbean Basin Initiative: Update," *Policy Focus,* No. 3, 1985.

The White House. Office of the Press Secretary. *Fact Sheets on the Initiative in President Reagan's Speech at Queens Park, St. George's, Grenada.* Washington: February 20, 1986.

World Bank. *The Caribbean: Export Preferences and Performance.* Washington: 1988.

(Various issues of the following publications were also used in the preparation of this appendix: *Caribbean Action; Caribbean Insight* [London]; and *CBI Business Bulletin.*)

Glossary

colono(s)—As used in the Dominican Republic, refers to a small independent sugarcane grower. In other Latin American countries, the word usually designates a settler or a tenant farmer.

Dominican Republic peso (RD$)—Dominican monetary unit, divided into 100 centavos. The Dominican government officially maintained a one-to-one exchange rate between the peso and the United States dollar until 1985, when the peso was allowed to float freely against the dollar for most transactions. In 1988, the exchange rate reached US$1 = RD$8.00; it subsequently leveled off to US$1 = RD$6.35 by 1989. The government decided in 1988 to reinstitute a fixed exchange rate that it would adjust periodically in accord with prevailing economic conditions.

807 program—Refers to items 806.3, 807, and 807–A of the Tariff Schedules of the United States that allow the duty-free entry of goods when the final product contains a certain portion of raw material or labor value-added in the United States and the Caribbean Basin. Item 807–A provides guaranteed access levels to specific Caribbean Basin countries.

encomienda—A fiduciary grant of tribute collection rights over Indians, conferred by the Spanish crown on individual colonists (*encomenderos*), who in turn undertook to maintain order and to propagate Christianity.

fiscal year (FY)—The Dominican Republic's fiscal year is the calendar year, except in the case of the State Sugar Council (Consejo Estatal de Azúcar—CEA), which runs in the cycle of October1 to September 30. Haiti's fiscal year is the same as that of the United States government, running from October 1 to September 30. Fiscal year dates of reference for these two countries therefore correspond to the year in which the period ends. For example, FY 1988 began on October 1, 1987, and ended on September 30, 1988.

gourde (G)—The Haitian monetary unit, divided into 100 centimes. The official exchange rate of US$1 = G5, established in 1919, remained in place in 1989. On the black market, however, the gourde traded at US$1 = G7 or higher.

gross domestic product (GDP)—A measure of the total value of goods and services produced by a domestic national economy during a given period, usually one year. Obtained by adding the value contributed by each sector of the economy in the form of profits, compensation to employees, and depreciation (consumption of capital). Only domestic production is included, not income arising from investments and possessions owned abroad, hence the use of the word "domestic" to distinguish GDP from gross national product (*q.v.*). Real GDP is the value of GDP when inflation has been taken into account.

gross national product (GNP)—The total market value of all final goods and services produced by an economy during a year. Obtained by adding the gross domestic product (*q.v.*) and the income received from abroad by residents and then subtracting payments remitted abroad to nonresidents. Real GNP is the value of GNP when inflation has been taken into account.

import substitution—Also known as import-substitution industrialization, an economic development strategy that emphasizizes the growth of domestic industries, often by import protection using tariff and nontariff measures. Proponents favor the export of industrial goods over that of primary products.

Industrial Free Zone(s)—Also known as free trade zones, or free zones, these industrial parks played host to manufacturing firms that benefited from favorable business conditions extended by a given government in an effort to attract foreign investment and to create jobs. In the Dominican Republic, free-zone enterprises paid no duties on goods directly imported into, or exported from, the free zone. These enterprises also enjoyed exemptions from Dominican taxes for up to twenty years, and they were allowed to pay workers less than the established minimum wage.

International Monetary Fund (IMF)—Established along with the World Bank (*q.v.*) in 1945, the IMF is a specialized agency affiliated with the United Nations; it is responsible for stabilizing international exchange rates and payments. The main business of the IMF is the provision of loans to its members (including industrialized and developing countries) when they experience balance-of-payments difficulties. These loans frequently carry conditions that require substantial internal economic adjustments by the recipients, most of which are developing countries.

liberation theology—An activist movement led by Roman Catholic clergy who trace their inspiration to Vatican Council II (1965), where some church procedures were liberalized, and the Second Latin American Bishops' Conference in Medellín, Colombia (1968), which endorsed greater direct efforts to improve the lot of the poor.

Lomé Convention—A series of agreements between the European Economic Community (EEC) and a group of African, Caribbean, and Pacific (ACP) states, mainly former European colonies, that provided duty-free or preferential access to the EEC market for almost all ACP exports. The Stabilization of Export Earnings (Stabex) scheme, a mechanism set up by the Lomé Convention, provides for compensation for ACP export earnings lost through fluctuations in the world prices of agricultural commodities. The Lomé Convention also provides for limited EEC development aid and investment funds to be disbursed to ACP recipients through the European Development Fund and the European Investment Bank. The Lomé Convention is updated every five years. Lomé I took effect on April 1, 1976; Lomé II, on January 1, 1981; Lomé III, on March 1, 1985; and Lomé IV, on December 15, 1989. Lomé IV included the Dominican Republic, Haiti, and Namibia in the convention for the first time.

936 funds—Funds deposited by United States-based corporations in the Government Development Bank of Puerto Rico in order to take advantage of Section 936 of the United States Internal Revenue Service Code, under which income derived from sources in Puerto Rico is exempted from United States income taxes. These funds may be used to help finance twin plant ventures with countries that have signed a bilateral tax information exchange agreement with the United States.

Paris Club—A Paris-based organization that represents commercial banks in the rescheduling of national debts.

San José Accord—An agreement between Mexico and Venezuela—signed in 1980 in San José, Costa Rica, whereby the two oil producers committed themselves to supply crude oil on concessionary terms to ten Central American and Caribbean nations.

terms of trade—Number of units that must be given up for one unit of goods received by each party, e.g., nation, to a transaction. The terms of trade are said to move in favor of the party that gives up fewer units of goods than it did previously for one unit of goods received, and against the party that gives up more units of goods for one unit of goods received. In international economics, the concept plays an important role in evaluating exchange relationships between nations.

twin plant—Productive arrangements whereby two or more producers in separate countries complementarily share the production of a good or service. Under the Caribbean Basin Initiative (CBI—see Appendix B), such arrangements with the

435

government of Puerto Rico potentially benefited from special investment or 936 funds (*q.v.*). The operations of twin plant ventures typically entailed the delegation of assembly or other labor-intensive production stages to plants in a CBI-designated country, from which these semi-finished products would then be shipped duty-free to Puerto Rico for final processing.

World Bank—Internal name used to designate a group of three affiliated international institutions: the International Bank for Reconstruction and Development (IBRD), the International Development Association (IDA), and the International Finance Corporation (IFC). The IBRD, established in 1945, has as its primary purpose the provision of loans to developing countries for productive projects. The IDA, a legally separate loan fund administered by the staff of the IBRD, was set up in 1960 to furnish credits to the poorest developing countries on much easier terms than those of conventional IBRD loans. The IFC, founded in 1956, supplements the activities of the IBRD through loans and assistance designed specifically to encourage the growth of productive private enterprises in the less developed countries. The president and certain senior officers of the IBRD hold the same positions in the IFC. The three institutions are owned by the governments of the countries that subscribe their capital.

Index

Abraham, Hérard, xx, xxiv
Acaau, Louis Jean-Jacques, 220
acquired immune deficiency syndrome (AIDS). *See* AIDS
Act of Chapultepec, 175, 361
Adams, John, 211–12
affranchis, 206, 207, 249
Africans (*see also* racial groups)
  Dominican Republic: 5; and black pride, 50; and culture, 49–50; in ethnic mix, 49
  Haiti: 206, 249; overthrow of slavery, xvii; Royal Dahomets, 216
African Swine Fever (ASF), 100, 235–36, 301
Agricultural Bank of the Dominican Republic (Bagricola), 115
Agricultural Credit Bank (BCA), 310
agriculture (*see also* crops)
  Dominican Republic: cash crops, 94–98; diversification of, 82; and employment, 89; and exports, 89–90; farming technology, 92–94; food crops, 98–100; forestry and fishing, 101; land tenure and policy, 90–92; land use, 92; livestock, 100–101; with mixed crops, 62–64; through rural cooperatives, 64
  Haiti: cash crops, 295–98; and credit, 294–95; and ecology, 291; and economy, 281; and employment, 290; and exports, 290; farming technology, 294; fishing, 302; food crops, 298–300; forestry, 300–301; land tenure and policy, 291–93; land use, 293–94; livestock, 301–2; as percentage of GDP, 290
Ahora, 156
Aid and Housing Institute, 48–49
AIDS (acquired immune deficiency syndrome)
  Dominican Republic: 72
  Haiti: 235, 248; incidence, 274–75; and tourism, 236, 281, 285, 314; transmission, 275

air force (*see also* armed forces)
  Dominican Republic: base locations, 180; command missions, 180–81; equipment, 180–81; origins of, 180; personnel, 180; post-World War II expansion, 180; training, 181
  Haiti: air corps, 372
Air Haiti, 313
airlines
  Dominican Republic: 117–18
  Haiti: 313
airports
  Dominican Republic: 117–18
  Haiti: 313
Alas del Caribe, 118
Aluminum Company of America (Alcoa), 107
American Federation of Labor-Congress of Industrial Organizations (AFL-CIO), 289
American Revolution: effect of, on Haiti, xvii
Amiama Tío, Luis, 32
Arabs
  Dominican Republic: immigration of, 51; and marital exclusion, 54
  Haiti: as ethnic minority, 250–51; intermarriage by, 251
Arawaks. *See* Taino Indians
Arias, Desiderio, 24–26
Aristide, Jean-Bertrand, xxiv, xxv
armed forces (*see also* air force, army, Garde d'Haïti, National Police, navy)
  Dominican Republic: attempts to reform, 144–45; and civic action program, 171; contemporary role, 163–64; costs, 163–64, 172–74; defense zones, 174–75; Directorate General of Forestry, 171; and emergency transport, 171; equipment of, 144, 173; General Juan Pablo Duarte Advanced School of the Armed Forces, 175; history and development of, 164–69; insignia of rank, 181; involved in war against drugs, 186; and judicial system, 175, 193; manpower, 172; organization of, 164, 174–75;

and potential external threats, 170–71; and potential internal threats, 171; radio station of, 156; ranks, 181; role of, in political regime, 144–45, 169–70; role of, in public life, 169–72; training, 175; uniforms, 181; Vocational School of the Armed Forces and Police, 175

Haiti: after Duvalier period, 359–61; equipment, 369–72; and foreign assistance, 364–65; in history, 354–55; insignia of rank, 369–71; modern politics of, 355–61; and national security, 353–54; organization and structure, 365–72; and political instability, 325; politics and Garde d'Haïti, 227–32; ranks, 369–71; role of, 361–64; spending for, 364–65; uniform of, 369

army (*see also* armed forces)

Dominican Republic: equipment, 178; headquarters, 175; manpower, 175; tactical organization, 178; training, 178–79; units, 175

Haiti: as government in rural areas, 336; politics of, 337–39, 355–61; and power of section chiefs, 336

Associated Press (AP), 155

Association for Microenterprise Development, 115

Association of Coffee Exporters (Asdec), 345

Association of Industries of Haiti, 345

Association of Landowners and Agriculturists, 146

audiencia, 5–6

authoritarianism (*see also* caudillo rule, personalism)

Dominican Republic: xix, 3, 18, 20, 129, 130, 131, 132, 150, 164; under Trujillo, 27–31, 32, 35

Haiti: xix, 203, 228, 325, 337, 339–40; under Duvaliers, 232–38, 326–28

autocolonization, 335

Autonomous Federation of Haitian Workers/Federation of Latin American Workers (CATH/CLAT), 289–90

Autonomous University of Santo Domingo, 70, 147–48

Avril, Prosper, xix, 326, 329–30, 339, 359, 360

"Baby Doc," 235, 326, 328, 357

baccalauréat, 273

Báez Machado, Ramón, 24

Báez Méndez, Buenaventura: rivalry with Pedro Santana Familias, 12–18, 166; rule over Dominican Republic, 166

Bahamas: migration of Haitians to, 247

Balaguer Ricardo, Joaquín, xxii–xxiii, 28–29, 32, 33–34, 152–53; and the Dominican military, 169; election of, 143; performance of, 143–44

balance of payments (*see also* foreign economic relations)

Dominican Republic: 122

Haiti: 317–18

bambosh demokrasi (revelry of democracy), 340

Bank of the Republic of Haiti (BRH), 287

banking and financial services

Dominican Republic: 113–15

Haiti: 309–11

banking laws, 288

Barbot, Clément, 357

bateyes, 62

Batista, Fulgencio, 31

bauxite. *See* mining

Bazin, Marc, xxi, xxiv, 285

beans, 99–100, 298, 300

Bennett, Ernest, 236

Bennett, Michèle, 236, 327

Bennetts, 236

Betancourt, Rómulo, 30

Biassou, Georges, 208, 210, 211

Billini, Francisco Gregorio, 19

Biological Weapons Convention, 175

birth control. *See* contraception

blacks. *See* racial groups

boat people, 247

Bobadilla, Francisco de, 5

Bobo, Rosalvo, 223

Bois Cayman (Alligator Woods), xvii, 208

Boisrond-Tonnerre, 213

Bolívar Palacios, Simón, 217

Bon Nouvel, 264

Bonaparte, Napoléon, 9, 212–13, 337

Bordas Valdez, José, 24

Borno, Louis, 226

Bosch Gaviño, Juan, xxii, 32, 152–53; confrontation with Duvalier, 234; military reaction to, 168; rivalry with Balaguer, 153

Boukman, 208

Bourbon dynasty, 7

Index

Boyer, Jean-Pierre, 10; enacted Rural Code, 218; governs Haiti (1818–43), 218–19; and land reform, 291; legislative opposition to, 219; named president of Haiti, 217–18; overthrown, 11, 219; and racial disharmony, 218; sailed for Jamaica, 219
brain drain, 284
brevet élémentaire, 270
Britain
    Dominican Republic: immigration from, 51; political role, 151
    Haiti: relations with, 347
brujos, 67
bureaucracy, as political interest group, 150
Bush, George, 347

Cabral Luna, José María, 18
Cáceres, José Núñez de, 10
Cáceres Vásquez, Ramón, 21, 22–24
caciques, 17, 19, 22, 23
cacos, 221, 338, 353
cadena, 46
Caesar, Julius, 210
cagoulards, 338
Calixte, Démosthènes Pétrus: candidate for Assembly, 229; commander, 227
campuno, 46
Canada: relations with Haiti, 348
Canary Islanders, 51
Cap Français, 206, 209
Cap François, 206
Cap-Haïtien, 203, 206, 216, 245–46
Cape Henry, 216
Caperton, William, 26, 224
Caribbean Basin Economic Recovery Act, 394
Caribbean Basin Initiative (CBI) (*see also* foreign economic relations), 121, 289, 393; administration proposal and congressional amendments, 393–95; agency network, 395–96; early assessment, 397–400; expansion of benefits and programs, 396–97; and free-zone manufacturing, 104; and nontraditional exports, 97
Caribbean Community and Common Market (Caricom), 121–22, 317
carreau, 292
Carter, Jimmy, 34

Casa Vicini, 60, 90
cash remittances
    Dominican Republic: 39, 47, 122
    Haiti: 248
Castro Ruz, Fidel, 30, 346
Catholic University Mother and Teacher (Universidad Católica Madre y Maestra), 70, 148
cattle. *See* livestock
caudillo rule (*see also* authoritarianism, personalism), xix, 3, 12, 28–29, 78
cellular mobile telephones, 118
cement, 109, 306
census, 245
Central Romana, 60, 90, 116
certificat d'études primaires, 270
Chamber of Commerce and Industry of Haiti, 345
Chamber of Deputies, 133–35
chickens. *See* livestock
children (*see also* family): health of, 72, 274
Chinese: immigration of, to Dominican Republic, 51; and marital exclusion, 54
Christian Democrat Party of Haiti (PDCH), xxi, 343
Christian Democratic International, 151
Christophe, Henri (Henry), xviii; chosen president, 216; and Haitian Revolution, 212; names himself King Henry I, 216; rejected for leadership, 217; ruled Haiti, 215–17; and school construction, 269; suicide of, 217–18
church and state, separation of, 131
Churchill, Winston, xxiii
Cibaeños, 17
civil liberties
    Dominican Republic: 32, 131, 132, 189–90
    Haiti: 330, 373, 375–76
civil war, xxii, 3, 32–33, 54, 79, 130, 132, 165–66
Claude, Sylvio C., xxi, xxiv
cocoa (*see also* agriculture, crops), 97, 296
Code of Criminal Procedure, 192
Codetel, 118
coffee (*see also* agriculture, crops), 96, 217, 295
Coffee Exporters Association (Asdec), 295
colonial rule, xvii
    Dominican Republic: xviii, 3–12, 16–18, 164–65; economic activity under, 77–78

Haiti: xvii, 203–7; colonial society, 206–7, 248–49; economic activity under, 77–78, 282–83; slave rebellion of 1791, 207–9
colonos, 60
Columbus, Bartolomé, 204
Columbus, Christopher, 3–4, 5, 203
Columbus, Diego, 5
Commercial Bank of Haiti, 310
communications (*see also* mass media) Dominican Republic: 118–19; and politics, 149
Haiti: 313–14
Communist Party of Haiti (PCH), 343
compadrazgo, 58, 65
compadres, 65–66
computer software (*see also* manufacturing), 119
comunidades de base, 68
Conciliation Commission, 331
Concordat, 67, 221, 269
Conseil Electoral Permanent (CEP), xx
Constant, Félix d'Orléans Juste, 229
constitutional development Dominican Republic: 130–32; and structure of local government, 139
Haiti: framework, 330–32; and public order, 374
constitutionalism, xix, 131, 203
constitutionalists, 33, 130–31, 152
construction Dominican Republic: 108–9
Haiti: 307
contraband traffic, 6
contraception Dominican Republic: 44–45; resistance to, 45
Haiti: 248
copper. *See* mining
corn, 99, 298
corruption (*see also* kleptocracy) Dominican Republic: 29, 36, 137–38, 142, 143, 144, 152, 186
Haiti: xix, 214, 220, 231, 233–35, 335
Cortés, Hernán, 6
cotton, 296, 298
credit. *See* banking and financial services
Creole, 257; attitudes toward, 260; and educational reform, 261–64, 272; increased use of, 260–61; as informal standard, 258; literature in, 264; origins of, 258; and social class, 258; usage patterns, 260; variations of, 258–60

crime Dominican Republic: combated by military, 186; corruption among government officials, 186; juvenile gangs, 186; and narcotics, 186; newspaper reports of, 186; and politics, 186–87
Haiti: 375–76; and narcotics, 363
criminal justice system Dominican Republic: constitutionally guaranteed rights, 189–90; judicial independence, 190; judicial requirements, 191; and national government, 164; penal law and procedure, 191–92; and politics, 190; pretrial delay, 191; prison system, 192–93; types of courts, 190
Haiti: judicial requirements, 334; jurisdictions, 334; legal framework, 372–73; public order, 374–76; types of courts, 334
Cromwell, Oliver, 7
crops (*see also* agriculture) Dominican Republic: cash, 94–98; exports of, 89–90; food, 98–100; mixed, 62–64
Haiti: cash, 295–98; food, 298–300
Cuba, 153; Dominican relations with, 157–58; and Haitian refugees, 362; immigration from, 51; as potential military threat, 170–71; and sugar, 95
curanderos, 67
currency Dominican Republic: 85–87
Haiti: 287–88
cyclones. *See* geography

Dahomets, 216
Danish, immigration of, 51
Dartiguenave, Philippe Sudre, 224, 226
death penalty: abolished in Haiti, 330
debt-equity swaps, 123–24
de Camps Jiménez, Hatuey, 152
Déjoie, Louis, xxiv, 232
democracy, xxiii Dominican Republic: democratic tradition, 129, 131, 132; democratic regimes, 130, 142; democratic system established, xxii
Haiti: absence of democratic tradition, xx; Haitian perceptions of,

340–41; lack of preparation for, xviii
Democratic Movement for the Liberation of Haiti (Modelh), 343
Democratic Revolutionary Party of Haiti, 343
Dessalines, Jean-Jacques, xviii, 9, 212, 213, 214, 337
Diederich, Bernard, 31
Directorate General of Forestry, 171
divorce, 66
diyari demokratik (democratic diarrhea), 340
doktè fey, 276
Dominican Agrarian Institute (IAD), 59, 90, 116–17
Dominican Airlines (CDA), 117–18
Dominican Center for the Promotion of Exports, 98
Dominican Central Bank (BCRD), 113, 123
Dominican Communist Party (PCD), 29–30, 154, 184
Dominican Constabulary Guard, 166
Dominican Development Foundation, 115
Dominican Electric Company (CDE), 110–11
Dominican Liberation Party (PLD), 35–36, 153, 154
Dominican Mortgage Bank, 114
Dominican National Aviation, 180
Dominican Port Authority, 117
Dominican Revolutionary Party (PRD), 32, 34–36, 82, 151–52, 154
Dominican Social Security Institute, 70
Dominican State Enterprises Corporation, 102
doré. See mining
drainage. *See* geography
Drake, Francis, 7, 205
drug trafficking (*see also* crime), 118, 363
Duarte, Juan Pablo: as governor of Cibao, 12; seized Santo Domingo, 220; as student, 11–12
General Juan Pablo Duarte Advanced School of the Armed Forces, 175
Dumesle, Hérard, 219
Dutch, immigration of, 51
Duvalier, François, xix, 203, 326; and armed forces, 356–57; declared president for life, 232; effect on economy, 283–84; named son his successor, 234–35; opposition to Roman Catholic Church, 267, 268; practiced voodoo, 233; presidential reign (1957–71), 232–35, 339–40; renounced U.S. aid, 234; rule of terror, 234; and *tonton makouts*, 232–33, 356–57; welcome of Protestants, 269
Duvalier, Jean-Claude, xix, 203, 326, 357; and armed forces, 357–59; and economy, 284; educational reforms of, 270; leaves Haiti, 238; misappropriated funds, 235–36, 285; named to succeed father, 234–35; presidential reign (1971–86), 235–38; as subject of plot, 237
Duvalier, Michèle, 236, 238
Duvalier, Simone, 234
Duvalier, Simone Ovide, 235, 236, 326
Duvaliers, 236, 237–38
"dynastic republicanism," 337

economic elites: as political force in Dominican Republic, 146–47
economic policy
    Dominican Republic: expenditures, on defense, 172–74; fiscal policy, 82–85; monetary and exchange-rate policies, 85–87
    Haiti: fiscal policy, 286–87; monetary and exchange-rate policies, 287–88
economy
    Dominican Republic: growth and structure, 77–82; labor, 87–89
    Haiti: corruption, 282, 285; growth and structure, 282–85; labor, 288–90; mismanagement, 285
education
    Dominican Republic: 68; and church operation, 70; and curriculum reform, 69; and enrollment growth, 69–70; higher, 68, 69–70; primary, 68–69; public and private, 70; in rural areas, 69; secondary, 68, 69
    Haiti: 269; commitment to, by urban lower class, 254; dropout rates, 272; enrollment figures, 270; higher, 273–74; and language changes, 261–64; modern changes, 270; postcolonial promotion of, 269; primary schools, 270–72; and Roman Catholic Church, 269; secondary schools, 273; teachers, 272; and urban elite, 269
Education Act of 1848, 269
Eisenhower, Dwight D., 31
El Caribe, 155

441

elections
Dominican Republic: 1849, 14;
1876, 18; 1880, 19; 1884, 19;
1899, 21; 1914, 24; 1924, 27;
1962, 32, 152; 1966, 33, 152;
1970, 34; 1974, 34; 1978, 34, 35,
130, 140, 142, 152; 1982, 35, 130,
140, 142, 152,; 1986, 36, 140, 143,
153–54; 1990, xxii
Haiti: 1946, 229–30; 1950, 231;
1957, 231, 326; 1961, 232, 326;
1964, 326; 1984, 327–28; 1987,
xx, 328–29, 353–54; 1988, 329,
353–54; 1990, xx
electoral system
Dominican Republic: 133, 139–41
Haiti: 331–32
electricity. *See* energy
electronics. *See* manufacturing
El Nacional, 155
El Sol, 155
El Tiempo, 155
encomienda, 4–5, 78
energy
Dominican Republic: 109–11
Haiti: 308–9
English: and class transcendence, 261; as
language of business, 261
Espaillat, Santiago, 14
Espaillat Quiñones, Ulises Francisco, 18
España Boba (Foolish Spain), 9
Estimé, Dumarsais, 203, 229; cited voodoo as a religion, 230; elected president,
230; nationalized Standard Fruit, 230;
proposed social-security legislation,
230; resigned to exile, 230–31
Estrella Ureña, Rafael, 28
ethnic groups (*see also* racial groups, social classes)
Dominican Republic: 49–52; modern immigration of, 50–52
Haiti: 249, 250–51
Evangelicals. *See* religion
Evangelista, Vicente, 26
exchange-rate policy. *See* economic policy
executive branch. *See* governmental system
exports. *See* foreign economic relations

Falconbridge, 107, 117
family
Dominican Republic: and adoption,

65; and marriage, 66; and migration, 46; and parent-child relationship, 67; and political dynamics,
141–42; and relative prosperity,
64–65; and social identity, 55; as
social unit, 64; and trust, 65; and
urban poor, 57–58
Haiti: and children, 256; and marriage, 256, 257; structure, in rural
areas, 256–57; and voodoo, 265–
66
family planning (*see also* contraception)
Dominican Republic: sponsored by
government, 44–45, 146
Haiti: 248
farming technology
Dominican Republic: 92–94
Haiti: 294
Faustin I, 220
Federation of Union Workers (FOS), 289
Ferdinand VII, 9
ferronickel. *See* mining
fertility
Dominican Republic: 44
Haiti: 248
Fiallo, Viriato, 32
Fignolé, Daniel, 230–31
financial services. *See* banking and financial services
financieras, 113, 114–15
fiscal policy. *See* economic policy
fishing. *See* forestry and fishing
Forbes, W. Cameron, 226
Forbes Commission, 226
foreign assistance
Dominican Republic: 124–25; military, from United States, 173–74,
175
Haiti: 318–21; and the armed forces,
364–65
foreign debt
Dominican Republic: 82, 122–24,
142
Haiti: 318
foreign economic relations (*see also* Caribbean Basin Initiative (CBI))
Dominican Republic: 77, balance of
payments, 122; foreign assistance,
124–25; foreign debt, 122–24; foreign trade, 119–22
Haiti: balance of payments, 317–18;
foreign assistance, 318–21; foreign
debt, 318; foreign trade, 314–17

foreign exchange earnings (*see also* foreign economic relations), 47
foreign relations
Dominican Republic: with Cuba, 157–58; with Eastern Europe, 158; with France, 159; with Germany, 159; with Haiti, 3, 156–57, 165, 347; with Israel, 159; with Jamaica, 158; with Mexico, 158; with Nicaragua, 158; with Puerto Rico, 157; with Republic of China, 159; with Spain, 159; with the United States, 158–59; with Venezuela, 158
Haiti: with Britain, 347; with Canada, 348; with Dominican Republic, 3, 156–57, 165, 347; with France, 347, 348; with Germany, 348; with the United States, 346–47
foreign trade
Dominican Republic: 119–22
Haiti: 314–17
forestry and fishing
Dominican Republic: 101; role of armed forces, 171
Haiti: 300–301, 302
France
Dominican Republic: as arms supplier, 173; political role, 151; relations with, 159
Haiti: colonialism, 205–7; policy of, on slavery, 248–49; relations with, 347, 348
freedmen, 8, 50
French, 257; attitudes toward, 261; in education, 264; and escape from poverty, 264; and social class, 258; usage patterns, 260
French Huguenots, 205
French Revolution: effect of, on Haiti, xvii, 337
French West India Company, 205–6
Frontier Treaty, 40

García Godoy, Héctor, 33
Garde d'Haïti, and military rule (1934–57), 226, 227–32, 355
gens de couleur (*see also* mulattoes), 207–9, 211
Geffrard, Fabre Nicolas, 220–21

Gendarmerie d'Haïti (Haitian Constabulary), 224, 355
General Agreement on Tariffs and Trade (GATT), 348
geography
Dominican Republic: area, 40; climate, 43–44; drainage, 41–43; regions, 40–41
Haiti: area, 243; climate, 244–45; drainage, 244; islands, 244; regions, 243–44
Gérin, Etienne-Elie, 214, 215
Germans, immigration of, 51
Germany
Dominican Republic: political role, 151; relations with, 159
Haiti: relations with, 348
Gilles, Serge, xxi
goats. *See* livestock
gold. *See* mining
Gonaïves, 246
González Santín, Ignacio María, 19
gourde. *See* currency, economic policy
government agencies, 138
governmental system (*see also* judiciary)
Dominican Republic: and constitutional development, 130–32; electoral system, 139–41; executive branch, 132–33; judiciary, 136–37; legislative branch, 133–36; local government, 139; public administration, 137–38
Haiti: between 1957 and 1989, 326–30; constitutional framework, 330–32; executive branch, 331; institutions, 333–34; judicial branch, 331; legislative branch, 331; rural/urban administrative split, 335–36; state functions, 334–35
gran abitan (large peasant) 336
grands blancs, 207
Grant, Ulysses S., 222
gro neg (big man), 336
gross domestic product (GDP)
Dominican Republic: 77; agriculture as percentage of, 89; construction as percentage of, 108; manufacturing as percentage of, 101; mining as percentage of, 106; transportation as percentage of, 115
Haiti: 281; agriculture as percentage of, 290; manufacturing as percentage

of, 302; mining as percentage of, 307; services as a percentage of, 310
gross national product (GNP): defense expenditures as percentage of, 172–73
groupman, 253
gubernatorial requirements, 139
Guerrier, Philippe, 220
Guillaume Sam, Vilbrun, 223–24
Guillermo Bastardo, Cesáreo, 19
Gulf and Western Corporation, 60
Guzmán Fernández, Silvestre Antonio, 34–36; approach to reform, 34–35; depoliticization of military, 34–35, 169; election of, 34; suicide of, 36; and tourism, 112

Haitian Academy, 331
Haitian-American Chamber of Commerce and Industry, 345
Haitian American Sugar Company (Hasco), 296
Haitian Armed Forces (FAd'H) (*see also* armed forces), xxiv–xxv, 353, 354, 362–63, 365–67, 374, 375
Haitian Army (*see also* armed forces), 230
Haitian Association of Voluntary Agencies (HAVA), 321
Haitian Communist Party (PCH), 229
Haitian Financial Development Society (Sofihdes), 310
Haitian General Banking Society (Sogebank), 310
Haitian Popular Bank, 310
Haitian Revolution, xvii–xviii, 207–13, 325; and agricultural losses, 283; and changes to social structure, 249; and the economy, 283
Haitian Revolutionary Front (FRH), 343
Haitians in Dominican Republic: immigration of, 51, 52, 157; Trujillo's action against, 52; treatment of, and controversy, 185–86; wages of, 52
Haitian Telecommunications Company (Teleco), 313–14
Habsburgs, 7
Harding, Warren G., 27
health
    Dominican Republic: acquired immune deficiency syndrome (AIDS), 72; and causes of death, 72; rural

services, 71; services, 70–72; services for military personnel, 172; and social security, 72
Haiti: acquired immune deficiency syndrome (AIDS), 248, 274–75; conditions, and urban poor, 254; nutrition and disease, 274; services, 275–76; welfare, 276
Pedro Henríquez Ureña National University, 70, 148
herbalism (*see also* voodoo), 276
hereditary presidency, 337
Heureaux, Ulises: as president, 18–21, 166
Hispaniola (La Isla Española), xvii, 3, 40, 77, 129, 151, 164, 203, 243, 282
Hitler, 29
Hoover, Herbert, 226
House of Deputies, 331
House of Trade (Casa de Contratación), 6
Hull, Cordell, 30
human rights, 268, 329, 345, 375, 376
human rights organizations, 345
Hungarians, immigration of, 51
Hurricane David, 35, 80
Hurricane Frederick, 80
Hurricane Hazel, 231, 300, 321
hurricanes, 43–44
Hyppolite, Florvil, 222

Imbert, José María, 12, 19, 32
Imbert Barrera, Antonio, 32
immigration, and assimilation, in the Dominican Republic, 50–51; of Haitians, 52; of various groups, 50–51
imports. *See* foreign economic relations
independence
    Dominican Republic: xviii, 310–12, 165
    Haiti: 9, 203, 213–15, 337
Industrial and Commercial Bank of Haiti, 310
Industrial Development Fund (FDI), 310
Industrial Finance Corporation, 115
industrial free zones (*see also* manufacturing), 44, 45
Industrial Incentive Law, 102
industry
    Dominican Republic: construction, 108–9; energy, 109–11; manufacturing, 101–6; mining, 106–8

Haiti: construction, 307; energy, 308-9; manufacturing, 302-7; mining, 307-8
infant mortality
Dominican Republic: 72
Haiti: 274
information services (*see also* manufacturing), 119
Inter-American Defense Board, 175
Inter-American Development Bank (IDB) (*see also* foreign assistance), 396
Dominican Republic: 159; transportation aid, 116
Haiti: 348; aid to survey geology, 307-308
Inter-American Treaty of Reciprocal Assistance, 175, 361
International Atomic Energy Agency (IAEA), 160
International Civil Aviation Organization (ICAO), 159
International Coffee Agreement (ICA), 96
International Coffee Organization, 96, 295
International Confederation of Free Trade Unions, 88, 289
International Court of Justice, 159
International Development Association (IDA), 159
International Development Bank (IDB), 159
International Finance Corporation, 159
International Labour Office (ILO), 289
International Labour Organisation (ILO), 159
International Military Education and Training Program (IMET), 365
International Monetary Fund (IMF): and Caribbean Basin Initiative (CBI), 396
Dominican Republic: xxiii, 80, 159
Haiti: 318, 348
International Telecommunications Satellite Organization (Intelsat), 118
Isabella (Queen), 5
islands, 244
Israel: relations with Dominican Republic, 159
Italians: immigration of, to Dominican Republic, 51

Jamaica, 7; relations with Dominican Republic, 158

Japan: immigration from, to Dominican Republic, 51; relations with Dominican Republic, 159
Jean-François, 208, 210, 211
Jeannot, 208
Jesuits, expelled from Haiti, 267
Jews, German, 51
Jews, Sephardic, 50
Jiménez, Manuel, 13
Jiménez Pereyra, Juan Isidro, 21-22, 24-26
Johnson, Lyndon B., 33
Jorge Blanco, Salvador, 35; and budget program, 143; effort to institutionalize the military, 169; succeeded Guzmán, 35
judiciary
Dominican Republic: government responsibility for, 164; lack of independence of, 190-91; lack of public confidence in, 191; and politics, 137; requirements, 136; Supreme Court, 136-37, 190; various other courts, 136-37, 190
Haiti: constitutional provisions, 331-32; Court of Cassation, 331; courts of appeal, 331; lack of independence of, 372-73; legal framework, 372-74; under military government, 333-34; and public order, 374-76

Kaposi's sarcoma. *See* AIDS
Kennedy, John F., 233, 234, 320
kinship. *See* family
kleptocracy (*see also* corruption), 235, 335
kounbit, 253
Knapp, Harry S., 26

labor
Dominican Republic: formal sector, 87-89; informal sector, 89
Haiti: 288-90
labor laws, 56, 88
labor unions (*see also* trade unions)
Dominican Republic: 88-89, 147
Haiti: 289-90, 345
La Filantrópica, 11
LaFontant, Roger, xxi, xxiv
La Información, 155
lakes. *See* geography

lakou, 256-57
land ownership
  Dominican Republic: 58-59
  Haiti: 252-53
land tenure and policy
  Dominican Republic: 90-92
  Haiti: 281, 291-93
land use
  Dominican Republic: 92
  Haiti: 293-94
language (*see also* under names of individual languages)
  Dominican Republic: 49
  Haiti: constitutional recognition, 331; Creole, 250, 254, 257-64, 341-42; 372; Creole, and Haitian Academy, 331; Creole, common in mass media, 341-42; English, 261; French, 249-50; 257-64, 372; national policy on, 261-64; Spanish, 261
La Ruche, 228
Las Casas, Bishop Bartolomé de, 204
La Trinitaria, 11
Lavaud, Franck, 229, 231
Laveaux, Etienne-Maynard, 211
La Victoria Penitentiary, 192
Lebanese (*see also* Arabs): immigration of, to Dominican Republic, 51; to Haiti, 250
Leclerc, Charles Victor Emmanuel, 212, 213
Leconte, Cincinnatus, 223
legislative branch. *See* governmental system
Léon, Gary, 360
Leopards Corps, 338, 353, 358, 366, 367
Les Cayes, 246
Lescot, Elie, 228
Levelt, Antoine, 229
Leyburn, James G., 219
Liberal Party (PL), 222, 342
liberation theology, xxiv, 146
liceo, 69
life expectancy
  Dominican Republic: 72
  Haiti: 274
Limited Test Ban Treaty, 175
Lincoln, Abraham, 346
Listín Diario, 155
literacy
  Dominican Republic: 69-70, 129

Haiti: and fertility, 248; lack of, foils Boyer, 218; and language, 264
livestock
  Dominican Republic: 100-101
  Haiti: 301-2
Lomé Convention, 122
loua, 265-66
Louis XIV, 205
Lundahl, Mats, xx-xxi
Luperón, Gregorio, 18, 19-20

Macandal, François, 207
MacGregor Sporting Goods, 304
machismo, 66, 132
Magloire, Paul E., 229, 326; became president, 231, 355; declared martial law, 231; fled to Jamaica, 231; restored elite to prominence, 231
Majluta Azar, Jacobo, 36, 142, 143
malaria, 226
malnutrition
  Dominican Republic: 72
  Haiti: 236, 274
Manigat, Leslie F., xxi, 326, 329, 360
manufacturing
  Dominican Republic: 77, 82, 101; and employment, 101; and export, 101; free-zone, 104-6; as percentage of GDP, 101; traditional, 102-4
  Haiti: 281, 302; assembly, 303-6; domestic, 306-7; and employment, 302; and export, 302; as percentage of GDP, 302
marriage
  Dominican Republic: dissolution of, 66; forms of, 66; and social class, 66
  Haiti: among lower classes, 256; among elite, 257
marrons, 207
Marxist organizations: and student politics, 148; and violent protest, 184
mass media (*see also* communications, radio stations, television)
  Dominican Republic: 154-56
  Haiti: 341-42
maternal mortality, 72
media. *See* mass media
Mella, Ramón, 12, 13
Mexico, and foreign debt, 123; relations with Dominican Republic, 158

middle class (*see also* social classes)
Dominican Republic: 55–56; as political force, 149–50
Haiti: 251–52; and political dynamics, 344–45
migration
Dominican Republic: 45; chain, 46; destinations, 46; international, 46; and rural society, 59; and sex differences, 46; steps of, 46
Haiti: 246–48
military. *See* armed forces
Military Assistance Program (MAP), 365
Military Aviation Corps, 180
milk. *See* livestock
minimum wage, 289
mining
Dominican Republic: 77, 79–80, 82, 106–8
Haiti: 307–8
Miranda, Francisco de, 217
mistè, 265–66
Molina Ureña, Rafael, 33
Monetary Board of the Dominican Central Bank, 85
monetary policy. *See* economic policy
Monroe Doctrine, 223
Morales Languasco, Carlos F., 22
mortality rate. *See* life expectancy
Mortgage Bank (BCI), 311
mountains. *See* geography
Movement for the Installation of Democracy in Haiti (MIDH), xxi, 343
Moya, Casimiro de, 20
mulattoes (*see also* racial groups, social classes): as elite, 215–18, 220; opposition to Dessalines, 214; rebellion, 208–9; role in revolution, 211–12; as ruling group, xviii, 220, 221, 222
Mussolini, 29

Namphy, Henri, xix, 237–38, 253, 326, 329, 330, 359
Napoleonic Code, 333
National Agricultural and Industrial Development Bank (BNDAI), 310
National Agricultural Industrial Party (PAIN), 343
National Airport Authority (AAN), 313
National Bank of Haiti (BRH), 287
National Civic Union (UCN), 32

National Civil Aviation Office (ONAC), 313
National Committee of the Congress of Democratic Movements (Conacom), 344
National Cooperation Front (FNC), 344
National Council for Free Zones, 105
National Council of Government (CNG), 238, 253, 272, 285, 316, 326
National Council of Higher Education, 70
National Department of Investigations (DNI), 188–89
National Economic Council for the Control of Drugs, 186
National Electricity Company (EdH), 308–9
National Housing Bank, 114
National Housing Institute, 48–49, 114
National Industrial Park Company, 304
National Institute of Agrarian Reform, 331
Nationalist Union, 343
National Party (PN), 221, 342
National Pedagogic Institute, 261
National Police (*see also* armed forces, police)
Dominican Republic: civic action by, 189; contemporary role, 163, 164, 193; establishment of, 187; functions of, 187–89; organization of, 187, 188; personnel statistics, 187; public image, 189; relation to armed forces, 187; and role of armed forces, 171; secret service, 188–89; and violent protests, 181–86
National Population and Family Council, 45
National Price Stabilization Institute, 86
National Progressive Revolutionary Haitian Party (Panpra), xxi, 343
National Republic Bank of Haiti, 287
National Road Maintenance Service (Serrin), 311
National Unity Party (PUN), 343
National Water Resources Institute (INDRHI), 94
navy (*see also* armed forces)
Dominican Republic: base locations, 179; equipment, 179–80; establishment of, 179–80; expansion of, 179; operational organization, 179; personnel, 179; training, 180
Haiti: 367, 369, 372

Netherlands Antilles, 308
newspapers
 Dominican Republic: 154, 155–56
 Haiti: 341
New Testament, in Creole, 264
Nicaragua: relations with Dominican Republic, 158
nickel. *See* mining
Nouel Bobadilla, Adolfo Alejandro, 24
nutrition (*see also* health): inadequacy of, 62, 274; school programs, 270

O'Donnell, Leopoldo, 16
Office of Citizen Protection, 331
Office of the United States Trade Representative, and Caribbean Basin Initiative (CBI), 396
Ogé, Vincent, 208
oil prices, and energy, 109
operation déchoukaj, 328
Organization of American States (OAS), 30, 139–40, 159, 348, 361
outmigration. *See* migration, population
Ovando, Nicolás de, 5, 204
Overseas Private Investment Corporation, 125

Palestinians (*see also* Arabs): immigration of, to Dominican Republic, 51; to Haiti, 250
"Papa Bon Coeur" (Father Good Heart) (*see also* Pétion, Alexandre), 217
"Papa Doc," 233, 234, 326
Paris Club, 123
Pascal-Trouillot, Ertha, xx, xxiv
paternalism (*see also* authoritarianism, patronage, personalism), 5
Patriotic Union, 343
Patriotic Unity Bloc (BUP), 344
patronage
 Dominican Republic: and bureaucracy, 150; and the elite, 55; and the middle class, 56; and public administration, 137–38; role in politics, 141–42, 144, 153; by storekeepers to rural farmers, 64
 Haiti: 334–35
Paul, Jean-Claude, 359, 360, 363
Peace Corps, 125, 320

peasants (*see also* social classes)
 Dominican Republic: political activity of, 148–49
 Haiti: 252–54
Peña Gómez, José Francisco, 152
Penal Code, 191–92
penal law and procedure (*see also* crime, criminal justice system, judiciary), 191–92
peninsulares, 204
Penn, William, 7
Pentecostals. *See* religion
Permanent Electoral Council (CEP), 330
personalism, xix, 29
 Dominican Republic: xxii, 29, 151–54
 Haiti: xxi, 203, 337, 339–40
Pessar, Patricia, 47
peso. *See* currency, economic policy
Pétion, Alexandre, xviii; chosen legislative head, 215–16; and Haitian Revolution, 212; and land reform, 216, 291; leadership failed, 217; promoted mulatto elite, 217; and school construction, 269
petro spirits, 265
petroleum. *See* energy
Peynado, Francisco J., 27
pharmaceuticals. *See* manufacturing
pigs. *See* livestock
Pimentel Chamorro, Pedro Antonio, 17
piquets, 220–21, 338, 353
plasaj, 256
police (*see also* National Police)
 Dominican Republic: 187–89
 Haiti, 224, 336, 374–76
political dynamics
 Dominican Republic: developments since 1978, 142–44; interest groups, 144–51; mass media, 154–56; military influence, 169–70; political parties, 151–54; political system, 141–42, 154
 Haiti: and the army, 337–39; between 1957 and 1989, 326–30; interest groups, 342–45; maintaining power, 337; mass media, 341–42; perceptions of democracy, 340–41; political parties, 342–44; presidential power, 339–40
political instability
 Dominican Republic: 18, 27, 31–32, 130, 141, 165, 219–24
 Haiti: 221–22, 325, 328–30, 376

political parties
Dominican Republic: 151–54
Haiti: 340, 342–44
political violence
Dominican Republic: 184–85
Haiti: xix, xx, xxi, xxiv, 220, 223, 358
politique de doublure, 216, 220
Pope John Paul II, 236–37, 268, 327
Popular Democratic Party of Haitian Youth (PDPJH), 343
Popular Socialist Party (PSP), 343
popular unrest
Dominican Republic: 31–32
Haiti: 236–38, 325, 328–30, 358
population
Dominican Republic: growth and size of, 44–45; and land reserves, 59; migration of, 45–47; urbanization of, 47–49
Haiti: demographics of, 245–46; migration of, 246–48; rural growth, 246; and social classes, 249; urban growth, 245–46
pork. *See* livestock
Port-au-Prince, 245, 254; major government spending in, 335–36; reported AIDS incidence in, 274; schools in, 273
poultry. *See* livestock
predatory state, xxi, 335
presidency
Dominican Republic: powers of, 133; requirements of, 132–33
Haiti: as political focus, 339–40
Préval, René, xxv
prison system (*see also* crime, criminal justice system, judiciary)
Dominican Republic: 192–93
Haiti: 376
Projé Pyebwa, 301
pronunciamientos, 141
Protestantism
Dominican Republic: 68
Haiti: 265, 268–69; role in life, 268–69; varieties of, 268–69; and voodoo, 268–69
Protocol of Revision of 1936, 243
Puerto Ricans: immigration of, 51
Puerto Rico: Dominican migration to, 46; relations with Dominican Republic, 157; share of exports, 119–20

racial groups (*see also* ethnic groups, slavery)
Dominican Republic: animosities about, 10; blacks, mulattoes, and whites, 49–50; modern immigration of, 50–52; and phenotypic characteristics, 50; and politics, 141–42; and social status, 39
Haiti: black middle class, 251–52; mulatto elite, 251–52; and the upper class, 250
rada spirits, 265
Radio Havana, 156
Radio Moscow, 156
Radio Soleil, 268, 341
radio stations
Dominican Republic: 154–56
Haiti: 341–42
railroads
Dominican Republic: 116
Haiti: 313
rainfall. *See* geography
Reagan, Ronald, 237, 320, 347, 393, 396
Reformist Party (PR), 33, 151, 152–53
Regala, Williams, 237–38, 359
Regla Mota, Manuel de la, 15
Reid Cabral, Donald, 32
religion (*see also* Protestantism, Roman Catholic Church, voodoo)
Dominican Republic: Evangelicals, 68; Pentecostals, 68; Protestantism, 68; Roman Catholicism, 67–68; voodoo, 68
Haiti: Protestantism, 265, 268–69; Roman Catholicism, 265, 267–68; voodoo, 265–66
repartimiento, 78
Republic of China: relations with Dominican Republic, 159
Reserve Bank, 113
Reuters, 155
Revolutionary Social Christian Party (PRSC), 153, 154
Revolution of 1843, 219
Revolution of 1946, 228
rice (*see also* agriculture, crops), 98, 298
Rigaud, André, 209, 210, 211, 212
Rio Treaty, 175
rivers. *See* geography
Rivière-Hérard, Charles: as president of Haiti, 219–20
roads. *See* transportation
Rochambeau, Donatien, 213

Rodríguez Echavarría, Pedro, 32
Roman Catholic Church
    Dominican Republic: activist priests, 67–68; harassment of, by Trujillo, 68; loss of influence, 146; marital annulment by, 66; newspapers, 156; numbers of clergy, 67–68; numbers of followers, 67; as political interest group, 145–46; as private educator, 70; radio broadcasts, 156; and Spanish culture, 6
    Haiti: attitude toward voodoo, 267; property confiscated, 10; as official religion, 265; and political links, 267–28; as publisher of Creole literature, 264; radio station of, 268, 341; role in life, 267–68; signing of Concordat, 267, 269; as supporter of peasant groups, 253; and voodoo adherents, 265
Roosevelt, Franklin D., 30, 224
Roosevelt, Theodore, 23
Roosevelt Corollary, 223
Rosario Dominicano, 106
Rosario Resources, Inc., 106
Royal and Supreme Council of the Indies, 6
Royal Patronage of the Indies, 6
rural cooperatives, 64

Saint-Domingue, xvii, 8, 283; colonial society of, 206–7
Salcedo Ramírez, José Antonio, 16–17
Salnave, Sylvain, 221
Salomon, Louis Lysius Félicité, 221–22
Sánchez, Francisco del Rosario: leadership of, 12
San José Accord, 110
Santana Familias, Pedro: bankrupting of Dominican Republic, 166; rivalry with Buenaventura Báez Méndez, 12–18, 166
Santo Domingo, 5–8; colony of, 8–12
Santos, Emilio de los, 32
Madame Sarahs, 295
schools. *See* education
Seaga, Edward, 237
seaports, 117, 312
seasons. *See* geography
Secretariat of State for Agriculture, 94
Secretariat of State for Education and Culture, 69

Secretariat of State for Public Health and Social Welfare, 44–45, 70
Secretariat of State for Public Works and Communications, 116, 118
security, national. *See* armed forces, crime, criminal justice system, judiciary, National Police, police
Senate
    Dominican Republic: 133–35
    Haiti: 331
serpette, 294
services
    Dominican Republic: banking and financial, 113–15; communications, 118–19; tourism, 111–13; transportation, 115–18
    Haiti: 281; banking and financial, 309–11; communication, 313–14; tourism, 314; transportation, 311–13
sex roles
    Dominican Republic: among children, 66–67; and machismo, 66; among parents, 67; and sexual behavior, 66–67
    Haiti: complementary, in rural areas, 254–56
sexual behavior: between *compadres*, 65–66; and male infidelity, 66
sharecropping, 293
silver. *See* mining
sisal, 296
slavery
    Dominican Republic: of Africans, 5, 49; import, 8–9
    Haiti: abolition of, 325; in colonial society, 206–7; import, 8–9; overthrow, xvii; policy, of the French, 203, 248; rebellion against, 207–9, 241; and social structure, 248–50
Smith, Adam, 282, 283
smuggling, 120
Social Christian Party of Haiti (PSCH), 344
Social Christian Reformist Party (PRSC), 149, 153
social classes
    Dominican Republic: elite (*la gente buena* or *la gente culta*), 54, 55; and employment, 56–57; *la gente de primera* and *la gente de segunda*, 54; masses, 54; middle class, 55–56, 149–50; and migration, 56–58; poor,

56–58; and racial stratification, 55; and women, 57, 58

Haiti: black slaves (*noirs*), freedmen (*affranchis*), mulattoes, poor whites (*petits blancs*), and white elite (*grands blancs*), 206–7, 249; middle class, 250, 251–52, 344–45; peasants, 252–54; ruling urban elite and military leaders, 249–50; upper class, 250–51, 344–45; urban lower class, 254

Socialist Bloc (BS), 154

Socialist International, 151, 152

social security coverage
Dominican Republic: 70, 72
Haiti: 276

sociedades inmobiliarias, 114

society
Dominican Republic: in late 1980s, 39–40
Haiti: colonial, 206–7; structure of, imposed by the French, 248–49

society, rural
Dominican Republic: and family ties, 58; and landholding, 58–59; and migration, 59; and mixed farming, 62–64; and population growth, 59; and social interaction, 58; and sugar plantations, 60–62; and women's household economic contribution, 60
Haiti: community councils, 253

society, urban (*see also* urbanization)
Dominican Republic: elite, 52–55; and marriage, 54; middle sector, 55–56; poor, 56–58
Haiti: lower class, 254

Society for the Rights of Man and the Citizen, 219

Sonthonax, Léger-Félicité, 210, 211

sorghum, 99, 298

Soulouque, Faustin, 13, 220

Soviet Union, 96, 120, 153

Spain: annexes Dominican Republic, 16–18; establishes colony in Dominican Republic, 3–8; political role, 151; relations with, 159; trade, 6; and War of Restoration, 54

Spaniards, 51, 203–4

Spanish, used in Haiti, 261

Spanish descendants, in society, 49–50

State Enterprises Corporation, 138

State Sugar Council (CEA), 60, 83, 138

State University of Haiti, 331

student politics, in Dominican Republic (*see also* education), 147–48

sugar (*see also* agriculture, crops)
Dominican Republic: and modern immigration, 50–51; prices, 80; quotas, 80; in rural society, 60–62
Haiti: 296; under Pétion, 217

Superior Court of Auditors and Administrative Disputes, 331

Superior Institute of Agriculture, 94

Sylvain, Franck, 231

Syrians (*see also* Arabs): immigration of, to Dominican Republic, 51; to Haiti, 250

Taft, William H., 24

Taino Indians (Arawaks)
Dominican Republic: 4–5, 49
Haiti: 203–5

tareas, 90

taxes
Dominican Republic: congressional power to levy, 135; evasion of, 83; on goods and services, 85; income, 85
Haiti: by Duvalier, 283; policy revisions, 287; Régie du Tabac, 235, 284; state power, 334, 335

Technical Secretariat of the Presidency, 48

Tejera, Luis, 24

telecommunications. *See* communications

telephone system. *See* communications

television (*see also* mass media)
Dominican Republic: attention on president, 132; various channels, 154, 155
Haiti: and Creole usage, 341–42; and English usage, 261; stations, 341

temperature. *See* geography

tiempo muerto, 95

Tlatelolco Treaty, 175

tobacco (*see also* agriculture, crops), 97, 235, 284

tonton makouts (*see also* Volunteers for National Security (VSN)), 338, 342; establishment of, 232–33, 353, 356; members' status, 376; murder in a church, 329; network, 342; political

role, 326, 342, 357; recruitment of voodoo specialists, 266; size, 357
Tortuga Island, 7, 205
tourism
   Dominican Republic: 77, 82, 111–13
   Haiti: 236, 281, 285, 314
Tourist Incentive Law, 112
Toussaint Louverture, François-Dominique: former slave, 209; led forces in Haitian Revolution, 208, 209–12; named commander in chief, 211; named governor general, 9; pledged support to France, 210; rescued Laveaux, 211; surrendered to Leclerc, 212
trade unions (*see also* labor unions)
   Dominican Republic: 88–89, 147
   Haiti: 289–90, 345
translation services (*see also* manufacturing), 119
transportation
   Dominican Republic: 115–18
   Haiti: 311–13
Treaty of Basel, 211
Treaty of Ryswick, xvii, 7
Treaty on the Control of Arms on the Seabed, 175
Treaty on the Non-Proliferation of Nuclear Weapons, 175
Treaty on the Prohibition of Nuclear Weapons in Latin America, 175
Trinidad and Tobago, 308
tropical storms. *See* geography
Trujillo Lovatón (Ramfis), Rafael, 31
Trujillo Molina, Héctor Bienvenido, 28–29, 31
Trujillo Molina, José Arismendi, 31
Trujillo Molina, Rafael Leónidas, xix, 3; administration of, 27–31; assassination of, 168; end of regime, 39; maintenance of large military, 167; military leadership of, 166, 167; ordered Haitians murdered, 227; personal command by, 167–68
tubers, 99, 298–300
tutumpote, 54

Última Hora, 155
Unified Democrat Party (PDU), 343
Unified Haitian Communist Party (PUCH), 343, 362

Union Bank of Haiti, 310
United Nations
   Dominican Republic: 159
   Haiti: 348
United Nations Educational, Scientific, and Cultural Organization (UNESCO), and Haitian educational reform, 272
United Nations (UN) Working Group on Slavery, 247
United Press International (UPI), 155
United States: and Caribbean Basin Initiative (CBI), 393–400
   Dominican Republic: intervention by, in civil war, 168–69; major aid donor, 124; migration to, 46–47; military aid from, 173; and military equipment, 173; occupation of (1916–24), 24–27, 166–67; political role, 151; relations with, 158–59; role in military, 166; share of exports, 119; share of imports, 121; and tourism, 112
   Haiti: agreement with, on immigrants, 247; and English language, 261; greatest aid donor, 282; migration to, 247; occupation, and economic benefits, 283; occupation of, xviii–xix, 224–27; restores aid program, 235; watching German activity, 222–24
United States Agency for International Development (AID), 89, 124–25, 291, 320, 321
United States Drug Enforcement Administration (DEA), 363
United States General System of Preferences, 121
United States Immigration and Naturalization Service (INS), 247
Universitas Santi Dominici, 70
University of Haiti, 273
University of Santo Domingo, 70
upper class (*see also* social classes): and political dynamics, 344–45
urbanization
   Dominican Republic: growth rates, 47–48; and housing, 48–49; in La Romana, 48; and political change, 148–49; in Santiago de los Caballeros, 48; in Santo Domingo, 48
   Haiti: 245

valleys. *See* geography
Vásquez Lajara, Horacio, 21–22, 27
Vatican (*see also* Roman Catholic Church, Concordat), 51, 151, 221
vehicles. *See* transportation
Velásquez, Federico, 21
Venezuela: and foreign debt, 123; relations with Dominican Republic, 158
vice presidency: requirements of, 132–33
Vicini Burgos, Juan Bautista, 27
Victoria y Victoria, Eladio, 24
Villatte, 210
Vincent, Sténio, 226, 227, 228, 338, 373
Voice of America, 156
Volunteers for National Security (VSN) (*see also* tonton makouts), 232–33, 326, 353, 356–57, 358, 374
voodoo
    Dominican Republic: 68
    Haiti: and health care, 276; *loua* or *mistè*, 265–66; *manbo* and *houngan*, 266; opposed by Roman Catholic Church, 267–68; practiced by Roman Catholics, 265; Protestant stance on, 268–69
voting. *See* electoral system, elections

War of the Castes, 212
War of Restoration, 17, 54
wheat, 99
welfare. *See* health, social security coverage
Welles, Sumner, 27
Wessín y Wessín, Elías, 33; overthrow of Bosch Gaviño, 168
Western Europe: relations with Dominican Republic, 159
whites. *See* racial groups
Wilson, Woodrow, 24, 226; planned to occupy Haiti, 223; and U.S. Marine control of Dominican Republic, 166
Windward Passage, 243, 346
witchcraft. *See* voodoo

women
    Dominican Republic: in armed forces, 172; economic activities of, 57; in labor force, 87–88; maternal mortality, 72; migration of, 46, 58; and rural family income, 60; among urban poor, 57–58
    Haiti: access to birth control, 248; anemia among, 274; and child care burden, 256; economic independence of, 256; incidence of AIDS in, 274; in labor force, 257, 288; legal rights of, 257; in manufacturing, 304; right to vote, 232; sex roles of, 254–55; as slaves, 206–7
Worker Peasant Movement (MOP), 229–30, 343
World Bank (*see also* Foreign assistance): and Caribbean Basin Initiative (CBI), 396
    Dominican Republic: 159, and energy efficiency, 111; and transportation, 116
    Haiti: and development, 321; educational support, 272; and foreign debt, 318
World Health Organization (WHO), 159; nutrition recommendations, 274
World Meteorological Organization (WMO), 160
Woss y Gil, Alejandro, 19, 22

xenophobia, 39

yaws, 226

zafra, 95
zinglins, 220, 338
zombies. *See* voodoo

Published Country Studies

(Area Handbook Series)

550-65	Afghanistan	550-87	Greece
550-98	Albania	550-78	Guatemala
550-44	Algeria	550-174	Guinea
550-59	Angola	550-82	Guyana and Belize
550-73	Argentina	550-151	Honduras
550-169	Australia	550-165	Hungary
550-176	Austria	550-21	India
550-175	Bangladesh	550-154	Indian Ocean
550-170	Belgium	550-39	Indonesia
550-66	Bolivia	550-68	Iran
550-20	Brazil	550-31	Iraq
550-168	Bulgaria	550-25	Israel
550-61	Burma	550-182	Italy
550-50	Cambodia	550-30	Japan
550-166	Cameroon	550-34	Jordan
550-159	Chad	550-56	Kenya
550-77	Chile	550-81	Korea, North
550-60	China	550-41	Korea, South
550-26	Colombia	550-58	Laos
550-33	Commonwealth Caribbean, Islands of the	550-24	Lebanon
550-91	Congo	550-38	Liberia
550-90	Costa Rica	550-85	Libya
550-69	Côte d'Ivoire (Ivory Coast)	550-172	Malawi
550-152	Cuba	550-45	Malaysia
550-22	Cyprus	550-161	Mauritania
550-158	Czechoslovakia	550-79	Mexico
550-36	Dominican Republic and Haiti	550-76	Mongolia
550-52	Ecuador	550-49	Morocco
550-43	Egypt	550-64	Mozambique
550-150	El Salvador	550-35	Nepal and Bhutan
550-28	Ethiopia	550-88	Nicaragua
550-167	Finland	550-157	Nigeria
550-155	Germany, East	550-94	Oceania
550-173	Germany, Fed. Rep. of	550-48	Pakistan
550-153	Ghana	550-46	Panama

550-156	Paraguay	550-53	Thailand
550-185	Persian Gulf States	550-89	Tunisia
550-42	Peru	550-80	Turkey
550-72	Philippines	550-74	Uganda
550-162	Poland	550-97	Uruguay
550-181	Portugal	550-71	Venezuela
550-160	Romania	550-32	Vietnam
550-37	Rwanda and Burundi	550-183	Yemens, The
550-51	Saudi Arabia	550-99	Yugoslavia
550-70	Senegal	550-67	Zaire
550-180	Sierra Leone	550-75	Zambia
550-184	Singapore	550-171	Zimbabwe
550-86	Somalia		
550-93	South Africa		
550-95	Soviet Union		
550-179	Spain		
550-96	Sri Lanka		
550-27	Sudan		
550-47	Syria		
550-62	Tanzania		